BETWEEN SERB AND ALBANIAN

For Arkle

MIRANDA VICKERS

Between Serb
and Albanian

A History of Kosovo

Columbia University Press
New York

949.71
VIC

Columbia University Press
New York

© 1998 by Miranda Vickers
All rights reserved.

Printed in England

ISBNs: 0-231-11382-X (cloth); 0-231-11383-8 (paper)

Cataloging-in-Publication Data available from the Library of Congress

'Kosovo is a plain where the Serbs bend over to work the soil, Albanians sweat in the mining shafts underground, Turks (largely spent and reminiscing about past fame) grow poppies and peppers, while the Gypsies fill the air with the sounds of life.'

(A.N. Dragnich and S. Todorovich, *The Saga of Kosovo*, East European Monographs, New York, 1984, p. 5)

CONTENTS

PREFACE AND ACKNOWLEDGEMENTS

International diplomatic recognition of the new political map that has taken shape in the former Yugoslavia has left many of the region's inhabitants deeply unsatisfied, and none more so than the Albanian population of Kosovo. The break-up of Yugoslavia and the collapse of communism in Albania coincided in 1991. These two factors brought the Albanian national question and the issue of the unification of the Albanian population of the former Yugoslavia with that of Albania to the fore. This in turn could have potentially explosive consequences for the other ethnically-mixed regions of south-eastern Europe.

The majority of Albanians, whether living in Albania or in the former Yugoslavia, believe that eventually and inevitably the Albanian nation will unite into a single state. But before this could become a reality the Serbs, Macedonians, Montenegrins and possibly Greeks, would need to re-negotiate their borders with Albania. This could be the cause of a catastrophic conflict throughout the Balkans. Since neither the Serbian nor the Albanian leaders in Kosovo will accept that the Province should return to the autonomy provided by the 1974 Constitution, only two alternatives seem possible: independence guaranteed by international force or a bloodbath.[1]

The term 'Kosovo' has been used as a metaphor by both Serbs and Albanians for the 'suffering and injustices' inflicted upon their nations throughout their turbulent history. However, relations between them in Kosovo have not always taken the form of confrontation. Balkan history in modern times has been a sequence of battles and wars, instigated by outside powers and internal interest groups deliberately exploiting nationalism and outright chauvinism. Differences of language and of religious tradition and custom have been over-emphasised. The victims of this process have invariably been the Balkan peoples, be they Slavs or Greeks, Alba-

1. *Kosovo: Oppression of Ethnic Albanians*, Minority Rights Group, London, 1992 p. 5.

nians or Turks. Ethnic and cultural differences exist and cannot be denied, but something else too brings these people together: a common layer of culture, the sediment of first Byzantine and then Ottoman domination. And buried deep under that layer lies the subjection and suffering of whole populations who underwent that domination.[2]

According to the Serbian academic Predrag Simic, Kosovo is 'an area that sublimes the collective identity of the Serbian people just as Jerusalem does, for instance, for the Jewish nation.'[3] This emotive attachment to the region stems from the Battle of Kosovo in 1389, when Serbia made its last great stand against the advancing Ottomans. The defeat the Serbs suffered at Kosovo made such a deep and lasting impact on them, greater than any other event in their history, that they appear condemned to avenge it. Thus Kosovo is known as the cradle of the Serbian nation. As Dragnich and Todorovich note, 'Kosovo is many diverse things to different living Serbs, but they all have it in their blood – they are born with it.'[4] Those same writers have nevertheless also correctly noted:

> 'In the past, as long as the Kosovo Albanians did not disturb the Serbs and their sacred monuments (in some instances Albanians actually guarded them), an atmosphere of 'live and let live' prevailed, and the multinational structure of Kosovo was not pertinent. In the Balkans ethnic imbalances are a fact of everyday life, ethnic jealousies a way of life, ethnic jokes the salt of life, and ethnic conflicts the curse of life. But all of this is a part of Balkan living.'[5]

So, although the tensions we find in Kosovo today are generated by conflict between the majority Albanian population and the Serbian authorities, one of the primary aims of this book is to examine how these tensions have been imported rather than originated by the inhabitants of Kosovo.

Albanian and Serbian scholars, most of whom are nationalist in orientation, have totally opposing theories about the ethnic development of Kosovo, and this has been an important issue in the background to the present crisis. The Serbs are convinced that before they arrived in the region in the sixth and seventh centuries,

2. A. Pipa and S. Repishti, *Studies on Kosova*, New York, 1994, p. 250.
3. P. Simic, *The Kosovo and Metohija Problem and Regional Security in the Balkans*, Institute of International Politics and Economics, Belgrade, 1995, p. 1.
4. A.N. Dragnitch and S. Todorovich, *The Saga of Kosovo*, East European Monographs, New York, 1984, p. 4.
5. Dragnitch and Todorovich, *The Saga of Kosovo*, p. 180.

Kosovo was almost uninhabited, and that Albanians only arrived in the area in the fifteenth century with the conquering Turks, and again in the seventeenth century after the exodus of a great number of Serbs. However, the Albanians are equally convinced that, as descendants of the Illyrians, they are the original inhabitants of Kosovo. The Province is also where the Albanian national movement was born in 1878 and where Albanian nationalism has its focus. The Albanians consider theirs to be by far the stronger historical claim to Kosovo since their ancestors, the Illyrians, are known to have inhabited the area for several centuries before the arrival of the Slavs.

The Albanian claim to Kosovo is also based on demography since they constitute more than 90 per cent of the total population, while the Serb's claim derives purely from history and emotion. Serb churches and monasteries dot the Kosovo landscape as a living testimony to their medieval Slav state. For Serbs to renounce Kosovo would be to deny their national and spiritual heritage. Although these arguments may not appear to all observers as of great relevance to any political arguments in the present, both sides continue to place great emphasis upon this, since they provide the basis for both Serbs and Albanians to regard Kosovo as the cradle of their national and cultural identity. This of course fuels the Kosovo crisis today.

After the collapse of the Ottoman Empire and the end of the First World War, almost half a million Albanians were included by force and against their will within the borders of the newly-created Kingdom of Serbs, Croats and Slovenes (later called Yugoslavia). Since the creation of that state, Serbian-Albanian relations in Kosovo have gone through several stages. Throughout the first stage, 1918-41, the Albanian minority had no specifically guaranteed minority rights, and lived under virtual Serbian domination. The élite structure of pre-Second World War Kosovo resembled a system of internal colonialism with a largely imported Serbian intelligentsia ruling the region's majority population of Albanian peasants and craftsmen. In the Second World War, a large part of Kosovo was united with Albania under Italian rule, and thus the situation was reversed with Serbs and Montenegrins in a vulnerable and inferior environment, as many Albanians openly collaborated with the occupying German and Italian administration to subdue the predominantly Slav resistance forces. The third stage, 1945-66, was a period of oscillations in these relations ranging from armed conflict to attempts at political resolution of disputes, including administrative restriction of the rights of Albanians and even violence.

Following the war, Kosovo's regional Communist Party was controlled almost exclusively by Serbs; Albanian party membership was extremely small at 0.16 per cent, and Albanian 'intellectuals' were merely hastily trained primary and secondary school teachers. This situation continued till the gradual emergence of a modern Albanian élite in the mid-1970s. This replaced the traditional élite comprising senior members of the clan organisations of a few landed families, whose wealth derived from the clan's past services to the Ottoman administration. The fourth stage, 1967–81, was the so-called post-Brioni period characterised by the acknowledgement and assurance of the minority rights of the Albanians.[6] At this time there was official encouragement for national emancipation and affirmation of Kosovo's Albanian population, and in the aftermath of the controversial 1974 Constitution this developed into a powerful Albanian national movement. It served in turn to alienate the region's Serb and Montenegrin population, who felt threatened by the new mood of Albanian self-assertiveness.

The fifth stage, 1981–92, was marked by the disintegration of federal Yugoslavia and the strengthening of all nationalist movements, which led to open conflicts and civil war in the territories of the former federation. The Kosovo crisis became acute as Serbia re-established its domination over Kosovo and the Albanians responded by seeking to create an independent Republic of Kosovo.[7] All areas of life in Kosovo have subsequently remained divided into two parallel worlds, one belonging to the legal system of government, and the other to an illegal system for organising all aspects of life. Intolerance and open hostility between these two worlds, and at the same time the potential for open conflict, have steadily increased.

Geographical description of Kosovo

The actual name 'Kosovo' is of Turkish–Albanian origin and was used to designate the Kosovo *vilayet* which, before the Balkan War

6. D. Janjic, *Conflict or Dialogue: Serbian-Albanian Relations and Integration of the Balkans*, Subotica, 1994, p. 140.
7. Janjic, *Conflict or Dialogue*, p. 132.

of 1912, covered the territory of Sandjak, Gornje Polimlje, Kosovo and Metohija, as well as northern Macedonia up to Veles, and eastern Macedonia up to the Bregalnica catchment. The area of present-day Kosovo is 10,887 sq. km. which is 12.3 per cent of the area of Serbia. The region consists of two separate geographic entities. The first is Kosovo, a valley between Pristina and Drenica, about 4 km. long and 14 km. wide. It is densely populated, with significant agricultural and mineral resources and a network of important transport connections for this section of the Balkans. The other is the territory known by Serbs as Metohija (in medieval times the term '*metoh*' denoted the holdings of the monasteries), which the Albanians include in a broader area called Dukagjni. It is about 80 km. in length and over 40 km. wide, and compared with Kosovo is primarily agricultural.[8] Thus the whole region is called by Serbs Kosovo-Metohija or 'Kosmet'. For our purpose in this book the term Kosovo is used throughout except where it is mentioned in a specifically Serbian context. For the sake of uniformity, place-names are left in the original Serbian, e.g. *Pec* – Peje; *Djakovica* – Gjakove, etc. Unless stated otherwise, the term 'Albanians' refers throughout to those persons who are ethnically Albanian and live in the region of Kosovo and other areas of former Yugoslavia.

Kosovo is particularly rich in mineral wealth, with 50 per cent of all known nickel deposits in the former Yugoslavia, 48 per cent of the lead and zinc, 47 per cent of the magnesium, 36 per cent of the lignite, and 32.4 per cent of the kaolin deposits. It is also rich in quartz, asbestos, limestone, marble, chrome and bauxite. Apart from its ample mineral resourses, Kosovo has abundant flora and fauna, including vast forests of wild chestnut, oak and beech, inhabited by lynx, brown bears and wild boars.[9]

However, chronic and persistent overpopulation has contributed to the region being one of the poorest in the Balkans. The far greater demographic strength of the Albanians in Kosovo compared to the Serbs has been a significant cause of the two nations' hostility to each other over the past two centuries. Albanians make up roughly 90 per cent of Kosovo's population. By 1981 Yugoslavia's Albanian population had grown from one third to nearly half of the entire Albanian nation, thus making them proportionately the world's largest irredenta. Albanians were the least integrated nationality in the former Yugoslavia and formed the lowest socio-

8. Simic, *The Kosovo and Metohija Problem*, p. 1.
9. Pipa and Repishti, *Studies on Kosova*, p. 126.

economic stratum in the country's poorest and least developed region. Kosovo has always been the most densely populated region of Yugoslavia, with 1,954,747 people in 1991 (20.5 per cent of the total for Serbia) and the country's – and Europe's – highest natural population growth rate. By 1991, the Province's 170,000 Serbs and Montenegrins accounted for just 9 per cent of Kosovo's population. The 1991 census, based on a statistical projection because the majority of Albanians boycotted it, recorded 1,686,661 Albanians in Serbia as a whole. According to official Yugoslav projections, Kosovo's ethnic Albanian population will reach almost 2,600,000 by 2001. This has serious implications for any unification process and for the general stability of the region as the Serbs, Bulgarians, Macedonians and Greeks all have declining, ageing populations (for fuller information, see tables in Appendix, pages 318-320).

According to many Albanians and some Serbs, the historical issue in Kosovo is only a pretext for the ethnic tension, while the real problem is that the province's strategic position is so important that Serbia cannot easily give it up or even accept a form of real autonomy. Kosovo borders on Macedonia which, although recently recognised by the Federal Republic of Yugoslavia, was up to a short time ago directly opposed to it, claiming the 'Former Yugoslav heredity'. But the essential factor is that Kosovo borders on the Republic of Albania which is militarily allied with Turkey against Serbia, and that the mountains separating the Kosovo plain from Albania and from Macedonia are the only natural protection in case of conflict with these countries. For these geo-political and military reasons it would be extremely difficult for Serbia to relinquish Kosovo.[10]

Natural barriers have historically divided the Albanian people into two distinct groups with different dialects and great variations in social structure. Those who live in the mountainous regions to the north of the Shkumbi river are called Ghegs, and among them are included the Albanians of Kosovo. Up till 1945, the social organisation of the Ghegs was tribal, being based on a small, tightly-knit clan system connecting various isolated homesteads. Those living south of the Shkumbi in the lowlands and plains are called Tosks, who by the time of the Ottoman conquest had abandoned the tribal system in favour of a village-based organisation, where they made up the bulk of the landless and subsistence level peasantry.

10. A. l'Abate, *Kosovo: A War not Fought*, Dipartimento di Studi Sociali, Universita degli Studi di Firenze, 1996, p. 6.

During the 1970s the Tirana administration set about the task of standardising the Albanian language, with the result that modern standard Albanian is based largely on the southern Tosk dialect.

The Gheg population of Kosovo (and northern Albania) is predominantly Sunni Muslim, with some 10 per cent being Roman Catholic. The Slavic population belong mainly to the Serbian Orthodox Church. As nationalist regimes in Yugoslavia alternated in power, some Albanians became 'Serbianised' and accepted the Orthodox faith, while a good number of ethnic Serbs and Montenegrins became 'Islamised' or 'Albanianised'. Confessional differences and discrimination are thus closely connected to ethnopolitical conflicts in the Kosovo region, and add to the already heady cocktail of inherently contradictory aims and interests of the region's Slav and Albanian communities.

Acknowledgements

I would like to thank all those Serbs and Albanians in Kosovo who, since my first visit there in 1985, have kindly talked to me of their experiences and knowledge of the region's past and present and helped me to get to know what must surely be the area of Europe least known to outsiders. I am grateful to the following for their specific contributions: Gabriel Partos, James Pettifer, Bob Churcher, Dusan Janjic, Mahmut Bakalli, Ilaz Ramajli, and to Mary Moats, for the use of her unpublished manuscript. I am also grateful to the publishers: Michael Dwyer, who commissioned the book, and Christopher Hurst, who edited it. Finally I acknowledge with gratitude the financial assistance I received from the Society of Authors (Authors' Foundation Awards).

London, January 1998   MIRANDA VICKERS

Kosovo in its Balkan setting

Kosovo

1

THE RULE OF THE NEMANJAS AND THE ARRIVAL OF THE OTTOMANS

'The earthly kingdom is shortlived, but the Heavenly one is forever.'
(Prince Lazar, on the eve of the Battle of Kosovo, 1389)

Following the Second World War, but especially since the serious riots which broke out in Kosovo in 1981, Serbian archaeologists have been hard at work seeking to refute the theory of the Illyrian ethnic origins of the Albanians. The battleground over the status of Kosovo has thus now been extended to pre-history. The long-standing Albanian claim for a continuity of descent from the ancient Ilyrians is now accompanied by arguments that Kosovo and Meto-hija form parts of an ancient Illyrian homeland that should naturally be joined with the rest of modern Albania.[1] The peoples whom the Greeks and Romans called Illyrians occupied an extensive tract of territory bordering on the Adriatic from Epirus in the south and Macedonia in the south-east to Istria in the north. The Albanians claim that they are consequently descended from the Illyrians and are the indigenous inhabitants of Kosovo. The Albanian language, which belongs to the Indo-European group, has distinctive vocab-ulary, morphology and phonetic rules which have engaged the attention of many philologists, of whom several have confidently asserted its descent from ancient Illyrian.[2]

The continuing political collisions between Albanians and Serbs have had a marked impact on Illyrian studies. It is no novelty that debates over the ethnic affinities of ancient peoples in southeastern Europe should be bound up with the antipathies of Serbs, Bulgars, Greeks and Albanians, but the question of Kosovo has become more serious than at any time since it was first posed at the Congress of

1. John Wilkes, *The Illyrians*, Blackwell, Oxford, 1992, p. 27.
2. Ibid., p. 278.

1

Berlin in 1878.[3] The theory of their Illyrian origins propounded by modern Albanians is centred on their unbroken descent from an Illyrian people already formed in Bronze Age times, and in a geographical area that includes the modern state of Albania, together with the Albanian-inhabited regions of former Yugoslavia: Kosovo, western Macedonia and southeastern Montenegro. This fact is corroborated by a number of items of evidence from the names of places and people, evidence of an Illyrian presence in the Kosovo-Metohija region. The Albanians also claim that the Dardanians – ancient inhabitants of Kosovo, northern Macedonia and southern Serbia – were an Illyrian people, whereas Serbian archaeologists hold that they represent an intermingling of both Illyrian and Thracian elements.[4] The issue has been consistently obscured by political and ideological arguments which have prevailed over academic ones.

Serbian historiography claims that the Albanian population was formed from a mele of peoples including remnants of Illyrians but also a mixture of peoples who inhabited the western Balkans during the classical and medieval period. Serbian scientific and political institutions strive to substantiate that since their arrival in the Balkans in the sixth century, the South Slavs have dominated the Kosovo region, and that the Albanians only arrived as late as the end of the seventeenth century and primarily during the eighteenth century. According to this theory, a few small Albanian communities lived up till the fifth century AD in Kosovo and in Macedonia as far north as Skopje, but they then retreated south into the mountains of Albania following the Slav invasions. They began returning in the thirteenth and fourteenth centuries, becoming larger communities after the Ottoman invasion under the protection of Islam. Strong insistence on the demographic argument aims at presenting the Albanians as colonisers and persecutors of Serbs, who have a historic right over Kosovo and therefore a right to live there, whereas the Albanians are immigrants and therefore have no historic right to live there. In general Albanian historians do not deny that some Albanians occupied Serbian lands (the North Albanian provenance of many Kosovars is attested by their own family histories).

3. Ibid., p. 11.
4. For the Albanian view see A. Hadri, 'L'historiographie yougoslave sur l'état illyrien,' *Iliria* (Tirana), IV, 1976, and for the Serbian response see M. Garasanin, 'L'historiographie yougoslave sur l'état illyrien (à propos de la communication de Ali Hadri dans *Iliria* IV, Tirana, 1976)', G CBI XVIII/16, 1980.

But they tend to minimise the size of the colonisation, while letting their opponents read between the lines that, after all, these immigrants were going back home, the lands they occupied having belonged to their Illyrian ancestors, the Dardanians,[5] who shared a long eastern border with the Thracians in the central Balkans during the Hellenistic period.

There was a pre-urban Dardanian society between the sixth and fourth centuries BC with urban settlements developing between the fourth and first centuries. Recent research has proved that close contacts with the Hellenic world began towards the end of the seventh century BC with imports from Chios. It has also been observed that hill settlements in Kosovo gradually disappeared towards the middle of the fourth century BC as they also did in the Skopje valley (Skopje castle, Nerezi, Varvara, Studencan). No instance of the destruction or forced evacuation of a settlement has been noticed, which makes their desertion as a result of the urban-isation of Dardanian society the more likely explanation.[6] Serbian archaeologists assert a number of theses on the origins of the Alba-nians, the most widely accepted being that the Albanians were not Illyrian but a mixture of Daco-Moesian, appearing during the early Middle Ages as a result of intermarriage between nomadic shepherds and local un-romanised remnants, including those of the Illyrians and the Dardanians. In the past, Serbian researchers had not always been of one mind in allocating the Kosovo region to the ancient Daco-Moesians. The prominent Serbian archaeologist Milutin Garasanin, in a survey of prehistoric Serbia in 1973, openly admits that on the basis of their personal and place names, the Dardanians can, with a degree of certainty, be considered Illyrians, and that a Thracian and perhaps a Dacian element are evident only in the east-ern parts of their territories.[7] In the matter of distribution, Thra-cian names are found mainly in eastern Dardania, from Skupi (Skopje) to Naissus (Nis) and Remesiana, although some Illyrian names do occur. The latter are entirely dominant in the western areas, Pristina-Mitrovica and Prizren-Pec.[8]

Whether the Dardanians were an Illyrian or a Thracian people has been much debated and one view suggests that the area was

5. Pipa and Repishti, *Studies on Kosova*, 1984, p. 242.
6. E. Shukriu, *Kosova Historical Review* (Tirana), 3/1994, pp. 12-13.
7. Milutin Garasanin, *Preistorija na tlu SR Srbije*, vol. II, Belgrade, 1973, p. 523.
8. John Wilkes, *The Illyrians*, p. 86.

originally populated by Thracians who were then exposed to direct contact with Illyrians over a long period. The theory of the Illyrian origins of the Dardanians is based primarily on classical written sources and personal and place names. In Kosovo archaeological research has so far concentrated mainly on the excavation of Neolithic, Iron Age and some classical and medieval sites. Few Bronze Age sites have been excavated and all of them appear to be of an Illyrian character. Research into the Iron Age, which has been the most intensively researched period in Kosovo, has shown that a culture with distinct features that can without doubt be called Dardanian existed in the eighth century BC in the territories that written sources later called Dardania.[9] In the first century BC the Dardanians appear as troublesome neighbours of Roman Macedonia, and around 70 BC the Roman army waged war against them with exceptional cruelty. Their final submission to the Romans may have occurred when Macedonia was in the charge of Antony (40-31 BC), though any record of that achievement is likely to have been suppressed by his rival Octavian.[10] Thus the Illyrians disappeared into the Roman Empire.

In the fourth century AD the Roman province of Dardania was created, which included Kosovo and Skopje, while the towns of Tetovo, Gostivar, Struga and Ohrid were included in the province of New Epirus. The Albanian-inhabited areas of what is today Montenegro were a part of the province of Prevalitana. The Romans generally left the Dardanians to their own devices, and they thus managed to retain their characteristics and traditions. Under Roman occupation Saxon miners were brought to Kosovo from Hungary. Throughout the third and fourth centuries AD, the Illyrian regions suffered numerous invasions from the Huns, the Visigoths and the Ostrogoths. When, in 395, Rome was split into eastern and western empires, southern Illyria went to the Eastern Empire and the Eastern Church, while northern Illyria went to the Western Empire, under the ecclesiastical authority of the Pope. By the sixth century AD the Slavs had begun to cross the Danube into the Balkans. However, the large Avaro-Slav migrations of the sixth and seventh centuries did not cause the disappearance of the pre-existing societies in the central Balkans. At first Kosovo was little affected by these migrations, which started from the Danube crossing by Singidunum (today's Belgrade), mainly heading for the shores of the Black Sea,

9. E. Shukriu, *Kosova Historical Review*, 3/1994, p. 11.
10. Wilkes, *The Illyrians*, p. 210.

Thrace and eventually Constantinople. Smaller numbers passed down the route via the Morava and Vardar valleys to reach Thessaloniki, and only isolated groups penetrated the western regions.

The dispersal of Slavs in the southern Balkans following the unsuccessful siege of Thessaloniki in 586 resulted in an occupation of Praevalitana and the region south of the Shkumbi river, a distribution indicated by place-names of Slav origin. These invasions seriously weakened the Byzantine Empire and by the end of the sixth century, following further invasions by Slav tribes, the indigenous tribes began to move their settlements from the exposed lowland plains to the comparative security of higher ground. Many mining communities dispersed as colonists left the area. Those that remained became subsistence farmers. Following the collapse of the Roman Empire and the weakening of the Byzantine Empire, the Illyrian-speaking peoples expanded again into the Mat valley and the Muzeqe plain. By then they were known to their southern neighbours as Albani, and their language as Albanian.[11]

During the tenth century the central Balkan regions became the scene of conflict between the Byzantines and the Bulgarian tsars Simeon and Samuel. By the end of the century the Empire of Samuel comprised most of the land between the Black Sea and the Adriatic, including all the Albanian inhabited regions. However, in 1018 the Bulgarians were defeated in a battle on the outskirts of Beligrad (Berat) by the Byzantines, who then re-established their rule over the Albanian-speaking regions. In 1054 the Christian world finally split into the Eastern Orthodox and the Roman Catholic Churches, and as a result the Albanian people of the Balkans came under the influence of the Greeks and Slavs on the one hand and of Rome and Venice on the other. Catholicism began to spread through the pastoral tribes of what is now northern Albania, and Latin was reinstated where Greek had formerly dominated as the cultural and ecclesiastical language. The Albanian world now became closely integrated to Byzantium, which greatly valued the economic and strategic importance of the Albanian-inhabited regions linking the vital trade routes from the Adriatic coast with Constantinople.

11. N. Hammond, 'The Relations of Illyrian Albania with the Greeks and Romans' in T. Winnifrith (ed.), *Perspectives on Albania*, London, 1992, p. 39. The second century geographer Ptolemy mentioned an Albanian tribe with a city named Albanopolis. The name of these Albanians was extended in the eleventh century to the rest of the ancient Illyrians.

The following century social and ethnic divisions occurred. Those Slavs entering the western Balkans split into three groups, comprising the Slovenes, who occupied territory to the north, and farther south the Croats and Serbs. The Croats established an independent state which lasted until it was absorbed into the Kingdom of Hungary in 1102, while the Slovenes accepted the rule of the Frankish kings. Much more central to the future of the Balkans was the evolution of Serbia. Its early history was marked by quarrels between various tribal chiefs (*zupans*), which led internally to disorder and externally to clashes with the neighbouring Bulgarians. Being predominantly agriculturalists, the Slav tribes settled in river valleys and plains. The interior was thinly peopled by pastoralists: Wallachians (Vlachs), Illyrians, Thracians, Dardanians and other (earlier) settlers. The Slav invasions pushed the 'indigenous' population back to the highland pastures, and by the eleventh century, almost all arable soil in the northernmost part of what is now Albania and in the region of present-day Kosovo was in Slavic hands.[12]

Up till 1180, when the Emperor Manuel Comneni died, Kosovo had been governed by Byzantium. The castle of Zvecan near Mitrovica that guarded the great mining centre of Trepca, played a major role in the twelfth century struggle of Byzantium against the Serbs. The original homeland of the Serbs was in the mountainous area around Raska, near the present-day region of Novi Pazar. During the latter part of the twelfth century, the Serbs moved south and eastward beyond Raska towards present-day Kosovo. Eventually, in about 1166, a major change occurred in Serbia. The old dynasty was replaced by a new one headed first by a certain Tihomir, who was quickly replaced by his brother Stefan Nemanja. This new dynasty was to reign in Serbia till 1371.

Kosovo, the centre of the Nemanjic state

Attempts to gain access to the Albanian coast were prominent in the politics of the medieval Serbian state. The urbanisation and consequently the development of the Serbs began as they drew nearer to the coast and established their administrative and religious centres in Shkoder, Prizren and Decan. In the decade 1180-90, taking

12. R. Gremaux, 'Politics of Ethnic Domination in the Land of the Living Past, Kosovo - Kosova', in G. Duijzings, D. Janjic and S. Maliqi (eds), *Confrontation or Coexistence*, Peace Research Centre, University of Nijmegen, 1996, p. 16.

advantage of the internal disorders of Byzantium under Andronicus, of the Hungarian attack launched in 1183 with which Nemanja was allied, of the Norman invasion in 1185, and of the Third Crusade in 1189, Nemanja was able to conquer Kosovo and Metohija, including Prizren, and penetrate into northern Macedonia, taking Skopje and the upper Vardar. No territory remained under the former Dukljan dynasty; Zeta was incorporated into Nemanja's state of Raska. Having reached the coast, he acquired southern Dalmatia, including the towns of Kotor, Ulcinj and Bar. From Zeta he also advanced into northern Albania, obtaining the region of Pilot lying between Prizren and Lake Shkoder.[13] Thus Serbia came into possession of a consolidated territory bordering Hungary along the low mountain range on the north side of the West Morava river and extending south well into Kosovo and Metohija and west to the coast, including Zeta, Trebinje, Hum and southern Dalmatia. The Byzantines were clearly on the defensive.[14]

Situated at the crossroads of the main Balkan routes connecting the surrounding Serbian lands of Raska, Bosnia, Zeta and the Shkoder littoral with Macedonia and the Pomoravlje region, Kosovo now became the cultural and administrative centre of the Nemanjic state following the fall of Constantinople to the Fourth Crusade in 1204. From the twelfth century Catholicism had begun to penetrate through the coastal areas to the interior of the Albanian-inhabited territories of the north-east, but since state and religion were synonymous, the Nemanjas set about imposing the Orthodox faith on their subject peoples. A large number of Catholic churches and monasteries were enlarged and converted into Serbian ones. In the course of time the Orthodox church divided into several national churches corresponding to the states or peoples of the region. Thus the Serbian Orthodox Church acquired an independent identity in the thirteenth century, becoming closely tied to the power of the state and a strong supporter of state policies.[15]

Throughout the twelfth century, Serbia experienced a growth in economic development. Progress in agriculture was based on rich soils left by former lakes located in fertile basins as in Kosovo (upper Ibar river), Metohija (upper Drin river) and Tetovo (upper Vardar

---

13. J.V.A. Fine, *The Late Medieval Balkans*, Ann Arbor: University of Michigan Press, 1994, p. 7.
14. Ibid., p. 26.
15. Mark Krasniqi, 'The Role of the Serbian Orthodox Church in Anti-Albanian policies in Kosova', *Kosova Historical Review*, no. 3 (Tirana), 1994, p. 15.

river). Progress in mining also occurred based on deposits of gold, silver, copper and tin. After the fall of Constantinople in 1204 the centre of the Nemanjic state moved to the comparatively rich and densely populated regions of Kosovo and Metohija. Here were established the Nemanjas' cultural and administrative centres which required the seat of the Serbian Orthodox church also to move to Pec on acquiring autocephalous status in 1219. The successors of the first archbishop, Saint Sava, built several additional chapels around the Church of the Holy Apostle, laying the ground for what was to become the Pec patriarchy. Through their various theoretical writings and liturgies, these monastic communities helped to foster and strengthen not only the beliefs of the Orthodox Church but also the spiritual form of the Serbian nation. King Milutin left behind the largest number of endowments in Kosovo, one of the greatest of which is Gracanica monastery built in 1321 near Pristina.[16]

In Kosovo, especially in its eastern part, most Albanians were gradually assimilated into the Eastern Orthodox faith by numerous methods, including the baptism of infants with Serbian names and the conducting of all religious ceremonies such as marriages in the Serbian language. In Montenegro entire tribes such as the Kuc, Bjellopavliq, Palabardha, Piprraj and Vasovic were assimilated; those who resisted assimilation retreated into the hills of what is now northern Albania. It is probable that during the twelfth century the definite differentiation occurred between the Gheg linguistic group north of the Shkumbi river and the Tosk group to the south of it. This division was clearly indicated in 1210 by the choice of this valley as the northern border of the territories 'conceded' by Venice to Michael of Epirus. At the same time Roman Catholicism, coming from Dalmatia, spread throughout northern Albania, while the south remained under the jurisdiction of the Orthodox Church.[17] The formal adoption of Catholicism, besides drawing a clear line of demarcation between Albanians and Serbs, also had a further important effect: it incorporated the resistance of the Albanians into the powerful anti-Serb coalition of the Catholic monarchs of Europe that the Papacy attempted to construct especially at the start of the fourteenth century. There is no doubt that the Serbs' breach with the French Angevins, hitherto their allies, played a decisive role in the creation of this front. Common interests gave rise to major campaigns against the Serbs, such as the

16. D. Batakovic, *The Kosovo Chronicles*, Belgrade, 1992, pp. 37-8.
17. Pipa and Repishti, *Studies on Kosova*, p. 8.

Crusades of 1319 and 1331, when the alliance of the Papacy, Naples and Hungary was eagerly joined by Albanian and Croat nobles.[18] The Albanians were not to create any structure resembling a state till the fifteenth century. However, organised in tribes under their own chieftains, they dominated the mountains of most of what is today known as Albania.

Virtually the whole territory of southern Kosovo during the Middle Ages became the property of the big monasteries. The information contained in the founding charters of these monasteries show that in the first half of the fourteenth century the population gradually moved from the mountains to the west and north of Kosovo down into the fertile valleys. Not far from Pec stands the enormous and beautiful church of Decani, built in 1327-35 for Stefan Uros III; its wealth of decoration includes almost 10,000 painted figures and twenty biblical cycles representing the largest surviving collection of icons created within the Byzantine sphere of influence.[19] Each Serbian ruler built at least one monastery. The 1330 Decani charter lists in detail households and chartered villages. The Decani estate was an area of sweeping size which included parts of what is today northeastern Albania. It is these self-sufficient monastic complexes that are cited as proof of the ethnic and homogeneous settlement of Kosovo by Serbs.

The empire of Stefan Dusan

The civil wars in Byzantium in the mid-fourteenth century had destabilised the European provinces of the Empire, thus opening the way for the Balkan conquests of the most powerful of all the Serbian kings, Stefan Dusan (1331-55), an undertaking easily accomplished with the aid of the local nobility. The conquest by the Serbs of the Albanian-speaking lands within the area formed by Antivar (Bar), Prizren, Ohrid and Vlora was mainly accomplished in 1343 when Dusan launched a great invasion of the territory now known as Albania. With the proclamation of the empire, the patriarchal throne was permanently established at the Pec monastery in 1346. Serbia's rulers subsequently dotted the fertile land lying between

18. Pellumb Xhufi, 'The Albanians in the Serbian Nemjana Kingdom', *Kosova Historical Review*, no. 4, 1994, p. 19.
19. For a detailed description of the monasteries and of Kosovo see A. Kindersley, *The Mountains of Serbia: Travels through Inland Yugoslavia*, Newton Abbot, 1977.

Pec, Prizren, Mitrovica and Pristina with churches and monasteries, and the whole region eventually acquired the Serb name Metohija (from the Greek *metoh*, meaning an estate owned by the Church). Thus the Metohija region became the spiritual nucleus of the Serbian nation. There followed a policy of enforced conversion of both Catholic and Orthodox Albanians to the Serbian national church – conversion to the Serbian church being a priority of Serbian state policy, as can be shown by the Code of Stefan Dusan. This Code – a form of constitution of the mediaeval Serbian kingdom – contained so-called 'anti-heresy clauses' demanding that all subjects of the Serbian kingdom and members of foreign communities be baptised into the Serbian church. The Code laid down the role of the Serbian king as the defender of the Serbian church and the extirpator of 'heresy'.[20]

In 1346, following the incorporation of Epirus and Thessaly into his Empire, Dusan was crowned emperor of the Serbs, Greeks, Bulgarians and Albanians. The Serbian bishopric of Pec was then proclaimed a patriarchate, thus establishing the Serbian Church's independence from Constantinople.[21] Stefan Dusan made a great effort to encourage commerce and industry, which was skilfully achieved by the importation of foreigners as well as by diplomacy and treaties. Saxons, Ragusans (from Dubrovnik), Venetians, Greeks and Albanians all worked in his rich mines such as Novo Brdo, or garrisoned his fortresses. Never before or since has Serbian power or territory been so great. Today Serbian patriots look back to the age of Dusan as the most glorious in their history and regard him as a hero. His name was to become synonymous with the aspirations of the Serbian nation. Under the Nemanjas, protected highways united Prizren with the Danube and the Adriatic. There was constant communication between Prizren, Kotor, Ragusa and even Venice. The Serbian rulers facilitated the passage of merchants through their lands. For two centuries Prizren was the seat of the Serbian sovereign, and was one of Serbia's chief trade centres where many Serbian merchants as well as traders from the coast resided, including Dubrovnik's consul for all of Serbia.

Prizren naturally became Dusan's capital, and in its vicinity he built between 1347 and 1352 a church dedicated to the Holy

20. Pellumb, Xhufi, *The Albanians in the Serbian Nemanja Kingdom*, p. 18.
21. The 'Book of Serbian Aristocracy', preserved at Chilandari, the Serbian monastery on Mount Athos, lists all the prominent members of the Serbian community living in Kosovo before the Ottoman occupation.

Archangels as his final resting place, the only structure he had an opportunity to build as donor. No expense was spared on the interior, which was resplendent in marble, gold leaf, silver stars and mosaics.[22] Unfortunately for the Serbs, Stefan Dusan never learned to hold his great empire together. He divided his territorial conquests into provinces, each under the control of a powerful chieftain. All goes well in such a consolidated state while there is a strong ruler at the helm, but once the 'iron hand' is removed, as happened after Dusan's death in 1355, internal conflicts inevitably emerge. The Empire, comprising small semi-independent states under such powerful families as the Dukagjin, Balsha, Thopia and Kastrati, lacked uniformity and cohesion, thus gradually crumbled, especially after it was attacked by the Ottomans, an enemy completely united under the authority of a single leader. Following Dusan's death, Kosovo came under the rule of King Vukasin Mrnjavcevic, the co-ruler of the last Nemanjic, Tsar Uros. In the years after 1371 Prizren declined to some extent, since it had become part of a smaller principality and was separated from the principal mines, which no longer lay under the same ruler as the town. After 1371 merchant colonies at individual mines, like Novo Brdo, grew in size and importance, and much of the trade between the mining centres and the coast was carried on directly rather than being routed through Prizren.[23]

The arrival of the Ottomans

During the late fourteenth century, disunity in the Balkans resulting from internal division and domestic squabbles was a prelude to the real danger that was materialising from the south-east. A new power now made its appearance as a factor in the history of Europe. The Ottoman Turks, an Asiatic people, had gradually worn away the weakened Byzantine Empire and in 1354 invaded the peninsula from Asia Minor. They began their inexorable trail of conquest by moving up through the Maritsa valley and capturing Macedonia in 1380. Lacking unity the various Balkan national rulers failed to recognize the problem and thus to stem the tide. The imminence and extent of the Ottoman threat had not been accurately estimated

22. A.N. Dragnich and S. Todorovich, *The Saga of Kosovo*, Westview Press, Boulder, CO, 1984, pp. 41–2.
23. Fine, *The Late Medieval Balkans*, p. 383.

by either the Byzantines or the Balkan rulers, whose main efforts were absorbed in wars among themselves.

By 1370 the Serbian state was very different from the empire Dusan had left at the time of his death. Thessaly, Epirus and Albania had seceded entirely, and internal feuds between the various autonomous Slavic and Albanian lords had allowed the Ottomans, throughout the 1360s, to penetrate deep into Thrace with little opposition. They were unable to form a sufficiently strong and united coalition to fight the Ottomans when the latter confronted them on 26 September 1371 at the Battle of Marica, near Crnomen, where the Ottomans scored their greatest success up to that time. This battle, which heralded the decisive Ottoman invasion of Serbian-controlled lands, was far more significant in opening up the Balkans to the Turks and in weakening Serbian resistance than the later and more famous Battle of Kosovo (1389). Due partly to their unpreparedness, the Serbian forces were annihilated and in consequence the rest of Serbia disintegrated. Parts of it were grabbed by the still feuding warlords who, distrusting each other, struggled to fill the vacuums created by the collapse of central power.

The Battle of Marica made the disintegration of the rest of Serbia easier; the central government, such as it was, lost the bulk of its forces in the battle, while the nobles who had not fought retained their forces unimpared. In 1386 the Ottomans invaded Serbia and captured the key communication 'crossroads' of Nis. In the ensuing peace treaty the Serbs agreed to pay the Ottomans an annual tribute and provide 1,000 mercenaries for the Ottoman army. At last, and too late, the Balkan states realised that they had to unite against the Ottoman threat. The Bosnian king (Tvrtko) sent a detachment of soldiers to aid the Serbs, and in the fastness of Montenegro a combined force of Albanians and Serbs utterly defeated the Ottoman army. Its leader Sultan Murad I (1362–89), then absent in Asia Minor, swore revenge. He dashed back to Europe and assembled an enormous army to march against the Serbs.

The battle of Kosovo

This was the background to the battle destined to decide the fate of the Balkans. It took place in Kosovo Polje (the Field of Blackbirds – the Serbian *kos* means blackbird) outside Pristina, on St Vitus Day, 28 June 1389. On the eve of the battle, the northern parts of

Kosovo were in the possession of Prince Lazar Hrebeljanovic and parts of Metohija belonged to his brother-in-law Vuk Brankovic. The Turks first demanded that Lazar accept Ottoman suzerainty and pay tribute. He refused and, realising that he would be faced with an invasion, sought aid from his neighbours Tvrtko and Vuk Brankovic. Tvrtko sent a large contingent under the command of Vlatko Vukovic, the commander who had defeated the Turkish force at Bileca. Vuk Brankovic came himself, leading his own men. Thus the Serbian army was composed of three contingents under these three leaders, none of whom was then a Turkish vassal.[24] It is said that Vuk accepted the offer agreeing to desert with his troops in the course of the coming battle, and he has accordingly been cast as a traitor in Serbian folk history. The Ottoman chroniclers, however, fail to mention these specific facts. Nevertheless, morale was certainly low in the Serbian camp, which led not only some Serbian but also several Bulgarian princes to offer their services to the Sultan. But in spite of this a large coalition army led by Serbian, Hungarian, Bulgarian, Bosnian and Albanian nobles gathered on the wide plain of Kosovo to confront the Ottoman army. Albanian princes were at that time close allies of the Serbs, the result of their shared desire to oppose the Ottomans. In many districts the Slavonic and Albanian elements existed side-by-side, and numerous examples are known of close economic and political ties between Serbs and Albanians during the medieval period.

Sultan Murad succeeded in surprising Lazar's army. The sudden attack caused considerable disorder among the Christian troops who were forced on the same afternoon to disperse in total confusion and disarray. Both Murad and Lazar were killed in the head-on collision between the two armies (approximately 30,000 troops on both sides). As the battle ended, what remained of the Turkish army held the field while the surviving Serbian (Lazar's and Brankovic's) and Bosnian (Vlatko Vukovic's) troops withdrew. However, the Turks then withdrew as well, for Bayezid needed to hurry back east to secure his position as the new sultan against his brothers; also, he did not have enough troops remaining to carry on an offensive against the Balkan Christians. Thus, since the Turks also withdrew, one might conclude that the battle was a draw. They had indeed lost a vast number of troops, but they had many more in the east and were able in the following years to return and raid, and continue

24. Ibid., p. 09.

their successful push into the Balkans. The Serbs were left with too few men to resist successfully, and although they did not lose the battle, they lost the war over the next two to three years because they could no longer resist the Turks effectively; and their losses at Kosovo were, of course, the main reason why they had so few men left to defend Serbia.[25]

Although no true military victor emerged from the battle, Tvrtko's emissaries told the courts of Europe that the Christian army had defeated the infidels, although Prince Lazar's successors were exhausted by their heavy losses and immediately sought peace by agreeing to become vassals of their new sultan. Vuk Brankovic resisted them until 1392, when he was forced to do the same. The Ottomans took Brankovic's lands and gave them to a more loyal vassal, Stefan Lazarevic (the son of Prince Lazar), thereby creating a rift between their heirs. Stefan appointed as his successor his nephew Djurad Brankovic, whose rule was marked by fresh conflicts and finally the fall of the whole of Kosovo to the Ottomans in 1455.[26] A feeling of despair permeated Lazar's lands after the prince's death and, conscious of the need to combat pessimism in Serbia and create hope for a bright future, the monastic authors of the day wrote eulogies and sermons in praise of Lazar in which they interpreted the events of the time for their own contemporaries. They portrayed Lazar as God's favoured servant and the Serbian people as the chosen people of the New Testament – the 'new Israel'. Like the Hebrews in Babylonian captivity they would be led out of slavery to freedom.[27] According to accounts in epics, Lazar dreamed on the eve of the battle that he was offered either a heavenly or an earthly kingdom and, being a man of his time, he chose the heavenly one. It was also prophesied that he would be betrayed in the battle.

Because the epic account was designed to parallel the New Testament, a Judas Iscariot also had to be found. Thus it was he who on the morrow would betray his master when the prophesy was revealed; Milos Obilic was accused by Vuk Brankovic of being the one in secret contact with the Turks. When Lazar faced Milos with the charge, Milos denied it, saying, 'Tomorrow my deeds will show that I am faithful to my lord.' To prove his loyalty, shortly before dawn on 28 June, Milos slipped out of his camp and announced himself to the Turkish sentries as a Serbian deserter. Taken to the

25. Ibid., pp. 410-11.
26. Dusan Batakovic, *The Kosovo Chronicles*, Belgrade, 1992, p. 40.
27. T.A. Emmert, 'The Kosovo Legacy', *Serbian Studies*, vol. 5, no. 2, 1989, p. 5.

Sultan, he pulled out a knife hidden in his garments and stabbed Murad, fatally wounding him. We do not know whether there had actually been any accusations in the Serbian camp before the battle, but it is a fact that a Serb named Milos Obilic (or Kobilic) did desert and murder the Sultan.[28] Lazar's death is depicted as the triumph of good over evil – a martyrdom for the faith and the symbol of a new beginning. Responding to contemporary needs, the medieval writers transformed the defeat into a kind of moral victory for the Serbs and an inspiration for the future. The Serbian epic tradition only developed these ideas further and established them firmly in the consciousness of the Serbian people.[29]

These epics influenced the Dalmatian historians who wrote about the great battle in the seventeenth century, but because their early versions had propagandistic motives and religious overtones, they are inevitably suspect. Not only were they partisan on behalf of the Serbs and Christians against the Turks and Muslims, but they also gave prominence to certain Serbian families against others. Therefore, much concerning the Battle has remained controversial.[30] The church also romanticised the Nemanjic tradition for the masses, and by removing any of the negative aspects of feudalism helped to convey the image of a once glorious state. The Serbs therefore viewed the collapse of the medieval Serbian state as the central event in their history and found its explanation in the Battle of Kosovo. Indeed, the epic cycle of Kosovo became the longest, most beautiful and most important of all the Serbian epics.[31] It was not so much the loss of the battle itself as the subsequent loss of statehood that so impressed the minds of ensuing generations of Serbs. These epic myths eventually became institutionalised as part of the nineteenth-century Serbian national programme, as poetic licence did away with historical fact. Nearly five centuries later two British travellers, after hearing a succession of accounts of the Battle, declared: 'Every Serb between the Danube and the Adriatic is as familiar with the names of all here mentioned as with those of his own brothers.'[32]

As late as 1866, only 4.2 per cent of the Serbian population were able to read and write – in rural areas the proportion was as low as

28. Fine, *The Late Medieval Balkans*, p. 410.
29. Emmert, 'The Kosovo Legacy', p. 5.
30. Fine, *The Late Medieval Balkans*, p. 409.
31. Emmert, 'The Kosovo Legacy', p. 7.
32. G. M. Mackenzie and A.P. Irby, *Travels in the Slavonic Provinces of Turkey-in-Europe*, vol.1, London, 1877, p. 186.

1.6 per cent. Decasyllabic epics chanted by bards and easily memo-
rised by generations of listeners were instrumental in preserving the
Serbian national identity; the heart of the national consciousness
being the Kosovo myth and its covenant. By transforming the
national defeat into a metaphor for survival, the poems about
Kosovo served a double function, providing a rationalisation of the
past that was a salve to wounded pride and at the same time
containing a radical programme for the future. The Tsar's curse on
all those who do not fight for Kosovo would serve as a reminder to
Serbs for all time.[33] Five hundred and sixty years later, following
the Second World War, a 25-metre-high monument was erected in
25 acres of pasture on Kosovo Polje where every summer hundreds
of thousands of bright red poppies bloom, supposedly the blood of
the fallen Christian heroes. Each year the battle's anniversary on 28
June (Vidovdan) is still commemorated.

Subjection to Ottoman control in Kosovo

The years following the Battle of Kosovo were marked by an
increase in Ottoman military activity; certain territories were
directly annexed and suzerainty was imposed on various hitherto
independent princes and tribes. Taking advantage of the increasing
internal troubles in Byzantium, Bulgaria and Serbia, the Ottomans
began to extend their conquests deep into the Balkan peninsula. In
1393 the capital of Bulgaria, Turnovo, was captured and a short
time later the whole territory of Bulgaria came under Ottoman
rule, but it was only in 1455, two years after their capture of
Constantinople, that the Ottomans directed a major assault against
Serbia, capturing Southern Serbia, the Kosovo region and the rich-
est mine, Novo Brdo, which was estimated at the time of its capture
to yield an annual revenue of 120,000 ducats. Among Serbia's losses
in 1455 was Pec, seat of the Serbian Patriarch.[34] After the final fall
of Serbia to the Ottomans in 1459, all the Serbian eparchies came
under the jurisdiction of the Greek Archbishopric of Ohrid. Many
ecclesiastical buildings were plundered and some were immediately
converted into mosques, among them the church of Our Lady of
Ljeviska in Prizren. Many of the great monasteries were looted.

---

33. D. Kostovicova, *Parallel Worlds: The Response of Kosovo Albanians to Loss of
    Autonomy in Serbia, 1986-1996*, Keele European Research Centre, 1997, p.7.
34. Fine, *The Late Medieval Balkans*, p. 569.

Tsar Dusan's magnificent Church of the Holy Archangels was all but razed to the ground, and its rich marble was re-used to build the huge Sinan Pasha mosque in the centre of the town. Today, more than 500 years later, the ruined church's forlorn, grass-covered stones lie scattered along the canyon of the bustling little river Bistrica, providing a playground for Albanian youngsters. The great monasteries of Decani and Gracanica escaped destruction, but their patrimonies were reduced to a handful of surrounding villages.

With the arrival of the Ottomans, Prizren and Pristina became important stages on the revitalised trade route from the Dalmatian coast to Macedonia and Constantinople. The new Ottoman administrative system divided up most of the land according to the Ottoman military fief (or *timar*) system, which was totally controlled by Ottoman feudal landowners and their officials. In 1432 a land registration was carried out dividing the territory of Albania into 335 *timars* or fiefs, each usually comprising two or three villages which were then distributed among the leaders of the civil, military or religious administration. Dibra and its surroundings became a separate *sandjak* (administrative district) while the region now known as Kosovo was included in the *sandjak* of Skopje. The expansion of the Serbian state southwards had led to a corresponding movement of the Serbian population into present-day Kosovo and Albania, but with the arrival of the Ottomans this process was reversed and migration came to be directed northwards. These events set in motion a series of northward local migrations of Serbs, and by 1481 a large part of the Slav population of Kosovo had migrated to what is now Hungary and Transylvania.

The continued development of mining in Kosovo caused the rapid development of several towns such as Novo Brdo, Janjeva, Trepca and Pristina and a corresponding population shift towards them. Although Ottoman colonists were sent to Kosovo, there were relatively few of them and they settled primarily in and around Prizren. By the first half of the fifteenth century Albanians had begun gradually to move their cattle down from the mountain pastures to the plain of Kosovo where they established small farming settlements. Migrants came mostly from the surrounding mountainous regions to settle in the lowland plains and valleys. As people moved to the towns, others came from the hills and occupied the abandoned villages. No one who has travelled in the formidably inhospitable mountains of present-day northern Albania and western Macedonia can fail to appreciate the chronic lack of suitable land on which to sustain even the smallest population. There are thus two types of new Albanian settlement in Kosovo – one in pastureland and the other in the towns. With the Treaty of 1489 between Venice and the Porte, recognising Ottoman sovereignty over Albania, almost half the Albanian population emigrated to Italy, and to evade the Ottomans thousands more retreated into inaccessible mountain regions, or migrated to Greece where they settled in Thessaly, Attica and as far south as the Peloponnese.

Albanian historiography asserts that Albanians were the majority in Kosovo even before the Ottoman conquest: 'The documents of the period after the Ottoman occupation of Kosovo, in 1455, and especially the land registers, provide many facts that show that these regions were inhabited by the Albanian population, while the Serbs who came as colonists, or as a ruling stratum during the Serbian occupation of these regions, constituted a minority, insignificant numerically but dominant from a political and social standpoint.'[35] In fact, the documents do not show any such thing. The Ottoman *defter* (register of landed property) of 1455 for the lands of the Serbian Brankovic princes (i.e. most of present-day Kosovo plus small areas of adjoining Sandjak and Serbia proper) record an overwhelming Slavic (Serb) majority.[36]

Although Albanian researchers claim with some justification that common Christian names do not necessarily imply Slavs, and a 'Todor or a Djuradj, son of Martin' could be either Albanian or Serb, it would be hard to imagine that a 'Radihna, son of Dabiziv' or a 'Prijezda, son of Relja' had any Albanian ancestry. It is more to the point that wherever Albanians appeared in 1455, they were often though probably not always identified as such. For example, in the village of Siptula, near Pristina, there were a 'Petko, Albanian' and a 'Mihal, Albanian'. In short, their nationality was not the usual one in the area.[37] The number of Albanian migrations into Kosovo began slowly to increase during the early sixteenth century.[38]

---

35. Selami Pulaha, 'The Scientific Truth about the Autochthony of the Albanians in Kosovo', *New Albania* (Tirana), no. 4, 1982, p. 20.
36. See Hamid Hadzibegic, Adem Handzic and Esref Kovacevic (comp.), *Oblast Brankovica: Opsirni katastarski popis iz 1455 godine*, Sarajevo, 1972.
37. Ivo Banac, *The National Question in Yugoslavia*, Cornell University Press, Ithaca, NY, 1984, pp. 294-5.
38. For accounts of medieval settlements in Kosovo and northern Albania see R.Mihaljcic, *Selista*, Zbornik Filozofskog Fakulteta, Belgrade, 1967; B. Hrabska, *The Registration Book of the Shkoder Sandjak of 1485*, Poljoprivredna proizvodnja Kosovo i susednih krajeva sredinom XV veka, Belgrade, 1974.

In an effort to cope with the Empire's increasingly diverse ethnic-religious groups, the Ottoman administration devised a socio-cultural communal entity, the *millet*, based on religious adherence rather than ethnic identity. The first *millet* – the Ortho- dox – was established in 1454 by Sultan Mehmet II who granted rights and freedoms in perpetuity; these were inherent in the *millet* and not subject to renewal, abolition or limitation. An Armenian and Jewish *millet* followed later.[39] Thus non-Muslims were brought into the Muslim organisational system but remained able to retain their own cultural and religious freedoms. The adoption of this system was essentially in response to the hetrogeneous nature of society in the Balkans, and used by Mehmet II to neutralise differ- ences and secure a degree of harmony. The *millet* and not the church was responsible for maintaining ethnic and linguistic iden- tity. Within the Orthodox *millet*, the Serbs could preserve their language, religion and ethnic individuality because religion not nationality was the fundamental factor in the Ottoman concept of governance.[40]

During the fifteenth century the great majority of Albanians were still Christians, and Serbs and Albanians lived together in considerable harmony. They venerated the same saints, worshipped in the same churches, and respected a past of shared values. Even today elderly Albanians recall that their fathers would never begin any project on a Tuesday, the day of the Serbian defeat at Kosovo.[41] The Albanians brought with them into Kosovo the maxims of the *Kanun of Leke*, which for the clans of northern Albania took precedence over all other laws, and for that reason both the church and the state opposed the application of the *Kanun*. In the areas bordering on Dukagjin, especially in the plains, where the Ottoman government had managed to establish a degree of domination, compromises occurred between the

---

39. A 'Latin Milet' was later given to the Roman Catholic population of north- ern Albania with the protection of the Habsburg Emperor. The first agreement to that effect was concluded on 14 July 1615 in Vienna between Emperor Matthias and Sultan Ahmet I.

40. For a comprehensive account of the *millet* system see Kemal Karpat, 'Millets and Nationality: The Roots of the Incongruity of Nation and State in the post-Ottoman Era', in B. Braude and B. Lewis (eds), *Christians and Jews in the Ottoman Empire*, vol.1, New York, 1982.

41. A. N. Dragnich, 'Serbian Culture in Kosovo in Past and Present Times', *Serbian Studies*, vol. 4, no. 4, 1988, p. 75.

Kanun and the *Shariat*.[42] Tradition ascribes the *Kanun* to Leke Dukagjini (1410–81), contemporary and comrade-in-arms of the Albanian national hero Gjergj Kastrioti Skanderbeg. However, Albanian customary law evolved over many centuries, both before and after the lifetime of this particular historical personage. The influence of Illyrian law should not be ignored. As the direct precursors of the Albanians, the Illyrians undoubtedly retained their legal norms despite coming under Roman domination, since it is established that the Roman governor of Illyria permitted the use of local laws when these did not conflict with the principles of Roman law. Even after Diocletian, when the provinces were forced to submit to increased Romanisation, the old laws were retained at least in memory and must have been transmitted orally to succeeding generations.[43]

The turbulent era of struggle against Ottoman expansion, in which Leke Dukagjini participated, also coincided with fundamental changes in the structure of Albanian society, especially the final disappearance of the aristocratic class (Leke belonged to it) and the emergence of a well-defined clan (*fis*) system.[44] While the *Kanun* of Skanderbeg was confined to a fairly limited area, that of Leke Dukagjini was observed over a wide area: in the mountains of Lezhe, in Dukagjin, in Shkoder, in Djakovica in Kosovo, and even among the Albanian populations in parts of Serbia, Montenegro and Macedonia. In certain overwhelmingly Muslim areas such as Krasniq and Lume the *Kanun* lost some of its power, and Ottoman customs came to replace older traditions. But on the whole the precepts of the *Kanun* of Leke Dukagjini were respected in all rural areas of the north, including Kosovo. As Syrja Pupovci says in his valuable introduction to the 1972 reprint of the *Kanun*, 'In essence,

---

42. *Kanun* is one version of a fluid compilation of customs, which vary in time and district. For a detailed study of the *Kanun* see Shtjefen Gjecov, *Kanuni i Leke Dukagjinit*, transl. Leonard Fox, Charles Schlacks, Jr, California, 1994. Shtjefen Gjecov, a Franciscan priest, codified the *Kanun* in a comprehensible and practical form for the use of scholars and other interested individuals. This work presents the fundamental customary law applied in almost all areas of Albanian settlement in the Middle Ages.

43. The *Kanun* of Leke Dukagjini was by no means the only code of customary law used by Albanians. In other areas, especially Kruje, Diber and Mat - the old strongholds of the Kastriots - a *Kanun* of Skanderbeg was in force, while various regions of central and southern Albania had their own separate legal codes, *Kanun of Leke Dukagjinit*, p. xvi.

44. Ibid., p. xvi

the preservation of customary law was one of the most important elements in helping the Albanian people to maintain their individuality under Ottoman domination.'[45] For those Serbs who remained in Kosovo the first century of Ottoman rule saw no great social change. In 1557 the patriarchate of Pec was renewed, thanks to Mehmed-Pasha Sokolovic, a Grand Vizier at the Porte of Serbian origin.[46]

45. *Kanuni i Leke Dukagjinit*, Rilindja, Pristina, 1972, p. ixxx., quoted in ibid., p. xvii.
46. Sokolovic was also responsible for building the bridge over the Drina at Visegrad, later celebrated by the Serbian Nobel laureate, Ivo Andric. This event marked a religious revival among all Serbs, especially those in Kosovo, which once again became the spiritual home of the Serbian nation.

2

THE GREAT SERB MIGRATIONS AND THE CONSOLIDATION OF OTTOMAN RULE

The Ottoman conquest of the Balkans resulted in significant but piecemeal population movements, as local inhabitants moved either south or north, while new ethnic elements emerged from the east. In Kosovo the Ottoman army was accompanied by members of Turkish-Tartar tribes who settled mainly in the towns. These were later joined by Gypsies and by Circassians, whom the Ottoman authorities encouraged to settle in the newly colonised Balkan region. This is the cause of the relatively cosmopolitan atmosphere that developed in such towns as Prizren, which retained its richly diverse population mix right up to the exodus of Turks in the 1950s. By the end of the sixteenth century, herdsmen from the northern Albanian mountains had begun descending to the plains of Kosovo where they gradually established themselves in small settlements. The majority came from the harsh Dukagjin region to escape from blood feuds or a shortage of grazing land. This steady trickle of Albanian families down into Kosovo certainly caused no dramatic demographic transformation in the ethnic makeup of Kosovo's population, despite the use in contemporary Serbian historiography of phrases such as 'marauding tribes from the Albanian highlands,'[1] which gives the impression that hordes of violent Albanians, bent on rape and pillage, were pouring into Kosovo.

As late as 1610 there were still ten times more Catholics in Kosovo than Muslims. The centres of Roman Catholicism in Kosovo were at Gjilan, Pec, Djakovica and Prizren, where many Catholics were descended from Ragusans who had migrated in the Middle Ages. This Catholic population was periodically replenished by fresh arrivals from the Albanian highlands. Ecclesiastical reports of the time give useful statistics on the religious distribution of some of the major towns of Kosovo at this time. For example,

1. D. Batakovic, *The Kosovo Chronicles*, Belgrade, 1992, p. 44.

Pristina, though not a parish, had twenty Catholic households (this fact is contained in the report of a Catholic priest, Pietro Mazrreku, who preached in south-western Kosovo in 1623). In addition numerous 'Turks' – especially those who owned a *timar* (landed estate tied to obligations of military service) fief – and many Serbs also lived there. In 1638 the households of Prizren were divided as follows: twenty-two Catholic, thirty-four Orthodox and 3,000 Muslim. Also in 1638, the households in Djakovica numbered twenty Catholic, twenty Orthodox and 320 Muslim. These reports, as one would expect, also contain accounts of Albanian expansion and settlement primarily by the Catholic Albanians. Mazrreku writes in 1623-4 that ten Catholic families from Albania had recently moved to Pristina; and ten left Pulat to settle in Prokuplje. In 1638 six families with twenty people emigrated from Pulat to Prizren. Fifteen Albanian families from Dukagjin – 120 people in all – settled in Suha Reka, a village near Prizren. In 1638 Bardhi found two families with a total of thirty-six members who had recently emigrated to the village of Dobrush from Dukagjin. All the Catholics in Kratovo were Albanian immigrants from Debar.[2]

By the middle of the seventeenth century, therefore, many hundreds of Catholic Albanian families had migrated from over-populated areas such as Debar into Kosovo where they adopted the Serbian and, occasionally, the Turkish languages, but it appears that they were being gradually Islamised rather than Serbianised. In Novo Brdo and Trepca the end of large-scale mining seems to have led to a decline in Catholicism. In 1623 Mazrreku reported that thirty years earlier these towns were rich in gold and silver deposits, which had attracted Catholics from Albania, Bosnia and other places. Yet by 1633, Trepca's Catholics could no longer even support a priest,[3] due to the growing number of conversions to Islam. The number of conversions increased mainly because of the sharp rise in the poll-tax on Christians in the strategically important western fringes of the Empire. Catholics were seen by the Porte as enemies, and thus the raising of the poll tax on the region's Christians appears to have been a deliberate policy to encourage the rapid conversion of Albanian Catholics to Islam. The Ottoman Empire saw Catholicism as an adversary with which it could not come to terms. Close to Papal

2. A. Pipa and S. Repishti, *Studies on Kosovo*, Columbia University Press, New York, 1984, p. 30.
3. Ibid., p. 26. 'Policies in Kosova', *Kosova Historical Review* (Tirana), no. 3,1994, p. 16.

Rome, the powers of the West could organise an attack in the name of Catholicism, and when the Ottoman-Venetian war of 1645 broke out, the Albanian Catholics, encouraged by the high clergy, sided with Venice. Severe measures were taken against them in consequence, and many converted to Islam or, in some cases, joined the Orthodox Church and thus remained faithful to the Ottoman Empire. In 1649 another pro-Venetian insurrection was crushed by the Ottoman forces, giving rise to another wave of apostasy among the Catholics. The persecution was sufficiently harsh to force the missionaries to leave Albania.[4]

Following the Ottomans' defeat before Vienna in 1683, and the Morean war in 1684 in which their troops suffered a severe defeat from the Venetians, came a period of forced conversion in which the Pasha of Pec deported hundreds of mostly Catholic inhabitants from northern Albania to the plain of Serbia where most were compelled to convert to Islam. This marked the beginning of the Ottoman Empire's war on various fronts with the Habsburg Empire, Venice, Poland and Russia, culminating in the humiliating Treaty at Karlowitz in 1699. This anticipated the right of Vienna to intervene in favour of the Catholic Church, which thus became the guardian of the language and cultural heritage of Catholic Albanians in northern Albania and Kosovo. Before this there had been little need to enforce Islamisation, since most lowland areas were largely controlled by newly-arrived Ottoman settlers and army garrisons. However, more and more Catholic Albanians were now converting to Islam, especially in the towns. Part of the Serbian population also converted as a means of avoiding the increasingly heavy taxes imposed on the Christians.

Both Serbs and Albanians were under constant political pressure to embrace Islam to escape not only the financial burdens but also the increasing military ones which were being forced upon Christian men. At the same time, the women continued to profess Christianity. Such conversions are described by many travellers such as Gregory Massarechi, a Catholic missionary from Prizren, who wrote in a report of 1651 that in the village of Suha Reka on the left bank of the White Drin, where there had once been 150 Christian houses, he only found about thirty-six Christian women, the men having all gone over to Islam.[5] This phenomenon, known as

---

4. S. Skendi, *Religion in Albania during Ottoman Rule*, Balkan Cultural Studies, Boulder, CO, 1980, p. 155.

5. H. Baerlin, *A Difficult frontier*, Leonard Parsons, London, 1922, p. 19.

crypto-Christianity, appeared throughout the Balkans in this period; the crypto-Christians lived in regions near those inhabited by Muslims and professed Islam, but satisfied their consciences by practising Christianity in private and only emerging as Muslims during outbursts of anti-Christian fanaticism. In Kosovo the crypto-Christians, who were called *laramane* (motley), were concentrated in the Pashalik of Prizren and lived chiefly around Pec and in the plain of Kosovo. Crypto-Catholics point to the involuntary nature of conversion to Islam, and long after all family members had converted, many Christian customs were still observed. This ambiguity prevailed until Ottoman religious tolerence declined at the beginning of the eighteenth century. So for the Albanians their religious status was a tenuous and fluid concept, aptly expressed by their saying 'Ku eshte shpata eshte feja' - 'Where the sword is, there lies religion'. An Albanian academic, writing in 1994, accurately assessed the Albanian attitude towards religion: 'Albanians have never been good believers in any religion. Their faith lies in a high traditional morality, not in religious dogmas'.[6]

Religious division in Kosovo

Before the era of nationalism, religious differences marked the sharpest and most important dividing line between Serbs and Albanians. The importance of religious affiliation was also reflected in social reality: many Albanians in Kosovo regarded Islam as the religion of free people, while Christianity - in particular Orthodoxy - was that of slaves.[7] As for the position of the Serbs in this religious dilemma, they appear to have been subjected to a not too subtle nurturing of their moral consciousness by Orthodox monks and priests. Parallel with the Orthodox Church's national policy in traditionally patriarchial societies, popular tales gradually matured into oral epic chronicles. Sung to the accompaniment of the gusle (lute), these glorified national heroes and rulers, cultivating the spirit of non-subjugation, cherishing the hope of liberation from the Ottoman yoke. Folk-poems about the Battle of Kosovo, the tragic fate of the last Nemanjics, the heroism of Prince Lazar and his knight Milos Obilic, and especially about the virtuous and fearless

6. M. Krasniqi, 'The Role of the Serbian Orthodox Church in Anti-Albanian Policies in Kosova', *Kosova Historical Review* (Tirana), no. 3,1994, p. 16.
7. D. Batakovic in Duijzings, Janjic and Maliqi (eds), *Kosovo – Kosova*, p. 3.

King Marko Mrnjavcevic, who was always defeating Turks and saving Serbs, expressed a particular moral code which in time crystallised into a common attitude to life, defined in the first centuries of Ottoman rule.[8]

The continued increase in conversions of Albanians to Islam, and the consequent increase in power which this gave them in relation to their Christian neighbours, marked the first steps along the separate roads for them and the Serbs. Ecclesiastical reports of the latter half of the seventeenth century describe the appalling social conditions in Kosovo. Missionaries and other clergy had to travel in harsh winter snows to avoid the almost annual summer epidemics of the plague. They also went well armed and under cover of darkness to avoid attack by bandits. At this time many Albanian families became relatively wealthy from the spoils of war brought back from Ottoman military forays in distant Kurdistan and Arabia. Those Albanians who served with the Ottoman forces returned with luxurious items such as gold, silver-inlaid arms and magnificent Arab horses, the decendants of which can still occasionally be seen today pulling ploughs and carts in Kosovo. Intolerance towards Christians increased after the Russo-Ottoman wars at the end of the eighteenth century. The Ottomans regarded the Orthodox Christians of Kosovo as allies of the Russians, and so put pressure on them to convert to Islam. In consequence of the abolition of the Pec patriarchate in 1766, the Serbs of Kosovo found themselves under the jurisdiction of the Greek Patriarchate of Constantinople, with the result that conversions to Islam further increased. Without the Pec patriarchate to propagate the notion of Serbian statehood, Serbs believed, with some justification, that their national concept was in serious danger. By the beginning of the nineteenth century forcible conversions to Islam became widespread. A report sent by the Catholic Archbishop Matteo Krasniqi to the Propaganda Fide in Rome told of how Islam was forced upon the population of Rugove (above Pec) in 1815. Three families tried to resist, with the heads of the households adopting Muslim names but continuing to attend mass in the city. They were tried and executed in public on 13 November 1817.[9]

The Eastern parts of Kosovo, with their compact Serbian settlements, were the last to undergo Islamisation. The first generation of Islamised Serbs continued to preserve their language and tradi-

8. Batakovic, *The Kosovo Chronicles*, p. 46.
9. Pipa and Repishti, *Studies on Kosovo*, p. 33.

tional customs in secret, but later generations, living in an increasingly Albanian environment, gradually began adopting Albanian dress and, outside their narrow family circle, using the Albanian language. By the beginning of the nineteenth century the entire Orthodox Serb village of Gora near Prizren had converted to Islam. Although the Christians regarded conversion as a necessary and temporary evil, many were already marrying Albanian Muslim wives by the third and sometimes only by the second generation. In the Golo Brdo, the 'Bald Mountains', thirty villages and hamlets were inhabited by Islamised Serbs who, with very rare exceptions, only spoke the Serbian language. Their conversion to Islam was largely due to the Greek Orthodox Church, which in the mid-nineteenth century left the region without a single priest so that the children remained unchristened and the people in disgust went over to Islam. Eventually, these Islamised Serbs married into Albanian families and were thus assimilated into the Albanian community. According to many Serbian accounts, the Albanians themselves protected Orthodox cemeteries from desecration because they knew that the remains of their own ancestors might lie there.[10]

Movement of Christian populations

During the Austro-Ottoman wars in the latter half of the seventeenth and the early eighteenth century, events occurred which drove a great part of the Slav population from Kosovo. In 1690 Austrian troops advanced through Serbia and Kosovo and onwards as far east as Skopje where the Ottomans eventually defeated them. Fearing harsh reprisals from the Porte, a massive social upheaval took place. Unable to fight the Ottomans, the greater part of the inland Serbian population accepted from the Austrian Emperor Leopold I an offer of asylum in the Habsburg territories. In 1690, therefore, 37,000 Serbian families from the Kosovo region, under the leadership of the Patriarch Arsenius Crnojevic III, left for exile in Hungary, having received assurances that the Serbs would be granted special political and religious status there. Others settled in the regions of Syrmia, Slavonia, the Banat and Backa. This was the beginning of the transfer of Serbia's religious, cultural and political centre of gravity northwards and finally to Belgrade. Many Alban-

10. For a detailed account of these events see D.T. Batakovic (ed.), *Savremenici o Kosovu i Metohiji, 1852-1912*, Belgrade, 1988.

ian Catholics from the Klementi clan also emigrated northwards with the Serbs and settled in the Srem district in the west of Vojvodina, in Hrtkovci and Nikinci. There they were assimilated by the Croat population, while preserving the memory of their Albanian background.[11]

A part of Kosovo's remaining Catholic Albanian population also migrated southwards into the regions of Berat and Vlora in southern Albania. Like many migrating Serbs at the time, they believed that their move was only temporary and that they would soon be able to return to their abandoned homes. Thus were set in motion the forces that strove to separate these two peoples who had lived alongside each other in relative harmony for nearly 900 years. Differences in faith produced friction only after the *millets* had lost their original structure in the profound changes of the eighteenth and nineteenth centuries with the rise of new commercial élites in the towns, and the development of a secular intelligentsia. The political significance lay in the latter two groups being the first among the non-Muslims, along with the Christian merchants, to press for reform of the *millets*. The shift away from religion to language as a bond of unity of a community was against the very essence of the *millet*. Thus the emphasis placed on language and ethnicity opened the way to secularism and nationalism.

As the Serbian population fled to the relative safety of Hungary, hundreds of Kosovo's villages became deserted and the Pec patriarchate was left without its highest clergy. The subsequent demographic upheaval caused by the mass exodus of Serbs, later known as the Great Migration, opened the way for the resettling of Kosovo by Albanians, lured down from the hills by the fertile land and encouraged by the Ottomans. They settled in Kosovo, Novi Pazar and Nis – also in Pec, which for six centuries had been the see of the Serbian Church and now, like Djakovica, became a predominantly Albanian town. From the eighteenth century Albanian migration into Macedonia also intensified, after which many of the Slav population remaining in Kosovo converted to Islam.[12] Those Albanians who migrated to Kosovo in the seventeenth and eighteenth centuries were dispersed in small family groups over a wide area. Thus they lost the

11. Duijzings, 'The Martyrs of Stubla: Religion and the Politics of Identity in Kosovo', unpublished Ph.D. thesis, Univ. of Nijmegen, p. 20.
12. For an account of the process of Islamisation of the Serbs of Kosovo see Atanasije Urosevic, 'Gornja Morava i Izmornik' in *Srpski etnografski zbornik*, Naselje, vol. 28, Belgrade, 1935.

security provided by the tight-knit clans from which they originated in northern Albania, but they made up for it by adopting the patriarchal *zadruga* system of large family cooperatives, often of up to fifty members, which was common among the South Slavs.

Meanwhile military pressure on the Ottomans increased on all fronts. The war with Russia had barely ended in 1711 when the Ottomans renewed hostilities with Venice in 1715, and a year later they were once more at war with Austria. After the war between the Porte and Austria in 1739, the Serbian population came under renewed pressure to convert to Islam. This resulted in their undertaking another great exodus under Patriarch Arsenius IV Sakabenta. Several hundred Serbian families withdrew from the mining settlements around Janjevo, Pristina, Novo Brdo and Kapaonik. Albanians also migrated to escape Ottoman rule. Albanian settlers founded their new communities mainly in Italy, Greece and along the Dalmatian coast such as the village of Arbanas, founded in 1726 by Albanian settlers from Brisk and Shestan west of Lake Shkoder.[13] The choice between converting to Islam or finding a powerful master who would protect them if they accepted the status of serfs caused both Serbs and Albanians to move beyond Ottoman control to a life that would possibly be more tolerable. During this period the population of Kosovo was also decimated by plague, and the combination of this with the previous migrations left hundreds of villages deserted and much land reverting to nature. The demographic upheaval which followed the Serb migration witnessed the arrival of more migrants from the impoverished highlands of northern Albania on to the empty, rich, fertile lands devastated by war.

The situation of Kosovo's Orthodox Christians began to improve somewhat following the Russo-Ottoman Treaty of Kucuk Kaynarca (1774), whereby Russia claimed protection of the Sultan's Orthodox subjects. The influence of the small but vigorous Serbian intelligentsia in Hungary, its patriotic writings and struggle for a literary language was mediated to the Serbs at large mainly through the Church which while continuing to serve as an instrument of Ottoman feudalism and suppression, still kept Serbian traditions alive, and they in turn fuelled the nascent Serbian national consciousness. The continual evolution of the Serbian folk-epic was important in this period for the development of this national consciousness and instilled into it, apart from a spirit of revenge

13. R. Elsie, *The History of Albanian Literature*, vol. II, New York, 1995, p. 65.

against the Ottomans, an idealised memory of the Serbian past.
Nevertheless, the folk-poets were mostly illiterate and ignored
economic and political issues, and therefore could not directly stimulate any intellectual or political movement.[14] This remained so up
till the Serbian insurrection against the élite Ottoman Janissary corps
in the Belgrade *pashalik* (land under the authority of *pasha* or *bey*)
in 1804 under the leadership of Karadjordje (Black George).[15]

In the aftermath of the Serbian revolution of 1804-15, Kosovo
acquired a special political importance for hereditary Albanian
pashas, who now feared with some justification that the flames of
rebellion might spread to other Serb-inhabited areas. The Porte
therefore encouraged the Muslim pashas to curb any rebellious
moves which the Serbs might make in regions under their control.
Nevertheless, the growing political independence of Serbia, which
by 1833 formed an autonomous principality under Ottoman sovereignty, revived the hopes of Serbs in Kosovo, many of whom,
during the first reign of Prince Milos (1830-39), ventured up to
the principality in search of land. There they hoped to settle and find
relative security, which by then was becoming scarce for virtually all
living under Ottoman rule. Prince Milos made efforts to ease the
position of his compatriots through ties with the family of
Mahmoud Pasha Rotulovic of Prizren and the Mahmud Begovic
family of Pec, and attempted also to revive the waning spirits of the
dwindling number of Orthodox clergy in Kosovo by bestowing
gifts upon the impoverished monks and permitting them to collect
donations for their monasteries in Serbia. He is to be credited with
the restoration of the Visoki Decani palace in 1836.[16]

The chaos of almost continual warfare and upheaval left Kosovo
relatively depleted of people, and the great monastic estates began
to revert to nature through lack of care and maintainance - this state
of affairs appears to have been replicated throughout the region.
Life for the average peasant, already weighed down by high taxes,
was harsh and in many ways intolerable. Throughout the nineteenth
century there was no public safety on the roads of Kosovo, which

14. For an interesting account of Serbian folk-epics see H. Rootham, *Kossovo:
    Heroic Songs of the Serbs*, Oxford, 1920.
15. The Janissaries, fearing the loss of their privileged status, opposed the reform
    programme of Sultan Selim III, which attempted to create a new army and with
    it a new financial system. For a full account of the Serbian revolution see M.B.
    Petrovic, *A History of Modern Serbia, 1804-1918*, New York, 1976.
16. Batakovic, *The Kosovo Chronicles*, p. 92.

were controlled by outlaw bands. Travel was only possible under the protection of a strongly armed escort, but this cost too much for most people and local Muslims as well as Christians begged the Porte itself to provide protection. However, the punitive Ottoman expeditions sent to deal with such rebellious lawlessness proved totally ineffective and Kosovo degenerated into an anarchic region where outlaws reigned supreme. The latter, known throughout the Balkans as *haiduks* or 'social bandits', comprised not only fugitives from the law, debtors and adventurers, but also those fleeing from blood-feud vendettas. They were the product of a general insecurity of life and property, foreign rule and a terrain and economy that favoured lawlessness in general and brigandage in particular. These outlaw bands offered an easy alternative refuge to any individual who was under pressure from his landlord, the state or the blood-feud. They operated in tightly-knit bands, often with the full cooperation of the local inhabitants. In good weather they lived in the forests and hills, but since banditry was generally seasonal, they often retreated in winter back into normal village life.

In such an environment of constant warfare at the far reaches of the empire, the authorities were sorely hindered in their attempts to mount concerted measures against the outlaws, one of whose prime targets were the Ottoman tax-collectors who were certain to be in possession of sizeable sums of money. Many cases of both Christian and Muslim bandit activity against them are to be found. As the centralised Ottoman feudal system gradually decayed, the bandits' actions, though uncoordinated, caused a state of perpetual conflict between the authorities and large sections of the population, Christian and Muslim; furthermore the cost of measures taken to control banditry in the Balkans was a factor contributing to the eventual bankruptcy of the Ottoman treasury.[17] In order to halt the deterioration caused by the migrations, which seriously decreased tax revenue, the Porte ordered a relaxation of restrictions on the lives of Christians.

The Muslim population under pressure

In 1835-6, after crushing the power of the insubordinate Bosnian beys, the Ottoman army finally eliminated the independent pashas of Kosovo - Mahmoud Pasha Rotulovic of Prizren, Arslan Pasha of

17. For more on the role of banditry in Balkan society see J. Koliopoulos, *Brigands with A Cause*, Clarendon Press, Oxford, 1987.

Pec, Seifudin Pasha of Djakovica and finally the heirs to the Pristina-based Djinic clan, on whose side the feudal lords of Pec, Debar and Djakovica fought. The law on the *timar* system was abrogated and the administration was henceforth entrusted to army commanders, and measures were implemented to centralise it, along with the tax system. The *sandjaks* of Shkoder, Prizren and Pec were put under the control of the Rumelian *vilayet* whose seat was at Monastir.[18]

As the nineteenth century progressed, it became ever clearer that the Muslim 'aristocracy' of the Balkans was doomed, as the central Ottoman authorities began further moves to cripple the power of the beys and pashas from central Albania and Kosovo by deporting a number of them to Asia Minor and destroying their fortresses. The successor to Mahmoud II, Sultan Abdul Mejid (1839-61) issued, in 1839, the famous *Hatti-sherif* of Gulhane that was to become a sort of 'charter of freedom' for subjects of the Ottoman empire. Christians were now officially equated with Muslims. It anticipated the introduction of a regular military obligation, centralisation of government and fiscal reorganisation, as well as the Europeanisation of the judiciary and of education.[19] The reforms met with strong Albanian resistance, especially against conscription in the Ottoman army.

In response, many Albanians began to re-convert to Catholicism to avoid conscription and to take advantage of the introduction of equal rights for Christians. They were also influenced by the growing involvement of the European powers in Balkan affairs. However, such re-conversions were strongly opposed by conservative Ottoman circles both in Kosovo and in Constantinople, and in 1846, on the instigation of the local Ottoman pasha, twenty-four families of Albanian crypto-Catholics or *laramans* – more than 160 people – were deported from the Kosovo parish of Letnica to Anatolia after repudiating their Muslim disguise and revealing their formerly concealed Catholic identity. Such actions were taken to deter other Muslims or pseudo-Muslims from openly espousing the Catholic faith, and to halt the reform process which conservatives feared would encourage further cases of collective apostasy.[20]

Ottoman fortunes were now at a low ebb. The Porte was increasingly unable to control its provincial officials and local Muslim notables. The reforms introduced in 1839 had been

18. D. Batakovic, *The Kosovo Chronicles*, pp. 82-3.
19. Ibid., p. 83.
20. G. Duijzings, 'The Martyrs of Stubla... ', p. 1.

designed to revitalise the Empire, which was plagued by administrative chaos and military weakness, but the majority of Muslims
felt keenly their loss of absolute power. Resistance was particularly
intense among the Albanians, and in 1844 revolts broke out in
Skopje, Pristina and Tetovo and were only suppressed after some
violent clashes. In having, like the Christians, to obey the new military draft and the new tax laws, the Muslims of these regions saw
in the reforms a serious threat to their privileges. A second phase
of reform, the *Hatt-i-Humayun*, proclaimed in 1856 after strong
pressure from the Great Powers, stressed the equality of all citizens.
By introducing certain European standards of organisation, together
with increased secularisation of the laws and institutions, it was
hoped to preserve and strengthen the Empire. Most importantly, the
Empire's Christians were to be appeased by the introduction of
equal rights for all citizens, thus stemming the tide of nationalism
sweeping through the Balkans. The right granted to establish their
own churches and schools encouraged the Serbs of Kosovo to
collect donations in order to open their own schools and maintain
their decaying monasteries and churches. The first Serbian secular
schools were also allowed to open in Kosovo from the mid-1830s.

As Ottoman rule declined, domestic unrest became more prevalent. Meanwhile, economic development within the Empire became
increasingly concentrated in the hands of its non-Turkish subjects.
The Ottoman abhorrence of commerce left most Turks in urban
areas engaged in traditional industrial handicrafts. The reforms
brought a revival of business for the merchants and craftsmen in
towns throughout Kosovo, and a slow process of urbanisation developed as people drifted into the towns and received training in various crafts or otherwise entered commerce. The 'Turkish' towns of
the Balkans began to receive an ever-greater segment of Slav professionals. The commercial Christian sectors prospered, while the
Ottoman aristocracy decayed as they gradually lost their material
base. Cities like Skopje, Prilep, Prizren, Ohrid, Bitola and Thessaloniki were attracting dynamic and agressive Christian, Jewish and
Armenian elements. In the new open society, the tables were turning economically against the Ottomans, who were losing their land
and not securing in the cities the lucrative prospects of the new capi-
talism on the march. They grumbled, sat smoking their chibuks and
drinking coffee, and watched Christians taking the initiative.[21]

21. Dragnic and Todorovich, *The Saga of Kosovo*, p. 78.

During the Crimean War of 1853-6, anti-Orthodox and anti-Slav sentiment in the Empire reached its peak. In Kosovo Albanians acted as guides for the English Consul who came to the districts of Pec and Decani looking for recruits, and along with other Muslims they were offered good pay to act as mercenaries. Serbs as Christians were not entitled to bear arms and thus had little means of defence. The Monks of Decani and the Pec patriarchate turned to the government of Serbia for protection. There were also some more cases of conversion of Slavs to Islam at this time again to avoid further persecution, but many more chose to emigrate amid the chaos of the war. In some cases, whole villages fled to Serbia or Montenegro. The Serbian government set about trying to win over influential Albanians to their cause but in that period, apart from intermittent reports from monks and teachers, little was known of the political situation of Serbs in Kosovo, who by then were left almost completely to their own devices. A few Ottoman officials lived in the towns, while most of the chief officials were Albanians. Muslim peasants appeared no better off than their Christian neighbours. Christian merchants, landowners and higher ecclesiastics began cooperating closely with the Ottoman authorities, as did their Muslim counterparts, leaving both the Christian and Muslim peasantry to bear the burdens of taxes and military service. Ottoman regiments were often to be found idling in the small towns of Kosovo. Many of them were Cossack deserters from the Russian army or Poles (who hated the Serbs and Montenegrins, regarding them as clients of Russia) and Hungarians.

Prizren

Meanwhile, Prizren had once more become the region's most important town. It lay on the edge of a broad valley so close to the mountains that at least half of it clambered up a steep slope crowned by the huge grey Kaljaja fortress. In the centre of the town the quays on each side of the fast-flowing river were lined with the spacious harems of the wealthier Turks. Trade and crafts flourished, and the leather workers, goldsmiths and tailors sold their highly-prized products in the bazaars of Serbia, Montenegro, Kosovo and Macedonia. Situated on an important crossroad between Shkoder and Thessaloniki, the town had a multi-ethnic population that included Serbs, Albanians, Turks, Jews, Gypsies and a people known as the Cherkess, who called themselves Adige and originated from a region of the north-west Caucasus near the sourse of the river Terek. They had been converted first to Christianity by the Georgians in the thirteenth century, and later to Islam by the Tartars in the sixteenth to seventeenth centuries. They first came to the Balkans via Varna and settled in Drama and the plain of Seres and other areas of Aegean Macedonia. Like the Albanians, they were cattle-breeders rather than farmers. In the second half of the nineteenth century, following the Russo-Ottoman wars, they were settled further west in the Balkan region in sensitive frontier areas, mainly in the garrison towns of Vucitrn and Pristina.[22]

Because of the presence of regular troops and the admixture of Ottoman families, and the fact that sons of richer families went to Constantinople for education, the Albanians of Prizren were less unruly towards both the central government and the Christian population than those in the districts around Pec and Djakovica. The Turkish language, while ignored in Pec and Djakovica, was widely spoken in Prizren because of the substantial Ottoman presence. Although Albanians, both Christian and Muslim, spoke Albanian at home and in public, schools in their language were not allowed, not even after the Hatt-i Humayun edict of 1856 promising equal treatment in education to all the peoples of the Empire. It was in the interest of the Porte and the Patriarchate of Constantinople to keep Albanians divided on the basis of creed.[23] This contrasted with the new private Serbian schools now appearing. Merchant and craftsmen guilds in Prizren, Pristina and Pec helped to fund and equip them and to encourage better-trained teachers to come to this remote backwater. Prizren, the economic centre for Serbs in southern Kosovo, was home to the oldest and most renowned Serbian church-school community which had been established in 1836 for the purpose of countering Greek Orthodox propaganda. A number of promising students from Kosovo were able to train for the teaching profession with scholarships received from the wealthy Prizren merchant Sima Andrejevic Igumanov (1804-82).[24]

22. When the Ottomans retreated after the Balkan wars in 1913, the Cherkess departed with them, except for a small number who remained in Kosovo, mainly in Donji Spacovac. Their names have been preserved in many town and village names, e.g. Cherkess chou, Tikves, Novo selo in Zeleznik. etc. For further information on the Cherkess see G. Elezovic, *Glava o postanku i poreklu naroda arnautskog*, Belgrade, 1936, pp. 256-63, and T. Dordevic, *Cerkezi u nasoj zemlji*, *Glasnik Skopskog naucnog drustva*, Belgrade, 1928, pp. 143-53.
23. Skendi, *The Albanian National Awakening*, p. 18.
24. Batakovic, *The Kosovo Chronicles*, p. 98.

In 1871 a Serbian seminary opened in Prizren. The Serbian government could not provide any overt political assistance, but it systematically aided churches and schools by sending teachers and encouraging the best students to continue their studies. The Prizren seminary educated teachers and priests to serve all Serb communities living under Ottoman control, and became the hub of activity on national affairs. Unknown to the authorities, it also established regular contact with the government in Belgrade, from which it received instructions and means for political action.[25] Its inauguration proved to be a secure bulwark against attempts by the Constantinople Patriarchate to Hellenise Kosovo's Serbian population and by the Bulgarian Exarchate (1870) to establish strongholds of support in the Gnjilane region. Until a Serbian consulate opened in Pristina in 1889, the seminary was the sole focus of Serbian political life in Kosovo, and books, journals and newspapers were delivered from Belgrade with the aim of consolidating national awareness. But from the very beginning of its operations, the Ottoman authorities suspected the seminary of being the centre of Serbian national action, and so, out of caution, political contacts with Belgrade were carried out through the Russian consulate in Prizren, which secured the transmission of confidential correspondence.[26]

The Prizren seminary soon became the seat of overall spiritual and educational life and the stronghold for political work on national affairs. But more importantly, for the first time contact had been established with the government in Belgrade, which as a consequence was able to exert immediate influence on national operations among Serbs in Kosovo. From its inauguration in 1871 till the Serbian reoccupation of Kosovo in 1912, the seminary worked in pursuance of instructions given by the Serbian government. Its operations came initially under the jurisdiction of the Ministry for Education and Religious Affairs, and later of the Foreign Ministry. All its expenses were paid by the Serbian government, but funds towards its maintainance also came from the church and from the endowment of Sima Igumanov.[27] Thus the school had a propaganda mission to enhance national consciousness, to prevent conversion, and generally to continue the programme of national enlightenment. Still, although there was little difficulty in

25. Ibid., p. 55.
26. Ibid., pp. 98–100.
27. Ibid., p. 99.

attracting teaching staff to the lively, cosmopolitan atmosphere of Prizren, the Slav community found itself in constant search for female school teachers to serve in Kosovo. The primary obstacle was the high salary that a woman educated in Belgrade would require to bury herself in such a wild place as Kosovo. Secondly, there was the ambition to marry, which removed young women from their teaching posts as soon as they were able to save a dowry. Thus in most Serbian schools the only teachers were monks and nuns.

The primary object of Serbian foreign policy at this time was the complete removal of the Ottoman presence from the country; specifically this meant ending the Turkish occupation of several fortresses. With that object achieved, planning for the acquisition of neighbouring Serbian lands, including Kosovo, could begin. To prepare for these moves the Serbian ruler Prince Mihael Obrenovic wished to contract alliances with the other Balkan Christian peoples so as to form a front against the Ottomans.[28] During the 1860s Serbia's Foreign Minister, Ilija Garasanin, wary of secret agreements then being forged by Russia and Austria with the Porte, and the negative role the Albanians were assigned in that game, decided to court various northern Albanian leaders, especially among the Catholic population. As a result, Belgrade diplomacy and Serbian money became very active among the Mirdite clans in order to entice them away from Italian and Austrian influences. No less than five separate Albanian clan leaders were Garasanin's guests in Belgrade in one year.[29] However, his policy of wooing the Albanians was abruptly halted by the assassination of Prince Obrenovic in 1868.

Weakening of the empires

As the century progressed the vulnerability of both the Ottoman and Austrian empires became steadily more apparent. The nationalist revolutions of 1848-9 and 1866-7 had demonstrated to the Habsburg rulers the basic weaknesses of their regime. The gradual territorial withdrawal by the Ottoman Empire, which had begun in 1699, accelerated during the nineteenth century despite numerous efforts by its leaders to recoup former power through modernisation and internal reforms. In order to consolidate its weakening position

28. Charles and Barbara Jelavich, *The Establishment of the Balkan National States, 1804-1920*, University of Washington Press, Seattle, 1977, p. 64.
29. Dragnic and Todorovic, *The Saga of Kosovo*, p. 82.

in the western fringes of the Balkans, the Porte enforced the law of 1865 on the organisation of its administration under which it planned to create a substantial and compact group of Muslims in the Albanian-inhabited provinces of Monastir, Janina, Shkoder and Kosovo. It was hoped that these would be ideologically, politically and socially committed to the Empire's basic interests, and provide a source of recruitment to secure peace on its increasingly vulnerable frontiers. The Albanian-inhabited regions, which also included large populations of other nationalities,[30] were split in 1866 into the three *vilayets* of Shkoder, Monastir and Janina, the fourth, Kosovo, being added in 1878. Each had its own governor and garrison. Thus it was hoped to make any alignment of the Albanians impossible for the foreseeable future. As the Albanians occupied such a strategic position in the Balkans, the Porte wished to avoid creating a definite demarcation to the still vague geographical notion of 'Albania'.

At a time of growing international interest in the fate of the Ottoman Empire two British women, the Misses Irby and Mackenzie, set off to discover and record life in the European provinces of the Ottoman Empire. In 1867 they published an account of their travels in many ways favourable to the 'clean, hardworking, honest Christian population', while chastising the 'indolent, slothfull, slovenly, idle Muslims', among whom were included the Albanians of Kosovo. Theirs was a view, widely held at the time, of civilisation versus barbarism. Europe represented to the two travellers everything then known as civilised, leading them to exclaim: 'Having now seen how Old Serbia lost her Christian and quasi-civilised inhabitants, we will examine how it came to be tenanted by barbarians and Islam.'[31] Christians were invariably perceived by foreign visitors as the most enlightened and civilised members of the Kosovo community whereas stereotype images of the Albanians were reinforced by the likes of the journalist Henry Baerlein: 'A primitive people like the Albanians admire warlike attributes beyond all others.'[32]

With Kosovo known above all else in the 1860s and '70s for ruin and lawlessness, Irby and Mackenzie contrasted the miserable

30. The population of Kosovo during the nineteenth century is hard to determine. Ottoman annual censuses were generally unreliable, the real number of family members being concealed in order to evade certain taxes. Muslims in particular refused to have their wives and female children listed.
31. G.M. Mackenzie, and A.P. Irby, *Travels in the Slavonic Provinces of Turkey-in-Europe*, vol. 1, London, 1877, p. 217.
32. H. Baerlin, *A Difficult Frontier*, Leonard Parsons, London, 1922, p. 35

condition of the Serbs in Kosovo to the relative prosperity of those living in the free Serbian state. In Pec the two English ladies were shocked as Serbian schoolchildren literally fell at their feet with a grovelling action that they found revolting: 'We asked how in the world they came to suppose we should wish to be thus received? Their teacher answered, "The Turks taught it us: their dignitaries require us Christians to prostrate ourselves before them." '[33] A great obstacle to prosperity for the Serbian community of Prizren was that its most vigorous members left to try their luck in free Serbia. Why then did they not all go and live there? The reason was that although some of the Serbs did go to Serbia, they often returned because all that their families possessed, whether a parcel of land or a shop, remained in Ottoman-controlled Kosovo. Also, they were considered by the Serbs of Free Serbia to be lazy and unreliable, perhaps on account of having mixed with Muslims for so long. More significantly the government of Serbia strongly discouraged Kosovo Serbs from moving to Serbia since this would have meant abandoning Kosovo entirely to Muslims.

At this time the governor of the towns of Kosovo was either an Ottoman official or, in many cases, an Albanian who had served in the regular army. The Mudir of Pristina in the 1870s was an Albanian. These officials had a few local supporters (*cavasses*) who frequently supplemented their income by robbing the population. The head of a Christian community was usually its primate or chief elder, known by the Turkish appellation *kodgia bashi*. Apart from helping to apportion taxes and adjudicating in civil cases, such Christian leaders had little political power, but they wielded considerable social influence. Irby and Mackenzie recorded:

> 'The mudir, or pasha, buys his post to begin with and is then left to enjoy it for so short a time that his chief aim was to reimburse himself as quickly as possible. Everyone knew this, so Muslims and Christians alike plied him with bribes, but besides enriching himself, he also had to raise the Sultan's taxes. If the Muslims would not pay their share he must doubly fleece the Christians; for the Muslims were not to be trifled with, as, should he offend them, they may bribe some higher authority to remove him from his post. In Pristina this was constantly the case; the mudir we found there was the second in a year, and before we left the district he was already deposed.'[34]

The condition of the region was now so bad as to reduce all its

---

33. Mackenzie and Irby, *Travels in the Slavonic provinces...* , p. 199.
34. Ibid., vol. 1, p. 223.

inhabitants to despair. The Albanians would not obey the Ottoman authorities, hence the disorderly state of the region. The prime object for the Albanian, whether as a *bekji* (village watchman) in times of truce or as a *bashibazouk* (irregular auxiliaries of Ottoman troops) in times of disturbance, was to get what he could by force in a world which gave him no other means of earning his livelihood. In the summer of 1867 Albanians murdered the governor of Pec whilst he was collecting the Sultan's revenue. The beleaguered Serb community of Pec told Irby and Mackenzie:

> 'We are suffering what no tongue can tell, what flesh and blood will endure no longer; our lives and property, our wives and children are at the mercy of a pack of robbers. Our governors and medjliss, our judges and police, all are thieves, villains and blood-guilty.'[35]

A Serb elder explained that:

> 'A consul who would stand up for the Christians would benefit us; but such consuls as I have known at Prizren are powerless and do no good. I do not say that things cannot improve, but I say that unless they utterly change we Serbs of Pec must do as our fathers did – we must go.'[36]

The dwindling Slav population, unwelcome in free Serbia and terrified in their increasingly lawless environment, thus had little choice but to retreat into their community, keep their heads down and pray for international intervention.

Albeit long after their neighbours, national consciousness was also now beginning to stir among the Albanians in the build-up to the so-called Eastern Question. The Albanian beys were becoming ever more disenchanted with the Ottoman administration. The Porte did not want the unity of Islam broken, or a national consciousness to form in any part of the Muslim world which would in the end prevail over religious solidarity. For this reason the Porte, while relatively tolerant towards other nationalities, was not so with the most faithful and favourite, and extended its policy of prohibition of the use of national language and schools to the Christian Albanians, in contrast to the policy towards other Christians. The Porte was aware of the closeness of relations between Christian and Muslim Albanians, and that these would be furthered by their common language and national sentiment.[37]

35. Ibid., vol. 2, p. 55.
36. Ibid., vol. 2, p. 56.
37. S. Skendi, *The Albanian National Awakening*, Princeton University Press, 1967, p. 133.

Before the advent of the Eastern Question, Serbs and Albanians, though never in such an intimate relationship as the different Albanian religious groups, did nevertheless share strong social similarities expressed in numerous common customs and traditions and in their shared struggles against the Ottoman authorities; often they even had blood ties. The extent to which the Albanian people recalled these close relationships is expressed in a statement made to Dositej Obradovic, Serbia's first Minister of Education, on a journey through Albania: 'Together with the Serbs we form one family and clan.'[38] In the border regions between Kosovo, Montenegro and the Sandjak the inhabitants were usually bilingual, sharing many common cultural traits such as the frontier epic songs known throughout the region, which praised heroes whether Albanian, Bosnian or Serb. Mistrust between the Serbs and Albanians deepened as the Balkans began to vibrate with national unrest. As the Serbian government strove to encourage the national consciousness of the Kosovo Slavs, the process of national awakening had tentatively begun among the Albanian population. But several more decades would lapse before any Albanian national uprising could be even partly implemented.

38. D. Tukovic, *Srbija i Albanija*, Belgrade, 1914, p. 113.

3

KOSOVO AND THE OTTOMAN DECLINE

The question of Kosovo became internationalised in the Great Eastern Crisis of 1875, which raised the issue of the very survival of the Ottoman Empire and brought this remote European province directly to the attention of the Great Powers. Following a series of Christian uprisings against the Ottomans in Bosnia and Hercegovina in 1875, a reform plan proposed by Austria-Hungary was imposed upon the Porte in order to prevent or at least forestall Russian intervention. A new Sultan, Abdul Hamid, had come to the throne in 1876 when the Empire's internal and external crisis was at its height, and put an end to the previous policy of modernising reform (*Tanzimat*), and began a long period of autocratic power. He attempted to re-found the legitimacy of the Ottoman state and dynasty upon its defence of Islamic values and interests. He thus favoured the Muslim element in the Balkans more than any of his nineteenth-century predecessors, and re-awakened in the Muslim population that sense of belonging to a privileged community, now threatened by Christian insurgency within and by the irredentism of the newly emergent Balkan states. In Kosovo this meant, in essence, encouraging the Albanian population to settle scores with the local Slav-Orthodox element.[1]

The Prizren League and Albanian nationalism

Meanwhile, advancing internal decay, as well as external pressure, had severely weakened the Porte. Capitalising on this weakness, the Serbian and Montenegrin principalities took advantage of the Russo-Ottoman war of 1877-8 to invade Kosovo, thus bringing the Serbs and Montenegrins into their first serious conflict with Albanians. Thousands of Kosovo Serbs crossed over into Serbian

---

1. M. Dogo, 'National Truths and Disinformation in Albanian-Kosovar Historiography' in Duijzings, Janjic and Maliqi (eds), *Kosovo - Kosova*, p. 45.

territory to enlist in the Serbian army; those Serbs and Montenegrins who remained in Kosovo largely managed to avoid conscription into the Ottoman army by bribing military officials. Facing
little opposition, the Serbian army advanced steadily, occupying the
towns of Nis, Lescovac, Vranje and Prokuplje, before entering
Kosovo. During this period thousands of Albanians were forcibly
expelled from the region of Toplice in the Sandjak of Nis, and many
of the region's mosques were destroyed, while as many Serbs fled
southern Kosovo ahead of unleashed *bashibazouks*, who began to
take vengeance upon the remaining Serbian inhabitants. The operations of the Serbian army in Kosovo provoked a wave of refugees
in the opposite direction as an estimated 30,000 Albanians deserted
those parts of the region which the Serbian army occupied. Alongside the retreating Ottoman troops were thousands of displaced
Albanians who arrived in Kosovo as refugees. Unaware that Russia
and the Porte had agreed to a truce, the voluntary Serb regiment
of Major Radomir Putnik took Gnjilane, while the advance guard
of the Serbian army reached the Gracanica monastery near Pristina
towards the end of January 1878. There a solemn liturgy was
performed to honour the victory of the Serbian army and Prince
Milan, and a commemoration was held for the heroes of 1389.
However, the concluded truce was inclusive of the Serbian army
whose units were thus compelled to withdraw from Kosovo.[2]

Following the defeat of the Porte in March 1878, Russia
imposed on the Ottoman administration the harsh Treaty of San
Stefano. This was designed to curb Austro-Hungarian influence in
the Balkans, to satisfy the Pan-Slavists who wished to see the liberation of all Slavs, and to strengthen Russia's position in the area.
Under the terms of the Peace Accord signed by Russia and the
Porte at San Stefano on 3 March 1878, the bulk of the liberated
territory was to be assigned to a greatly enlarged Bulgaria stretch-
ing as far west as Korca. Serbia, who now gained her complete
independence from the Porte, had her border extended to include
Mitrovica and a large part of the Sandjak of Pristina, while the rest
of Kosovo remained under Ottoman control. Montenegro received
the predominantly Albanian-inhabited regions of Pec, Ulqin, Hoti,
Plava, Guci and Podgorica. Indignant at the assignment of
Albanian-inhabited territory to the Slavic states at San Stefano, the
Albanians hastily formed local committees of defence throughout

2. Batakovic, *The Kosovo Chronicles*, p. 108.

the *vilayets* of Kosovo, Shkoder and Monastir. In response, Albanian nationalist activists decided to call an urgent general meeting of all Albanian leaders. And so on 10 June 1878, over 300 delegates, mostly from Kosovo and Western Macedonia, but including a handful of representatives from southern Albania, arrived in Prizren.

The meeting, which founded the 'Prizren League', was predominantly attended by very conservative Muslim landowners, who favoured the maintenance of the sovereignty of the Porte over their domains as security against the partitioning of their lands by their Balkan neighbours. Through them the Porte hoped it could still exercise an influence in its own interests. Initially, therefore, the Porte encouraged the League as it, too, was naturally opposed to the agreement forced upon it at San Stefano. Sultan Hamid hoped to use the League to instill a form of pan-Islamic ideology as a counterbalance to the growing national discontent spreading througout his wavering empire. It was in this sense that the Prizren League was to play a crucial role as a form of Albanian military frontier between the Porte's remaining Balkan domains and Serbia and Montenegro. For the Albanians, the primary purpose of the League was to organise political and military opposition to the dismemberment of Albanian-inhabited territory, and to petition the Sultan to unite the four *vilayets* of Janina, Monastir, Shkoder and Kosovo into one political and administrative unit. Although what was considered Albanian territory at that time was not easy to define, the League remained unified over the question of defending Albanian territorial integrity. As the meeting at Prizren drew to a close, the delegates dispersed to form regional committees in their local areas.

The threatened disintegration of the Ottoman Empire caused a good deal of alarm among the European Powers. Britain, France, Austria-Hungary, Germany and Italy all assumed that the enlarged Bulgaria created at San Stefano would become simply an extension of Russia. They were concerned that whichever Power controlled the strategic region of Istanbul and the Straits would eventually dominate the Sultan's Christian subjects. At stake were the balance of forces in Central Europe and the Mediterranean, together with European rivalries in Asia. In order, therefore, to find an acceptable solution to the 'Eastern Question', the Powers compelled Russia to submit to a new peace settlement at the Congress of Berlin, presided over by Bismarck, in June 1878. In the hope of diminishing Russian influence in the Balkans, the Congress drastically reduced the frontiers of Bulgaria. The new, smaller Bulgaria was confined to the area between the Danube and the Balkan mountains, and was recognised as an autonomous principality under the nominal suzerainty of the Sultan. Southern Bulgaria was formed into a new, and less autonomous province of the Ottoman Empire, known as Eastern Rumelia. The Berlin Congress more or less stifled Russia's ambitions in the Balkans. She therefore turned her attentions eastward, where before long she came into conflict with the newly emerging power of Japan. All the Albanian-inhabited areas were returned to the Porte's control. Serbia's claims on Albanian territory were curtailed as she was refused the Sandjak of Pristina and retained only the areas she had occupied before the war.

In the aftermath of the truce signed by Serbia and the Porte, Serbian troops withdrew from Kosovo. Throughout the month-long Berlin Congress, Kosovo's Serbs sent petitions to the Congress delegates asking for the *vilayet* to be united with Serbia, while Albanian representatives travelled to the European capitals where they vigorously argued for Kosovo to be united with the other Albanian-inhabited *vilayets*. At this stage the Porte continued to support the Prizren League in the hope that it might exert pressure on the Powers to reconsider the entire 'Eastern Question' and recognise the dangers that would result from any further extension of the independent Balkan states, thereby helping to prop up weakened Ottoman rule in the region. The League became the first bulwark against the expansionist policies of the neighbouring Balkan states, uniting the fledgling Albanian nationalist movement in its demands for administrative and cultural autonomy within the framework of the Empire. However, the failure of the Ottoman state to defend its interests in the face of the European Powers caused the leadership of the Albanian League to turn gradually to ideas of total autonomy. Before long, the League decided to defy the authority of the Porte's officials by refusing to send military recruits, and begin acts of civil disobedience and armed force substituting for political protests.

The majority of Albanians had not wished to see the Ottoman Empire dismembered or to seek an independent state. Autonomy within the Empire seemed the best guarantee of their local interests and national safety. Now, even many northern conservative Albanian nationalist leaders began to give serious attention to the question of autonomy. Because the northerners had long enjoyed certain local autonomy they, more than the southerners, resented the centralising policies of the Porte.[3] Before long around 16,000 Albanian men in arms were preparing to confront the Ottoman authorities and army. The Porte's first attempt to challenge the League's forces caused a massive Albanian rebellion in August 1878, during which one of the Porte's most renowned diplomats, Mehmed Ali Pasha, who had arrived to interpret the decisions of the Berlin Congress, was murdered in Djakovica. Such was the fury of the Albanians that his host, the president of the local committee of the Prizren League, Abdullah Pasha Dreni, was also killed. Throughout the following year anti-Ottoman demonstrations continued in southern Kosovo. A young Englishman, Edward Knight, who in the summer of 1879 explored Montenegro and northern Albanian-inhabited regions, later described how the Porte had all but lost its hold on northern Albania, including Kosovo:

> 'The government is very weak here, neither feared nor respected, merely tolerated. Albania is in a state of positive anarchy, the gendarmerie is on strike, the soldiers refusing to salute their officers, neither having received pay for months, while the natives hold seditious meetings publicly and unmolested in the mosques of the garrison towns, in which rebellion against the Porte is fearlessly advocated. Nowhere is the rotten condition and utter helplessness of the Porte more apparent than here'.[4]

The policy of courting the Albanian leaders pursued by the Serbian foreign minister, Ilija Garasanin, in the 1860s was reactivated in the '70s by the Russian ambassador to Istanbul, Ignatiev, who even offered to use his own fortune to win Albanians over to joining the Slavs. For the same reason Montenegro's Prince Nikola Petrovic Njegos courted the Catholic Mirdite ruling family Bib Doda in the 1880s, admitting that he did so in the hope that 'when it comes to hurrah' Albanians would join the Montenegrins in the fight against the Ottomans. Thus the Serbian government, Belgrade agents and numerous semi-official organisations all worked hard to attract Albanian support for the common struggle against the Porte. They especially hoped for a sympathetic response from northern Albanians,

3. For more detail on the formation of the League, see M. Vickers, *The Albanians: A Modern History*, London, 1995, and S. Skendi, *The Albanian National Awakening*, Princeton University Press. There was less support for the League in southern Albania where the threat of territorial loss was not so great. Nothing had been granted to Greece by the San Stefano Treaty and thus action for unification was not as urgently needed as in the north.
4. E. Knight, *Albania: A Narrative of Recent Travel*, London, 1880, p. 117.

whose Christian faith might prompt them to join the fight against the Ottomans and Islam rather than against Christian Serbia. But this did not happen,[5] the main reason being that Albanians were Albanians before they identified themselves as either Catholics or Muslims, as numerous foreign travellers noted in the nineteenth century.[6]

Meanwhile, the anti-Christian tenor of the League worried many non-Muslim Albanians, who wavered over joining it.[7] During the 1880s a Mr Kirby-Green was the British Consul-General for North Albania, and the loneliness of his job made him particularly glad to receive Mr Knight and his companion. Monitoring the political situation, he had observed the religious divisions beneath the surface of the League, and hearing that the two Englishmen intended to go to Prizren he warned them:

> 'Prizren, let me tell you, is the headquarters of the Albanian League, an organisation of the most fanatical Mussulmen of the country. These men are now worked up to a high pitch of religious zeal, and hatred of the Christians. Prizren is, with perhaps the exception of Mecca, the most dangerous spot for a Christian in all Mohammedan countries.'[8]

At that time the Mujahidin were actively encouraging a policy akin to ethnic cleansing. As the situation in Kosovo worsened, more and more Slav families decided to emigrate to Serbia, and in the wake of their departure, the region of south-western Kosovo was settled by Albanian Catholics known as Fandas, whose original homeland was along the upper reaches of the Fan i Fandit river. Many families, amounting to several thousand people consequently left the district and settled in the Pec, Djakovica and Prizren regions; they were forced to migrate to Kosovo at this time because their territory contained little arable land, which caused widespread poverty. These particular emigrants did not convert to Islam although their new neighbours were almost exclusively Muslims, who generally regarded their new neighbours with fear. According to a British Military Intelligence Report of the First World War, these settlers were called '*Fanda*' by their Muslim neighbours, 'who are much afraid of them owing to their courage and the relentless way they avenge an insult'.[9]

5. Dragnich and Todorovich, *The Saga of Kosovo*, p. 89.
6. See Vickers, *The Albanians,* p. 15.
7. The majority of Catholics eventually joined the League, but only after it had become obvious that the the waning power of the Porte would lead to their absorption in an Orthodox Slavic state, either Serbia or Montenegro.
8. Knight, *Albania*, p. 115.
9. *The Tribes of Northern Albania: A Handbook of Serbia, Montenegro, Albania*, Admiralty War Staff Intelligence Division (no. I.D.1096), June 1916, p. 399.

In the aftermath of the Bosnian insurrection in 1875, the forces of the League were being swollen daily by refugees from Bosnia and deserters from the Ottoman army. The League's men, confident in their growing strength, extended their programme by calling for autonomy in order to resist the advances of both Austria from the north and Greece from the south. There were also well-founded fears that Montenegro would try to extend its frontiers to take in Prizren and Shkoder. The League's leaders were appalled by what they perceived as the Porte's betrayal over the Albanian-inhabited areas ceded to Montenegro. As a result, the League took upon itself the task of uniting the Albanian-inhabited regions since the Porte was demonstrably unable to do so. Albanian resistance began in earnest in Kosovo on 4 January 1881, when the Prizren contingent, commanded by Sulejman Vokshi, first occupied Skopje and from there moved north to Mitrovica and parts of the Sandjak of Novi Pazar. By the end of the month the forces of the League were in control of Pristina. They eventually expelled the Ottoman administrators from the whole of Kosovo and proclaimed themselves the provincial government. From Kosovo they prepared to march south.

The growing Albanian movement directly challenged Ottoman rule and created conditions that would inevitably invite foreign intervention. As a consequence, the Sultan was advised to crush the League as soon as possible. Having reached an agreement with Greece over Thessaly, the Porte was now free to turn its attention to destroying the Albanian League.[10] On 23 March members of the League Committee in Constantinople were arrested and deported to the island of Rhodes. A month later, an Ottoman army of 10,000 men, commanded by Dervish Turgut Pasha, an advocate of centralisation, marched into Kosovo, and after stiff resistance occupied Prizren. The League's headquarters were hastily transfered to Djakovica, but resistance there lasted only a few days.[11] Albanian nationalists were from then on regularly arrested and all local organisations linked to the League were disbanded. The exacting of taxes,

10. The negotiations over the future of Epirus dragged on for almost two years until Greece and the Porte eventually reached agreement in 1881 whereby Greece would receive Thessaly and Arta in Epirus, but not the Janina *vilayet*.
11. There were similar moves to destroy the southern branch of the League. Within weeks military tribunals had judged its leaders and exiled most of them to remote parts of Anatolia. Abdul Frasheri fled but was captured at the end of April. His death sentence was commuted to life imprisonment, but he was released by the Sultan in 1885 following a general amnesty. He died in 1894.

the corruption of Turgut Pasha, the high cost of living, and the restriction of former freedoms caused deep discontent among the population, and the spirits of the people in Prizren and the surrounding districts were low.

The continued suppression of the Albanian movement, combined with the increasingly centralising policies of the Porte, led to the leaders of the Albanian League making continued calls for open opposition to the Porte, denying the authority of its officials and refusing to send army recruits. Although the Porte effectively destroyed the League, it could not destroy either the spirit of rebellion or the national awareness it had aroused. These steadily grew, and the League's ideals continued to exercise a powerful influence on Albanian intellectuals for several decades. The motivating force behind this early expression of nationalism was less a wish to disturb the *status quo* than self-preservation. Nevertheless, the series of local revolts, which had characterised the decade following the creation of the Prizren League, were sparked off not by national concerns but by the Albanian refusal to heed attempts by Ottoman officials to collect old taxes and impose new ones, only a small part of which was spent on local needs while most found its way directly into the state treasury. Albanians were indignant at having to pay taxes at all but more so at being required to pay no less than Christians.

At the end of September 1884 an Albanian rebellion broke out in the district of Prizren, against an attempt by the Porte's authorities to list the population and its properties to determine the amount of new taxes to be paid. After widespread violence in the town of Prizren, the Porte tried to placate the Albanians by freeing some political prisoners, but the result of this was that travel outside the major towns became extremely dangerous. In 1887 an Australian who wished to travel from Prizren to Djakovica was strongly advised not to do so by Ahmet Hamdi Bey, head of police in Prizren. He wrote:

> 'The Bey tried hard to dissuade me, but I remained obstinate. At last he made an earnest appeal. "I have no power", he said, "to forbid your going, and no claim to ask a favour from you, nevertheless, I should take it as a very great kindness if you would give up this journey. Just at the present moment the risk of going there is enormous, and if anything happens, the blame will fall on me."'[12]

12. H.A. Brown, *A Winter in Albania*, London, 1888, p. 251.

The long years of Ottoman occupation of Kosovo had created
an atmosphere of profound stagnation. The Porte provided neither
schools nor roads, and with the exception of a few ramshackle
barracks and custom houses the region was left much as the
Ottomans had found it. During the last decades of the nineteenth
century, in addition to the arrival of the Fandas, the population of
Kosovo was swollen by several thousand more Albanian families,
who had trekked over the Northern Albanian Alps to settle permanently in the towns and villages in the fertile plain between Pec
and Prizren. New Albanian villages were also beginning to appear
along the northern borders of the Kosovo *vilayet*. The prime motive
for this migration into Kosovo appears to have been, as in the past,
the severe shortage of pasture and cultivable land. The same British
intelligence report cited above states that the small size of the district
belonging to the Berisha clan 'caused many to emigrate, particularly
in the direction of Djakovica to the North-West, where they
occupy many villages. These have often turned Mohammedan.'[13]
The Catholic Shala clan, whose territory centred around the
extremely mountainous district of Thethi in the North Albanian
Alps, was formerly very large, but the scarcity of cultivable land
forced many families to migrate down into Kosovo, especially to Pec
and its neighbourhood where there were hundreds of Shalyan families; Isnich, a village near Decani, was entirely composed of them.[14]
We see therefore that the population of Kosovo was by now becoming predominantly Albanian. In a dispatch on 27 July 1880 to Lord
Granville, the Foreign Secretary, Lord E. Fitzmaurice, his representative on the Eastern Roumelian Commission, wrote: 'In my
dispatch of the 26 May last I expressed the opinion that the whole
of the former vilayet of Prizren, which included Debar, Djakovica,
Pec, Kosovo, Prizren and Pristina, was distinct from the Slavonic
countries lying east and south of it, and was predominantly
Mohammedan and Albanian in character.'[15]

With 46,000 inhabitants Prizren had continued to grow into one
of the largest and most important Balkan towns. Owing to the skill
of its metalworkers, it had become the main centre for the manu-
facture and trading of weapons. In the Serbian *mahala* (quarter),
which spread up the steep slope below the huge fortress, all the

13. *The Tribes of Northern Albania*, p. 397.
14. Ibid., p. 411.
15. J. Swire, *Albania: The Rise of a Kingdom*, London, 1929; reprinted New York,
    1971, p. 53.

inhabitants regardless of their ethnicity spoke Turkish as the language of everyday converse. Most urban Albanian families also spoke Turkish at home as it was considered a mark of urban sophistication. It was of great use as a lingua franca because of the variety of other languages now spoken in Prizren. A new commercial swing had come to Kosovo with the opening of the railway line from Mitrovica to Thessaloniki in 1873. With the exception of its fine, decorative silverwork for which it was famous, Prizren's handicrafts showed a decrease in sales due to competition from cheap European goods brought to Kosovo by Jewish merchants from Thessaloniki. A foreign visitor to Kosovo in 1887 noted how Christians now dominated the town's commercial activities:

> 'There are an immense number of Slavs and other members of the
> Greek Church in Prizren. The business of the town is almost
> entirely in the hands of Christians. The Roman Catholics have a
> considerable number of shops but the greater portion belong to the
> Greeks.'[16]

The town's vibrant, cosmopolitan character was reflected in the people's everyday dress: the fezzes and bloomers of the Turks; the Albanians, with their white skull-caps and flaming sashes; the tall Montenegrins, with their gay jackets and tiny round hats; the people of the Sandjak, with glaring, pirate-like turbans; the Serbian peasant women, with their vari-coloured stockings, multiform *opanki*, exquisitely embroidered short skirts and jackets, and bright headgear; the Serbian men in their brown and black homespun trousers, tight in the leg and voluminous in the seat: all flowed in barbaric masses of colour through the streets of Prizren.[17]

Nevertheless, despite the relative prosperity and wellbeing of the town-dwelling Slavs, the majority of Kosovo's Serbs and Montenegrins still lived in rural districts and had few comforts. They remained in a distinct and recognisably inferior position; even their houses were not permitted to be more conspicuous than those of their Muslim neighbours or overlook them. Travelling through Kosovo in 1885, another visitor, William Forsyth, noted:

> 'The few remaining rural-dwelling Christians had a sorry time of it.
> They are heavily taxed and the condition of the countryside is bad
> enough to reduce to despair all its inhabitants. It is no wonder they
> look with longing eyes to their brethren in the Principality of free

16. Brown, *A Winter in Albania*, p. 236.
17. F. Jones, *With Serbia into Exile*, London, 1916, p. 296.

Serbia, but it is said that the government there discourages emigration from Old Serbia because this would tend to abandon the region wholly to the Albanians. Thus what the free Serbians would call a feeling of patriotism is indulged in at the expense of the sufferings of their unfortunate fellow Christians.'[18]

In order to enforce Sultan Abdul Hamid II's Pan-Islamic policy, groups of Muslim theological students would tour the villages of Kosovo, especially during the Ramadan fast. Serbian merchants and craftsmen living mainly in the towns fared better than their kinsfolk in the countryside, but even so they kept a low profile and preferred whenever possible to remain within their own quarters.

The administration of Greek metropolitans over the Raska-Prizren eparchy, encompassing almost all of Kosovo, greatly hindered Serbia's work on national affairs among Serbs living under Ottoman rule. In 1885 negotiations began between Belgrade and the Patriarchate in Istanbul, on the question of a Serb being appointed as Metropolitan in Prizren. Despite the lack of success in the discussions, the Serbian government neverthess began to send young men to train for future religious duties in the Ottoman Empire. Austro-Hungarian influence in the Kosovo *vilayet* gradually grew through Catholic missions in northern Albania and Kosovo, and Vienna's consulates in Prizren, Skopje and Shkoder.

Meanwhile, Serbia's position in the Balkans was now weakened. The only protection for Serbs in Kosovo came from Russian diplomats, since under Article 23 of the Berlin Congress Russia, as the traditional guardian of the Orthodox population in the Ottoman Empire, had the right to protect Christians. However, Russia's waning influence in the Balkans following the Congress had an unfavourable impact on the Serbs under Ottoman rule. Owing to the Austrophile policy of Milan and Alexander Obrenovic, Serbia lost valuable Russian support at the Porte in its efforts to protect the Serbian population.[19] By the time that the quincentenary of the Battle of Kosovo was commemorated in June 1889, Serbia was under Austrian influence and its plans for unification were necessarily thwarted. As the day of the commemoration drew near, tensions began to mount in those South Slavic areas controlled by Austria-Hungary. From April 1889 onwards, no travel was permitted in the Empire except to bearers of a Great Passport, and no

18. William Forsyth, *The Slavonic Provinces South of the Danube*, London, 1876, p. 71.
19. Batakovic, *The Kosovo Chronicles*, p. 58.

Serbs were given such passports for travel in any southerly or easterly directions. Imperial police began to guard all roads leading to Serbia and forbade passage to any Serb wishing to travel in the days before the actual celebration.[20] Nevertheless, the commemoration was more successful than anyone could have imagined. Despite all the attempts at repression, the anniversary became a popular symbol in the liberation struggle of all South Slavs under foreign rule. To many who still yearned for their freedom the Kosovo epic sounded a note of hope. In Vienna, South Slav youths gathered in their clubs to remember the heroes of Kosovo. The celebrations united the Slavic and Orthodox world. A Slavophile newspaper in Russia called Kosovo the 'Serbian Troy' and urged all Russians to recognise it as such. In St Petersburg a requiem was held in St Isaac's Cathedral, and black flags flew from churches in Athens.[21]

During the 1880s the Great Powers had begun to reform their alliance groupings in the hope of establishing a new equilibrium among themselves. The French occupation of Tunisia in 1881 prompted Italy to join with Germany and Austria-Hungary in the Triple Alliance of 1882, which was designed to counter further Russian and French expansion, mainly in the Balkans. When the Triple Alliance was renewed in 1887, it was accompanied by a separate Austro-Italian Treaty, pledging the two parties to preserve the *status quo* in the Balkans, which they regarded as the basis for the maintenance of peace in the area. However, this did not dispel the mistrust between Italy and Austria-Hungary, both of which recognised the strategic importance of Albania. Austria-Hungary planned that if the Ottoman Empire collapsed Albania would be autonomous but under its protection, to prevent it falling under another Power's influence. This foreign influence was most likely to come from Italy which likewise did not wish to see Albania in the grasp of Austria-Hungary. Italy's interests appeared to depend on extending its sphere of influence across the Adriatic to compensate for the failure of its other colonial ventures. Towards the turn of the century, Albanian national literature had begun to appear in Italy among the Italo-Albanians, the Arbaresh, who in 1794 had founded an Albanian-language school in Calabria; they actively strove to publicise, throughout Italy and Europe the aims of the Albanian national movement through their journal *Flamuri Arberit* (Flag of

20. T.A. Emmert, 'The Kosovo Legacy', *Serbian Studies*, vol. 5, no. 2, 1989, p. 12.
21. Ibid., p. 16.

Albania). However, the Italo-Albanians were out of touch with political realities within the Ottoman Empire in believing that by introducing Albanian as the official language of the five *vilayets,* they could define Albania as a national territory, thus ignoring the non-Albanian elements.[22]

In response to the Powers' growing interests in the region, several prominent northern Albanians decided to reactivate their political activities and in January 1889 over 400 delegates from all parts of Kosovo gathered in Pec where the Prizren League was re-formed under the new name of the League of Peja (the Albanian name for Pec), presided over by Haxhi Mulla Zeka, a landowner from that district.[23] In a similar manner to the background of the Prizren League's agenda among Kosovo's Albanians, the Peja League had essentially a Muslim rather than any nationalist character, showing little regard for the demands for reform being made at that time by the Albanian – and Macedonian – Christians. There developed a struggle between moderate and more radical factions; the moderates argued primarily for cultural reforms, while the radicals demanded political reform – genuine autonomy. However, the northern tribes still possessed only a rudimentary national consciousness, and thus the main purpose of the meeting was to protect Islam. The national idea still had to compete with tribal particularism, but Christian Albanians were united by their intense mistrust and dislike of Ottoman rule. Although the predominantly Muslim Kosovars, who were conservative by nature, identified themselves religiously with the Ottomans, the Porte still regarded all Albanians with deep suspicion, and ordered Ottoman officials to watch all their moves and forcibly suppress any signs of renewed agitation.

Meanwhile, tension in the Balkans increased considerably as the Powers intensified their pressure on the Porte to put reforms into effect in Macedonia. The region then known as Macedonia was bounded to the north and east by the Sar and Rhodope mountains, on the south by the Aegean sea and the Pindus mountains and on the west by Lakes Ohrid and Prespa. Its population of 2 million comprised almost every ethnic group to be found in the Balkan peninsula – Bulgars, Turks, Serbs, Gypsies, Albanians, Vlachs, Jews, Greeks and Macedonian Slavs. It also contained the most important

---

22. Skendi, *The Albanian National Awakening*, p. 249.
23. At the beginning of 1902, Hadji Mulla Zeka was killed by a certain Adem Zaim in what was believed to be a clan dispute.

and strategic port in the Balkans, Thessaloniki. Because of Macedonia's immense strategic importance, the Balkan states – Bulgaria, Greece and Serbia – all wished to aquire a major portion of it, for whoever controlled it would be the strongest power in the peninsula. Each of these three Balkan states also claimed Macedonia as its own for historical reasons, since the region had been an essential part of their past empires. The Serbo–Bulgarian war of 1885 worsened relations between those two countries and made Macedonia even more of a tinder-box, and from then onwards it became the all-absorbing concern of the Bulgarians, who plotted for its annexation.[24]

By now it was becoming apparent that the Ottoman Empire had run its course, and in consequence both Russia and Austria-Hungary became even more concerned to consolidate their spheres of influence in the Balkans. Bulgaria's absorption of Eastern Rumelia in 1885 effectively did what the Russians had been prevented from doing at San Stefano. Complete disorder now reigned in Kosovo. The waning power of the Porte caused an increase in Albanian incursions into Serbian territory, where frontier garrisons were constantly being reinforced. Despite numerous calls from the Serbian government to the Porte to end these incursions, the situation worsened. Further south the Pec patriarchate and other Serbian monasteries were reduced to paying the customary protection-money to Albanians to ward off attacks by robbers and bandits. When the seat of the Kosovo *vilayet* was moved to Skopje in 1888, the Serbian consulate in Prizren remained a solitary diplomatic watchtower in a weakly supervised district. In 1889 a Serbian consulate finally opened in Pristina, and from this time on the Serbian government was able to monitor goings-on in Kosovo more closely. However, the assassination of the first Serbian consul, Luka Marinkovic, in the streets of Pristina in June 1890 indicated how unwelcome the consulate was. Put under pressure by Serbian and Russian diplomats, the murderers of the Serbian consul, *muhadjirs* (Muslim zealots) from Prokuplje, were tried and imprisoned, but those who had planned the assassination were never apprehended.[25]

The Serbian vice-consul in Pristina Milan Rakic now argued that the only feasible solution to the lawlessness was for Serbs to

---

24. S.E. Palmer and R.R. King, *Yugoslav Communism and the Macedonian Question*, Shoestring Press, Hamden,CT, 1971, p. 7.
25. Batakovic, *The Kosovo Chronicles*, pp. 128-9.

continue paying for Albanian guards to protect Serbian monasteries and villages. Serbian diplomats demanded the disarming of Albanians and reinforcement of Ottoman garrisons in areas with mixed Serbian-Albanian populations, and progress was made in halting the anarchy in Kosovo through the mediation of Russian diplomats in 1892, who requested that the Porte secure public safety and protect Christians. But, apart from the writing of detailed reports describing the situation in Kosovo, Serbia's sole diplomatic success was the election of a Serbian candidate as the Raska-Prizren Metropolitan in 1896, following a series of anti-Serbian Greek bishops who had held the see since 1830.[26]

Cultural developments

Despite the general anarchy, rapid progress was made. On 1 May 1889, Kosovo's first Albanian-language school was opened in Prizren, although it was still illegal to teach in the Albanian language. The Ottoman government had been alarmed by the Albanians' drive not only for political but also for cultural autonomy as the spirit of the Prizren League lived on through intensive cultural activity. Some thirty Albanian-language newspapers and journals were established in the years up to 1908 within the Empire and abroad, and some Albanian-language schools were opened. Educationally, Islam had hindered rather than helped the majority of Albanians, since all religious communities within the Empire had their own schools except the Albanians, who were taught as Turks. If the people were to be united, new schools had to be non-denominational.[27] From 1902, new laws made possession of an Albanian book and even the use of Albanian in correspondence a punishable offence. Thus all the Albanian-language schools were closed. The Albanians responded by forming secret societies to promote the teaching of their language, which the Greek ecclesiastical authorities also suppressed.

26. Ibid., p. 58.
27. The first Albanian school for boys, both Christians and Muslims, was opened in Korca in 1885. The first Albanian school for girls was founded in 1891, again in Korca. Before long, however, the Porte decided to curtail Albanian educational activities, and the Muslim pupils were forced to leave the school. The Orthodox clergy also put pressure on parents to withdraw their children by threatening them with excommunication.

A few years before the founding of the Prizren League, several Albanian intellectuals in diaspora centres such as Bucharest and Istanbul had gathered to discuss the pressing question of an Albanian orthography, and the creation of Albanian schools inevitably raised this question in an acute form. Differences of opinion had arisen between those favouring the Arabic script, while others preferred the Greek and yet others the Latin alphabet. At this time a number of different alphabets based on the Latin, Greek or Arabic scripts were in use, adding further to the division. So exasperated was Vasa Pasha Effendi, a Catholic from Shkoder and an advocate of the Latin alphabet, that he wrote in a poem: 'Albanians, you are killing your brothers, you are divided into a hundred parties. Some say I am a Christian, others, I am a Turk, yet others I am a Latin, I am a Greek or a Slav or something else. But you are brothers all of you. The priests and Hodjas have confused you, unite in one faith; the faith of Albanians is Albanianism.[28]

Since Serbs were in the Orthodox *millet*, they were not recognised as a separate national group, and thus the independent Bulgarians sought to present all Serbian schools as Bulgarian. However, under an Imperial decree on education issued in 1896, the Serbs in Kosovo and other Ottoman regions could open their own schools and thus indirectly acquired recognition of their nationality. The first Serbian bookshop opened in Pristina in 1893. Following the death of the Greek Metropolitan Meletije, a Serb, Archsyncellus Dionisije Petrovic (1896-1900) was consecrated to the Raska-Prizren bishopric through the joint effort of the governments of Serbia and Montenegro, bolstered by Russian diplomacy in Istanbul. On orders from the Serbian government, the new metropolitan carried out a wide reorganisation in ecclesiastical and educational institutions, opened new schools, renewed teaching staff, created new church-school communities and united activists on national affairs.[29] These seedbeds of national propaganda were springing up throughout Kosovo and Macedonia as Serbia and Bulgaria contended for influence over the population. The Greek-Ottoman war of 1897 marked the approaching disintegration of the Ottoman Empire. By 1898 the position of the Serbian peasant in Kosovo was parlous. Much of the Albanian unrest in Kosovo was believed to have been stirred up by the Austro-Hungarian intelligence services

---

28. Vasa Effendi, *La Verité sur l'Albanie et les Albanais. Etude Historique et Critique*, Paris, 1879, p. 98.
29. Batakovic, *The Kosovo Chronicles*, p. 132.

in order to provoke sufficient chaos for Vienna to intervene and
occupy the region.

Travelling through southwest Kosovo shortly afterwards, the
English anthropologist Edith Durham summed up the tenuous presence of the Serbs in Kosovo and the Albanians' determination to rid
the province of its remaining Slav element:

> 'The Albanians are almost solely Albanophone, whereas the scattered
> Serbs usually speak both languages and when addressed in Serb often
> replied at first in Albanian. Were it not for the support and instruc-
> tion that has long been supplied from without, it is probable that the
> Serb element would have been almost, if not quite, absorbed or
> suppressed by this time. Ineradicably fixed in the breast of the Alban-
> ian...is the belief that the land has been his rightly for all time. The
> Serb conquered him, held him for a few passing centuries, was swept
> out and shall never return again. He has but done to the Serb as he
> was done by.'[30]

Durham also noted how the Serbs tried to maintain a foothold in
the district of Prizren:

> 'The school, a fine building, recently enlarged and repaired, holds a
> hundred students. Many come from Montenegro even. I went over
> it sadly. It seemed sheer folly to make a large and costly Serb theo-
> logical school in a Muslim Albanian town, and to import masters
> and students, when funds are so urgently needed to develop free
> Serb lands.'[31]

Leon Trotsky, a war correspondent for *Pravda* during the Balkan
Wars, wrote:

> 'The Albanian villages are much better, much richer than the
> Serbian ones. The Serbs, even the rich ones, don't build fine houses
> in villages where there are Albanians. If a Serb has a two-storey
> house he refrains from painting it so that it shan't look better than
> the Albanian houses.'[32]

In the new century the movement for Albanian administrative
autonomy gathered momentum. It was now generally realised that
the Porte would be unlikely to grant the Albanians administrative
autonomy of its own accord, and the various Albanian leaders
therefore decided to take matters into their own hands by organis-

30. Edith Durham, *High Albania*, London, 1909, repr. 1985, p. 294.
31. Ibid., p. 275.
32. L. Trotsky, *The Balkan Wars - 1912-1913*, New York, 1980, p. 123.

ing sporadic and random raids on isolated Slav settlements and Ottoman garrisons. In May 1901 Albanian bands pillaged and partly burned Novi Pazar, Sjenica and Pristina. The Serbian populations suffered most, through their proximity to Albanians who, when occupying Kolasin, massacred a considerable number of Serbs.[33] In an attempt to halt the killings of Slavs, a group of Albanian notables from Pec and Djakovica arrived in Belgrade at the invitation of the Serbian government. Among them was the Pec leader Mehmed Zaim. There they were lavished with gifts of money and arms and promised assistance in their struggle against the Porte if they would help to end violence in Kosovo.

At the end of 1902 Russia opened a consulate in Mitrovica, nominally to protect the Slavs from violence, but in reality to monitor more closely Austria-Hungary's increasing influence over the Albanian Catholic population. Alarmed at the rapid weakening of Ottoman authority, the Powers hastily tried to effect a new series of reforms they had drawn up, through which means they hoped to ease the plight of the beleaguered Christian population and perhaps diffuse an explosive situation. Nevertheless, even though a Christian gendarmerie was eventually introduced, its men were not allowed to carry arms and spent their days lounging around the police stations, the objects of scorn to Muslim Albanians. The Kosovars, conservative by inclination and suspicious that foreign interference favoured the Slavs, vehemently opposed the Austro-Russian programme of reforms for Macedonia, which involved their own lands. In particular, they could not tolerate the idea of having Christian Slav gendarmes policing their territories. In March 1903 they rose in revolt and occupied Vucitrn and Mitrovica, where they attacked the Ottoman garrison. The Porte dispatched various commissions to conciliate them, but they would not listen. The newly-appointed Russian consul in Mitrovica, Grigorie Stepanovic Shtcherbin, was assassinated on 31 March by an Albanian.

For the Serbs this murder was a national tragedy. They had seen him as a protector and a representative of the power they had hoped would end the anarchy and violence. The train bearing his coffin was accompanied by several thousand Serbs, and religious ceremonies were held in churches throughout Kosovo.[34] The forces sent by the Porte to implement the reforms paid little heed to the continuing

---

33. Skendi, *The Albanian National Awakening*, p. 201.
34. Batakovic, *The Kosovo Chronicles*, p. 153.

lawlessness. If the Muslim Albanians attacked the Serbs as Orthodox Christians, it was because they resented seeing government positions, under the reforms, pass from Muslim to Christians, who till then had been under their rule – and these Christians had a Serbian state to back them.[35] The disorders now spread rapidly to Pristina, the Sandjak of Novi Pazar and the northern part of the *vilayet* of Shkoder, but were, as usual, rudimentary and uncoordinated. *Drita*, the Albanian diaspora newspaper in Sofia, described the real situation effectively and succinctly: 'Gjakova fights and dies, while Peja is in ignorance. In Lume houses are in flames, while other places hear nothing about it.'[36] In response to the deteriorating situation, on 2 August 1903 some 25,000 Macedonian Slavs also staged an uprising orchestrated by the Internal Macedonian Revolutionary Organisation, IMRO, which aimed to seize the *vilayet* of Monastir (Bitola) and so liberate Macedonia from the Ottomans. With most of the central Balkans now in revolt, the Porte sent in the *bashibazouks*, most of them Albanian, to crush the various uprisings, which they did with great brutality.

With the murder of King Alexander Obrenovic in 1903, the Karadjordjevic dynasty returned to the Serbian throne, and this signalled a new period of independence *vis-à-vis* Austria-Hungary. Petar Karadjordjevic abruptly changed Serbia's foreign policy in favour of a pro-Russian stance and renewed national propaganda among Serbs living under Ottoman rule. As a result Serbia immediately found itself in conflict with Vienna and the Porte over the reform issue. In response Austria-Hungary stepped up its propaganda among Albanians, who in turn responded by instigating incessant revolts and uprisings. Armed rebellions had also now become a chronic feature of daily life throughout Macedonia as Bulgarian, Greek and Serbian bands continued their fight to gain territory for themselves and impose their nationality on the territory's inhabitants.

As the situation in Macedonia worsened, a Committee for the Liberation of Albania was hastily formed in Monastir to inject some sense of direction into the fragmented Albanian political movement. At the beginning of 1906, a branch of the Committee was established in Djakovica, headed by, among others, the great chieftain Bajram Curri (1862-1925), a native of that place. Committees

35. Skendi, *The Albanian National Awakening*, p. 295.
36. Ibid., p. 213.

were also established in the other Albanian-inhabited *vilayets*. Not long afterwards the Albanians formed their own guerrilla bands known as *cheta*. The Ottoman Empire was now well into its death throes. Sultan Abdul Hamid pathetically embodied all the spiritual despair, all the moral decadence, all the physical degeneracy of his regime. Over the whole spirit of the Hamidian Empire, over its barren reforms and equally barren reactions hung this gloom of despair, this shadow of impending death.

4

THE YOUNG TURKS AND
THE BALKAN WARS

Towards the end of the nineteenth century a new political factor had
emerged within the Ottoman Empire, with roots going back to the
1860s. This was the Young Turk Movement, which formed a liberal
opposition to the regime of Sultan Abdul Hamid. The Young
Turks, a product of the earlier reforms and the better education
provided in schools modelled on Western lines, sought to revitalise,
restructure and regenerate the Empire. An emerging sense of 'Turkish' national identity had by now made its appearance and the redis-
covery of texts in the Koran supporting government by discussion,
combined with a new literary movement based on French models,
created an atmosphere of change and progress. Thus the foundations
were being laid for an eventual Turkish national state distinct from
the Ottoman Empire.

Kosovars and the Young Turks

In 1906 the Young Turks established their headquarters at Thessaloniki and formed a Committee of Union and Progress. Before
long, branches sprang up in neighbouring towns and many Albanian members of the Young Turk Committee were also members of
the local Committee of the Prizren League. They sought a return
to the 1876 constitution which had granted the Empire's ethnically
and culturally diverse population the national rights they had been
demanding. Gradually the movement extended its influence in the
army, until a general and spontaneous uprising heralded a military
coup which overthrew the Sultan and brought the Young Turks to
power in July 1908. This revolution was greatly assisted by Albanians, especially those from Kosovo, since the Young Turks had
promised to relieve them of their heavy taxes and award them full
constitutional rights, together with their traditional privileges. They

also gave assurances that Albanians would remain in possession of their arms and have schools in their own language, and that provincial autonomy would be granted to the various nationalities. Elections for the new parliament were followed by the adoption of a constitution that ended the absolutist regime.

Throughout the Empire there was a general expectation that change was under way. The new constitution was hailed throughout Kosovo, as indeed throughout the Empire, with wild enthusiasm. A general *besa* (truce) was proclaimed throughout the Albanian-inhabited regions, and almost a year passed with no private or inter-tribal feuds.[1] The promises of the Young Turks were greeted by both Serbs and Albanians, Christians and Muslims, as an opportunity for national affirmation and free political organisation. To the Albanians the proclamation of the constitution marked the beginning of a new era of freedom and equality. The *chetas* (armed groups) came down from the hills, many political exiles returned, and Albanian newspapers appeared in the variety of alphabets used to write the Albanian language, but generally the Kosovo Albanians had little confidence in the durability of the new regime, and saw it as a means to an end. They had not been unduly dissatisfied with the rule of Sultan Abdul Hamid, who till the advent of the Eastern Crisis, had behaved towards them as an indulgent father (they called him '*baba mbret*', father king), respecting their laws and customs and allowing them to carry arms and pay low taxes. He even distributed honours, positions and titles to their chiefs.[2] So, while many Albanians were on their side, the Young Turks still had to reach an understanding with the bulk of the Muslim population of Kosovo, who were not inclined to abandon the Sultan.[3]

However, it was not going to be easy to win over the staunchly conservative Kosovars, many of whom believed that the constitution was a *bid'at* (innovation against religious law) The Young Turks responded to this by declaring further that the constitution did not oppose the Koran and that Islam consecrated the right of the parliament to restrict the power of the Sultan. Nevertheless, the Young Turks would not have won the Kosovars to their side had they not promised to satisfy their demands. They committed themselves to respect the old privileges over taxation to allow the Albanians to

1. J. Swire, *Albania - The Rise of a Kingdom*, London, 1929, repr. New York, 1971, p. 83.
2. Skendi, *The Albanian National Awakening*, p. 392.
3. Ibid., p. 341.

retain possession of their arms and to open Albanian schools, and they accepted the inviolability of the Sultan.[4] The new Young Turk parliament included twenty-six Albanian deputies, the majority of whom were prominent figures with a strong regional following such as Ismail Kemal, Hasan Pristina and Essad Pasha Toptani. These deputies all worked for decentralisation of government, and thus for a brief time the Albanians enjoyed Ottoman benevolence.

The new spirit of freedom led to a demand for published material in the Albanian language. A Congress was therefore convened on 14 November 1908, at Monastir, with delegates from all the Albanian-inhabited regions and the Albanian diaspora abroad to approve an Albanian alphabet. Two currents finally emerged, favouring respectively the Latin alphabet and the Istanbul (Arabic) script. The Latin alphabet was seen by many more liberal delegates as a way of uniting Christian and Muslim, Gheg and Tosk, and making them more conscious of their common heritage. The Young Turks naturally backed the Istanbul form, and organised demonstrations to that end, but eventually it was agreed to adopt both forms, hardly an ideal solution, but one which at least enabled material published in the north to be read in the south and *vice versa*. The Muslims of northern Albania, especially those in the *vilayet* of Kosovo, took little part in this debate and could not understand the cultural efforts of their more emancipated brothers in the south. They were rather reluctant to adopt a script that was not that of the Koran and they were also disinclined to see Albanian taught in the schools, since they recognised Turkish as the only official state language even though the majority could not fully understand it.

In general the Muslims of Shkoder and Kosovo were pro-Ottoman and pro-Islamic, and repeatedly this allegiance to the old order proved an obstacle to Albanian national development. They were regarded by most observers as the most backward and fanatical of all Albanian religious groups, as was shown by their boycott of another Congress held in Elbasan that September to study further questions relating to their education and culture. Attended by thirty-five delegates, all from central and southern Albania, it officially endorsed the Monastir decision to use the Latin alphabet rather than the Arabic script for written Albanian. It was considered more suitable than either Arabic or Greek characters, and easier to

4. Ibid., p. 343.

learn. It also corresponded more closely to the sounds and conso-
nants of the Albanian language. Moreover, Albanians were anxious
to avail themselves of every opportunity to establish the individuality of their nation, divorce themselves from Orientalism, and bring
themselves into closer contact with the West.[5]

The southern Tosks therefore had an extremely difficult task not
only trying to persuade the Kosovars to participate in nationalist
activity, but in generating interest in national issues in the first
instance. In 1908 the Austro-Hungarian consul in Prizren,
Prohaska, reported a poor response to the nationalist propaganda
spread by the southern Tosks. The people were under the heavy
influence of the old clans and their leaders who had little interest in
the national issue. However, he reported the existence of certain
nationalist activities among younger students. In some areas, like
Prizren, nationalist ideas were condemned because of a strong
Ottoman influence; there a man's Islamic beliefs were considered of
far greater importance than his feelings of Albanian nationalism.[6] A
Kosovar who visited his compatriots in the early period of the
constitutional regime and was disappointed with the situation wrote
critically: 'But even those who call themselves Albanians in Kosovo
have been blinded by fanaticism and do not know what is Alba-
niandom, or language, or nation. Only in Gjakova, and particularly
in Skopje, did one find a real national Albanian movement.[7] The
obstacles to Albanian national development were clearly twofold: on
the one hand, the religious division among the people and the
differences in culture between north and south, and on the other the
efforts of the Young Turks to deepen the existing divisions and use
them in their own interest.[8]

Following the announcement of the new constitution, a period
of relative peace reigned throughout Kosovo as both Serbs and
Albanians at first believed that their lot was about to improve
dramatically, but this did not last long. The establishment of a
constitutional empire was considered as having solved the Eastern
Question on a basis of equality (though with an imperialistic basis),
guaranteed by new representative institutions. However, before long
the Ottoman revolution proved to be a Turkish national renais-

5. Swire, *Albania*, p. 63.
6. Kiraly Belsk and D. Djordjevic (eds), *East Central European Society and the
   Balkan Wars*, New York, 1986, p. 166.
7. Skendi, *The Albanian National Awakening*, p. 391.
8. Ibid., p. 404.

sance, and as such came into violent collision with Balkan nationalism. The main obstacle in the reformed Empire was the difficulty of reconciling new and old: liberty, equality and fraternity with the principle of Muslim and *Rayah* (Christian peasants); the constitutional regime with the 'good old rule' of Istanbul; the Young Turks with the Old Turks; the followers of Comte with the faithful of the Khalif; and the intelligentsia with Islam.[9] Thus within months of consolidating their power, the Young Turks reneged on their promises to the Albanians and the Empire's other subject peoples. Within the Young Turk leadership a strongly pan-Ottoman inclination prevailed, which considered all subjects of the Empire an inseparable whole, and the regime now planned to enforce the uniform Turkification of the various Ottoman dependencies. It therefore became increasingly difficult to publicise non-Ottoman national ideas or to discuss political affairs of any kind in the newly-formed Slav and Albanian cultural clubs and societies. The pan-Ottoman ideology of the Young Turk leadership, centralisation of the administration, introduction of regular military service and a new tax policy ruffled the Albanians, who felt that the resolute Young Turks had no understanding of their special rights. Thus the 'honeymoon' between the Albanians and the Young Turks began to wane.

Originally the Young Turks carried out their promises and at the end of 1908 they not only enacted electoral laws but allowed elections to be held. However, it was not long before deep divisions appeared in their relations with the Albanians. The electoral law of September 1908 stipulated that the candidates should present themselves as Ottomans and have a knowledge of the Turkish language. This ruled out the majority of Kosovo's population excluding the élite, whether Muslim or Christian. The Albanians continued to advocate more decentralisation of the Empire and autonomy for their national regions, while the Young Turks adopted a series of measures designed to reinforce central power. A clash was therefore inevitable because the Young Turks were totally opposed to nationalism within the Empire and believed that only enforced Turkification of all subjects would keep the Empire intact and strong.

Meanwhile, the situation in Macedonia had worsened as Bulgarian insurgents increased their activities. Macedonia had

9. Lord Courtney of Penwith (ed.), *Nationalism and War in the Near East*, Carnegie Endowment for International Peace, Oxford, 1915, p. 120.

become the arena for bitter Balkan racial and social warfare and a locus of infection for European political war fever. When the Powers decided in June 1908, to revive the programme of reforms for Macedonia, the Young Turks saw a renewed threat to the Empire. The reforms could lead to an autonomous Macedonia, which would include Albanian territory, and eventually its loss. The Young Turk revolution had thwarted Austro-Hungarian and Italian plans for extending their influence in Albania. Austria's main fear was that Serbia, under Russian patronage, would assimilate Bosnia-Hercegovina, thereby creating a Greater Serbia. Vienna saw the control of Bosnia-Hercegovina as essential to provide security for its Dalmatian coast and to curb Serbian and, even more important, Russian influence. Thus, on 5 October 1908 Austria-Hungary announced its annexation of Bosnia-Hercegovina.

By the end of the year Kosovo was seething with intrigue and the heady atmosphere of impending war, and Prizren swarmed with spies from every consulate reporting on the actions of fellow diplomats. Edith Durham, who was staying there, observed:

> 'Each nation that designs to pick up the pieces when Turkey in Europe bursts up, keeps a Consul on the spot. A Russian represents Slav interests, to claim the land as Old Serbia. An acute Austrian is posted there to forward his country's plan of 'Advance, Austria', and Italy has had to plant a man to see what he is doing.'[10]

In the diplomatic crisis which followed the annexation of Bosnia-Hercegovina, Russia was galvanised into organizing the Balkan states to oppose Austria-Hungary, which now firmly believed that if the Balkan *status quo* could no longer be preserved, it must insist on the possession of Bosnia-Hercegovina and the Sandjak of Novi Pazar in order to keep Serbia and Montenegro from uniting. An independent Albanian state must therefore be created.

The Entente Powers, without having any direct claims on the region, nevertheless feared further Austrian expansion towards and even beyond the prized port of Thessaloniki. To secure its political and economic independence Serbia needed an outlet to the Adriatic Sea, and the Austrian annexation of Bosnia-Hercegovina was thus a bitter blow since it considered the region as its own national land. Austria-Hungary, not the Ottoman Empire, was now the

10. E. Durham, *High Albania*, Edward Arnold, London, 1909; repr. Virago Press, 1985, p. 270.

enemy. The Serbs had found in the port of Thessaloniki their only
escape from the economic wars waged against them by the Austrians which had culminated in the veto placed on the Serbo-Bulgar-
ian commercial treaty of 1905 and the 'pig war' of 1906. Keeping
this economic escape-route open was of more immediate importance to Serbia than establishing politically its remote reversionary
interest in the intervening territory. In their attempt to force Serbia
to renounce the recently signed customs union with Bulgaria, the
Austrians closed their border to all livestock exports, most of which
were pigs. After 1908, their economic and political pressure on
Serbia intensified, and the danger of further encirclement grew.
Thus Serbia's foreign policy goals were, first, to make the division
of the Balkans between Russia and Austria-Hungary impossible
and, secondly, to prevent the emergence of an autonomous Macedonia which might then fall to Bulgaria.

As the war clouds grew ever thicker, the few Serbs still living in
Kosovo desperately tried to assert their presence in the province. By
then, except for small pockets, they were to be found living only
along the Serbian and Montenegrin frontiers in towns like Pec,
Mitrovica and Beraria. While travelling in Kosovo, Edith Durham
wrote of the Serb plight in the district of Prizren:

> 'The white castle of Tsar Lazar was but a dream in the night of the
> past. Around us in the daylight was the Albanian population, wait-
> ing under arms, to defend the land that had been theirs in the
> beginning of time ... I felt that so far as Prizren and its neighbour-
> hood were concerned, the cause was lost, dead and gone - as lost
> as is Calais to England and the English claim to Normandy. ... And
> for I do not know how the manyeth time I cursed the Berlin
> Treaty, which did not award to this people the truly Serb lands of
> Bosnia and Hercegovina, where they could have gathered their
> scattered forces and developed, but gave them to be crushed under
> Austria.'[11]

The Ottoman Empire's loss of Bosnia-Hercegovina and Bulgaria
was a severe blow to the morale of the Young Turks, who after all
had come to power to save the Empire. In April 1909 the Empire's
conservative old guard staged a brief counter-revolution which
overthrew the Young Turks and restored the former absolutist
regime, but it gained little support outside the capital and was soon
crushed by Young Turk troops. Sultan Abdul Hamid was, in turn,

11. Ibid., p. 275.

deposed and his younger brother Mahmoud, a tool of the Young Turks, was installed in his place.

Disillusionment with the Young Turks and Formation of the Balkan League

By now disenchantment with the constitution had become increasingly widespread as the Young Turks began to show their true nature. Having consolidated its power, the regime now planned to enforce the uniform Turkification of the various Ottoman dependencies, and a general sense of disillusionment eventually led to open revolt, particularly in Kosovo. Without originally intending war with either Arabs, Albanians or Macedonians, the Young Turks were driven by the imminence of war in their Empire into a series of wars which united against them all the national and separatist forces it contained. They now hastened to propagate the idea of the unity of the peoples of the Empire, under the name of 'Ottomanisation'. Extensive reorganisation was planned for the armed forces, together with a uniform system of education throughout the Empire in which Turkish was to be the main language of instruction in the higher schools for all nationalities. There was to be compulsory military service for all nationalities, plus a considerable increase in taxation to pay for all these expensive reforms. Throughout the summer of 1909 the Kosovo Muslim clans, led by the Mitrovica chieftain Isa Boletini (1864-1916),[12] were in rebellion against the Young Turks for threatening to withdraw from them privileges that Sultan Abdul Hamid had recognised. They objected especially to census registration, which the Albanians saw as a prelude to compulsory military service and tax collection.

The Kosovars were among the earliest supporters of the Young Turk revolution, yet they had quickly been compelled to defend their rights and privileges against it. The Young Turks had anticipated trouble from the Albanians of Kosovo, and once their intentions were revealed, Djavid Pasha was appointed military commandant of the Mitrovica region to deal with them. His first act was to carry out operations in the mountainous region north of there, mainly with the object of capturing the redoubtable Isa Boletini, who possessed supreme authority among the Albanians of the

12. For an account of the life of Isa Boletini and in particular his role in organising insurgent activity in Kosovo, see Fatmir Musaj, *Isa Boletini*, Tirana, 1987.

Kosovo *vilayet*. Fierce fighting against him and against Bajram Curri of Hashi, Islam Sipahi of Ljuma and other Albanian leaders continued throughout August and September. Eventually Djavid succeeded in fighting and burning his way into the Ljuma district, disarming the tribesmen (who generally surrendered only obsolete weapons) as he went. At the end of September 1909 he fell back to Mitrovica, congratulating himself that he had scotched the Albanian insurrection. However, it was only the beginning.[13]

Although the Ottomans razed Boletini's village - Boletin - to the ground, the chieftain himself escaped. The defeat of his rebellion seems to have been largely due to the Albanians' tactical inferiority to the Turks. Being generally obsessed with the possibility of being surprised, taken in the rear or occupying a position commanded by higher ground, they preferred to occupy bare hill-tops which provided an easy target for the Turks, and seldom used cover.[14] After five months the Ottoman forces regained control of Kosovo, but many of the insurgents found refuge in Montenegro. The large number of refugees who followed them put Montenegro at risk of conflict with the Porte but the situation nevertheless suited the King of Montenegro, for apart from binding the Albanians to his country, they would naturally be weakened by the continued fighting, and thus be more willing to collaborate with him in his inevitable conflict with the Porte. To some degree therefore the Serbian and Montenegrin governments helped the Albanian rebels by taking in refugees and giving them arms in order to undermine Ottoman rule and curb Austro-Hungarian influence on their leaders.

By now much of the Albanian population of Kosovo was deeply disaffected. Determined to avenge the actions of Djavid, they launched yet another insurrection in April 1910 after the population had refused to pay new and severe taxes levied from Istanbul on imported goods. The revolt began in Pristina and quickly spread to the region of Urosevac where large demonstrations were organised against perceived betrayal and the loss of privileges. The Porte replied by sending to Kosovo 20,000 men, many of them Kurdish irregulars, led by General Shefket Turgut, to stamp out the rebellion and disarm the people. The severity of the suppression - whole villages were burnt and Albanian leaders were flogged in public - only ensured that unrest would continue.[15] Nevertheless, the Alban-

---

13. Swire, *Albania*, pp. 92-4.
14. Ibid., p. 95.
15. *Foreign Office Handbook*, no. 17, London, 1920, pp. 44-5.

ian resistance movement was mostly dictated by local particularisms. There was still no universally recognised Albanian authority to coordinate and direct the nationalist cause. The tribes continued to act independently, at their own discretion, and in defence of their own particular interests.[16] The Young Turks now instituted a reign of terror throughout Kosovo and northern Albania, prompting Russia to warn the Ottoman government not to extend hostilities against Montenegro.[17] The turmoil caused by the fighting in 1911 led to an estimated 150,000 people fleeing Kosovo, of whom roughly 100,000 were Serbs, just under a third of Kosovo's estimated overall Serbian population. From then on the dismemberment of the Ottoman Empire began in earnest with Italy's declaration of war on the Porte in September 1911 in the hope of capturing Tripolitania (modern Libya), which was largely undefended, and the Ottoman forces were easily defeated. The other Balkan states saw in the Porte's weakness their chance to take advantage of the situation and realise long-cherished territorial designs on Ottoman territory. In its desperate need for support, the Porte entered into political negotiations with the Albanians.

By the autumn of 1911 Albanian *chetas*, comprising both Christians and Muslims, were operating throughout the Albanian regions. The Serbian and Montenegrin governments worked actively to support these Albanian guerrilla bands, so as to prevent any reconciliation and subsequent alliance between the Albanians and the Porte, which could result in the creation of an autonomous Albania. Indeed, the newly-formed Serbian secret organisation, *Ujedinjenje ili Smrt* (Union or Death), popularly know as the Black Hand, offered Albanian leaders such as Isa Boletini arms and money to encourage them to revolt. For some time Boletini hesitated to come to any arrangement with the Serbs, being understandably wary of their declaration that they desired only to liberate the subject races of European Turkey, but eventually Dimitrijevic Apis, the leader of the Black Hand, was successful in allaying his suspicions, causing him to doubt the advisability of being satisfied with the concessions already wrung from the Porte, and inducing him to believe that the Serbs and Albanians together should free the land of the Ottomans

---

16. Swire, *Albania*, p. 96.
17. Fearing that the events in Kosovo could be repeated elsewhere, the Ottoman authorities turned their attention to central Albania. Here the population was forcibly disarmed, military tribunals were set up and heavy sentences were imposed on the hundreds of Albanians arrested for nationalist activities.

for their common benefit.[18] Serbia was determined to try to neutralise the Albanians and win them over to its own side. With this in mind, shortly before the Balkan Wars, Serbian officers stayed with Isa Boletini and Idriz Seferi, another Kosovar leader who had established friendly relations with Serbia during the latest Albanian uprisings. It was believed in Belgrade that those Albanians living in border areas would remain calm for the time being, and would later act as the nature of the situation demanded: in other words, with a Serbian victory they might either remain neutral or take action in Serbia's support. Various Serbian declarations therefore proclaimed that Albanians should be protected and regarded as friends, but only as long as their conduct merited such treatment.[19]

To ensure his protection, Boletini included several Serbs in his bodyguard. At night he was guarded by two Serbs at his outer door, two at the second door, and ten Muslim Albanians within. Thus for a short time the Serbian minority were on relatively good terms with the insurgent leaders, who maintained rigid discipline among their men; Idriz Seferi shot several of his followers for robbing Serb houses.[20] The Porte was aware of the tentative alliances being made between Serbia and the Kosovo Albanians, and tried once more to appease the Kosovars by promising financial support for Albanian cultural activities. But by this time the repressive measures of the Young Turks and the breaking of their earlier promises had only increased the hold of nationalist and separatist ideas upon the majority of Albanians. It was now obvious to all that with revolutionary nationalism sweeping the disintegrating Empire, the Porte had only a precarious hold over its rebellious subjects, and Abdul Hamid, conscious that a point of no return had been reached, retreated behind the high walls of Topkapi palace to plot his survival.

A Serbian agent, Grigorije Bozovic, working in Kosovo in the summer of 1912, noted:

> 'The negative aspect of the Albanian movement as far as the Serbs are concerned, is that the Albanians are on the verge of becoming a nation, and they wish to settle their issue in Kosovo, and that they are neither the conquerors nor the conquered. We fall between them and the Young Turks, and both will throw their rage at us. A

18. Swire, *Albania*, p. 128.
19. D. Mikic, 'The Albanians and Serbia during the Balkan Wars' in B.K. Kiraly and D. Djordjevic (eds), *East Central European Society and the Balkan Wars*, New York, 1987, p. 171.
20. Swire, *Albania*, p. 129.

positive move, however, is that the Albanians are gradually beginning to unfetter themselves from Turkish fanaticism; Muslim solidarity and hypnosis are slackening; they are very aware that they are at enmity with the Turks and, most important, they speak of Serbia with sympathy and regard it as an amicable country.' [21]

The previous Serbian assumption had been that the Albanians were not a nation but rather a number of mutually estranged tribes sharing neither a common language, social customs or religion. Milan Milojevic, Serbian Consul in Pristina at the time, echoed Bozovic by observing: 'that it was a great error to treat the Albanian movement as an insignificant phenomenon in the context of the developing Balkan crisis'. He believed that the Albanians had gradually begun to establish an increasingly explicit notion of themselves as a separate people, and he emphasised that this must be taken seriously.[22] This was obviously a turning point for Albanian relations not only with the Ottomans but also with the Serbs. Consequently, just before the beginning of the First Balkan War, Serbia escalated its wooing of the Kosovo Albanians, as well as of the Catholic Mirdite tribe further south.

The Young Turks, in their rush to build a unified state, had failed to take into account the growing national sentiments of the Albanians and, instead of looking for collaboration, consistently provoked the Albanians to insurrection by their arrogant and insensitive handling of their grievances. And so with active assistance from the Serbian government yet another Albanian insurrection, this time more widespread, broke out in January 1912. Led by Hasan Pristina (1873-1933),[23] who came from the powerful Siskovic clan in Vucitrn, this was by far the best organised and most effective Albanian revolt against the Ottoman authorities since the formation of the Prizren League. Albanian soldiers deserted in ever-increasing numbers from the Ottoman army as the towns of Prizren, Pec, and Pristina fell to the rebels. The occupation of Skopje in August by nearly 30,000 rebels led by Isa Boletini caused alarm in Istanbul as the Porte struggled to appease the Albanians. By September all of Kosovo and central and southern Albania were in the hands of the rebels. With the Albanian successes the Ottoman administration was paralysed and the government in Istanbul was

21. D. Batakovic, *The Kosovo Chronicles*, Belgrade, 1992, p. 164.
22. Mikic, 'The Albanians and Serbia', p. 168.
23. For an authoritative account of the life of Hasan Pristina, see T. Abdyli, *Hasan Pristina, ne Levizjen Kombetare e Demokratike Shqiptare 1908-1933*, Pristina, 1990.

forced to resign in favour of Mouktar Pasha and his followers, who opposed the radical Turkification policies of the Committee of Union and Progress. The situation grew quickly worse, with mutinies breaking out in the majority of Ottoman garrisons.

The new Ottoman administration induced many Albanians to abandon their rebellion by promising further reforms and free elections, but others with longer memories refused to moderate their demands. Nevertheless, the Albanians did not accept Serbian Premier Nichola Pasic's offer in 1912 of an 'agreement leading to the association of Serbs and Albanians in the Kosovo *vilayet*.' Such an agreement would have guaranteed, within the Serbian state structure, freedom of religion; use of the Albanian language in schools, in the courts, and in community and district administration; and a separate Albanian assembly, which would pass laws dealing with religious, educational and legal matters.[24] The Albanians still feared the likely occupation of their lands by the Balkan states if they proved victorious, and thus chose to play for time while they built up their own arms. Consequently, they carried on a dialogue with Belgrade and accepted Serbian financial assistance, but at the same time agreed to the Porte's belated offer to grant the non-Turkish populations the right to be governed by administrators who spoke their language. Thus the Albanian insurrections in Kosovo during 1912-13, prepared the way for the forthcoming victory of the Balkan Allies over the Porte.

At this time, an Albanian intellectual, Ismail Kemal, formerly a prominent official in the Ottoman administration, believed that the preservation of Albanian-inhabited territory depended on the rivalry among the Great Powers, and that Austria-Hungary was Albania's only potential defender. But, at the same time, Austria-Hungary, striving to maintain the *status quo*, advised the Albanians that their security was best assured by remaining within the Ottoman Empire. It feared, in particular, that because Kosovo stood as a buffer against Serbian expansion southwards, the weakening of the Kosovars would strengthen Pan-Slavism. Serbia's future expansionist territorial ambitions to the north and west had been severely frustrated by its denial of Bosnia and access to the Adriatic. Its hopes now concentrated on intervention in Macedonia. Thus the Balkan states made swift political moves to take advantage of the deteriorating situation: to this end, with Russia's encouragement, several alliances were made between

24. Mikic, 'The Albanians and Serbia', p. 170.

Bulgaria, Greece, Serbia and Montenegro. In March 1912, seeing their best chance to realise their national ambitions, the states formed a common alliance and agreed to divide the European Ottoman possessions between themselves.

The first accord was between Serbia and Bulgaria, which agreed on Serbia's annexation of Kosovo and northern Albania but left much of Macedonia unassigned. This was followed in May by a treaty between Bulgaria and Greece against the Porte, and in October by one allying Montenegro with both Serbia and Bulgaria. Thus was formed the Balkan League, its principal objective being the ejection of the Ottomans from Europe. The principle motive for the actual establishment of the League, however, was the reaction of Serbia and Russia to Austria-Hungary's annexation of Bosnia-Hercegovina; a Balkan bloc was needed to keep Austria in check. Ever since the Congress of Berlin in 1878, Albania had become the crucial southern meeting point of Austro-Italian collaboration and rivalry. From 1911, Italy placed the real focus of its diplomacy in the Adriatic, in which Albania was of particular importance since the Italians regarded Saseno island, off the port of Vlora, as the 'Gibraltar of the Adriatic'.

Another motivating factor in the formation of the Balkan League was the rise of Albanian national identity. The Balkan states feared the formation of an autonomous Albania which, if the Porte were defeated, would be far harder to carve up between the Balkan allies than if it remained merely an Ottoman province. Hasan Pristina has been chastised by latter-day Albanian historians for accepting the agreement with the Porte which called a halt to his insurrection, seeing it as a premature capitulation. But there were good reasons for Pristina to conserve his strength because the impending threat from the newly-formed Balkan League required a regrouping and reorganisation to ward off this new danger to Albanian-inhabited territory. Hasan Pristina was also weakened because not all the Albanian regions took up arms, some still being content with organising small armed bands which undertook only a few insignificant raids.

The First Balkan War

The reverses inflicted on the Ottoman armies by both the Italians and Albanians had encouraged the Balkan states to press forward with their war preparations; but when, to their dismay, the Albanians appeared to have won virtual autonomy, they resolved to act at once, before they became reconciled with the Porte, organised their resources, and established their claim to national consideration by the Great Powers. Therefore, to the complete surprise of both the Porte and the European Powers, Montenegro on 8 October 1912 suddenly opened hostilities with the Porte by attacking Albanian territory. A declaration of war by Serbia, Bulgaria and Greece immediately followed. The outbreak of the First Balkan War saw the western flank of the Ottoman Empire relatively undefended with the bulk of the Ottoman army deployed along the coastline of Asia Minor and Syria. The Albanians hoped to follow a course of neutrality and non-engagement but found this impossible as the Ottoman army collapsed faster than had been anticipated and the Balkan allies penetrated deep into Albanian-inhabited territory. Following the old dogma 'better the devil you know', the Albanians fought with the Empire against the Balkan armies.

At the outbreak of this war thousands of young Serbian volunteers rushed to join the army, yearning to avenge the Battle of Kosovo. The declaration of war had opened up the exalting prospect of participating in the national rebirth – an ideal bequeathed to them by their forefathers. The realisation that Kosovo might finally be liberated after more than five centuries fired their imaginations and emotions, and the Serbian army was unstoppable. Consider the recollections of one young soldier as he was told that his unit was heading for Kosovo:

> 'The single sound of that word - Kosovo - caused an indescribable excitement. This one word pointed to the black past - five centuries. In it exists the whole of our sad past - the tragedy of Prince Lazar and the entire Serbian people. Each of us has created for himself a picture of Kosovo while we were still in the cradle. Our mothers lulled us to sleep with songs of Kosovo, and in our schools our teachers never ceased in their stories of Lazar and Milos. My God, what awaited us! To see a liberated Kosovo. When we arrived on Kosovo Polje and the battalions were placed in order, our commander spoke: "Brothers, my children, my sons! This place on which we stand is the graveyard of our glory. We bow to the shadows of fallen ancestors and pray God for the salvation of their souls." His voice gives out and tears flow in streams down his cheeks and grey beard and fall to the ground. He actually shakes from some kind of inner pain and excitement. The spirits of Lazar, Milos and all the Kosovo martyrs gaze on us. We felt strong and proud, for we are the generation which will

realise the centuries-old dream of the whole nation: that we with the sword will regain the freedom that was lost with the sword.'[25]

Stirred up by Austro-Hungarian agents, the Albanians prepared to resist the Serbian army as it advanced towards Kosovo but, after minor skirmishes, led by Bajram Curri, Isa Boletini and Riza Bey, they withdrew into the northern Albanian mountains. The Montenegrins meanwhile moved towards Pec and Djakovica. With a profound sense of national elation Serbian troops finally entered Pristina on 22 October.[26] The Serbian population were also exuberant as they greeted the Third Army, who immediately attended a mass at Gracanica in thanksgiving for Kosovo's liberation. Proclamations were then issued to the Albanian population to keep calm and surrender their weapons. Many fled rather than do so, having already heard of the appalling atrocities committed by the Serbs and recorded by numerous writers and journalists as they marched towards the Adriatic — Leon Trotsky was given the following account by a Serbian army officer:

> 'The horrors actually began as soon as we crossed into Kosovo.
> Entire Albanian villages had been turned into pillars of fire,
> dwellings, possessions accumulated by fathers and grandfathers were
> going up in flames, the picture was repeated the whole way to
> Skopje. There the Serbs broke into Turkish and Albanian houses and
> performed the same task in every case: plundering and killing. For
> two days before my arrival in Skopje the inhabitants had woken up
> to the sight of heaps of Albanian corpses with severed heads. Among
> the mass of soldiers you see Serb peasants who have come from
> every part of Serbia on the pretext of looking for their sons and
> brothers. They cross the plain of Kosovo and start plundering, from
> the area around Vranje the population has crossed over en masse into
> the Albanian villages to pick up whatever may catch the eye. Peasant
> women carry away even the doors and windows of Albanian
> houses.'[27]

Serbian historiography attempts to excuse such atrocities by arguing that they were provoked:

> 'During the border fights which got under way two days before the
> declaration of war, the Albanians used deception, raising false white

25. T.A. Emmert, 'The Kosovo Legacy', *Serbian Studies*, vol. 5, no. 2, 1989, p. 20.
26. For a detailed account of the situation in Kosovo during the Balkan Wars, see J.Tomic, *Rat u Albaniji i na Kosovu, 1912-1913*, Novi Sad, 1913.
27. L. Trotsky, *The Balkan Wars, 1912-1913*, New York, 1980, p. 267.

flags; this led to significant losses on the part of the Serbian army and provided a motive for subsequent reprisals.'[28]

However, this same account also tells of the peaceful and constructive role the Albanian population played during the Serbian advance through a part of Kosovo:

> 'A local leader, Sadik Rama, who had close ties with the Serbian Consul in Pristina during the 1912 uprising, contributed to the Albanian's peaceful conduct during the Serbian Army's march through Drenica and Prekoruplje. To his credit, the settled Albanian population in 150 villages did not fire a single shot, and some 400 rifles were gathered at the monastery of Devic without the use of any military force.'[29]

In truth the Albanian population were paying the price for having sided with the Porte against Belgrade. When victorious King Peter visited Decani shortly afterwards, he lit the gigantic candle that was to be set burning only when the Battle of Kosovo was avenged. The Serbs were so dazzled with the bright glow of recovered lands that they almost failed to notice that hardly any Serbs were left in 'Old Serbia': the overwhelming majority of the population were now Albanians.[30]

Following the Ottoman army's defeat at Kumanovo, Kosovo's Albanians put up strong resistance in the districts of Urosevac and Prizren, but the fiercest resistance, led by Bajram Curri and Riza Bey, occurred in the southern region around the town of Djakovica. These somewhat isolated Albanian *chetas* were ultimately forced to retreat over the mountains into Albania or gradually reintegrate themselves into ordinary civilian life as Albanian resistance was finally eliminated as an organised political force. Until the fall of Pristina, Albanians had fought fervently against the Serbian army. Their national leaders were totally unprepared for the sudden collapse of the Ottoman army and the loss of Kosovo to the Serbs but had been severely hampered by the disruption of communications and the lack of any central Albanian authority. In the Lab, Pristina and Prizren districts, Serbian civil rule and administration were quickly established, while the Montengrins incorporated the districts of Pec and Djakovica. Vienna hastily warned Serbia not to

28. Mikic, 'The Albanians and Serbia', p. 171.
29. Ibid., p. 172.
30. I. Banac, *The National Question in Yugoslavia*, Cornell University Press, Ithaca, NY, 1984, p. 292.

extend military operations beyond Prizren. There was now a real and justifiable fear in Serbia that the creation of an independent or even autonomous Albanian state would be used by Vienna as a tool against Serbia. Serbia's prime goals were access to the sea and a harbour in its own territory, and it did not oppose, as such, the creation of an autonomous Albanian state. What did matter, however, was that the ruler of that state should be friendly with Serbia, and consequently the Serbian military authorities made a renewed attempt to win over any opponents of the Porte. Hence the renewed courting by Belgrade of such Albanians as Essad Pasha Toptani and the Mirdite leaders.

Reluctantly the Powers had to acknowledge that, with the Ottoman Empire on the point of collapse, the *status quo* could no longer be maintained. Austria's concern intensified as it became aware of the extent of the crisis on the southern border of its territory, and it contemplated, in the event of an Ottoman defeat, occupying Kosovo itself, as it had done Bosnia-Hercegovina, thereby preventing the union of Serbia and Montenegro. The Habsburg Empire's principal concern was that Greece and Serbia would partition Albania at the Shkumbi river. The Foreign Minister, Berchtold, enunciated the Empire's policy that in no circumstances must Serbia be allowed to expand to the Adriatic. This principle reflected the fear that a Serbian port could become a Russian port (or, as Archduke Franz Ferdinand feared, an Italian port); a sense of the dangerous effect on the South Slavs of the Monarchy of Serbia's prestige rising too high; and the desire to restrict Serbia's economic independence by forcing it to channel its drive to the sea through Austro-Hungarian territory.

If Austria-Hungary's notion of an independent Albania was not to yield completely before the territorial gains of the victorious Balkan allies, then swift action was required. It realised that the Habsburg interests in the area could only be secured by an independent Albania, which would halt Serbia's territorial expansion towards the coastal region between Durres and San Giovanni di Medua. Thus, with the diplomatic support of Vienna, eighty-three delegates, Christian and Muslim, from all over Albania gathered at the Congress of Vlora on 28 November 1912. There, in precarious circumstances, Skanderbeg's black-eagled emblem was raised, and the independent state of Albania was proclaimed. None of the most prominent Kosovar leaders was present: Isa Boletini and Bajram Curri were still fighting the Serbs and Montenegrins, while Hasan Pristina, Idriz Seferi and

twelve others were held in Kalemegdan prison in Belgrade. As we
have seen, it had not at first been the goal of Albanians to establish an
independent nation-state; only the series of catastrophic defeats
suffered by Ottoman military forces compelled them to do so for
their own survival. For the Albanians the actions of the Young Turks
had driven and speeded up their national movement, which might
otherwise have matured gradually over fifty years or more. In the
mean time, further up the coast, the Serbian army was approaching
the port of Durres and the realisation of its ultimate goal of gaining
an exit to the sea was in sight. The Vlora government's position
became ever more precarious as the Balkan Allies penetrated deeper
into Albanian territory, but as the Serbian army approached the
Albanian coast, Austria-Hungary warned that it would not be
permitted to occupy any Adriatic seaport.

The Conference of Ambassadors

Austro-Hungarian intervention in the Balkans was prevented by
the Conference of Ambassadors hastily convened in London at the
end of December 1912. Presided over by the British Foreign Secretary Sir Edward Grey, it debated three main issues: the international
status of Albania, the organisation of the new state, and the establishment of internationally acceptable frontiers. The Albanian delegation argued for an ethnically compact Albania to include the
towns of Pec, Djakovica, Prizren, Mitrovica, Pristina, Skopje and
Monastir. Although Nikola Pasic insisted that Serbia would never
relinquish the area between the towns of Debar and Djakovica,
Serbian troops nevertheless had to withdraw from the Adriatic
coast, following the advice proffered by the Russian Foreign Minister Sazonov, who warned the Serbs: 'Watch out. Don't insist on
Durres, because you might lose Belgrade. Vienna has lost its head.'
Neither Russia nor its allied powers could allow the question of a
European war to be decided by Serbia.[31]

Austria argued vehemently that Shkoder's inclusion was essential to the new state's economy. In response to German pressure not
to jeopardise the Conference, Austria made a series of concessions
until Russia finally agreed to the inclusion of Shkoder in Albania,
while remaining adamant that the small, purely Albanian market
town of Djakovica in Kosovo, which Austria claimed for Albania,

31. Dragnich and Todorovic, *The Saga of Kosovo*, pp. 103–4.

should remain in Serbia.[32] Public opinion in Russia was deeply anti-Austrian, and had rallied to the support of fellow Orthodox Slavs. For weeks the peace of Europe hung on the fate of Djakovica, which appeared of dubious benefit to Serbia; one visitor described it as 'the most primitive, not to say primeval, town in the least civilised of European countries, but the Serbs insisted that it was an integral and important part of Old Serbia'.[33] Austria-Hungary was determined to prevent a hostile power replacing the Porte in Albania, which if independent and firmly under its influence, could counter Serbia in the Balkans.

The Conference nevertheless awarded the Balkan allies large areas of Albanian-inhabited territory, without regard to its ethnic composition. In January 1913 the Porte, following the Austrian example, began serious but belated attempts to organise anti-Serbian activities among the Albanians of Kosovo. Several Turks and Albanians were sent from Istanbul to Prizren to prepare for the arming of Albanians and a general programme of agitation. In an attempt to counter these moves, and to halt growing anti-Serbian agitation, Belgrade tried once again to encourage 'pro-Serbian sentiments' among influential Albanians. However, what many Serbian historical accounts define as the 'financial assistance' offered to promote these pro-Serbian sentiments was no more than bribery. Doubtless such payments calmed those within the regional influence of the bought-off beys, but the ferocity of the Serbian army in Kosovo resulted in widespread anti-Serbian resistance. Caches of weapons were hidden in Albanian villages or carried into the woods by the numerous Albanian 'outlaws' on the run for tax-evasion (at that time there was even a tax on sheep and chickens) or from blood-feud vendettas. In March, in another move to appease the Albanians, the Serbian Ministry of War released several prominent Albanian leaders, including Hasan Pristina, from imprisonment in Belgrade's gloomy fortress.

The Second Balkan War

Meanwhile, at the end of May after seven months of constant warring, the Powers finally compelled the Balkan states to lay down

32. J.F. Kontos, *Red Cross, Black Eagle: A Biography of the Albanian-American School*, New York, 1981, p. 5.
33. R. Crampton, *The Hollow Detente - Anglo-German Relations in the Balkans, 1911-14*, London, 1979, p. 87.

their arms and accept the terms of the Treaty of London, under which the Porte would renounce all its European territories west of a line between Enos on the Aegean and Media on the Black Sea. Thessaloniki and the island of Crete went to Greece. Thus the Ottoman Europe was reduced to Istanbul and the surrounding territory in eastern Thrace. Nevertheless, the Balkan League was doomed to break up once the Empire had been defeated. Rival claims prevented Bulgaria from agreeing a territorial settlement with Greece over Thrace, Thessaloniki and southern Macedonia. In addition, Bulgaria saw Serbia as the chief obstacle to the realisation of its aspirations in the rest of Macedonia, where the claims of both countries collided. The proposed division of Ottoman territory had allocated to Serbia the land north of the Sar mountains, while Bulgaria was to receive all regions east of the Struma river and the Rhodope mountains. This left the greater part of Macedonian territory unassigned.

The Balkan allies signed their peace with the Porte on 30 May 1913, and Serbian troops began withdrawing to strategic positions in the country's borderlands. Although a new Balkan bloc was still needed to keep Austria in check, the defeat of the Ottoman Empire left nothing to hold the League together. Both Serbia and Greece were frustrated by the creation of Albania, which they had hoped to partition between themselves. They therefore sought compensation in Macedonia, which in turn led to confrontation with Bulgaria, which was convinced it could win a swift military victory. At dawn on 30 June 1913 with no formal declaration of war, Bulgarian troops attacked the Serbian and Greek armies in Macedonia. This was a disastrous mistake since Romanian, Montenegrin and Ottoman troops quickly entered the war against the Bulgarians, who were soon forced to capitulate and to sacrifice nearly all the gains they had made in the first war. The Treaty of Bucharest, concluded on 10 August 1913, provisionally settled the contest over the division of the Albanian and Macedonian territories. As was to be expected, the terms were extremely damaging to Bulgaria. Adrianople and most of Eastern Thrace reverted to Ottoman control, Romania took southern Dobrudja, Greece extended its border to about 50 miles north of Thessaloniki and to the east beyond the port of Kavalla. In the west Greece annexed Epirus including Janina. Serbia almost doubled in size with the acquisition of most of Slavic Macedonia.[34]

34. C. and B. Jelavich, *The Establishment of the Balkan National States, 1804-1920,* Washington, DC, 1977, p. 221.

The Second Balkan War so embittered relations among the former allies that conditions became even more explosive than in preceding years. The Ottoman Empire and Bulgaria hungered for revenge, making them easy prey for alliance with Austria and Germany. On 15 September 1913, the Serbian government ordered its army to retreat to the line beyond the Black Drin until the establishment of final borders. Its claim to northern Albania had now become even more tenuous. Nevertheless, during the following months, Serbia tried to persuade the International Commission, which had confirmed the details of the Albanian-Serbian border, to allow the construction of a railway to the Adriatic. These efforts, however, were disrupted by the outbreak of the European war in 1914, and the border remained as it had been determined by the Conference in London.[35] The conclusion of the Second Balkan War, however, left fundamental issues still to be resolved: Macedonia remained a continual source of discord among the Balkan states; the new Albanian state failed to encompass all the areas predominantly inhabited by Albanians; and Serbia remained cut off from the Adriatic.

Now that the Balkan Wars were over, serious discussion had to begin over the final frontiers of the new Albanian state, and in the spring of 1913 the Ambassadors' Conference finally concluded its plans for the country. Albania was to be neutralised, and would remain under Ottoman suzerainty at first, but, after a period of years, be granted full independence. However, it soon became obvious that the Porte would eventually lose all of Macedonia and thus its territorial connection with Albania. It was thus deemed necessary to grant Albania full independence under a constitutional monarchy which the Powers would guarantee. Consequently the Treaty of London of 30 May 1913 formally recognised an independent Albania, but the final settlement of the new state's frontiers was postponed. The Powers now found themselves faced with the impossible task of reconciling the competing claims of the victorious Serbs, Greeks and Montenegrins with those of the Albanian population.[36] The Albanian frontier issue was particularly complex because the troops of the Balkan alliance were still in occupation of the regions in dispute. A Northern Albanian Frontier Commission was appointed by the Ambassadors to survey the region and make

35. Mikic, 'The Albanians and Serbia', pp. 190–1.
36. *Foreign Office Handbook*, no. 17, HM Stationary Office, London, 1920, p. 50.

recommendations regarding the Albanian-Serbian-Montenegrin frontiers. A Southern Commission was also appointed to negotiate the Albanian-Greek frontier.

A delegation representing the provisional Albanian government argued with the Frontier Commissioners for the new frontier to follow the then existing one with Montenegro to its easternmost point, and thence onwards so as to include the towns of Pec, Mitrovica, Pristina, Skopje and Monastir with their hinterlands. The line then extended to a point south of Lake Prespa, from which it turned almost due south, leaving Kastoria on the east to Greece; it thus reached the Greek frontier a little east of Metzovo. For the rest, the line followed the then existing Greek frontier down to the Gulf of Arta.[37] The frontier proposed by Austria closely followed the Albanian claim, but the Powers, anxious not to provoke Russia, which supported the Serb and Greek claims, would not adopt it but instead compromised with a delimitation half-way between the Austrian proposal and that of the Balkan allies.

In December 1913 the Powers agreed to sign the Protocol of Florence whereby Serbia, in return for withdrawing from Albanian territory, would with Austria's reluctant agreement be ceded the districts that included the towns of Pec, Prizren, Djakovica and Debar. Greece would receive the large southern region of Chameria (Epirus). The frontiers of the new Albanian state agreed in Florence satisfied neither the Albanians nor their Balkan neighbours. Serbia was deprived of an Albanian port, Montenegro lost Shkoder, and Greece had to relinquish its claim to southern Albania including Korca, Gjirokaster and Saranda, while the Albanian state was reduced to the central regions, plus Shkoder and its surrounding territory. More than half of the total Albanian population was left outside the borders of the new Albanian state.

Britain never maintained that the Albanian frontier was a just and equitable one, but believed that preserving the peace of Europe took precedence over ethnographic considerations. The fairness or otherwise of the allocation of Albania's frontiers can be judged by a speech made by Sir Edward Grey to the House of Commons on 12 August 1913, in which he openly stated that the basic objective of the agreement on the borders was to satisfy the Great Powers, but that many criticisms could be raised by anyone who really knew Albania and viewed the issue from that country's standpoint. About

37. Ibid., p. 97.

the unfairness of the Albanian frontier, one observer ominously noted: 'there remains in the heart of the Balkan Peninsula an ulcer poisoning the European system, and bidding fair to render inevitable a bloody operation.'[38] The bitterness and resentment felt by the Kosovars was echoed in the parting words of Isa Boletini upon leaving with the Albanian delegation from the Ambassadors' Conference: 'When spring comes, we will manure the plains of Kosovo with the bones of Serbs, for we Albanians have suffered too much to forget.'[39] With the small Albanian state hemmed in between the advancing armies of the Balkan allies, the new country's fate could not have been more precarious. Another observer wrote that the future of the new state was as much in doubt as that of a young lamb stalked by hungry wolves and protected by the vague benevolence of a distant assembly of patriarchs.[40]

38. Swire, *Albania*, p. 162.
39. Margaret Fitzherbert, *The Man who was Greenmantle: A Biography of Aubrey Herbert*, Oxford University Press, 1985, p. 114.
40. F. Scheville, *A History of the Balkans*, 1922, repr. Dorset Press, 1991, p. 512.

5

THE WAR OF 1914-1918

The amputation of Kosovo from Albania caused deep shock and anxiety among the majority of Kosovo's Albanians. Aside from the obvious psychological effects, the new frontier had severe economic implications for all northern Albanians, regardless of the side of the border on which they found themselves. Serbia now prohibited Albanians from crossing its new border and thus deprived large rural populations from their traditional markets, which were reached by an ancient trade route running from Shkoder to Djakovica and on to Prizren, but were now on Serbian soil. Djakovica was the market town for the Nikaj, Merturi, Gashi, Krashnich, Tropoja and Puka tribesmen, who were now either flogged or shot when they attempted to cross the frontier. A four day's tramp to Shkoder was their only alternative.[1] To the east many more Albanian clans were cut off from their market towns such as the Lurja, who occupied the source of the Zali Milthit and extended over the saddle into the valley of the Mala (Lurja Mala), which it occupied down to the Drin. Debar, the market town for this clan, was now included with Macedonia.

In response, various northern Albanian tribes rebelled in protest at their exclusion from age-old market centres in Serbia; thus already by the beginning of August 1914 a series of small-scale skirmishes were taking place on the Albanian-Kosovo border. The continuous violation of the frontier by the Albanians was also caused by the fact that the Serbs, when withdrawing from Albania on orders from the Powers, took with them livestock belonging to Albanians, who then pursued their animals over the border. It was in Serbia's interest that continued unrest should prevail in northern Albania, thereby preventing the new state from becoming a viable entity. Nevertheless, there were deep divisions between the various Albanian leaders over which policy to follow in order to preserve

1. J. Swire, *Albania - The Rise of a Kingdom*, London, 1929; repr. New York, 1971, p. 153.

Albanian-inhabited territory in Kosovo. Bajram Curri, Riza Bey and Isa Boletini toured the northern clans seeking advice and support, but the powerful Catholic Mirdite would not cooperate, and advised the Kosovo leaders not to incite an uprising against the Serbs. Their leader Gjon Marka Gjoni had his own scheme for creating a Serbian-backed independent Mirdite republic.

During this immediate pre-war period, both Serbia and Austria-Hungary continued to court the Albanian leadership. Armed with money for bribes, Austro-Hungarian agents travelled through Albania looking for potential supporters. Because the new Albanian government of Ismail Kemal was fundamentally committed to seeking a change in the borders of Albania established by the Ambassador's Conference, the Serbian government was therefore unwilling to reach any agreement with the Vlora authorities. Instead it courted a variety of Albanians who were eager to become independent rulers of central Albania; the most notable of these was Essad Pasha Toptani, whom they perceived as most likely to assist them in achieving their objectives in northern Albania.[2] Serbian diplomacy had tried unsuccessfully to bring about an Albanian state headed by Essad Pasha, that would be pro-Serbian, albeit one centred around a single easily bribed adventurer. Belgrade now concentrated on wooing the Mirdite.

War begins a new shake-up in the Balkans

The Balkan Wars had introduced a period of disruption along the frontier regions of Austrian-controlled Bosnia-Hercegovina contiguous to Serbia and Montenegro. These rural border regions contained a hazardous mix of banditry, peasant dissatisfaction and Serbian nationalist agitation. To this emotive mixture was added the idea of 'Trialism' whereby Austia-Hungary viewed the South Slav territory as a third part of the Imperial government of the

2. Essad Pasha was born in Tirana in 1863 into an influential Muslim family that owned extensive property around Tirana. His reputation as an opportunist with a voracious appetite for power was acknowledged throughout Albania, and even among his allies, the Serbs. Before 1912 Essad had supported the Young Turk movement and represented Durres in the Ottoman parliament. He was a deputy to Hussein Riza Pasha, the commander of Shkoder, whom Essad murdered in an ambush he set up while the Ottoman army was surrounding the town in 1912. He thus got command of Shkoder, securing his position by signing the treaty with Montenegro.

Austrian Emperor Franz Josef, together with the Kingdom of
Hungary, in a unified Empire under its control. Such a concept
would block independent Serbia's plans for further territorial accumulation. This dangerous situation provided the spark that ignited
the European war when Gavrilo Princip, a Bosnian Serb and
member of the Mlada Bosna (Young Bosnia) organisation, assassinated the next heir to the Habsburg throne, Austrian Archduke
Franz Ferdinand and his wife when they were visiting Sarajevo on
28 June 1914, the anniversary of the Battle of Kosovo. Austria
declared war on Serbia a month later, which in turn led to the
outbreak of the First World War.

The period since the end of the Balkan Wars had seen Albania's
frontiers fixed in theory but not in practice; the outbreak of the
Great War curtailed the activities of the two Border Commissions,
one to the north and the other to the south, set up at the Ambassador's Conference to determine the exact line on the ground and
erect boundary-marks. As we have seen, this boundary had been
defined in very vague terms, and was based on political rather than
ethnographic or geographical considerations. Such was the difficulty of communications in those parts that news of the outbreak
of war in 1914 did not reach the Northern Commission until four
days later. Neither Commission had been able to complete any
survey or erect beacons in places where no accurate map or any
civil registration of ownership of properties existed.[3]

The outbreak of war gave the neighbouring countries the
opportunity to seize what land they could amid the confusion of
armies rapidly mobilising throughout the region. It also greatly
hindered Serbian attempts to establish and consolidate their administration over Kosovo. The news that Austria–Hungary had declared
war on Serbia was greeted with satisfaction throughout Albania,
especially in the north where the population had persistently peti-
tioned Austria–Hungary for support against Serbian and Montenegrin territorial aspirations. The Serbs continued to regard the
Albanian state as an abortive creation which deprived them of territory, and they had a similarly low regard for the Albanian people,
whom they associated with the Ottoman Empire because of their
predominantly Muslim faith. Kosovo now saw vicious fighting
between Serbs and Albanians, with atrocities being committed by

3.   Colonel F. L. Giles, *Boundary Work in the Balkans*, Royal Geographical Society,
     London, 1930, p. 303.

both sides. As guerrilla warfare went on relentlessly, a continuous flow of Albanian refugees from Kosovo drifted into Albania.

The final dismemberment of Albanian-inhabited territories was recognised by the Western Allies on 26 April 1915, in the secret Pact of London. To encourage Italy to enter the war on the side of the Entente, the Pact, which the Bolsheviks made public in 1917, agreed to divide up Albania between Greece and Italy, leaving a small autonomous state in the central regions. Under the terms of the treaty Italy was granted possession of Sazan (Saseno) island, the port of Vlora, and a mandate over central Albania. It was agreed in addition that if Italy acquired Trentino, Istria and Dalmatia, as stipulated in the pact, then Greece was to take southern Albania, and Serbia and Montenegro would partition northern Albania. Greece and Serbia were also to establish a common frontier west of Lake Ohrid through the annexation of Albanian territory. The central portion was to be set up as an autonomous but not independent state, which would be represented in foreign affairs by Italy.[4]

As the war progressed, Austro-Hungarian troops occupied a large part of Kosovo, while Bulgaria took control of the districts of Pristina, Prizren, Kacanik, Gnjilane and Urosevac. Serbia was forced to fight on two fronts because of the combined German-Austro-Hungarian offensive against it in the autumn of 1915, and Bulgaria's entry into the war on the side of the Central Powers and subsequent incursion into Macedonia, which threatened to cut off the retreat of the Serbian army to Greece. The Serbian retreat and Bulgaria's penetration deep into Macedonia prompted hundreds of Albanian recruits in the Serbian army to desert; many joined the Bulgarians who gave them arms. With Austro-Hungarian advance-guards, they subsequently attacked Serbian soldiers in the Ibar valley, and by the beginning of October, in spite of having successfully defeated three major Austro-Hungarian offensives, Serbia was in a military position that had become untenable. The Serbian Supreme Command, with all connections to Thessaloniki severed by the Bulgarians, decided to withdraw its entire army through Albania.

The Great Serbian Retreat

Faced with the Austrian and Bulgarian offensives on two fronts, the Serbian army had no alternative but to make its epic and tragic

4. C. and B. Jelavich, *The Establishment of the Balkan National States*, p. 318.

retreat down through Kosovo and across the snow-bound mountain passes of north Albania. With the army went the sick King Peter I carried on a stretcher, and a mass of the Serbian civilian population fleeing the bloody massacres by Austro-Hungarian troops, the Germans sweeping down from Raska, and the Bulgarians striving to cut off their line of retreat between Pristina and Prizren.[5]

Mingling with the army were thousands of Serbian civilian refugees who had witnessed Bulgarian atrocities and heard of the fate of Belgium. They saw the army withdrawing through their villages and, sensing impending disaster abandoned their homes and joined the retreat bringing with them only as much as they could load on to carts and horses with oxen tied behind. The Serbian army's epic retreat through Kosovo and the Albanian Alps to Durres in October 1915 was accompianied by an American writer, Fortier Jones, who had volunteered to join the American Relief Organisation then working in Serbia, only to find that his arrival coincided with the Serbs' departure. He travelled with them and was greatly moved by what he witnessed: 'From Mitrovica to Pristina is scarcely more than twenty-five kilometres, yet I am sure that never before in human history has more suffering, heroism, and patriotism been crowded into so small a space.'[6]

Jones described the desolation and misery of the army's passage across the Kosovo plain, having gone for days with hardly any food and through snow blizzards which froze their soaked clothes stiff. The Austrians bombed the columns of refugees on the plain in the first aerial bombardment of civilians.

> 'There was no wood for fuel and no fodder for the animals ... only a dead-white landscape devoid of variety or form, through the centre of which thousands of people and animals crept, everyone of us suffering, the majority hopeless. Scores of dead animals were strewn along the road, and many others not yet frozen or completely starved lay and moaned, kicking feebly at the passers-by. As the day wore on, I saw many soldiers and prisoners, driven almost insane, tear the raw flesh from horses and oxen, and eat it, if not with enjoyment, at least with satisfaction.'[7]

5. For an authoritative account, accompanied by a large selection of pictoral evidence of the barbarous massacres of Serbian civilians by Austrian troops see: R.A. Reiss, *Austria-Hungary - Report*, Simpkin, Marshall, Kent and Co., London, 1916.
6. Fortier Jones, *With Serbia into Exile*, London, 1916, p. 206.
7. Ibid., pp. 230-1.

He arrived in Pristina with the bedraggled Serbs:

> 'We moved on down the hill into the town, no longer a town, it was
> an inferno. The tens of thousands rushing before the Bulgarians, and
> the tens of thousands ahead of the Germans met and mingled at
> Pristina before pushing on their augmented current to Prizren. In
> Pristina there was not even the semblance of law that had obtained
> at Mitrovica. The Government was crumbling, a nation was dying,
> and all such superfluities as courts of justice and police were a thing
> of the past.'[8]

After the gruelling trek across the Kosovo plain they arrived in
Prizren:

> All three Serbian armies were converging on the Albanian and
> Montenegrin frontier between Prizren and Pec, some were planning
> to take the route across Albania to Shkoder, the rest to go through
> Montenegro by way of Pec, Androvica and Podgorica to Shkoder.
> The road to Monastir had been cut; the General Staff had already
> announced the evacuation of Prizren and were preparing to go to
> Shkoder by the Albanian route. Beside the tremendous number of
> prisoners, there were more refugees gathered at Prizren than at any
> other place during the retreat. When the refugees looked at the
> mountains ahead and heard the guns behind, they realised finally that
> Serbia was lost, abandoned to three strong invaders, betrayed by
> three strong allies. This was the general sentiment. I heard it contin-
> ually from civilians, soldiers, officers and government officials. 'Why
> did not Russia come? Where are the French? Has England forgotten
> us?' These questions were so common as to become a sort of
> national threnody.[9]

The Serbs had hoped to win through to Shkoder where the
Allies promised to wait for them with food and supplies. The route
of the Serbian Army passed through central Albania, via Elbasan. At
the same time, the Bulgarians were pushing into Albania from the
east. On the whole, the Albanians refrained from physically attacking the pitiful columns of Serbs, whose journey was described by
an English observer:

> The roads southward from Shkoder lay through a country that was at
> any rate nominally friendly. Here the influence of Essad Pasha, the
> one central authority left in Albania whose name commands any
> widespread respect, was exercised on behalf of the Allies. But this
> did not prevent the inhabitants of the plain from following the

8. Ibid., p. 238.
9. Ibid., p. 291.

example of the Albanians of the mountains in regard to the extortion of money. At the ferries they demanded gold, and those who could not pay might remain where they were and die. Those who went through that whole retreat say that the last stages through the marshes and mud of central Albania were the worst of all. When at last Vlora was reached, thousands still died neglected, before they could be taken off by the French and British ships. From Vlora the army of 150,000 strong finally left Albania and crossed over to Corfu'.[10]

An estimated 100,000 Serbs died on the gruelling trek through Kosovo and Albania. The majority lay unburied, covered by either snow or mud, until only their bones were found the following spring.

Following the Serbian retreat, Kosovo was divided into two Austro-Hungarian occupational zones: Metohija entered the General Government of Montenegro, while a smaller part of Kosovo with Mitrovica and Vucitrn became part of the General Government of Serbia. The greater part of Kosovo - Pristina, Prizren, Gnjilane, Urosevac, Orahovac - was included in the Bulgarian Military Region of Macedonia. In Mitrovica a large number of Albanians volunteered to join the Austro-Hungarian military command, where they were organised into small detachments. Between 1916 and 1918 the Austro-Hungarian occupation authorities in Kosovo allowed the opening of more than 300 Albanian-language schools in an effort to undermine the Serbian presence in the region. In the Bulgarian-occupied regions of Kosovo even the Albanians kept as low profile as possible due to the harshness of the Bulgarian administration. The Serbs later claimed that Albanians had gouged out the eyes of frescoes in Serbian churches which had suffered attack during the Austrian offensive, but were unaware of how blasphemous such an act would have been for any Albanian, Muslim or Catholic. Damage to frescoes was invariably the work of Ottoman or Bulgarian troops, when the latter turned Gracanica monastery into a stable and in doing so severly damaged the frescoes. This act horrified the Albanians under whose strict Code of Laws, the *Kanun* of Lek Dukagjini, severe punishment is prescribed for all who fail to respect churches of whatever denomination.

In the autumn of 1918 the tide began to turn against the disintegrating Austro-Hungarian Empire, and the Austrian and Bulgarian armies retreated. Together with French troops, Serbian *komitadji*

10. R.G.D. Laffan, *The Serbs: The Guardians of the Gate*, New York, 1989, p. 227.

companies re-entered Kosovo in October and after several fierce battles established martial law. Soon after the peace was signed at the beginning of November 1918, an illegal Committee for the National Defence of Kosovo (*Komiteti i Mbrojte Kombetare e Kosoves*, later known simply as the Kosovo Committee or KK), which had existed in a loose form since May 1915, was set up in Shkoder with the primary objectives of campaigning against the border decisions of the Ambassador's Conference, for the liberation of Kosovo and for the unification of all Albanian-inhabited lands. A further objective was to organise raids into Serbia and smuggle arms to insurgents over the border. It was assisted financially by Italy and led by Hoxha Kadriu from Pristina, and consisted mainly of political exiles from Kosovo. Two of the most prominent members were Hasan Pristina and Bajram Curri.[11]

The Serbian army now in its turn set about wreaking revenge on the Albanian population. In November, it ravaged the area of Podgor Metohijski (near Pec), massacring women and children and destroying 138 houses. Another 700 Albanians were killed at Rozaj (in the Sandjak), and 800 in the region of Djakovica. In mid-February 1919, fifteen villages in the Rugovo Gorge, the main route between Metohija and Montenegro, were destroyed by cannon fire. Also in February, the same methods were used to suppress uprisings in the Plav and Gusinje districts, leading to a mass flight of Albanians, who, like their Dardanian ancestors, sought the high grounds in the Prokletije range, from there many of them fled south to Shkoder.[12] On 14 March 1919, a Member of Parliament in London, Colonel Guinness, drew the attention of the House of Commons to the Serbian attacks on Albanians in the Pec and Djakovica districts which, though allotted to Montenegro in 1913, had never been subdued or occupied by the Slavs, but no investigation was made and the atrocities continued. In retaliation, guerrilla warfare against the Serbs was carried on relentlessly both in Kosovo and in Montenegro.[13]

11. Isa Boletini and his family went to Podgorica to negotiate with King Nicholas. It appears that a fight broke out there between Albanians and Montenegrins, in which Boletini, his family and three friends were killed.
12. Hoover Institution Archives, C.W. Furlong Collection, Box 3: Outcard no. 454. The Committee for the National Defence of Kosovo: Letter to David Lloyd George (no date, probably late winter or early spring 1919). Banac, *The National Question in Yugoslavia*, p. 298.
13. Swire, *Albania*, p. 290.

In a letter to the editor of the *New Statesman*, a Mr Cunnington wrote of his experience in Shkoder in January 1919 when the Serbs and Montenegrins overran Gusinje:

> I was in Scutari at the time and had the duty of examining the 2,000 Albanian survivors fleeing from Gusinje and of reporting what had occurred. The bedridden were burnt alive in their houses, the women were outraged and afterwards, in a spirit of Serb playfulness, were ripped open, filled with petrol and set alight; the small children were collected together and tossed by bayonet point into bonfires. A British officer sent officially to investigate, a week later, was arrested by Serb-Montenegrin forces and treated with gross indignity. Ultimately, our minister in Belgrade forced the Serbian government to apologise abjectly. The officer reported that the towns of Gusinje, Plava and Djakovica have been destroyed and most of their Albanian inhabitants have vanished.[14]

In a rather feeble defence of the Serbs' actions, the British journalist, Henry Baerlein, who had acted as an adviser to the Belgrade government at the Paris Peace Conference, claimed:

> 'The Albanians in the region of Shkoder made a series of violent onslaughts during December 1919 and January 1920. So persistent were those attacks that the Yugoslav government decided that their army must occupy such defensive positions as would put a stop to these everlasting incidents.'[15]

The Serbian leadership defended its position by treating any disturbances as treason aimed at the destruction of the new state, and strong repression by the gendarmerie continued to be applied against all elements that disagreed with the central regime. This policy led to large numbers of Albanians seeking refuge in the territory of independent Albania, thus increasing the difficulties and embarrassment of the weak and impotent Albanian Government. Meanwhile, Hasan Pristina, then President of the Debar branch of the Kosovo Committee, wrote to the British Foreign Office about the 'horrors committed by Serbian troops against the Albanian civilian population of Kosovo and Debar.'[16] Describing events following the 1918 Serbian 'reoccupation of Kosovo', he wrote: 'On the 28–30 August 1920, in the Debar region of Ljuma 7,800 Albanian houses were set ablaze killing 250 people, and at the beginning of

14. *The New Statesman*, 22 January 1921.
15. H. Baerlein, *A Difficult Frontier*, London, 1922, p. 32.
16. PRO, FO, 371/5725-96398, 7 February 1921.

December in the Kosovo district of Vucitrn 250 homes were destroyed by fire killing 120 people.' Pristina went on to protest against the Belgrade government encouraging 'the immigration of Cossacks from the army of General Wrangel into the region of Drenica', claiming that the arrival of the Cossacks was 'causing discord between Albanians and Slavs', and implored the British to intervene to 'stop the extermination of the Albanian race and the occupation of their regions by Serbs.'[17]

The Kingdom of Serbs, Croats and Slovenes

The Peace treaties of 1919-20 divided the old dynastic empires into what were alleged to be nation-states, but in fact they contained large national minorities. The defeated powers of Austria-Hungary, Turkey and Bulgaria faced the inter-war period deeply aggravated by what they regarded as an imposed peace, and the new successor-states feared reprisals from them in attempts to overturn the peace agreements. The new Yugoslav state, which had been proclaimed at the Declaration of Corfu in July 1917, was now officially defined as 'one nation' with 'three names' - the Kingdom of Serbs, Croats and Slovenes. Thus it was essentially defined as a Slav state, and the ethnic, religious and language differences of the various components of the large non-Slav population were intentionally neglected. A constitutional monarchy was established on the basis of universal manhood suffrage with a population of 12 million including 400,000 Albanians. According to the 1921 census based on the Albanian mother-tongue, out of 436,929 inhabitants in Kosovo, 280,440 or 64.1 per cent were Albanians, of whom 72.6 per cent were Muslims, 26 per cent Orthodox and 1.4 per cent Catholic.[18] These census figures, however, are unreliable and it has been suggested that the Albanian population could have been much higher. The new kingdom was to be organised on a pattern closely resembling that of pre-war Serbia, being governed from Belgrade under an extension of the Serbian administrative system. The Serbs saw themselves as liberators of the South Slavs and therefore justified their intended domination of subsequent South Slav national life.

After prolonged debate over the Yugoslav-Italian border, Britain and France finally agreed that Italy should be given control of Istria,

---

17. Ibid.
18. *Popis stanovnistva u Krajlevni Srba, Hrvata i Slovenaca*, Sarajevo, 1924.

Rijeka and Zadar and have a mandate over central Albania. In return Yugoslavia would be given much of northern Albania, including Kosovo and the Drin valley, while Greece gained parts of southern Albania. The question of the Albanian frontier then remained dormant till 1920, when the Albanians asked for a neutral International Commission to delimit and demarcate their frontier in north-western Macedonia with the newly formed kingdom of Serbs, Croats and Slovenes because of the friction which had arisen there between the two countries. The commission duly appointed for this purpose consisted of British, French and Italian military representatives, Japan waiving its right to be represented. Technical work was carried out by survey parties from Yugoslavia and Albania (the latter hired Italians for the task, having no surveyors of her own).[19] A boundary pillar was built at suitable intervals along the frontier.[20]

Meanwhile, the Yugoslav Constitution of June 1921 was based on the 1920 elections, which resulted in ninety-four seats for the Serbian Democrats, eighty-nine for the Serbian Radicals, fifty-eight for the Communist Party, fifty for the Croatian Peasant Party, twenty-seven for the Slovene and Croatian Clerical Parties, twenty-four for the Bosnian Muslims, and ten for the Social Democrats. The new government was thus formed by the Serbian Democrats while the Croatian Peasant Party decided not to participate in the Assembly. The Communists were totally excluded.[21] Thus the new Constitution reflected the aspirations of the Serbian Centralists but was unacceptable to the majority of Croats, Slovenes and Communists. Much authority was transferred to the King. As in pre-war Serbia, power was to be centralised in Belgrade and remain largely in the hands of the Serbian political élite. In an attempt to create a feeling of Yugoslav unity, the country was divided up into nine

19. Giles, *Boundary Work in the Balkans*, p. 304.
20. The Greek-Albanian frontier was completed on the ground by December 1923. After the winter recess work was resumed on the northern frontier in May 1924, and the Yugoslav-Albanian portion was effectively completed that summer. Diplomatic disputes prevented a conclusion from being reached until another two years had elapsed. The summer of 1925 saw the completion of all technical work on the Yugoslav-Albanian frontier, but the final documents were not signed, and the Commission remained in existence till August 1926.
21. The Communist Party of Yugoslavia (CPY) was established in 1919 by a merger of the Social Democratic parties that existed before 1914. As in other European countries, the 'left' elements separated in 1919 and formed the CPY as a section of the Communist International. In the 1920 elections the CPY obtained 12.3% of votes and 13.8% of representatives elected.

provinces. The boundaries were intended to weaken or destroy traditional loyalties, but they were in fact gerrymandered so that Serbs would form a majority in six provinces, Croats in two, Slovenes in one, and Muslims and Albanians in none.

At the same time, the future of the Albanian population of south-eastern Europe was firmly sealed by statesmen representing the European Powers, many of them wholly ignorant of Balkan affairs. While powerful Yugoslav, Italian and Greek propaganda was deployed to influence the outcome, the concerns of the Albanians over the future of their newly-forged state received little attention. They were persistently ignored for two main reasons. First, the part played by Serbia in the Great War had prejudiced the Entente Powers in favour of its claim over Kosovo. During the Great War, Serbia had lost one fifth of its population. The Entente Powers were convinced that Serbia should be rewarded for its recent heroism and sacrifices. In June 1918, while the war still had several months to run, the United States had recognised the anniversary of the Battle of Kosovo as a day of special commemoration in honour of Serbia and all other oppressed people who were fighting in the Great War. The meaning of Kosovo was the subject of countless sermons, lectures and addresses throughout the United States. In a special service in New York City's Cathedral of St John the Divine, the Rev. Howard C. Robbins compared the Serbs to the people of Israel and observed that Serbia 'voices its suffering through patience far longer than Israel's and it voices a hope that has kept burning through five centuries.'[22]

Serbia had also become the darling of the public in both Britain and France.[23] A nationwide tribute was arranged in Britain in 1916 to celebrate the Kosovo anniversary. A shop was opened in London to sell literature about Serbia, which publishing houses had printed in tens of thousands of copies and information was widely disseminated by other means, including films. Posters based on a cartoon in *Punch* of 'Heroic Serbia' were displayed throughout the country. The Serbian national anthem was even played in some theatres.[24] The Serbs were thus well placed to argue that they needed Kosovo to re-establish their cultural identity after the horrendous wartime casualties and trauma their nation had suffered during the war, and

22. T. A. Emmert, 'The Kosovo Legacy', *Serbian Studies*, vol. 5, no. 2, 1989, p. 22.
23. The author's English grandparents kept a Serbian flag in a small vase on the overmantel of their London kitchen until their deaths in the 1970s.
24. Ibid., p. 21.

they did so successfully. Following the proclamation of the Kingdom, Serbs found themselves for the first time in their history living
within the framework of a single state, which they felt they had a
right to lead after their tremendous sacrifices during the war. The
Albanians on the other hand had great difficulty adjusting to the new
situation where they were governed by yesterday's sub-class. The
Balkans had been continuously at war for eight years, and during this
time old and new hatreds had deepened between Serbs and Albanians. A sense of fear, anger and betrayal now pervaded the Albanian villages of Kosovo. Immediately after the creation of the
Kingdom of the Serbs, Croats and Slovenes, Albanian philanthropic
and cultural societies were closed, along with all Albanian schools.

While the vicious border skirmishes continued, Europe's newspapers carried the news that Serbian troops were advancing beyond
the 1913 frontier. Aubrey Herbert, a former British colonel who
campaigned on behalf of Albanians, described the situation in Albania in February 1921:

> 'In the north more than 120 villages have been destroyed by
> Yugoslav troops; the refugeees from these villages are in a state of
> complete destitution, which the Albanian government, with its
> limited resourses, is doing what it can to relieve. The unfortunate
> people are enduring the utmost misery and are threatened with star-
> vation in the immediate future.[25]

In July 1921 the Kosovars submitted a petition to the League of
Nations begging for reunion with Albania. The document, covering seventy-two pages, described atrocities committed by the Serbs,
with the name and address of each victim. It stated that throughout the *vilayet* of Kosovo 12,371 people had been killed and 22,000
imprisoned since 1918.[26] In an insipid response the League's
Commission of Enquiry into border disputes reported from the
Yugoslav-Albanian frontier that both sides had committed unim-
portant and inadvertant violations of the 'zone of demarcation' due
to inaccurate maps and misinterpreted orders, but that both the
Yugoslav and Albanian authorities seemed anxious to avoid such
violations. Further, the Commissioners proposed that a joint
Yugoslav-Albanian military Commission should be appointed to
deal with any further incidents in the zone, to which both sides at
once agreed. Open warfare – other than skirmishes – between the

25. *New Statesman*, 5 February 1921.
26. Swire, *Albania*, p. 291.

Albanians and Yugoslavs thus came to a close. At the beginning of March, Yugoslavia officially recognised the Albanian government and appointed a Minister to Tirana.[27]

The Kachak movement

The new Serbian authorities attempted to consolidate their deeply unpopular administration in Kosovo, but found great difficulty in disarming the Albanian population whose growing resistance, now being actively assisted by Italy, became known as the *Kachak* movement.[28] The primary objective of the movement, which posed a major obstacle to efforts at stabilising the new political situation, was to persuade the international community to agree to Kosovo being annexed to Albania. The leading coordinator of the *Kachak* (outlaw, from the Turkish *kachmak*, meaning runaway or hide) movement was the Kosovo Committee which established branches in every town in the province. Some very dramatic *Kachak* raids encompassing all regions of Albanian settlement, from Tuzi in Montenegro to Debar in western Macedonia, were launched during the first five post-war years.

The Kachak movement was made up predominantly of Albanian emigrants from Kosovo, and was referred to by the Serbs as an outlaw organisation and by the Albanians as a national–liberation movement. In fact it had elements of both. The outlaws took to the hills and waged guerrilla warfare against the authorities, not only terrorising local officials but stealing cattle from settlers on a massive scale. Operating separately were a number of regular outlaw bands which raided and looted the remote and poorly protected frontier regions, avoiding taxes and military service. The 1921 amnesty for all crimes except murder produced only partial results: the outlaws surrendered just before winter but by spring were back in the forests again, thus following traditional *hajduk* practice. Many of the *Kachak* leaders were indeed robbers in the tradition of *hajduks* or popular heroes. The greatest and most celebrated *Kachak* leader was Azem Bejta (1889-1924), who kept his native Drenica, the central district

27. Ibid., p. 384.
28. For a detailed account of the Kachak movement see L. Rushti, *Levizja Kacake Ne Kosove (1918-1928)*, Pristina, 1981, and Hajredin Hoxha, 'Proces nacionalne afirmacije albanske narodnosti u jugoslaviji', *Casopis za kritiko znanosti*, Ljubljana, 51,52/1982.

of Kosovo, in permanent revolt during the early 1920s. Bejta and his wife Shote, who hid her sex by assuming a male name (Qerim) and attire so as not to offend the patriarchal mores of her people, were the leaders of a powerful movement that in late 1918 alone commanded some 2,000 fighters and 100,000 other adherents.[29] On the advice of Bajram Curri and Hasan Pristina, Bejta urged Albanians not to pay taxes and to refuse service in the army for as long as their rights were violated. According to Serbian sources, the response was tremendous: 'The kacaks were springing up like toadstools. Whenever somebody gets a court or administrative summons, he joins the kacaks; and also when he is drafted.[30]

As it turned out, Bejta's resistance, popular as it may have been, was halted not so much by government repression as by the self-contained policy of Ahmed Zogu and Albanian conservatives. Italy had now become Yugoslavia's chief rival in Albania. In 1922 Zogu, then Albania's Minister of the Interior and known to be an opponent of the *Kachaks*, started disarming the tribes of Albania's northern highlands and within the neutral frontier zone towards Yugoslavia where, notably at Junik, the *Kachaks* and Bejta had their bases. In March 1922 Bajram Curri, Hasan Pristina and Elez Jusufi, an important *Kachak* leader, tried to overthrow the Tirana government, but failed. In January 1923, soon after Ahmed Zogu had become the premier of Albania, Curri and Pristina once again failed in an attempt to overthrow him – some 500 *Kachaks* from Kosovo notwithstanding. Between the two armed revolts, Zogu entered into a secret agreement with Belgrade, promising among other things to do away with Curri, Pristina, and the *Kachaks*. Curri's third effort, in the wake of the Zogist-inspired assassination of Avni Rustemi (the assassin of Essad Pasha Toptani), was part of the June revolution of 1924, which brought the nationalist and progressive government of Fan Noli to power. Azem Bejta and his main force of 1,000 *Kachaks* were betrayed to the Yugoslav gendarmes at the very end of the disorders that marked the change of regime. Bejta fell on July 15, and on 24 December Zogu was back in power at the head of a regime sponsored by Belgrade. He quickly suppressed the Kosovo Committee, had Zia Dibra murdered 'while attempting to escape', sent his gendarmes to kill Bajram Curri, and scattered the other Kosovar leaders. Nine years later, in 1933, his agents killed

29. Banac, *The National Question in Yugoslavia*, p. 303.
30. Ibid., p. 302.

Hasan Pristina in Greece.[31] Zogu proclaimed himself King of Albania in 1928 and henceforth concentrated his energies on keeping himself in power, leaving the Albanians of Kosovo to their fate. So ended any hope of assistance from Tirana for the Kosovars' struggle for unification with Albania – a situation that has been repeated through successive administrations in Tirana right up to the present day.

Because of their overwhelming support for the *Kachak* movement, Albanians in general were viewed in the new Yugoslav kingdom with the utmost suspicion as a subversive element that would revolt at the first opportunity. Meanwhile, a flurry of activity came once more to that isolated corner of Metohija, a mile from the bustling town of Pec, where an agglomeration of churches made up the seat of the Pec patriarchate. Having been virtually ignored since the Ottomans finally abolished it, the Patriarchate now again enjoyed a wintry glory when, in 1924, the first Patriarchate of the new Yugoslavia was installed. At the same time the Serbian authorities stepped up their supression of the *Kachaks* by rounding up many extended families of up to fifty members and detaining them all together on pain of death until their 'outlaw' relatives surrendered. This method was probably the only way to bring the *Kachaks* to heel and it proved highly effective since these very small and highly mobile units, which enjoyed such immense popular support, were able to disappear with ease into the mountains after skirmishes with the police or army.

According to an eyewitness, the village of Dubnica in the district of Vucitrn, was surrounded on 10 February 1924 by the orders of the Prefect Lukic and of Commander Petrovic, and then set on fire so that all the inhabitants were burnt alive. What had happened was that the gendarmes had wanted to capture the robber Mehmet Konio, but by escaping the bandit had deprived them of their prey. The authorities held responsible not only the relations of Mehmet Konio, who were all massacred, but the entire village. In this fire, twenty-five people died, of whom almost all were women, children under the age of ten, and men over fifty.[32]

The *Kachak* movement began to dwindle in 1924 when, after the capture of Azem Bejta, one of the more liberal governments in Belgrade issued a sweeping amnesty decree that included more

31. Ibid., p. 305.
32. PRO, FO, WO 204/9463 196888.

serious crimes. The amnesty and improved relations with Albania helped to bring about the demise of the Kachak movement which, despite being ruthlessly suppressed, had served to reinforce an increased sense of national consciousness among the Albanians of Kosovo. It lingered on in small pockets of resistance till the late 1920s. From now on the Albanian (and Turkish) population in Kosovo had to become reconciled to living in a state where, instead of having the privileged status they had enjoyed under Ottoman rule, they acquired only civil equality with what had previously been the infidel Christian *rayah*.

6

THE COLONISATION PROGRAMME

As the 1920s progressed, a fundamental problem emerged within the Yugoslav state over the question of national identity. Despite the hopes of some intellectuals and political leaders before 1914, a Yugoslav nationality did not come into existence. At this time the national balance was approximately 43 per cent Serbian, 23 per cent Croatian, 8.5 per cent Slovenian, 6 per cent Bosnian Muslim, 5 per cent Macedonian Slavic, and 3.6 per cent Albanian, with the final 14 per cent composed of the minorities: Germans, Hungarians, Vlachs, Turks, Jews and Gypsies. Despite much previous rhetoric, these people did not consider themselves one nation.[1] It must be noted that during the inter-war period the question of the status of Montenegrins, Macedonians and Albanians was not an important issue in domestic politics. Montenegrins were treated as Serbs, and Macedonia was 'South Serbia'. The sensitive Albanian question played a role in foreign relations, but not in internal affairs.[2]

At first, the official state policy towards the Albanian population was one of assisted assimilation through the Serbian language education system. Albanians were denied the right to use their Albanian language for official matters, or in any other form of cultural activity, and all schooling was conducted in Serbo-Croat. However, this policy was abandoned after it became apparent that instead of aiding assimilation, it was educating a potential opposition élite. From the mid-1920s therefore Belgrade began discouraging public education for Albanians, permitting them only catechetical instruction, conducted by Muslim imams and Catholic priests. The authorities were convinced that these predominantly Muslim *mektebs* (primary schools) and *medreses* (secondary schools), popularly known as 'Turkish schools', would keep the Albanians backward and ignorant. Again this calculation was wrong. Although

1. B. Jelavich, *History of the Balkans*, vol. 2, Cambridge University Press, 1983, p. 151.
2. Ibid., pp. 153–4.

103

in Kosovo Albanians made up only 2 per cent of the high-school population in state schools, they succeeded in turning the 'Turkish schools', where instruction was ostensibly only in Koranic Arabic and Turkish, into formidable centres of underground national education and oppositional activity.[3]

Alexander's dictatorship

On 6 January 1929 King Alexander abrogated the 1921 constitution and dissolved the Assembly, thereby establishing a dictatorship in the country. The official name of the Kingdom of the Serbs, Croats and Slovenes was now changed to Yugoslavia, which was divided into nine regional units (*banovina*) in place of the earlier thirty-three regions. The *banovina* were then sub-divided into districts. For example, the districts of Gracanica, Gnjilane, Nerodimlje, Sar Planina, Podgora, Gora, Podrimlje (Orahovac) and Djakovica were included in the Vardar *banovina* with its seat in Skopje. The districts of Pec, Istok and Mitrovica belonged to the Zeta *banovina* with its seat in Cetinje, and the districts of Lab, Vucitrn and Drenovica were included in the Morava *banovina* with its seat in Nis. Thus Kosovo was split between three *banovinas*. This administrative and territorial division remained in force up till 1941.[4] Like the Ottomans in the past, Belgrade feared, in the wake of the Kachak rebellion, creating a single predominantly Albanian-inhabited administrative region. The once important and proud town of Prizren now became a quiet provincial backwater on account of its peripheral position so close to the Albanian border.

An example of how severely the new dictatorship dealt with Albanian nationalist activity can be seen in the treatment of the Franciscan priest Shtjefen Gjecov who, after the war, was assigned to the post of parish priest in Zym, near Prizren. His constant preoccupation with teaching Albanian language and culture to local people, after the Yugoslav government closed the few Albanian-language schools that had existed during the war, caused him to be seen by the Yugoslav regime as an ardent nationalist and thus as a natural enemy. His situation became much more perilous after January 1929 when the local police threatened and abused him for

---

3. Banac, *The National Question in Yugoslavia*, p. 299.
4. 'Relationship Between Yugoslavia and Albania', *Review of International Affairs*, Belgrade, 1984, p. 19.

several months until he was finally summoned before the sub-prefect in Prizren. When he arrived in the city, this official denied any knowledge of the summons. Gjecov left immediately with a few companions to return to Zym, but on the way he was ambushed and killed. The date of his death was 14 October 1929.[5]

Colonisation of Kosovo begins

The inter-war period in Kosovo was dominated by the policy of the Serbian colonisation, which began in 1918 and lasted till 1941. This programme was in two stages. The first, from 1918 to 1928, coincided with the Kachak movement, and in the second, from 1929 to 1941, serious attempts were made by Belgrade to base Albanian emigration on official international agreements. Of the many motives behind the colonisation programme, that of strategic, security and defence considerations were arguably the most important. Yugoslavia continued to regard the state of Albania as an abortive creation depriving it of territory, but felt threatened also by Italy, which it correctly believed was planning to make Albania a buffer state. From the military-strategic standpoint therefore it was necessary to secure Yugoslav possession of territory of which the Albanian-inhabited regions comprised one of the most important positions in the country, the point from which the Balkan rivers flow to the Adriatic, the Aegean and the Black Sea. Whoever held this strategic position could largely determine the fate of the central Balkans, especially of the main Balkan communication line from Morava to Vardar. It was thus imperative that such areas were kept free from occupation by hostile elements. Having experienced so many years of continuous warfare, it was considered necessary to secure Kosovo's borders with the most vigorous and trustworthy Serbs. So, during the two waves of settlement, in 1922-29 and 1933-38, 10,877 families were settled on 120,672 hectares of land. For the incoming settlers 330 settlements and villages were built with 12,689 houses, forty-six schools and thirty-two churches.[6]

Under the Decree of 24 September 1920 on the Colonisation of

5. *Kanuni i Leke Dukagjinit*, trans. L. Fox, Charles Schlacks, CA, 1989, p. xviii.
6. Useful studies on the colonisation programmme include: M.Verli, *Reforma Agrare Kolonizuese ne Kosove,1918-1941*, Illyria, Bonn/Tirana, 1991; M. Roux, *Les Albanais en Yougoslavie*, Editions de la Maison des Science de l'Homme, Paris, 1992; and M.Ivsic, *Les Problèmes Agraires en Yougoslavie*, Rousseau, Paris, 1926.

the Southern Regions of Yugoslavia, and the Law on the Colonisation of the Southern Regions of 11 June 1931, the colonists were
granted up to 50 hectares of land, free transport to the place of settlement, some basic tools, the free use of state or communal forests
and pastures, exemption from any taxation for three years, and occasionally houses. Agrarian reform, in Kosovo as in the rest of
Yugoslavia, meant the dismantling and redistribution of the big
estates belonging to private individuals, religious institutions and the
state. Throughout the long period when reform was being implemented, far more land was allocated for redistribution than was actually redistributed. This was not because it was expropriated on a
massive scale, but because Kosovo had large areas of uncultivated
state, communal and free land available as a result of the general
conditions of insecurity in the region through the last years of
Ottoman rule.[7]

However, land was easily expropriated from the Albanians on
the pretext that they had no documents proving their title to ownership. Under the vague pretext of agrarian reform, land which was
'abandoned' or deliberately so described as such was liberally distributed to Serb and Montenegrin colonists. This even included land
temporarily left untilled for the rotation of crops. Pastures, forests and
common land used by the Albanian peasantry were siezed under the
pretext of their being 'land in excess of need'. This was a particularly severe blow to small farmers with just a few acres, since their
livestock depended on the open pastures and commons for fodder,
and the family needed the forests for fuel. By contrast, the new Slav
colonists were given tracts of woodland and the right to the use of
state pastures and forests. Albanian owners were supposed to be
compensated with land of equal quality, but what they got was
usually of inferior quality, and although they could appeal against the
decisions of the agrarian reform authorities, they could never recover
their original land because the law guaranteed the colonists possession against any subsequent legal claims by former owners. Moreover,
when Albanians were unable to prove their rightful ownership of the
land – a frequent situation in a traditional society where property was
often held in common – they lost all claim to possession.[8]

The initial phase of colonisation was accomplished with volun-

7.   M. Dogo, 'Kosovo-Kosova: National Truths and Disinformation in Albanian-
     Kosovar Historiography' in Duijzings, Janjic, and Maliqi (eds), *Kosovo - Kosova*,
     p. 38.
8.   Banac, *The National Question in Yugoslavia*, p. 300.

teers, but before long some settlers who had been given land in the Metohija region were trying to sell their property back to the Albanians, preferring to try their luck on the richer and less dangerous plains of Vojvodina. The majority of those who settled in the Metohija region were Montengrin shepherds who had little knowledge of farming skills, but who co-operated better with the local Albanians than did the Serbian immigrants, since they often had common customs and lifestyle; many Montenegrins learned to speak Albanian to facilitate dealings. The most successful colonies were those established in Kosovo proper where the land was more fertile with a favourable climate and an abundance of good water. The only drawback was the absence of forests; this gave free play to the winds, which blew away the seeds after planting.

By the end of the first phase of the colonisation programme Djordje Krstic, Chief Agrarian Commissioner responsible for the colonisation of Kosovo, noted: 'in the Lab district of northern Kosovo, the colonisation had thoroughly changed the ethnic composition of the entire region in which, in 1913, there had not been a single Serbian inhabitant.'[9]

According to Kristic:

'Our best elements from various parts of the country have settled in Kosovo where they have formed homogenous as well as mixed colonies. The colonisers are real peasants who have gone there to work, and are prepared to face any difficulties. They have had good results in a short time. Most of them have built houses, and some have restored old houses. They work the land well, and some have brought with them agricultural implements. As an example of the economic development. I will quote the declarations made by a certain Gavrilo Tapachevic from Piva. When I asked him how he fared, he answered: 'See how I fare! My grandfather Joja Pejov Tepachevic talked with pride when he owned 1,000 kilogrammes of wheat, and I in this bad year [1927] shall have a railway wagon full.'[10]

One significant result of colonisation was how it changed the ethnic composition of Kosovo's towns. Kristic wrote:

'Among the results obtained is that of the progress of the towns. Urosevac is no longer the Albanian town it was before, for a large number of Hercegovines have settled there, and they will before long become the dominant element. Pristina is on the way to

9. D. Krstic, *The Colonisation of Southern Serbia*, Sarajevo, 1928.
10. Hamid Kokalari, *Kosova, Djepi i Shqiptarizmit*, Tirana, 1944, p. 33 (whole book: PRO WO 204/9463 196888).

becoming a modern town and is making great progress. Pec, where before it was difficult to see one of our people, is today crowded with our colonisers, who seem to give a new life to the town, and very soon they will change the town's entire character.[11]

In the first months of 1928, 938 families settled in Kosovo, 552 of them in the region of Pristina. But an obstacle to the success of the programme was the antagonism of the local Albanian population, who regarded the settlers as robbers and foreigners. Antagonism was also shown to the newcomers by the local Slav population, who often spoke Albanian, were used to collaborating with Albanians, and had adopted some of their customs. They were not in favour of this new Slav element in their districts, who had an alien mentality and aimed to reinforce Serbian sentiment wherever they settled. The newcomers were also rivals to them because of their new tools and methods; they had the support of the political authorities and were granted the best land confiscated from Albanian emigrants, which the local Slavs wanted for themselves.[12] The Albanians used the term 'native Serbs' of those whose families had lived in Kosovo before 1912, and had lived in relative harmony with their Albanian neighbours.

Along with the programme of colonisation, Albanians were also officially encouraged to emigrate. With a growing danger of instability on its south-western borders, the Yugoslav government set about enforcing the emigration and deportation of the Albanian population to Turkey. But many did not leave for Turkey or the state of Albania, and went off to live in the hills where they became ready recruits for remnant *Kachak* bands, venturing down periodically to the lowlands to carry out minor acts of sabotage to communications and such like. It was virtually impossible to colonise the wild district of Gjilani with its hostile Albanians. There was much insecurity at the time of the colonisation of Drenica which was without any state authority whatsoever, and only after Azem Bejta, the famous *Kachak*, was killed in 1924 could the colonisation of the region begin with the construction of the Serb colony of Serbica.[13]

11. The colonisation programme was less successful in Macedonia, and the ethnic structure of the towns less altered because the colonies settled there were smaller.
12. Hamid Kokalari, *Kosova, Djepi i Shqiptarizmit*, Tirana, 1944, p. 35.
13. It was Serbian colonists in the late 1920s who founded the villages of Milosevo, Obilic, Devet Jugovici and Lazarevo near Pristina, named after the heroes of the Battle of Kosovo.

Other social developments

During the inter-war period, Kosovo experienced virtual economic stagnation. Around 87 per cent of the economically active population, both Albanians and Slavs, were engaged in farming. but agricultural production remained extremely primitive and productivity low, while the largely illiterate rural population grew rapidly. Despite its rich mineral wealth, Kosovo's mining industry was slow to develop. The most prominent mines, including that of Trepca – the biggest and best known – were owned by Selection Trust Ltd. of London, and most of the others were in the hands of British, French and German capital. Of the entire capital invested in Kosovo between the two world wars, 72.8 per cent was foreign.[14] Although Kosovo was rich in ores, this wealth only began to be expolited after 1930. It had only two brick kilns, three small power-stations, five sawmills and ten flour mills. Despite the low level of industrial development, rural Kosovo, like the rest of the Balkans, was all but self-sufficient. Its undulating plains were mostly cultivated with wheat and maize. The farms consisted of solid houses with well-filled yards surrounded by high and defensible walls. At the colourful weekly bazaars peasants from nearby villages, wearing various traditional costumes, sold richly-coloured hand-woven cloths and rugs, cheese, honey, vegetables and livestock. Albanian women sat cross-legged behind baskets filled with brightly-patterned knitted stockings and other woollen objects. Small shops sold leather goods, pottery and the region's famous filigree silverwork.

It appears from traveller's accounts that the great churches and monastic estates had been largely forgotten – a consequence of the ever-diminishing Serbian population. Visiting Kosovo in 1925, Lena Yovitcic, the daughter of a Serb father and a Scottish mother, was saddened by the state of neglect in which she found the church of Gracanica. Most of the monastic buildings were in ruins, and nothing was apparently being done to preserve the ancient edifice. Yovitcic described the equally abandoned atmosphere of Kosovo Polje:

> 'Something about the vastness of Kosovo and the hush that makes itself felt in that region is very impressive, and seems to harmonise with one's sense of the fitness of things. From the tombs of the standard-bearers who fell on Kosovo one can see the simple stone monument raised to the memory of the avengers of Kosovo in 1912-13. Further on is the shrine which marks the spot where

14. Pipa, and Repishti, *Studies on Kosova*, p. 126.

Sultan Murad met his death at the hands of Milos Obilic. Otherwise there is nothing remaining to speak of the momentous struggle. Ever since the Battle of Kosovo, Murad's shrine has been guarded from generation to generation by a long line of decendants from one single Turkish family. The post of guardian, handed down from father to son, has never had a break in the chain, and the old Turk now keeping watch on the lonely plains is proud of the trust inherited from his ancestors. He has five sons, so there is no reason to suppose that the old tradition will die out.'[15]

Yovitcic described the role ascribed to Albanians in policing the wild districts still plagued by remnants of the *Kachak* rebellion, as well as by ordinary robbers:

'From here the road rises in zig-zags and goes through a lonely pass which is still the happy hunting ground of Albanian brigands. Many a traveller has been attacked on this bit of the road, which explains the armed policemen, with their guns and belts full of cartridges, stationed at every few yards. Albanians in national dress also stand on guard; they are obliged to take their share in protecting the road, and should they not give warning of the approach of their marauding kinsmen, they pay the penalty with their lives. Since this method has been adopted, we were told that the raids have been few and far between.'[16]

Unlike the tribal structure that still prevailed in northern Albania, the Albanians of Kosovo lived in *zadrugas* as did their Serbian and Montenegrin neighbours. The *zadruga*, which began disappearing in the rest of Yugoslavia after the Second World War, resembled a miniature state in which the executive power was vested in the head of the household – this was the family's most respected member. An average family community would have between fifty and ninety members. When a decision was needed that affected the entire family about work, production, family relations, etc., it was taken by a council consisting of all the male members and presided over by the head of the community. The parlour in which adult men discussed matters and spent their evenings took on the appearance of a parliament in miniature. In such family communities food was prepared and bread baked collectively. Meals were served out of a single vessel on low round

15. L.A. Yovitchitch, *Pages from Here and There*, Belgrade, 1926, pp. 129-30. In 1996 the present author found an elderly Turk, apparently from the original family of guardians, sitting in the porch of Murad's tomb.

16. Ibid., p. 130.

tables, where men ate separately from women and children.[17]

Within the *zadruga* was a complex network of relationships. The hierarchy was sharp, any difference in age producing a difference in status. An older brother had more authority than a younger one; a daughter-in-law introduced into the *zadruga* earlier had more authority than one who came later. All men were higher in rank than all women; all marriages were arranged by the elders; everything was the property of the *zadruga*. The only private property consisted of clothes and bedding, items brought in as the trousseau of the daughters-in-law. Anything earned by *zadruga* members outside their home was automatically handed over to the Senior (the eldest male).

The Albanian *zadruga* shared most of the characteristics of the classical form, but also had some specific features of its own. First of all, life within it was shaped by Islam. It also helped to keep the rules of Islam alive, for example; the seclusion of daughters and wives from all males who did not belong to the household; keeping the fast of Ramadan; and the circumcision of sons and marriage of sons and daughters in the proper manner. Women were segregated in their living and cooking room, where they also worked on handicrafts and entertained female guests. This patriarchal way of life was still the norm in many Kosovo Albanian villages well into the 1990s.

While other Yugoslav regions with Muslim populations had a few *zadrugas* before the war, and these were generally small, the Albanians showed that Islam and *zadrugas* were compatible, perhaps because the houses in the Kosovo region were much larger than elsewhere and members did not have to live in such close proximity. Many Albanian *zadrugas* had large houses which were as high as towers; these were called *kulas*. One great room was a guest hall, where the Senior sat near to the open fireplace and the other men sat around in precise sequence. The sleeping rooms for the couples were in lower buildings next to the *kula*. The large houses often had small windows and loopholes for guns, since they might have to resist attackers seeking vengeance or loot. The *kulas* were indeed like fortresses, with as many as twenty 'guns', i.e. adult men ready to fight.[18] One of the striking features of Albanian domestic life was the proverbial hospitality and the loving care and devotion shown

17. R. Marmullaku, *Albania and the Albanians*, Hurst, London, 1975, p. 147.
18. V. St. Erlich, 'The Last Big Zadrugas in the Kosovo Region', in R.F. Byrnes (ed.), *Communal Families in the Balkans: The Zadruga*, Notre Dame University Press, 1976, pp. 246-7.

to guests and visitors. Each person who approached the house was accepted as an honoured guest without being questioned about his identity or his interests. Most visitors were the fathers and brothers of the *zadruga's* daughters-in-law. Whoever entered the house was under the protection of the *zadruga* which would never surrender him to blood feud enemies pursuing him for vengeance. These customs of hospitality with tribal roots coloured all aspects of Albanian *zadruga* life.[19]

The secret life of Albanian women in Kosovo, with its manifest restrictions and stifling boredom, was scarcely ever recorded. We must therefore be grateful for a detailed account by an English woman who visited the town of Pec during the First World War. The woman had asked her Serbian guide if she might be shown around an Albanian harem, and the chief of police, a friend of the guide, asked a rich Muslim to let the foreigner visit his wives. The Muslim graciously assented, saying that he would do it as a great favour to the chief of police and that no European woman had ever visited a Pec harem. The Englishwoman's companion described her privileged visit to the harem thus:

> Outside a cavernous doorway sat the chief of police and the wealthy Albanian. The introduction was ceremonious and the Muslim, losing no time, took Jo through the doorway into a courtyard. At the other end was a door guarded by a responsible-looking Albanian. He stood aside and she entered yet another court full of trees. She passed through a lower story packed with grain and ascended into a simple room with a seat built all round it. The Albanian waved his hand to the seat, called to his wives much as a sportsman summons his dogs, and left. They came in, three women simply dressed in chemise and flowered cotton bloomers. Their voices shook with excitement and they were quite upset because Jo got up to shake hands with them. They spoke nothing but Albanian having only a few words of Serb. One had been a beauty but her teeth were black and decayed, another was a healthy-looking wench, the third was plain. A plump dark-eyed girl came in, daughter of the first wife. She spoke Serb and interpreted for the wives. They wanted to know everything but knew so little about anything that they could grasp nothing. 'Where had Jo come from?'- she tried London, Paris, no use they had never heard of them - two weeks on the sea - they didn't know what the sea was, nor ships, nor boats. They had never left Pec and only knew the little torrent. The girl said that women did not learn to read and write. That was for men only. Jo asked

19. Ibid., p. 248.

them what they did. 'Nothing.' 'A little sewing,' they owned with elegant ease.[20]

The Communist Party

The Communist Party of Yugoslavia (CPY) had been formed in 1919, but during the inter-war period it was forced to operate clandestinely, after the Law on the Protection of the State was passed in 1921. Its programme for the nationality question was based on the Marxist dogma of the right of nations to self-determination, and the concept of equal political rights among nations. In 1923, a resolution of the CPY (then known as the Independent Workers' Party of Yugoslavia) stated that it was the Party's duty to lead a common and open struggle for the right of secession. This resolution and other discussions among Yugoslav communists led to considerable disagreement over the national question and how it should influence the organisation of a future Communist state. At the end of the nineteenth century and in the first half of the twentieth, the Serbian and Yugoslav left had treated Serbian-Albanian relations within the scope of its aim to have the national question resolved through the creation of a Balkan confederation. The dilemma of the communists was cut short by the Comintern which decided at its Fifth Congress in 1924 that the state of Yugoslavia, as a 'product of world imperialism', should be broken up. From then on, the national policy of the CPY was founded on the Leninist theory about 'the reactionary nationalism of hegemonic nations and the progressive nationalism of oppressed people'. From this it concluded that 'Greater Serbian nationalism' had to be countered, and that communists should cooperate to this end with all anti-Serbian nationalist movements. At its Fourth Congress in 1928, the CPY adopted the position of the Comintern that Yugoslavia should be dismembered since it was a country 'created in the Balkans by world imperialism for counter-revolutionary purposes aimed against the Soviet Union'.[21]

20. J. and C. Gordon, *Two Vagabonds in Serbia and Montenegro*, Penguin, London, 1939, pp. 124-5.
21. P. Simic, *The Kosovo and Metohija Problem and Regional Security in the Balkans*, Institute of International Politics and Economics, Belgrade, 1996, p. 8. This position was modified only in 1936 when the Comintern took a turn towards a 'national front' policy for Yugoslavia's preservation and defence. In doing so, however, the initial position that Yugoslav communists must support the Albanian national movement was not changed until the beginning of the Second World War.

In the early 1930s a number of Communist students from Belgrade University began operating in Pec and its surrounding districts, and in August 1935 the first party cell of four members was founded in Mitrovica where various CPY members had been active since 1930. This cell soon developed into the local party leadership. At the same time party organisations were set up in Djakovica, Urosevac, Prizren and Pristina.[22] Under the Comintern's constant and vigilant pressure, the CPY came to recognise the right of national self-determination, including secession, of the different nationalities, a line which was most fully elaborated at the Fourth Congress held in exile in Dresden in 1928. Between 1929 and 1934, during the dictatorship of King Alexander, all political rights were suspended and the Party was almost destroyed by police terror. When political liberties of a limited kind were revived after Alexander's assassination in 1934, the Comintern line on Yugoslavia had changed and with it the nationality policy of the CPY. No longer hostile to the European *status quo*, Moscow under Stalin responded to the Nazi rise to power by emphasising collective security and the politics of popular fronts. The Party now stressed Yugoslav unity: the right to self-determination was put to one side, and advocating the secession of disaffected regions was condemned once again as nationalism.[23]

Following the opening of the first mines in Kosovo in the early 1930s, the CPY attempted to activate some revolutionary activity among the new mining workforce – especially at Trepca, the only place in Kosovo with any real industrial proletariat, the other mines tending to employ mainly seasonal workers. Before long communists dominated the trade unions and were successful in organising a twenty-day strike over working conditions at Trepca in May 1936. After the destruction of the Montenegrin Party organisation in 1936 the Central Committee of the CPY decided to set up a regional leadership for Kosovo. Its founding conference for the region was held in Pec in July 1937, attended by twenty-one delegates of whom two, Ramiz Sadiku and Ramiz Djema, were Albanians. A Montenegrin, Miladin Popovic, later to play an important role in the development of Communism in Albania, was elected head of the Pec regional committee. By the following year local party organisations had been established in Pristina, Prizren and

22. *Relationship Between Yugoslavia and Albania*, Belgrade, 1984, p. 22.
23. B. Magas, *The Destruction of Yugoslavia*, London, 1993, p. 27.

Djakovica, and the total membership of the CPY in Kosovo was now 239 of whom 55 per cent were classified as peasants, 30 per cent as workers and 12 per cent as intellectuals. The membership at this time consisted mainly of Montenegrin settlers. Even Serbs were comparatively few, while only twenty-three out of the CPY's 239 members were Albanians.

The CPY made headway slowly and with difficulty among the Albanians, although the importance of winning Albanians over to Party policy was pointed out at every party meeting. There were several reasons for the Albanian population's reservations over joining the CPY: the persistent national oppression to which they had been subjected; the region's backwardness; the lack of any significant working class; the small numbers of the intelligentsia; and most important of all, the Albanian's accumulated mistrust of the Serbs and Montenegrins. Albanians were also heavily influenced by the beys, most of whom, such as Dzafer Deva in Mitrovica and Ilijas Agush in Pristina, were loyal supporters of the regime.[24] There was also widespread apathy among Albanians. The Regional Committee organised recruitment drives in June 1938, when it instructed the party organisations to agitate among the settlers and persuade them not to accept land taken from Albanian peasants. At the same time a tract written by students from Belgrade University was distributed throughout Kosovo, protesting against the regime's drive to deport Albanians from Kosovo to Turkey and confiscate their land.[25] Throughout 1939 and 1940, strikes continued at the Trepca mines as workers demanded better working conditions and increased pay.

At the 5th Party Conference, the last before the war, a gesture was made towards the Albanian population by detaching the regional Committee of Kosovo (itself formed in 1937) from the Montenegro Provincial Committee. Implicit in this measure was a recognition of the territorial autonomy of Kosovo and of the separate and distinct status of the Albanian population in Yugoslavia. It was felt that this step would not only facilitate the recruitment of Albanian cadres, but also assist Communist groups in Albania itself – a task for which the CPY was directly responsible to the Comintern and into which it put considerable effort before the Albanian Communist Party was founded in November 1941.[26]

24. *Relationship Between Yugoslavia and Albania*, p. 28.
25. Ibid., p. 25.
26. Magas, *The Destruction of Yugoslavia*, p. 28.

The second colonisation programme

According to the 1931 census, the population of Kosovo was 552,064, of whom 347,213 or 62.8 per cent of the population, were Albanians.[27] The areas most subject to forced expulsions of Albanians were those bordering the Albanian state. One of the greatest advocates for the removal of Albanians from Yugoslavia was the Serbian academic, Vasa Cubrilovic (1898-1990), a loyal follower of Ilija Garasanin (1812-74) and his renowned idea of '*Nacertanje*' propounded in 1846. This called for the unification of all the lands that were considered predominantly Serbian and Orthodox, including Bosnia, Hercegovina, Montenegro, Kosovo and parts of Macedonia. Meanwhile, Cubrilovic was highly critical of the methods employed in the colonisation programme, which had not produced the desired ethnic balance or any increased security along the Yugoslav-Albanian border. In a memorandum on the subject presented to parliament in Belgrade on 7 March, 1937, he blamed the failure of the colonisation programme in Drenica and Metohija on the settlement there of Montenegrins, rather than the more industrious Slavs from the north.

Nevertheless, he recognised the need to settle at least some Montenegrins in Kosovo to forestall pending social unrest. He wrote:

'Recently Montenegro has become a very grave problem. The poor land cannot sustain the population, which increased by 16 per cent from 1912 to 1931. The increase in the Montenegrin population has brought poverty, which has recently led to incessant social-political movements detrimental to the authority of our state and somewhat dangerous for future law and order. It is not in our interests to offer these people maize and pensions. The only solution is to move them to the fertile regions of Kosovo and Metohija because they are close to the Albanian in mentality and temperament. The main priority is to immediately grant the colonists title deeds to the property where they are to settle because one of the main reasons for the failure of our colonisation so far has been that colonists have not felt secure on the land where they have been settled, because title has not been given at once.'[28]

It was therefore not only strategic reasons but also fear of domestic unrest that prompted the colonisation programme. On a prophetic

27. *Popis stanovnistva u Krajlevni Yugoslaviji*, Sarajevo, 1934.
28. Vasa Cubrilovic, 'The Expulsion of the Albanians', *Kosova Historical Review*, no. 4, Tirana, 1994, p. 37.

note Cubrilovic added:

> 'The Albanians cannot be repulsed by means of gradual colonisation alone. We have had no success to speak of in any national assimilation of the Albanians in our favour. On the contrary, because they base themselves on Albania, their national awareness is awakened and if we do not settle accounts with them at the proper time, within 20-30 years we shall have to cope with a terrible irredentism, the signs of which are already apparent and which will inevitably put all our southern territories in jeopardy.'[29]

Having outlined the faults of the previous year's policies, Cubrilovic then proceded to list the proposals he suggested should be followed in order to speed up the expulsion and deportation of Albanians:

> 'If we proceed from the assumption that the gradual displacement of Albanians through our colonisation is ineffective then we have only one course to follow, that of their mass resettlement. In this case we must consider two states, Albania and Turkey. With its sparse population, its many undrained swamps and uncultivated river valleys Albania would be in a position to admit some hundred thousand Albanians from our country. With its large uninhabited and uncultivated territories in Asia minor and Kurdistan, modern Turkey has almost boundless possibilities for internal colonisation.'

Cubrilovic was writing at a time of acute instability in Europe, a fact he noted after saying that the international community had its own problems:

> 'the world today is used to things much worse than this and is so preoccupied with day-to-day problems that this aspect should not be a cause for concern. At a time when Germany can expel tens of thousands of Jews and Russia can shift millions of people from one part of the continent to another, the shifting of a few hundred thousand Albanians will not lead to the outbreak of a world war. Italy will no doubt raise more difficulties, but at present it is extremely occupied with its own problems in connection with Abyssinia and Austria and will not dare go very far in its opposition.'[30]

Therefore, in the mid-1930s, following negotiations with Turkey which expressed willingness to accept 200,000 Albanian emigrants from Yugoslavia, Albanian landholdings in the counties of Djakovica and Sar Planina were restricted to 0.16 hectare per

29. *Kosova Historical Review*, no. 3, Tirana, 1994, p. 40.
30. Ibid., p. 41.

household member, unless ownership could be documented. In the words of one official report, 'This is below the minimum needed for survival. But that was precisely what we wanted; that is, to prevent them [the Albanians] from living and thereby force them to emigrate.'[31] The second colonisation programme culminated with the signing in July 1938 of an agreement between Yugoslavia and Turkey on the emigration of some 200,000 ethnic Albanians, Turks and Muslims from Kosovo and Macedonia, to Turkey, which was keen at the time to populate the sparsely-inhabited areas of Anatolia and the tense areas bordering Kurdish-inhabited regions. However, the convention was never implemented: the funds needed to dispatch the emigrants were lacking.

The deportation of Albanians was efficiently organised. Some went to Albania and others to Arab countries, but the majority went to Istanbul via the Skopje-Thessaloniki railway and from there either by sea or rail to Turkey. Official Yugoslav historiography claims that the thousands of Albanians who emigrated from Yugoslavia during the inter-war period did so 'voluntarily' and because they were 'discontented with the new state and felt more at home in a Muslim environment.' In several ways this was a flagrant departure from the truth. Naturally, Albanians resented their new status in the new Yugoslavia, but they had little desire to uproot themselves from their fertile farms and villages and either move to an alien, impoverished and sparsely-populated region of eastern Turkey or become refugees in Albania.

The Turkish authorities settled the Albanians mainly in the interior of the country, especially in the east around the towns of Diyarbakir, Elazig and Yozgat, regions sadly different from the prosperous areas they had left behind in Yugoslavia. Nevertheless, a considerable number of the deportees managed from the start to make their homes in more suitable places such as Bursa, Istanbul, Tekirdag, Izmir, Kocaeli and Eskisehir, where they established prosperous communities.

We need to discover the real causes of the emigration. Room should be made too for the persistence of traditional links and the hope of new economic prospects, both connected to the image of Turkey, if not the reality. How else can we explain the fact that the migratory flow tended to be towards Turkey rather than

31. M. Pirraku, 'Kulturno-prosvetni pokret Albanaca u Jugoslaviji (1919-1941)', *Jugoslovenski istorijski casopis*, nos. 1-4, 1978, pp. 357-8, cited in Banac, *The National Question in Yugoslavia*, p. 297.

Albania?[32] In the Albanian state, meanwhile, Albanians from Kosovo and other Yugoslav territories settled mainly in the marshlands of the west, in the modern districts of Fier, Kavaje, Berat, Elbasan, Durres and Kruje.[33] It is not possible to determine the exact number of Albanians expelled from Yugoslavia until all the possible sources of data, particularly Turkish ones, can be examined, Nevertheless, data from the administrations of the Kingdom of Yugoslavia and the state of Albania, namely diplomatic records and other sources such as the records of political and religious bodies and the press, and demographic analyses, show that the total number of emigrants from Yugoslavia was between 200,000 and 300,000.[34]

Official Yugoslav sources play down the numbers of Albanians who left the country as fairly insignificant. Official figures from 1927-39 show 19,279 ethnic Albanian emigrants in Turkey and 4,322 in Albania. Compared to the 30,000 Serbs, Croats and Slovenes who emigrated for economic reasons to the United States and other transoceanic countries every year, the migration in question was not seen officially as particularly remarkable. However, the Albanian Consul-General in Skopje told a British Foreign Office source in February 1937 of his opinion that the Turkish-Yugoslav negotiations were making little progress, because the Turkish authorities had their hands full with the settlement in Turkey of Muslims transplanted from the Dobrudja and that they would not be willing to receive the 100,000 Muslims whom the Yugoslavs wished to send for at least another three years. He also noted that most of the Turkish population of Kosovo had returned to Turkey.[35]

The colonisation programme failed mainly because of the inadequate financial resources, unsystematic management and policy shifts following changes of government, together with an unspecialised bureaucracy which dealt with matters piecemeal. Cubrilovic, in a memorandum, called for the entire colonisation programme to be placed in the hands of the Army General Staff,

---

32. Dogo, *Kosovo-Kosova*, p. 37.
33. Lady Carnarvon, the mother of Aubrey Herbert, engaged in relief work among Albanian refugees from Yugoslavia after her son's untimely death in 1923. In 1926 she founded a village in Albania, situated near Kavaje, for the numerous refugees from Kosovo. The village was called Herbert (now Helmasi) in her son's honour.
34. Z. Shtylla, *Kosova Historical Review*, no. 3, Tirana, 1994, p. 20.
35. PRO, FO, 371/21112, 3921, 23 February 1937.

who would be able to direct it through a State Colonisation Council. He warned that chaos would follow if his advice were not heeded. He wrote:

> 'All Europe is in a state of chaos. We never know what the next day will bring. Albanian nationalism is increasing in our territories. To leave the situation as it is means, in the case of a world conflict or a social revolution, both of which are possible in the near future, to put a question mark over all our territories in the south.[36]

On the eve of the Second World War the Turkish parliament decided not to ratify the agreement with the Yugoslavs of July 1938 for three reasons: the fall of the Stojadinovic government in 1939, lack of financial means and the impending war. The colonisation programme was therefore an overall failure. At the end of the decade, a sociologist from the University of Zagreb noted that Yugoslavia's Albanians were considered anti-national and an 'unreliable element' because of their political role in the past. As producers of tobacco, they had suffered under the policies of state monopolies, the agrarian reform and bureaucratic hostility. Yet although they had fallen from their formerly high social position, the effects of this on family life were hardly noticable. People in Kosovo did not appear pauperised or de-classed. Crime, alcoholism, prostitution and the squandering of property were not serious problems. Patriarchal dignity and responsibility still remained.[37]

36. *Kosova Historical Review*, no. 4, 1994, p. 42.
37. Erlich, 'The Last Big Zadrugas... ', p. 249.

7

THE SECOND WORLD WAR

The Axis invasion of Yugoslavia began on 6 April 1941, with a savage bombing of Belgrade, and ended on 17 April with an armistice which was in effect an unconditional surrender. King Peter II and his government, newly installed on 27 March by the military coup and anti-Axis demonstrations which precipitated Hitler's decision to attack, had already fled the country *en route* to form a government-in-exile in London and later in Cairo.[1] Yugoslavia was then carved up between Germany's allies. Subsequently when Milan Nedic's collaborationist government was formed in Serbia on 29 August 1941, this area was gradually placed under the administration of the so-called 'Government of National Salvation'.

Following the occupation, the Kosovo-Mitrovica region remained under direct German control due to the importance of the Trepca mines, and with the districts of Lab, Vucitrn and Dezevo (Novi Pazar) was incorporated into the newly-created Kosovo Department. Here the Germans immediately set up an Albanian gendarmerie composed of some 1,000 men, while another 1,000 were registered as armed volunteers, known as *Vulnetara*, under the command of local officers. The eastern districts of Gnjilane, Kacanik and Vitin were allotted to Bulgaria, which set up its own administration, army and police force, while a large part of Kosovo together with the towns of Debar, Tetovo, Gostivar and Struga covering about 11,780 square km. and with a population of 820,000, was attached to Italian-occupied Albania in May 1941. An independent state of Croatia, governed by the Ustasha movement with Italian support, was created as an Axis satellite. Thus the kingdom of Yugoslavia ceased to exist.

As they set about consolidating their position in Kosovo, the Italians began organising Albanian units to be incorporated into the

1. D. Rusinow, *The Yugoslav Experiment*, Hurst, London, 1977, p. 1.

Italian army. Some of these were composed of Kosovars and Chams.[2] The pre-war Kosovo Committee reactivated itself and returned from exile and played an important role in collaborating with the occupation forces, who were able to portray themselves as liberators of the Albanians and the creators of a unified Albania. The Italians and later the Germans were easily able to capitalise on the profound desire of the majority of Albanians for national unification. The Albanian language was brought into use for local administration and schools for the first time. It was permitted to fly the Albanian flag throughout Italian-controlled Kosovo. These measures were naturally attractive to Albanians, and won the support of most Kosovars. The position of the Serb and Montenegrin minority, on the other hand, was bleak since they were collectively perceived by both the Italians and the Germans and by many Albanians as the enemy within. As a result, thousands of Slavs were arrested, interned or deported to forced labour camps, and many thousands more were killed. Settlers' houses were burnt down and their occupants forced to leave Kosovo.

Remarkably, it was only Slav settlers who were attacked. Original Serbian communities, then still referred to as '*raja*', were generally treated by most Albanians as traditional neighbours. According to Serb sources, attacks on Slavs by Albanians resulted in some 10,000 Serb and Montenegrin families being forced to migrate from Kosovo. Dozens of Orthodox churches were also destroyed and looted. Those Serbs and Montenegrins deported to forced labour camps in Pristina and Mitrovica worked in the Trepca mines, while others were sent to Albania to work on various construction projects. Throughout Yugoslavia a variety of collaborationist organisations began to emerge. In Kosovo the leaders of the pre-war Muslim Xhemijet Party founded a new Albanian political organisation with a pronounced irredentist programme - the Lidhja Kombetare Shqiptare (National Alliance of Albanians). The majority of those Kosovo Serbs who decided to stay and fight joined an emergent resistance organisation of former Royal Yugoslav officers known as the Chetniks, and led by Colonel Draza Mihailovic. They fought for King Peter and his government-in-exile and for the return of the traditional political and social system. The Orthodox Church, through which the Serbs were united as a nation, was

2. Muslim Albanians living in the region of north-western Epirus. One infamous Kosovar unit which fought in Albania against the Greeks was called '*Tarabosh*'.

sympathetic to Mihailovic, and became standard-bearer of the anti-Soviet/communist mood in Serbia and Kosovo.[3]

The Partisans and Kosovo

Opposing both the Axis forces and the Chetniks were the Communist Partisans led by the Party Secretary, Joseph Broz Tito. The Chetnik movement in Kosovo had around 1,500 men formed into two battalions, and operated in the mountainous regions on the borders of Kosovo. The Italian occupation force encouraged an extensive settlement programme involving up to 72,000 Albanians from Albania in Kosovo. Although the Communist Party of Yugoslavia (CPY) had committed itself at its Fourth Congress in 1928 to assisting 'the general struggle of the oppressed and fragmented Albanian people for an independent and united Albania',[4] the Fifth National Conference in 1940 reduced this stand to 'the formation of a peasant republic of Kosovo through the revolutionary overthrow of the imperialist and fascist Greater Serbian regime'.[5] Therefore, attempts by the CPY to recruit Kosovo Albanians were largely frustrated. The Kosovars shunned the CPY as an alien 'Pan-Slavic' organisation, which ignored their national aspirations. All the CPY could offer them was an undefined place in a federal Yugoslavia in which all peoples would be free and equal. As a result, the Partisan struggle in Kosovo was essentially a Serbian and Montenegrin effort, attracting only a handful of Albanians. With no base among the Albanians and with most Serbs sympathetic to Draza Mihailovic's Chetniks, the CPY had little choice but to keep its distance. The Italians, on the other hand, supplied the Albanian population, who feared a restoration of the old Yugoslav kingdom, with arms, gave them back land cleared of settlers, and thus provided a degree of economic as well as 'national' security.

The turning-point in CPY influence among the Albanians of Kosovo came towards the end of 1940 and in early 1941 when some initial contacts were made with the few small communist cells which had operated in Albania. From the beginning of July till

3. For an excellent and thorough account of the Chetniks, see J. Tomasevic, *The Chetniks: War and Revolution in Yugoslavia - 1941-45*, Hoover Institution, Stanford, 1975.
4. Dusan Lukac, *Radnici pokret u Jugoslaviji i nacionalno pitanje 1918-1941*, Belgrade, 1971, p. 274.
5. Ibid., p. 367.

December 1941, the CPY in Kosovo was in a very difficult situation owing to the fact that its contacts with the Party leadership of
Yugoslavia were scanty or non-existent. Although it made attempts
to make contact with the CC of the CPY through couriers sent to
Montenegro, they met with little success. The organisation of the
CPY in Kosovo was considerably weakened during April and May
1941 with the exodus of almost half the original 300-odd CPY
members there had been just before the war. In June 1941, following provisional contacts made in August 1939, the Albanian
communists re-established contact with communists in Kosovo and
talks were held in Pec on cooperation between communist groups
in Albania and the CPY Regional Committee. Since no unified
Communist organisation had been established in Albania, Tito,
under a Comintern directive, sent there two delegates, Miladin
Popovic and Dusan Mugosa, with the aim of drafting the
programme and first resolution of the fledgling Albanian Party.
Although the Yugoslavs found total ideological confusion and bitter
internal friction, they eventually succeeded in uniting the diver-
gent communist leaders and managed to weld together the factions
they favoured. A unified Albanian Communist Party (CPA) was
thus officially formed on 8 November 1941 with Enver Hoxha,
born in 1908 in Gjirokaster and one of the organisers of the Korca
branch of the ACP, being appointed the Party Secretary.

The Yugoslav emissaries' task was to control the political development in Albania. This meant encouraging division among the
differing currents of Albanian politics and countering aspirations
towards national unification by putting class and party allegiance
first.[6] There followed talks in Tirana in August 1941 between Dusan
Mugosa and Fadil Hoxha with representatives of the various Albanian communist factions. The talks centred on the urgent need for
unity between the communist groups in Albania and their cooperation with their counterparts in Kosovo. Fadil Hoxha was born on
15 March 1916 in Djakovica, and he lived there until he left for
Albania to attend secondary school. Because of his revolutionary
activity, he was forced to leave the Shkoder high school, but he
continued his education in the teacher training college at Elbasan,

6. Their most effective work was done in the organisational field, issuing the first
    instructions for the formation of Party cells and the recruitment of the first
    members. Before this, the number of Communist Party activists in Albania had
    never exceeded 150.

where he soon became leader of the Shkoder communist group. After the Italian invasion of Albania in 1939 he organised a battalion of volunteers to resist the Italians in Durres. For a while he worked in the Party headquarters in Tirana and formed party cells in northern Albania. On instructions from the Shkoder Communist group, he established contacts with the CPY's regional committee for Kosovo and Metohija. After the occupation of Yugoslavia in April 1941, he went to Kosovo and dedicated himself to the organisation of armed resistance.[7]

Because of the extremely difficult conditions in Kosovo during the early years of the war, the first acts of Partisan resistance to the occupying forces were carried out by underground diversionist units, rather than by the regular detachments formed in various parts of the region from July 1941. The CPY regional committee believed that conditions in Kosovo were not yet suitable for armed action on a large scale but that minor sabotage missions should begin. Small diversionist shock groups were therefore engaged mostly in cutting telephone wires and electric cables, seizing weapons, typewriters and other office material from fascist institutions, destroying tools, and so on.[8] With the objective of putting the Trepca mines out of action, in late July a group of miners blew up the cable car used for transporting ore, which ran from Zvecan to Stari-Trg, and then withdrew to the mountains of Kapaonik. There miners and forestry workers formed the Kapaonik Partisan detachment, which operated mainly outside the territory of Kosovo and was under the command of the General Staff for Serbia. In spite of difficult conditions for underground recruitment in Kosovo, special efforts were now made to gain at least a measure of support among young Albanians. In this the CPY was greatly assisted by the arrival in Kosovo of more dedicated young communists from Albania. During working hours these young men were legally employed mainly in the collaborationist state institutions, but in their free time they worked to recruit Albanian secondary school students to

7. Marmullaku, *Albania and the Albanians*, p. 141. After the war Hoxha performed various political duties in Kosovo where he enjoyed great prestige and popularity. From 1969 he became a member of the Executive Bureau of the Presidency of the League of Communists of Yugoslavia, and belonged to Tito's party caucus. He was nominated a member of the Presidency of the SFRY in Kosovo, the body which in the post-Tito period served as the collective president of the republic.

8. *Relationship between Yugoslavia and Albania*, Belgrade, 1984, p. 109.

the communist cause, particularly in the towns of Pec, Djakovica and Prizren.

The Partisans found that the fear among the Albanian population of a return to Serbian rule and hence of joining a Slav-led movement seriously weakened conditions for any serious armed struggle in Kosovo. This was despite the CPY's simple message to all Albanians in the Balkans that their only way of achieving liberation and national unification was by joining in the struggle with the CPY and thereby assisting the joining of Kosovo and what was now western Macedonia to Albania. Communism had a stronger influence on the Albanians of these areas after the foundation of the Albanian Communist Party (ACP). Having been left without direct connections with the Central Committee (CC) of the CPY from July 1941 onwards, the National Liberation Movement (NLM) in Kosovo was very much isolated from the fighting in other parts of Yugoslavia. According to Predrag Ajtic, a member of the wartime regional committee, the NLM in Kosovo was 'only a pale reflection' of the insurrection which had flared up throughout the rest of Yugoslavia.[9]

In the autumn of 1941 it became apparent that attempts were being made by the various Albanian patriot bands to organise themselves in resistance to the occupying forces, and the names of a few of their leaders began to filter through to the outside world. One of the best known was Muharem Bajraktari, once in the gendarmerie under Zog but dismissed about 1936; he had thereafter lived in Yugoslavia and France and only returned to Albania after the Italian invasion. He was given a military post in Tirana but soon resigned and retired to his native village in the Ljuma area where he organised a guerrilla band which operated at first spasmodically but later with great regularity.[10] During May 1942 an unsuccessful attempt was made to assassinate the new Albanian collaborationist 'Prime Minister' Mustapha Kruja, whereupon the Italian authorities declared a state of siege in Tirana. New restrictions were imposed on the entire Albanian population, including Kosovars, and the police were authorised to tear veils from women in the street as a precaution against disguised guerrillas. It became evident at this stage that Albanian guerrillas were working in collaboration with Draza Mihailovic. The Italians, in an attempt to alienate his supporters in Albania and Kosovo, spread stories of his maltreat-

9. Ibid., p. 48.
10. PRO, FO, 371/37144, XC196634, 27 September 1943.

ment of Muslim Albanians in southern Serbia.[11] A British intelligence source had heard rumours from the Partisans that Muharrem Bajraktari was in close contact with Mihailovic, a fact which he had explained by saying that Mihailovic had sent emissaries to him suggesting that they should collaborate against the Partisans, but that negotiations had broken down over the Kosovo issue. The source commented that although clearly eccentric and exceedingly ambitious, Bajraktari should not be dismissed simply as of no political significance. He was better-educated and much more intelligent than most of his countrymen. Above all, he undoubtedly commanded the devoted allegiance of the whole province of Ljuma, which contained thousands of the best fighters in Albania and had great strategic value by virtue of dominating part of the important Shkoder-Prizren road.[12]

According to a report from Istanbul received in London the same month, Bajraktari was maintaining contact with the Serbian Chetniks.[13] As a professional soldier, Colonel Mihailovic was aware of the strategic military value of Kosovo: as a possible key point in an Allied advance through the Balkans, it was a communication line that would be extremely vulnerable if it were not held by the Serbs but, for example, by the Bulgarians or Albanians. So by early 1942 he had established three task forces in the area, covering Metohija, Kosovo and the Ibar river basin. Mihailovic's allegiance was steadfastly to the King and to the Serbian people, but before his struggle was over he had been dismissed by the one and abandoned by the other. Mihailovic gambled all on his belief in an Allied victory, but meanwhile, intent on preserving Serbian lives, he favoured a minimum of fighting against the occupation forces till after the expected Allied landing. While he waited, he sought to liquidate the communists. This led eventually to a complex policy of collaboration involving the British and Americans, the Germans, the Italians, Nedic and anti-communist Albanians.

Throughout the spring of 1942 Partisan operations could not be extended beyond minor acts of sabotage because hundreds of Serbian and Montenegrin members of the NLM had been arrested and deported to concentration or forced labour camps. Many of them were put to work by the Germans in the chrome mines

11. See report on this in the *Sunday Times*, 7 June 1942.
12. PRO, FO, WO204/9536 196824, File 293, 3 September 1944.
13. PRO, FO, 371/ 37144, XC 196634, 27 September 1943.

around Kukes in north-eastern Albania; others escaped and went into hiding. Also, because of such difficult conditions within Kosovo, those who had joined Partisan detachments were compelled to operate outside Kosovo. In order to encourage Albanians from Kosovo to identify with the aims of the liberation struggle, the CC of the CPA and the Regional Committee of the CPY for Kosovo issued a joint proclamation on 4 March 1942, addressed to the Albanians of the region stating that they should not give assistance to the Axis forces but join the Partisan struggle against them. Indeed by the middle of 1942 many Albanians had begun to question the long-term intentions of the occupying forces, especially after the arrival in Kosovo of Nedic's army. The first Albanian Partisan detachment, entitled 'Zejnel Ajdini', was duly formed in September 1942 in the village of Ramnjani between Urosevac and Gnjilane. It comprised around twenty-eight young Albanians from Prizren and Djakovica whose primary task was propaganda work among the Albanian community.

Aside from numerous arrests, the NLM in Kosovo had gradually increased in strength by the summer of 1942 with the setting up of party organisations and military underground units in almost all districts. By August the Party organisation in Kosovo comprised forty-eight party cells with 463 members, 12 per cent of whom were Albanians, the rest Serbs and Montenegrins. The Pristina branch of the CPY Regional Committee now had thrity-five party cells and 275 members, and by September a Kosovo Partisan detachment had been set up as an active unit designed to rally sympathisers to the NLM and recruit directly for the various district organisations. Shortly after the formation of the Partisan-led National Liberation Council (LNC) in Albania in September 1942, the more conservative nationalists, concerned over the growth of the Communist movement, decided to form their own 'National Front', the Balli Kombetar (BK – adherents known as Ballists) led by Midhat Frasheri and Ali Kelcyra. This fiercely anti-Communist, nationalistic resistance movement was totally opposed to the return of King Zog, who had fled Albania after the Italian occupation in 1939, and favoured instead the establishment of a republic within the Axis-imposed boundaries of 1941, which would include Kosovo within Albania. As the BK leaders represented the pre-war social order, they were naturally concerned to protect the social, eonomic and political interests and privileges of the landowning beys. Unwilling to accept the consequences of reprisals, they sought to preserve rather than destroy. Among the BK anti-communist resistance the attitude was 'wait and see'. It concentrated on having a nucleus from which the old order and an ethnically enclosed Albanian state would re-emerge.

Due to the severity of enemy manoeuvres and reprisals, the communist Partisan detachments had to be constantly on the move from one area of Kosovo to another. In April 1943 the delegate of the CPY/CC and of the Army Supreme Command, Svetozar Vukmanovic-Tempo, arrived in Kosovo to set up a general staff for Kosovo instead of the provisional one hitherto in operation. Having proved himself an outstanding leader and organiser, he was appointed by Tito as commander of the National Liberation Army and Partisan detachments in the Kosovo region.[14] He propounded the idea of a Balkan general staff, but it only struck a responsive chord in Albania and not in Bulgaria or Greece: this was because he wrapped it up in much idealistic talk about self-determination. He had become convinced after seeing the situation in Kosovo and in the area around Debar for himself that there was little hope of rallying the Albanian population there to the national liberation cause unless the Albanian National Liberation Council led by the CPA were to play a part there. If the CPY and CPA worked together, and the Yugoslav and Albanian national liberation movements likewise, and if the people could be persuaded that victory in the fight for liberation would win them the right to determine their future national allegiance, a communist-led resistance movement might be kindled even in Kosovo.[15]

Having acquainted himself with the military and political situation in Kosovo, Tempo took a number of measures aimed at stabilising and strengthening the NLM in that part of occupied Yugoslavia. He insisted on strengthening the Partisan detachments in order to engage the enemy more effectively and to link them with their counterparts in neighbouring Serbia, Montenegro, Macedonia and Albania. However, owing to the severity of reprisals by the occupation forces against civilians, such links were not easy to forge or maintain for any length of time. Nevertheless, by May

14. For a detailed account of Tempo's mission see S. Vukmanovic-Tempo, *The Struggle for the Balkans*, London, 1990.
15. R. Hibbert, *Albania's National Liberation Struggle*, London, 1991, p. 24.

1943 the NLM leadership in Kosovo had begun cooperating more closely with military units in Macedonia, Montenegro, Southern Serbia and Albania. Tempo visited Enver Hoxha and the Albanian communist leadership three times in 1943, and the two leaders reached agreement without difficulty over the question of the formation of a Balkan general staff. Their conclusions on the subject – the text of which, according to Tempo, was drafted by Hoxha – required the Albanian LNC to send two detachments to northern Albania to cooperate with the Kosovo forces under Fadil Hoxha, and a further detachment to cooperate with the Macedonian command in the Debar-Kicevo area. The aim was clearly stated to be to mobilise the Albanian masses who, because of their hatred of the Serbs in these regions, were abstaining from the national liberation struggle. It was made equally clear that participation in the struggle would be a guarantee to the peoples of Kosovo that they would decide their future for themselves.[16]

The Slav population of Kosovo gradually began joining the NLM in the spring of 1943. It was the Albanians, however, who had to be recruited before any real progress could be made in Kosovo. In order to entice them to join the NLM, Tempo encouraged the formation of a special Albanian detachment which would wear the national colours of red and black and be under a general staff for Kosovo. Throughout 1943 small-scale Partisan guerrilla activities continued to disrupt economic life in Kosovo as large quantities of ammunition, buried in nearby conduits, were destroyed at Trepca. Drilling machines and electric power stations were also sabotaged, causing frequent breakdowns and interruptions of production. In Prizren district members of the NLM concentrated their efforts on severing telephone lines along the roads from Prizren to Djakovica and Urosevac. During the spring and summer of 1943, the CPY was hard hit not only by the arrest and internment of large numbers of communists, but also by the deaths of several outstanding leaders, including four members of the Bureau of the Regional Committee: Emin Duraku (23 December 1942), Stanko Buric (27 March 1943), Boro Vumirovic and Ramiz Sadiku (20 April 1943).[17] At the end of 1943, the Provincial Committee and the Regional Committees of the CPY and the general staff for Kosovo moved to

16. Ibid., p. 25.
17. *Relationship between Yugoslavia and Albania*, p. 124. *Kosovo Issue - A Historic and Current Problem*, Tirana, 1996, p. 105.

Malesija near Djakovica. They could offer only minimal assistance
to the harrassed settler population there, contacts being rare and
communications maintained mostly by letter.

The Mukje agreement

Meanwhile, the Allies were particularly concerned to unite the
opposing factions and thus avert a fractricidal war in Albania.
Therefore, despite strong protest from the Yugoslavs, they urged
the leaders of the Albanian National Liberation Council and the
Balli Kombetar to meet in August 1943 at Mukje in central Albania. Here an agreement was reached that provided for a joint
Committee for the Salvation of Albania. Both nationalists and
communists were to fight for the liberation of an 'ethnic' Albania,
which would include Kosovo. Although Enver Hoxha and others
within the Central Committee of the CPA believed in reaching
some form of agreement with the Ballists, a disagreement soon
arose over Kosovo's future. The CPY Central Committee, wishing
to encourage division between the different currents of Albanian
politics, intervened to annul the Mukje agreement of August 1943,
which, among other things, had sanctioned the Albanians' right to
self-determination and the creation of a unified Albanian state. The
Yugoslavs strongly objected to the term 'ethnic' Albania and to the
inclusion of Kosovo within a post-war Albania. They therefore sent
Tempo to Albania to bring the Albanian communists into line and
reinforce Yugoslav influence within the LNC. The latter formally
repudiated the Mukje agreement, thus weakening Allied attempts
to maintain unity within the Albanian resistance. The Yugoslavs
also demanded that the Albanian communists dissociate themselves
from their entanglement with the nationalist movement Balli
Kombetar: Tempo warned his Albanian comrades that the Ballists
had adopted the same tactics as the Chetniks in Yugoslavia, namely
avoiding confrontation with the occupier and waiting for the Allies
to land. It was not a good idea, therefore, to plan on setting up a
joint National Liberation Council that included BK.[18]

Both the Albanian and Yugoslav communists believed that they
could solve the problem of Yugoslavia's Albanians amicably once
they had defeated the Axis forces, and the Albanian communists
believed that the future of Kosovo could be decided in a post-war

18. Dragnic and Todorovic, *The Saga of Kosovo*, pp. 151-2.

plebiscite. By this time, it was becoming evident to the the CPY leadership that the issue over the post-war status of Kosovo was likely to become a source of discord between the Albanian and Yugoslav communist parties. So, to rectify the somewhat ambiguous statement on Kosovo made by Enver Hoxha at the 2nd Conference of the Albanian National Liberation Conference at Labinot in September 1943, the CC of the CPY sent a letter to its Albanian counterpart stating it intended to retain its Albanian minority within the new Yugoslavia, which was to be a 'land of free nations'. The letter explained:

> 'Armed struggle against the occupying forces can only be clearly indicative of what the people want in order to forge real democracy and brotherhood of the people, so there is no need to emphasise the fact that such a question cannot constitute a problem where we and democratic anti-imperialistic Albania are concerned. The New Yugoslavia will be a country of free people and there will, therefore, be no place in it for national subjugation of the Albanian minority.[19]

Consequently, there would be no national oppression of the Albanian minority. Twice the Yugoslav communists had endorsed the eventual return of Kosovo, the first time in 1928 at the 4th Party Congress at Dresden and again at the 1940 Party Congress in Zagreb. During the war, however, Tito radically revised the agreed plan for the future of Kosovo. Its right to secede was no longer on the agenda. Only the phrase 'self-determination' was now acceptable.

Following the breakdown of the Mukje agreement, the fragile mutual tolerance that had existed between Ballists and communists quickly evaporated. The refusal of the communists to argue for the return of Kosovo to Albania made it all but impossible for the Ballists to cooperate with the LNC in the resistance movement. The Allies too could not guarantee that Kosovo would be a part of Albania after the war, and this weakened their attempts to maintain unity within the Albanian resistance. When Italy capitulated on 8 September 1943, the majority of the Italian soldiers surrendered to the Germans, who by then had entered Albania from Macedonia and Greece. Italy's collapse brought Kosovo under German administration, and the region consequently underwent a tightening of control. Germany's recognition of Albania's 'neutrality', combined with the various concessions made to the highland leaders, helped prevent

19. V. Dedijer, *Yugoslav-Albanian Relations, 1939-1948*, Belgrade, 1984, pp. 126-7.

the creation of a communist-dominated united front. Germany also managed to ensure the benevolent 'neutrality' of many Ballists, and won the assistance of a considerable number of Ghegs through their support for the inclusion of Kosovo in Albania. Thus it became difficult for NLM activists, who had to be on the move day and night, to make any meaningful contact with the population and explain to them the newly-engineered situation. German propaganda reinforced the notion that the real enemies of all Albanians were the Orthodox Yugoslavs and Greeks, backed by Russia.

The Yugoslav Partisans inherited a substantial quantity of arms from the defeated Italians, and continued to operate from their mountain retreats. Overt supporters of Italy, such as Ferad Drage and his son Ali, now played a less important role. The most important member of the new regency was Mehdi Frasheri, while Rexhep Mitrovica, a well-known representative of the irredentist right wing became Prime Minister. The office of Minister of the Interior was occupied by Dzafer Deva, hitherto district chief in Mitrovica and undoubtedly the most powerful personality in Kosovo. He openly declared himself a friend of Germany, but at the same time was close to British political circles and their intelligence arm. By now almost all Albanians assumed that the Germans would be defeated, and therefore considered the LNC their chief enemy. Dzafer Deva stepped up the overall activities of Balli Kombetar, and created new military formations within it, among them the notorious 'Kosovo Regiment', and set about the military and political mobilisation of the Albanian people.[20] Towards the end of 1943 regular NLA units consisting of Kosovars were being formed in areas outside Kosovo, and in September 1943 the Kosovo battalion named 'Ramiz Sadiku' was formed in the village of Izvor near Kicevo, consisting of some 150 men from Kosovo who had been freed from the German concentration camp near Tirana. The following month saw the formation of the 'Boro Vukmirovic' battalion made up of escapees and prisoners from Tirana and the Porto Romano camp in Durres.

The second Prizren League

The Second Prizren League was organised on 16 September 1943 by Dzafer Deva, the most notorious member of BK, and attended by delegates from all the Albanian territories. In cooperation with

20. *Relationship between Yugoslavia and Albania*, pp. 233-4.

the German occupation authorities, it coordinated the activities of numerous Albanian nationalist movements, and life consequently became increasingly difficult for Kosovo's Slav population whose homesteads were routinely sacked by the '*Vulnetara*'. While the main proponent of violence against Serbs and Montenegrins at that time was BK, its creation, the SS 'Skanderbeg' Division, composed of Albanian soldiers and German officers, and so-called 'village police' units were also involved. The new League claimed to represent all Albanians living in Albania and Yugoslavia, with its main task being to organise the Albanian population to fight against both the Albanian and Yugoslav national liberation movements.

The Anti-Fascist Council of National Liberation, AVNOJ, met in its second session at Jajce on 29 November 1943, and laid the foundations for the post-war federal Yugoslav state. The Yugoslav government-in-exile was divested of all rights and a National Committee of Liberation of Yugoslavia was established as the sole government of the people. AVNOJ acknowledged the multinational nature of Yugoslavia and the vital need to preserve the Yugoslav identity. It was therefore decided that the nations and nationalities comprising it should remain united within the new Yugoslav federation as a community of equal nations and nationalities. Concerning attitudes in Kosovo itself, a British Foreign Office source noted:

> 'It cannot be too clearly emphasised that the dominating factor in
> the attitude of the Albanian population of Kosovo is their fear of a
> return to Yugoslav domination. However, relations between the
> Albanians and the original Serbian inhabitants of Kosovo, i.e. fami-
> lies who had been settled there for 4-500 years, were generally very
> good. The Germans have told the Albanians that they are there as
> friends and liberators and who will protect them from the Serbs; but
> that if the Allies win the war, Kosovo will certainly go back to
> Britain's ally, Yugoslavia. The majority of Albanians in Kosovo will
> have nothing to do with Marshal Tito. He appears to them as simply
> another manifestation of the Serb-Montenegrin menace, and his
> inclination towards Russia and Communism make him appear in
> their eyes simply as a tool of what they call 'Russia's Pan-Slav Impe-
> rialist policy'. The Communists freely admit their unpopularity in
> Kosovo, saying that what little support they enjoyed there came from
> Serb or Montenegrin elements; unquestionably, the most powerful
> group in Kosovo are the Albanian Irredentists, who are violently
> anti-Communist and who have supporters among all the other
> parties and among every class and occupation in the area. The Irre-

dentists do not form a single party, but rather a group, drawing their support from all parties except the Communists.'[21]

The Bujan conference

The activities of the Second Prizren League appear to have seriously upset the plans of the communist forces and the leaders of the National Liberation Movement in Kosovo and Albania. To minimise this organisation's authority, Fadil Hoxha published an article in the newspaper *Lirija* in October 1943 announcing that a national liberation council for these areas would meet to 'ensure us total freedom and independence'. The decision to hold such a conference was made at a meeting of the Council of the Kosovo YCP Provincial Committee at Sharr on 4-6 November 1943.[22] Thus the first conference to set up a National Liberation Committee for Kosovo convened on 31 December 1943 and remained in session till 2 January 1944 in a house in the village of Bujan in the Djakovica highlands on the Albanian border. It was attended by forty-nine communist representatives from Albania and Kosovo of whom forty-three were Albanians, three Serbs and three Montenegrins. At this conference, which was later to cause considerable controversy, delegates of the Albanian and Yugoslav communists invited the Kosovo Albanians to join in the struggle against fascism in the hope that their victory would open the way for unification with Albania. Although the stands taken at Bujan were criticised within the caucus of the CPY even before the end of 1944, they revealed two basic features of the CPY's policy on Kosovo at that time: its desire to have ethnic Albanians from there join the anti-fascist movement and its orientation towards incorporating Albania into Yugoslavia or possibly a Balkan communist federation after the war.[23]

The main objectives of the conference were to strengthen the existing village, local and district national liberation committees and create new ones; to increase political activity among Kosovo's popu-

21. PRO, FO, WO204/9536, 196824, File no. 293, 3 September 1944.
22. F. Rexhepi, *The Struggle of the Albanians of Kosovo and other areas of the Former Yugoslavia for Self-Determination and National Unification during World War II - The Kosovo Issue - A Historic and Current Problem*, Tirana, 1996, p. 105.
23. P. Simic, *The Kosovo and Metojia Problem and Regional Security in the Balkans*, Institute of International Politics and Economics, Belgrade, 1996, p. 9.

lation, especially people of Albanian nationality; and to discourage
the increasing emigration of Serbian and Montenegrin families
from the region. The Bujan Conference appealed in conclusion to
the peoples of Kosovo to unite against the Germans and a Resolution was adopted. This contained a paragraph which caused controversy not only at the conference but in post-war political debates:

> 'Kosovo and the Plain of Dukagjin represent a territory largely
> inhabited by the Albanian people, which still today, as always, wish
> to unite with Albania. We therefore consider it our duty to show the
> correct path the Albanian people must follow in order to realise their
> aspirations. The sole path by which the Albanian people of Kosovo
> and the Plain of Dukagjin can unite with Albania is by a common
> struggle with the other peoples of Yugoslavia against the occupier
> and his lackeys, because this is the only way to win the freedom in
> which all peoples, i.e. the Albanians too, will be able to declare their
> own destiny with the right to self-determination to the point of
> secession.'[24]

Here, explicitly stated in this document, was the acceptance of
the unification of Kosovo with Albania. The CPY and the Yugoslav
Army headquarters were quick to answer. Marshal Tito, secretary-
general of the CPY, and Tempo, his military lieutenant for southern Yugoslavia, both wrote letters that strongly criticised the Bujan
Resolution.[25] Ever since it has been treated by official Yugoslav
historiography as a political blunder: how was such a vague and
ambiguous statement allowed to be included in the final resolution
of this important conference? There are reasons which partly
explain this. There was a certain degree of optimism about the new
era which would follow the war. Fadil Hoxha, at that time member
of the Bureau of the Regional Committee of the CPY and
commander of the General Staff for Kosovo, says in his memoirs that
the question of frontiers was avoided, although no one would
accept the partitioning of Yugoslavia, but every potential Albanian
recruit for the NLM would ask 'What place will my people have in
this?' To this question Hoxha would reply:

> 'I would say we should fight under the leadership of the Communist
> Party of Yugoslavia to liberate this land. Even more definitely it is
> clear that if socialism wins in Albania as well as in Yugoslavia –

Kosovo will be in Albania. This was not my attitude but that of the Regional Committee.'[26]

In 1943, when the question of the future boundary between Yugoslavia and Albania seemed irrelevant, the CPY could afford to be generous in its promises. Albania itself might even be incorporated into Yugoslavia as a separate federal unit. Tito rejected the decisions agreed at Bujan because he believed that they raised issues prematurely which should be dealt with after the war. He knew that the Partisans would lose too many followers if the Albanian demands were met. It was therefore agreed not to alter the pre-war borders of Yugoslavia. Enver Hoxha also agreed that

'...the question of the future of Kosovo and the other Albanian regions in Yugoslavia should not be raised during the war ... that Kosovo Albanians should fight fascism within the framework of Yugoslavia ... that the problem of Kosovo will be resolved after the war by the two sister parties and the Albanian people themselves.'[27]

This document produced immediate unease. The Central Committee of the CPY, in a letter of 28 March 1944 to the leaders of the resistance movement of Kosovo and Metohija signed by Tito's closest aide Milovan Djilas, made an assessment of the first regional conference. It endorsed the orientation of the National Liberation Committee of Kosovo and Metohija, but indirectly criticised the part of the Bujan Resolution which referred to the aspiration of the Albanians from Kosovo and Metohija to join Albania. Similarly a letter had been sent to the CPY's regional committee for Kosovo and Metohija dated 2 October 1943, by Vukmanovic Tempo, who had stayed among the Partisans in Kosovo. He wrote:

'Regarding the question of the future borders between Yugoslavia and Albania, it will be resolved by brotherly agreement and co-operation between the NLM of Yugoslavia and the Council of National Liberation of Albania on the basis of the right of self-determination of nations. How the borders will be drawn will depend on the evolution of the political situation in Yugoslavia and Albania. At present we must not make any definite statements on the issue.'

After receiving a letter from the CC/CPY dated 28 March 1944, the leadership of the resistance movement in Kosovo undertook to amend that part of the resolution of the first conference of its

26. *Relationship between Yugoslavia and Albania*, p. 67.
27. E. Hoxha, *With Stalin*, Tirana, 1981, pp. 137-8.

National Liberation Committee where the problem of the union of these parts with Albania was referred to.[28]

The rights and wrongs of the Bujan Resolution have continued to be bitterly disputed up to the present time, especially among the Albanian diaspora. In a recent debate one Albanian-American, Vasil Camaj, echoed the view of the majority of Kosovars on this subject:

'It is not acceptable to be proud or propagate the political mistakes of the past. This is the case with the overstated propaganda about the Bujan Conference, where I believe, Albanian, Serb and Montenegrin Communists, instructed by Serb anti-Albanian politicians, helped to establish the second occupation of Kosovo and the other Albanian-inhabited regions of Yugoslavia. Who were the traitors? – the Ballists or the Bujan Communists, Fadil Hoxha, Mehmet Hoxha, Ymer Pula, Ali Shukrija, Xhavid Nimani and others like them, who fought for Serb-Montenegrin interests with the Communist star on their caps? In short, the Bujan Conference and the earlier meeting at Mukje in August 1943 were supported by Communist Albanians who set up alliances with Communist Yugoslavs and helped to divide Albanians again.'[29]

In reply, the Albanian-American academic, Sami Repishti, explained that the Bujan Conference was not a political blunder:

'It was politically correct! It was also a sincere effort on the part of many communist-orientated Kosovars and 'nationalists' to bring into the open, through a formal document, the prevailing sentiment among the entire Albanian population of Kosovo, namely, the right to self-determination for all peoples, as promised by the 1941 Atlantic Charter. The fact that the resolution was rejected by Tito, and strongly condemned by the Yugoslav Communist Party – committed to preserving (even extending) the territory of pre-war Yugoslavia – is an indication that the Resolution, in its spirit and its letter, was pro-Albanian and anti-Yugoslav. The dismantling of monarchist Yugoslavia being an act of violence was not accepted by the international community. Consequently, the 'union' of Kosovo with Albania in 1941 was not recognised by the Allies who were winning the war. Then a new group emerged in Kosovo which rejected fascist Italy's (and later Nazi Germany's) policies. They were mostly communists and their sympathisers. Their political programme, namely, an uncompromising war against the fascist invaders, had the full support of the Allies. With war developments favouring the Anti-fascist Coalition, the role of the communists in

28. Marmullaku, *Albania and the Albanians*, p. 144.
29. *Illyria*, 14–16 February 1994, p. 5.

Kosovo became more relevant. Gradually they became the main
political force recognised by the victorious Allies. By fighting against
fascism, they earned the moral right to represent the Kosovar population. And so they did, in the village of Bujan, where the overwhelming sentiment of that population was codified in a clear and
unequivocal statement: union with Albania! With this act, all
sections of Albanian society in Kosovo had reached the same conclusion. Here is the historic importance of the Bujan Resolution.'[30]

In the meantime a source for the British Foreign Office travelled
secretly through Kosovo and Albania during August 1944 and
reported:

'The question of the future status of Kosovo was one of a burning
anxiety in the minds of all – even of people living a long way from
Kosovo, people of such widely differing views as Enver Hoxha,
Mustapha Gjinishi, Ymer Disnica. All agreed on the importance to
Albania of a just settlement of the Kosovo problem – which they all
agreed could only be secured by a return to Albania of Kosovo.
They all implored me to obtain from the Allies a simple declaration,
not that Kosovo would be returned to Albania, but simply that the
future of Kosovo would be settled by a plebiscite held under Allied
supervision in the area; alternatively they requested a declaration
from the Yugoslav government in London that they would consent
to such a plebiscite... King Zog is not popular in Kosovo mainly
because people regard him as a nominee of the Yugoslav government, in exchange for whose support they believe he acquiesced in
the Yugoslav domination of Kosovo. The most outstanding political
figure in Kosovo (in 1944) is Gani Kryezyu, who is very pro-British
and seems a most able and intelligent man. He is one of the very few
people who could possibly weld together a powerful common front
against the Germans in Kosovo.'[31]

The Kryeziu brothers advocated a policy of protracted military
confrontation, for which he sought British support. Gani conducted
dealings with the British in more or less full view of the Partisans.
Therefore, both Enver Hoxha and Tito must have already resolved
that it would be better from their point of view if there were no
resistance in Kosovo rather than a successful one led by Gani
Kryeziu with British support. Thus the Kryeziu brothers' plans
were doomed.[32] British sources claim that the NLC knew that

30. Ibid., p. 5.
31. PRO, FO, WO204/9536, 196824, File no. 293 - 3 September 1944.
32. For accounts of the Kryeziu brothers' dealings with the British see Hibbert, *Alba-
    nia's National Liberation Struggle*, and Julian Amery, *Sons of the Eagle*, London, 1948.

terms like 'Ethnic Albania' and 'Greater Albania' were coined by the
Germans to lure the Albanians into a trap.

> 'What we, the LNC, try to do is to organise Kosovo into battalions
> and NLC brigades to fight the Germans now in cooperation with
> the Yugoslav Partisans whose war is directed against the Germans
> and whose aim is to give freedom to all the various Yugoslav
> peoples. These Partisans will themselves leave Kosovo free to choose
> her own way based on the Atlantic Charter, which has been guaran-
> teed by the U.S.A., U.S.S.R. and Great Britain. This is the only way
> the Kosovo question can be settled and Kosovo be given back to
> Albania.'[33]

The United League of Anti-fascist Youth of Yugoslavia (USAOJ),
at its Second Congress held in Drvar in May 1944, blamed the pre-
war Yugoslav regime for the tense state of inter-ethnic relations in
Kosovo. A letter signed by 1,150 USAOJ delegates stated among
other things:

> 'The anti-people's regimes of the old Yugoslavia, pursuing a criminal
> policy towards our peoples and subjecting the Albanian people of
> our region to the most brutal exploitation and physical extermina-
> tion, deliberately fanned chauvinistic hatred between the Albanian,
> Serbian and Montengrin people of Kosovo.'[34]

Until the first months of 1944 there were continued waves of
migration from Kosovo of Serbs and Montenegrins, forced to flee
following intimidation. It was not possible to organise self-defence
in the settler villages. The 21st SS 'Skanderbeg Division' (consisting, as already mentioned, of two battalions) formed out of Albanian volunteers in the spring of 1944, indiscriminately killed Serbs
and Montenegrins in Kosovo. This led to the emigration of an estimated 10,000 Slav families, most of whom went to Serbia, where
some settlers joined the Partisan forces while a larger number joined
Mihailovic. The Party organisation in Kosovo was considerably
weakened by the departure of the Slav settlers who were replaced
by new colonists from the poorer regions of northern Albania.
Recruitment to the NLM of Albanians thus began on a more
concerted scale. By January 1944 the Party membership for Kosovo
stood at around 400, of whom forty-five were Albanians.[35]

---

33. PRO, FO, WO204 /9536, 196824, 5 June 1944. An extract from an NLC
    document printed in Albania on 9 April 1944.
34. *Relationship between Yugoslavia and Albania*, Belgrade, 1984, p. 129.
35. Ibid., p. 128.

The final stages of the war

As the war drew to an end, the people of Kosovo witnessed the tide turning in favour of the Partisan forces. By the summer of 1944 units of the Yugoslav NLA began advancing from the Sandjak towards Kosovo and southern Serbia. In order to co-ordinate operations throughout this region, Tito sent a directive to the General Staff for Kosovo and Metohija changing its name to the 'Operative Staff for Kosovo and Metohija' on 2 September, 1944 under the command of the General Staff for Serbia. By agreement between the supreme command of the NLA of Yugoslavia and the General Staff of the NLA of Albania, two brigades of the latter crossed into Kosovo in unison with the NLA of Yugoslavia. Official Yugoslav accounts claim that this was done 'in order to promote trust between Albanians, Serbs and Montenegrins, and in any case, was a continuity of cooperation between the liberating armies of the two countries, which had begun as far back as 1942'.[36]

For the majority of Serbs as well as Albanians, the NLAs of both Yugoslavia and Albania now became the enemy. By the end of 1944 Ballists were operating openly in collusion with Draza Mihailovic's Chetniks. In the wake of the euphoria generated at Bujan, there was a great sense of betrayal among the Albanians. Their leaders could not understand why they were not uniting with Albania – to achieve this, after all, was the reason why they had agreed to fight with the Partisans. Those Albanians who had joined the CPY's call to fight fascism had done so in the belief that the CPY would realise the principle of self-determination to the point of secession after the war, as it had promised. In October 1944 the German army began retreating through Kosovo from Greece. The final battles for Kosovo's liberation were fought in October and November 1944, and the whole territory was liberated at the end of November by the victorious Yugoslav Partisans. The settling of accounts with the various collaborationist organisations, especially Balli Kombetar, then numbering around 9,000 men, quickly followed.

The Albanian uprising

Because of their co-operation with the Axis forces, the Kosovars were perceived as politically unreliable and thus a possible threat to

36. Ibid., p. 52.

the stability and territorial integrity of Yugoslavia. Tito realised that only by retaining Kosovo within Serbia's borders could he hope to win over the Serbs to communism. The Partisans therefore launched a large-scale military campaign in the region with the aim of consolidating their rule and dealing with the many suspected collaborators. The campaign was accompanied by the general mobilisation of thousands of Albanians, Serbs and Montenegrins, and their hurried despatch to the front to fight the retreating Germans in the Banat, Srem, Bosnia-Hercegovina, Croatia and Slovenia. Weapons were ordered to be collected together, and prominent Albanians, whose discontent had risen high at their treatment by the Yugoslav army, were arrested. The Kosovars reacted with a general insurrection against the Partisans, supported by remnant bands of Ballists and Chetniks.

The rising began after the Supreme Staff of the NLA and the Main Staff of Serbia ordered some of the Albanian brigades to march northwards. To ensure that this order would be carried out, the 7th Brigade, which included volunteers from Drenica, had been stationed in Podujevo. At this time reports began to arrive in Podujevo about a massacre of civilians in Drenica, and among the victims were said to be members of the families of soldiers serving in the 7th Brigade. The Partisans from Drenica were given permission by the Operational Staff for Kosovo to send a commission to Drenica to verify the report of a massacre, and when the commission delegate arrived in Drenica he found ample evidence that a large number of Albanian civilians had been killed. In the Klina river the population showed the delegates the bodies of some 250 men, bound together in groups of six, from the village of Skenderaj (now known as Serbica), many of whom had been hacked to death with axes. The commission presented its findings to the Staff of the Yugoslav detachments who, instead of taking measures to find the perpetrators of the massacre, opened fire on the commission delegate. Immediately following this incident and for the next two months, the region of Drenica became the scene of extremely bitter fighting.[37]

To suppress the revolt, the Supreme Staff of the NLA sent reinforcements to Kosovo, which was proclaimed a 'military zone' and had its command attached directly to the Supreme Staff of

---

37. For an official Serbian account of the Albanian insurrection of 1944-5 see Spasoje Djakovic, *Sukobi na Kosovu*, Narodna Kniga, Belgrade, 1984.

Yugoslavia. There followed the forced removal of hundreds of young Albanian men to the north of Yugoslavia, initially to form Kosovo brigades but who were subsequently absorbed into Yugoslav military units or into the ranks of the newly-established 'labour brigades'. On 2 December rebels from the Drenica region attacked Urosevac, Gnjilane and the Trepca mining complex. For the next two months these rebels, numbering at the most 2,000 men, resisted some 30,000 troops. In February 1945 the Yugoslav government declared martial law and a military directorate took over the administration and pacification of Kosovo. Although it is not possible to give an exact number of Albanians killed during this revolt, data collected by the National Democratic Committee of Albanians suggests that about 48,000 Albanians died in the six months of fighting. In their absence Serb and Montenegrin military units were brought to Kosovo and presented as liberators. The new military administration re-opened the Trepca mine and the economically vital Kraljevo-Kosovo Polje-Skopje railway line. These 'counter-revolutionary' forces were subdued and only around 200 or so remained in hiding in the remoter parts of Kosovo. The behaviour of these NLA troops towards the Albanians was sharply criticised at the first Congress of the Serbian Communist Party in the spring of 1945.

Although little is known of the political aims of the uprising, the intellectual leader of the rebellion, Imer Berisha, advocated the union of Kosovo and Western Macedonia with Albania. Official accounts spoke of fascists and collaborators being punished, and of the rising being 'a final attempt to raise a counter-revolutionary rebellion by remnants of the Ballists and other pro-fascist forces and a number of Albanians who had deserted from the brigades of the NLA of Yugoslavia and become outlaws'.[38] But what was really happening was a repetition of the hideous massacres that had occurred between Serbs and Albanians after the First World War. One of the worst atrocities occurred in Tivar in Montenegro, where 1,670 Albanians were herded into a tunnel, which was then sealed off so that all were asphyxiated. Kosovo, therefore, emerged from the war into the new Federal Yugoslavia under siege, and with its alienated Albanian population regarded, as in 1918, as a threat to the new state.

38. *Relationship between Yugoslavia and Albania*, p. 53.

8

KOSOVO IN THE NEW SOCIALIST YUGOSLAVIA

Although the civil war from which Yugoslavs emerged was multi-dimensional, all pervasive and brutal, a spirit of idealism prevailed throughout the Partisan higher echelons. Yugoslavia was now clearly the strongest Balkan state - indeed, the leading state outside the Soviet Union in Eastern Europe. It had an impressive army of 800,000 experienced fighters under a purely national command, and a revolutionary regime was in power that apparently had close and friendly relations with Moscow.[1] Flushed with victory, the CPY discussed the future of Kosovo and its status in the new Yugoslavia at the Assembly of National Representatives of Kosovo and Meto-hija held in Prizren in July 1945. Here it was agreed that the region should become a constituent of Federal Serbia. The Prizren Reso-lution boldly pronounced that the situation in Kosovo had calmed down, and that the Albanian population, like all the other peoples of Yugoslavia, had accepted neither the dismemberment of the region by the invader nor the dismemberment of Yugoslavia. It has been consistently and officially maintained that this Resolution, taken by delegates hurriedly assembled shortly after the crushed Albanian insurrection, was the fundamental legal expression of Kosovo-Metohija's 'expressed free will' for union with Serbia and, through Serbia, with the new state of Yugoslavia.[2]

There now followed several political acts aimed at winning over the Albanians to the communist cause. On 6 March 1945 the Ministry of Internal Affairs took a decision to prohibit for the time being an estimated 50-60,000 Serbian and Montenegrin settlers who had fled Kosovo during the war from returning to their homes because they were considered supporters of the pre-war Greater Serbian state. On the other hand, until Tito's split with Stalin in

1. Jelavich, *History of the Balkans*, vol. 2.
2. Pipa, and Repishti, *Studies on Kosova*, p. 209.

1948 the border was open to new immigrants from Albania. During that period an estimated 25,000 of them crossed over into Kosovo to join relatives, thus following a pattern encouraged by both the Italians and the Germans during the war.

This decision represented a step to correct a previous injustice to the Albanians, but it also produced a new injustice to the Serbs. In any case, it constituted an exception in the then legal system of Yugoslavia. At that time Yugoslavia strictly applied the laws on seizure of war profits acquired during enemy occupation and on treatment of property seized from occupiers and their collaborators (dated 24 May 1945) to entire ethnic groups which, like the Albanians, collaborated massively with the occupiers. These measures particularly affected the Germans, Hungarians and Italians (from Vojvodina, Slavonia, Dalmatia and Istria) who were designated as the 'fifth column' and forced to move out of Yugoslavia in large numbers.[3]

The final process of establishing the new Yugoslav Federation was completed that August at the Third Session of AVNOJ, when the Presidency of the Assembly of Serbia passed the Law on the Administrative Division of Serbia into Provinces, whereby the Autonomous Province of Vojvodina and the Autonomous Territory of Kosovo and Metohija were finally established. It is the predominant opinion among Serbian historians that there were at least three motives for the creation of the Autonomous Region of Kosovo and Metohija on 7 August 1945: these were, first, to resolve the status of Albanians in Kosovo; secondly, to make way for the incorporation of Albania into a Yugoslav-dominated communist federation;[4] and thirdly, to create a balance between the Serbs and the other nations of the country based on the Leninist doctrine for resolving nationality questions in multi-national states (the so called 'Weak Serbia - Strong Yugoslavia' policy). In support of this doctrine, the argument most often presented is that such autonomous regions were created only within the territory of Serbia and not within Macedonia and Montenegro, both of which also have areas with Albanian minorities, or indeed within any of the other Yugoslav republics such as Croatia and Bosnia-Hercegovina, also with ethni-

---

3. D. Janjic, *Conflict or Dialogue, Serbian-Albanian Relations and Integration of the Balkans*, Subotica, 1994, p. 136.

4. Tito, with support from the Bulgarian leader Georgi Dimitrov, had plans to set up a Balkan federation which would include Bulgaria, Albania and possibly Greece should the Communist guerrillas win victory there.

cally mixed populations.[5] At first, Tito had wanted to create a Balkan Federation that included Albania and Bulgaria – with Kosovo becoming part of Albania. The purpose of this idea was twofold: for the Yugoslav Communists it was the realisation of their old aspirations to dominate Albania, and for Tito himself it meant the achievement of his personal ambition to become ruler of the Balkans. The Communist leader of Albania, Enver Hoxha, saw the notion of a Balkan Federation differently – as the final unification of Kosovo and Albania through mutual agreement.[6]

The 1946 constitution

The new socialist state was defined by the 1946 constitution, based on the 1936 Soviet constitution, and intended to safeguard the rights of all nationalities and minorities from the political domination of any one ethnic group. In practice, however, it started out with two fundamental flaws in its construction. First, by not granting full territorial autonomy to the Kosovars, the Albanian national question was ignored. Secondly, Vojvodina was granted a higher status than Kosovo by being proclaimed an Autonomous Province with a governmental structure similar to that of a republic. In contrast, Kosovo-Metohija was classified an Autonomous Region with its local administrative units denied any independent decision-making; it had neither an independent legislature nor a supreme court as did Vojvodina. The official justification for this difference in status was that the presence of a greater number of culturally distinct national groups in Vojvodina called for a supreme court. Whereas the constitution of the Republic of Serbia stated that the Republic was created by the will of the people, the allegiance of Kosovo to Serbia was taken for granted. Thus Kosovo joined the new Yugoslav Federation as a mere appendage of Serbia.

The *raison d'être* of the Yugoslav communists was a carefully set balance of power among the peoples and minorities of Yugoslavia over a potential threat of Serbian predominance. The Serbian national question was complicated by the fact that the Serbian republic also contained the vast majority of Yugoslavia's national

5. P. Simic, *The Kosovo and Metohija Problem and Regional Security in the Balkans*, Institute of International Politics and Economics, Belgrade, 1996, p. 9.
6. D. Batakovic, 'The Serbia-Albanian Conflict: An Historical Perspective', in Duijzings, Janjic and Maliqi (eds), *Kosovo - Kosova*, p. 8.

minorities. But the Serbs themselves could not be united in a single republic without infringing the rights of other nationalities. The rights of the individual nations were to be guaranteed as much by the country's federal order as by its unity. Thus, the creation of the two Autonomous Regions of Vojvodina and Kosovo within Serbia was an attempt to solve the Serbian question. The communists did not wish to antagonise the largest ethnic group, the Serbs, or weaken what little appeal they had in Serbia by offending Serbian nationalism, and so a compromise was reached with article 103 of the new constitution whereby the rights and scope of the Autonomous Regions of Vojvodina and Kosovo were to be determined by the constitution of the Republic of Serbia. The constitution failed to elaborate in any detail the exact position of the autonomous units, but merely stated: 'The People's Republic of Serbia includes within its structure the Autonomous Province of Vojvodina and the Autonomous Region of Kosovo and Metohija.' The CPY saw the new constitution as an instrument of individual national equality and of Yugoslavia's unity.

Five nationalities were recognised under the constitution: Serbs, Croats, Slovenes, Montenegrins and Macedonians. Each republic, except Bosnia-Hercegovina, was considered a nation-state in the sense that it served as a rough equivalent of the homeland of the dominant nationality within its boundries. The minorities, however, had a special status and it was clear that the right of self-determination was not intended to apply, even in theory, to them. The basic rights of the minorities were provided for in a general way by Article 13 of the constitution, according to which the national minorities enjoyed the right and protection of their cultural development and the free use of their language. Albanian nationalism was also to be suppressed. The constitutional arrangements concerning Albanian-inhabited territories were decided arbitrarily and without reference to the general population in those areas. As in pre-war Yugoslavia, compact Albanian-inhabited territories were again divided among different administrative units. South-western areas bordering Albania were incorporated into the Republic of Montenegro, while South-eastern areas became part of the Republic of Macedonia. They were not included in the Kosovo Autonomous Region because of the regime's efforts to accommodate Macedonian nationalism, and geographical factors in the shape of the Sar mountains, which form a formidable barrier to communication between the two areas. The constitutionally inferior status of Kosovo, akin to that of the autonomous republics within the union republics in the Soviet model, was aggravated by Serbian domination of the region's political life for the next two decades.

Thus the 1946 constitution unnecessarily fostered a deep resentment among the Albanians, who maintained a hostile stand towards the National Liberation Movement simply because they did not understand the difference between the old and new Yugoslavia. Thus in the difficult period immediately after the war the Albanian nationality remained 'the most hostile element', and in dealing with them the new regime was guilty of extreme measures which at times differed little from those used by the occupation forces during the war. Various Albanian sources estimate that during 1944-6 36,000 and maybe as many as 47,000 Albanians were the victims of systematic mass executions by communists during the days of revolutionary fervour, and later through 'search and destroy' missions, 'pacification', 'disarming', and 'rehabilitation' programmes, police torture, and epidemics of typhoid fever affecting military units.[7] Fearing an outbreak of fresh revolts among the Albanians, the CPY ordered that officials in Kosovo suppress the followers of Balli Kombetar.[8]

The break with Moscow

In the first post-war years the arrogant Yugoslav leadership held themselves and their revolution in such high esteem that it could only be a matter of time before Stalin would become angered by the growing prestige attached to Tito, who toured the other East European People's Democracies extolling the virtues of his regime. The basic issue in the great quarrel of 1948 was simple: whether Tito and his Politburo or Stalin would be the dictator of Yugoslavia. What stood in Stalin's way was Tito's and hence the Yugoslav regime's autonomous strength, based on the uniqueness in Eastern Europe of Yugoslavia's do-it-yourself Communist revolution.[9] The

7. S. Repishti, 'Human Rights and the Albanian Nationality in Yugoslavia', in Oskar Gruenwald and Karen Rosenblum-Cale (eds), *Human Rights in Yugoslavia*, New York, 1986, p. 238.

8. Several Albanians who had been participants in the signing of the Bujan Resolution in 1944 paid with their lives for the ideal of the unification of Kosovo and Albania. Rifat Berisha died fighting in the hills of Drenica in 1948 and Xheladin Hana was murdered by UDBa in 1948.

9. Rusinow, *The Yugoslav Experiment, 1948-1974*, p. 25.

Yugoslavs, albeit unconsciously, challenged and diminished the authority of the October Revolution and the Soviet Union's historical position as the true home of Socialism. Stalin objected to the leading role the Yugoslavs were beginning to play *vis-à-vis* the other Balkan communist movements, especially in Greece where the uprising in 1946 was strongly supported by the CPY. However, it was the plans of Tito and the Bulgarian leader Georgi Dimitrov for a Balkan federation that finally precipitated the open rift in Soviet-Yugoslav relations. Stalin was enraged at such a show of independent foreign policy-making by his client states, and even more by their lack of consultation with him. As a result, Yugoslavia was expelled from the Cominform in June 1948.

One of the many consequences of Tito's break with Stalin was the increased threat posed by Yugoslavia's Albanian population. Enver Hoxha, having foreseen the developing break between Stalin and Tito, decided to throw in his lot with the Soviets, and thus Albania became the first of the communist states openly to attack Tito. The split between Yugoslavia and Albania in 1948, as a result of Yugoslavia's conflict with the Cominform, marked the end of speculations that Kosovo might be unified with Albania. It also halted the immigration of Albanians into Yugoslavia.

In order to dilute the developing national consciousness among Kosovo's large Albanian population, which was growing twice as fast as the Yugoslav average, the government promoted a policy of 'Turkification'. The policy was implemented in two ways: the opening in 1951 of schools teaching in the Turkish language, and again encouraging Albanians to emigrate to Turkey. The concept of a Turkish minority in Kosovo was officially introduced almost immediately after Tito's break with Stalin and Albania's siding with the latter in June 1948. The Cominform split in 1948 raised fears in Belgrade that anti-Yugoslav propaganda emanating from Tirana might have an appeal among Kosovo's Albanians. In order to encourage Albanians to leave, direct pressures were imposed, with the forcing of Albanians to declare themselves Turkish nationals. This created an atmosphere of fear and insecurity; thus many Muslim Albanians registered as 'Turks' to escape persecution, and were quickly shipped to Turkey. The newly-reactivated Yugoslav-Turkish agreement designed to encourage Albanian emigration to Turkey was signed in 1953.

Vasa Cubrilovic, by then a university professor and the most influential figure in the Serbian Academy of Arts and Sciences, once again argued for the expulsion of Albanians from Yugoslavia. In a report entitled 'The minority problem in the new Yugoslavia', addressed to the senior leadership of the National Liberation War including Tito, Milovan Djilas and Alexander Rankovic, he reactivated his pre-war thesis on the necessity of expelling Albanians from post-war Yugoslavia because of the strategic importance of holding on to Kosovo. He wrote:

> 'Kosovo and Metohija have always been considered as a strategic point in the Balkans. Situated in the central part of the Balkans, these areas divide Montenegro from Serbia and these two, in turn, from Macedonia. These lands of the Federative Yugoslavia will never be strongly tied to each other as long as they do not obtain a direct ethnic border. This is a particularly important question for Macedonia. Of the Vardar River, its upper flow is kept by Albanians, while its lower flow is in the hands of Greeks. We, the Southern Slavs, are holding only its middle flow. We must not cherish the illusions as to future development of relations in Europe. This horrendous war will hardly be the last. We will still remain at the crossroads and be exposed once again to the first stroke of some new war.'[10]

Cubrilovic argued that the biggest problem for Yugoslavia was how to break the minority blocks in important geopolitical positions. It was therefore not only Albanians who should be expelled; Germans and Hungarians also came in for attack:

> 'Following that terrible violence, which through the help of native Germans was committed by the Reich Germans over the Slavic lands, the Slavs have every right to demand cleansing of their land from the Volk-Deutschers. The new political border between ourselves and Austria must be an ethnic border between the Slavs and the Germans also. Even now the Soviet Union has been resuming population exchanges begun during the war, by displacing the Poles from the Ukraine and Bjelo-Russia over the new Soviet-Polish border, and bringing from there Ukranians and Bjelo-Russians into the Soviet Union. Referring to those examples, we too will have the right to ask from our allies that our minority question be solved in the same manner, through expulsion. This war and its movements of masses has also created the preliminary psychological mood for expulsions. Our minorities are aware of their deeds, therefore they will not even defend themselves for long if we expel them.'[11]

10. *Kosova Historical Review*, no. 1, Tirana, 1993, p. 39.
11. Ibid., p. 40.

Thus 500,000 Germans were expelled from Yugoslavia after the Second World War without any international reaction.

As a result of Tito's split with Stalin in 1948, the intended Yugoslav annexation of Albania became impossible, and Enver Hoxha became his most virulent opponent in the communist world. There followed a thorough purge of the pro-Yugoslav faction inside the Albanian Party, and this combined with a general persecution of all those among the general population with any Yugoslav connections, resulting in some 5,000 Albanians seeking refuge in Kosovo. Up to 1948, the ideological bond uniting Yugoslavia and Albania left the Kosovo question out of their respective agendas, but after Yugoslavia's expulsion from the Cominform, Tirana was encouraged to reactivate the 'unsettled' question of Kosovo. With Stalin's backing, the Albanian news media reported extensively on the 'persecution' of Albanians in Yugoslavia, whom it urged to 'overthrow' Tito.[12] A secret document from the British embassay in Belgrade at the end of October 1949 reported on the alleged activities of anti-Hoxha Albanian Committees in Yugoslavia, and recent speeches by Enver Hoxha also threw light on the subject. Speaking in Shkoder on 15 September 1949, he alleged that Tito was 'harbouring and feeding war criminals in Skopje and Pristina' for purposes 'well known to the Albanian government.' Although the activities of his enemies were like the 'blind leading the blind',[13] he added that Tito had prompted the escape from Albania of a few dozen enemies of little intelligence, enrolled them into diversionary bands in Yugoslavia and sent them back over the Albanian frontier to stir up trouble; some of these bands had 'repented' and revealed 'the despicable aims of the Titoists'. Others had succeeded in murdering 'some of our comrades, such as the great patriot Bardok Biba'.[14]

Social developments; cross-border Albanian relations

In the years immediately after the war, the foundations were laid for a gradual process of socio-economic development in Kosovo which, as in much of the rest of the Balkans, was devastated by the effects

12. *Zeri-i-Populit*, Tirana, 25 September 1949, p. 1.
13. For Hoxha's account of his relations with the Yugoslav regime see E. Hoxha, *The Titoites*, Tirana, 1982.
14. PRO, FO, 371/78217, 21 October 1949.

of the war. With more than 70 per cent of the region's meagre industry destroyed and not a single kilometre of road asphalted, enormous efforts were needed to repair the economy and create the material and social conditions that would stimulate development. The new regime set about forging a new 'Yugoslav' rather than nationalist dimension to popular folk mythology – based on the uniqueness of the Partisan revolution.

Thus, with the establishment of a socialist society in Yugoslavia, the Kosovo myth gradually lost its pertinence.[15] No more was Tsar Lazar's sacrifice lauded publicly; instead, commemoration of the Battle of Kosovo was strictly consigned to low-profile ceremonies in the Serbian Orthodox Church, which also lost its public prominence. New myths were created and celebrated, aided and abetted by the government's ideologues and survivors of the war, originating from the liberation struggle of the Yugoslav Partisans. For many years after the war the famous Partisan victory at the battle on the Sutjeska was revered as a kind of Yugoslav Kosovo.[16] To counterbalance the atmosphere of bitterness and revolt in Kosovo, the Yugoslav authorities gradually opened Albanian-language schools and encouraged the printing of a bi-weekly Albanian newspaper, *Rilindja* (Awakening). Thousands of Albanian children enrolled in school for the first time. Education in their mother-tongue, denied by previous regimes, was perceived as a national victory and the best way to preserve the region's Albanian national character. This conviction remained a permanent feature of Albanian thinking in the years to come.[17]

The 1948 Yugoslav census showed over 73 per cent of the 750,483 Albanians in Yugoslavia to be illiterate. The few who could read and write did so in the Serbian Cyrillic alphabet and knew nothing of their own alphabet. The new state not only opened schools for Albanian children – 157 between 1945 and 1950 – but provided courses for illiterate adults. A campaign was simultaneously waged against 'backwardness'; this, according to a contemporary official handbook, was 'to free the Shqiptar woman from prejudice (in the first place strip the veils which cover her eyes and face) and give her equal rights which will enable her to go to school, thus better fulfilling her role as a mother and making it

15. T. Emmert, *Serbian Golgotha: Kosovo 1389*, East European Monographs, no. CCLXXVII, New York, 1990, p. 140.

16. T.A. Emmert, 'The Kosovo Legacy', *Serbian Studies*, vol. 5, no. 2, 1989, p. 28.

17. S. Repishti, 'Human Rights...', p. 239.

possible for her as a woman to come into contact with people and assume public and social functions'.[18] The campaign to raise literacy levels was severely hampered by the acute shortage of teachers who could provide instruction in Albanian; except for the very few Albanians who had formerly attended Serbian schools, virtually no member of Yugoslavia's Albanian community could do so. It was therefore an urgent priority to train the first batch of Albanian school teachers. As regards higher education, there were naturally very few highly qualified educational experts among the Albanian population. By 1950 twenty Albanian students had registered at the Faculties of Philosophy and Natural Sciences in Belgrade, while the Pedagogic School enrolled forty-one Albanians. Scholarships were also awarded to encourage Albanians to register at high schools.[19]

Numerous cultural and educational societies, theatres and reading rooms were set up in the post-war years for Kosovo's Albanian population, and represented the first serious attempt to form an Albanian national culture in Yugoslavia. In 1950 Kosovo had 258 such societies with 3,150 members.[20] One such in Prizren, called '*Agimi*' (Dawn), had its own string orchestra, a drama group, a choir and a folk-dancing group. Another prominent society, the '*Meto Bajraktari*' from Pristina, gave sixty-four performances in 1950. The drama sections of these cultural societies had the dual function of laying the foundations for a new theatrical Albanian art and exerting an educational influence on the Albanian population as a whole. Albanian amateur theatres emerged in Prizren, Pec and Mitrovitsa, followed soon afterwards by the first professional groups; the Albanian National Theatre in Pristina, pioneer theatres in Mitrovica, Pec and Prizren, and a marionette theatre which gave performances both in Serbo-Croat and Albanian. They also gave performances in Belgrade to wide acclaim.[21] By 1951 Albanians emerged further

18. L. Stojkovic and M.Martic, *National Minorities in Yugoslavia*, Belgrade, 1952, p. 124.
19. Ibid., pp. 128-9.
20. These were modelled on cultural and educational societies formed by Albanians living in Istanbul and Bucharest in the second half of the nineteenth century. For a detailed account of Albanian cultural developments under Ottoman rule, see Stavro Skendi, *The Albanian National Awakening*, Princeton University Press, 1967.
21. Stojkovic, and Martic, *National Minorities in Yugoslavia*, Belgrade, 1952, pp. 130-1. For an enthusiastic review of the Pec theatrical group's performance of Molière's comedy *Les Fourberies de Scapin*, see *Borba*, 11 November, 1951.

on to the Yugoslav cultural scene at the festival of Yugoslav National Dances and Songs held in Opatia, with dancers from the remote mountain region of Rugovo near Pec performing their characteristically wild dances, using curved Turkish daggers, to an enthusiastic audience; they also appeared at that year's Edinburgh Festival. Thus the cultural horizons of both the Slavs and Albanians of Kosovo were being gradually widened.

Apparently there was much crossing of the Yugoslav-Albanian border in this period. After the break with Stalin, with the new international political threat and ideological disintegration within the country, the work of the State Security Service (UDB-a – Uprava Drzavne Bezbednosti) increased. In Kosovo it persecuted remnants of Ballist bands, but also concerned itself with Albanians as a whole, who were now seen as ideological enemies harbouring spies infiltrated from Albania. Ever since the suppression of the Kosovo rebellion in 1945, the Albanian National Democratic Committee had continued to work clandestinely for the liberation of Kosovo and its unification with Albania. The illegal organisation had a dense network of members from all the Albanian-inhabited regions of Yugoslavia. In the late 1950s the Yugoslav authorities uncovered it, and many of its members were killed or sentenced to several years' harsh imprisonment. In 1957 the intellectual Zekeria Rexha was arrested and deported to Albania. On 25 September in that year, the Albanian government requested Belgrade to extradite certain persons regarded as 'criminals' by the Albanian state who had taken refuge in Yugoslavia since the war, including Cen Elezi and Dan Kalloshi, alleging that they were 'carefully organised with hostile, if well known, aims against the interests of Albania'; Fikri Dine and Muharem Bajraktari were mentioned as other members of this 'group of spies'. However, it appeared that Dine and Bajraktari were not working for the Yugoslavs but for the Albanian Committee (formed by exiled BK and pro-Zog Legaliteti members) in Paris.[22]

Such allegations by Tirana were repeated with monotonous regularity. On the Yugoslav side the British had so far been able to find only one piece of positive evidence of the existence of Albanian refugee organisations in Yugoslavia. In October 1949 the newspaper *Borba* had reported the existence of a group of seventy Albanian political refugees who had formed a '*Koci Xoxe*'[23] work-

---

22. PRO, FO, 371/78217 10197, 21 October 1949.
23. Koci Xoxe had been Albania's Interior Minister until his 'trial' for pro-Titoist sympathies and execution in May 1949.

ing brigade and were then building a dam on the Moracha river in Montenegro. Some of these people, after escaping across the frontier, had apparently been working in Montenegro and Hercegovina on their own account before being organised into a brigade. At the same time the Albanian press published evidence of moves from Yugoslavia to Albania. In September 1949, the newspaper *Bashkimi* printed an article by a Yugoslav refugee, Pero Jovanovic, and a speech at a Youth Congress by Xhafer Vokshi, described as President of the anti-Tito Youth Organisation in Kosovo. The Cominform press had also given details of the recent arrest of four anti-Titoist workers in Kosovo.[24] The armed resistance of outlaws and their aids proved that a large amount of war material was still in private possession. When an extensive operation for the collection of these weapons was carried out in the winter of 1955-6, Serbs and Albanians suffered equally, though more weapons were found in Albanian than in Serb houses.

Belgrade continued to exploit the rupture between Yugoslavia and Albania by arresting thousands of Albanians, who were accused of being 'Stalinists'. This mainly affected the few Albanian intellectuals, who were regarded with deep suspicion and deemed a security risk to the country. However, it was not only Albanians who felt persecuted in Kosovo. The UDB-a continually arrested and harrassed Serbian Orthodox monks and priests, whose church came under attack as ecclesiastical lands were incorporated in the new agrarian reforms and monastic property was confiscated. In 1950 a large Orthodox church in Djakovica was destroyed to make way for the construction of a memorial to the Partisans. In the light of all this, the new 1953 Yugoslav constitutional law made a subtle change from the 1946 federal constitution. The Federation no longer referred to the institution of autonomy as a federal matter, and the constitutional powers of Vojvodina and Kosovo were thus delegated for the future to the constitutional-judicial system of the People's Republic of Serbia. With the abolition of the Yugoslav government's Chamber of Nationalities the same year, the significance of the two autonomous areas was reduced even further, as they became merely no more than ordinary districts of Serbia. But, even the Republics had little real autonomy at this time as Yugoslavia repressed not only Albanian but all other national aspirations through a strong centralist administration. Not surprisingly this

24. PRO, FO, 371/78217, 21 October 1949.

renewed dominance by the Serbs over Kosovo was also reflected in Party membership: in 1958 Serbs and Montenegrins jointly comprised 27.4 per cent of the population of Kosovo, but 49.7 per cent of local Party membership.

In the latter half of the 1950s nationally-related tensions, at first economically conditioned, began to be felt among the individual Yugoslav republics. The separate power centres of the Communist leadership had an impact for the first time in the individual republics whose economic interests had come to coincide with those of the population, including the non-communists. An example was the general dissatisfaction in Slovenia over large funds being channelled from this relatively developed republic via the federal budget to the less developed parts of the federation. The uncertainty of the Party in the face of the revival of national movements and conflicts caused it to look for theoretical concepts that might resolve these contradictions in the multinational state of Yugoslavia. It was felt that somehow a 'Yugoslav consciousness' had to be created, which could appeal to both patriotic and ethnic feelings. In 1957 Edvard Kardelj attempted to direct this search into politically acceptable channels. In a foreword to the second edition of his work on the Slovenian national question, which he had written before the Second World War, he advocated a socialistically determined 'Yugoslavness' (*Jugoslovenstvo*) that would form a 'consciousness' above the national feelings of the different peoples of Yugoslavia.[25]

As the trend towards regional interests became increasingly identified with the national interests of each republic's nominal nation, the CPY launched a campaign of 'Brotherhood and Unity', to encourage a patriotic Yugoslavism. There followed a review of the minority question by the Executive Committee of the Serbian Party in 1959, after which the status of the minorities was officially upgraded by referring to them as 'nationalities'. In the spirit of this new policy of fostering national harmony, it became the Yugoslav strategy that minorities could serve as a bridge between countries rather than being the source of conflict as in the past. Kosovo therefore found itself being promoted as such a 'bridge' between Yugoslavia and Albania. This policy made little headway till the late 1960s, for after Stalin's death in 1953 and the détente of 1955 between Tito and Khrushchev, the other Socialist countries began

25. Viktor Meier, 'Yugoslavia's National Question', *Problems of Communism*, March/April 1983, p. 51.

normalising relations with Yugoslavia – Albania alone stubbornly resisting this process. Consequently Belgrade seized the opportunity to crush any Kosovar dissident movement and the Albanians suffered renewed pressures of assimilation and de-nationalisation:

> 'The Albanian language was denied equal status with Serbo-Croat.
> The display of any Albanian national symbols and flags, and the commemoration of Albanian national holidays were prohibited.
> Also, the teaching of Albanian history, traditions and literature was considered a nationalist deviation.'[26]

In the midst of this repression, on 1 May 1956 four Albanian youths displayed the Albanian national flag in the town of Djakovica. This overt display of the flag, the first since December 1944, was an eloquent expression of Albanian alienation from Yugoslav society. Over the next few months Albanian national flags were secretly unfurled over government buildings and schools, and at night on trains travelling all over Yugoslavia. During the summer there were scores of trials of Albanians accused of flag-raising and nationalist agitation. Using the pretext of suppressing Albanian irredentism, the security police responded by putting further pressure on Albanians to emigrate, and between 1954-7 some 195,000 left for Turkey. At the same time, the UDB-a stepped up its campaign to confiscate weapons belonging to the Albanian population of Kosovo, affecting wide-spread resistance. For every Albanian the worst year of the post-war period was agreed to have been 1956, the year of 'collecting of arms,' when every Albanian household was estimated to own a gun and the police demanded from each house that a gun be handed in.[27] That year also saw a massive exodus to Turkey, and in the same period, a second powerful wave of colonisation took place in Kosovo as Serbian and Montenegrin families were encouraged to settle there. They came to take jobs in state-administrative departments, social institutions, public services and medical and cultural institutions. These new arrivals were mainly from South Serbia, Plava, Gucia, and the Podgorica region.

After the break with Moscow, Kosovo was considered too vulnerable a site for the construction of major industrial projects. But because the area was rich in mineral resources, investments were primarily concentrated in the extractive industries, making Kosovo

---

26. A. Hadri, *The National and Political Development of Albanians in Yugoslavia*, Zagreb, 1970. vol. 1, p. 551.
27. M. Moats, 'Yugoslavia Lost', unpubl. ms., 1996, p. 192.

essentially a supplier of raw materials to the wealthier parts of Yugoslavia. Kosovo contained a half of Yugoslavia's coal reserves and, as well as having sizeable chrome, lead, zinc and other deposits, it contained the largest lignite basin in Europe. The decisions made in Belgrade on Kosovo's economic policy were politically motivated, and as a result the region failed to develop a diversified economy. From 1957 significant amounts of capital were transferred from the developed regions to the less developed such as Bosnia, Macedonia, Montenegro and Kosovo. At first, these transfers were in the form of compulsory plan allocations, but the 'reform' of 1965 abolished the central investment fund and replaced it with the Federal Fund for the Accelerated Development of the Underdeveloped Regions. This fund received 1.85 per cent of each republic's gross social product for exclusive redistribution to the less developed regions. Kosovo received more than 40 per cent of these resources, which provided more than 70 per cent of the province's investment capital and about 70 per cent of its budget in 1971-5.[28]

Post-war government policy, in which speedy industrialisation was a first priority, produced rapid urbanisation throughout Yugoslavia, though less so in Kosovo and Macedonia. Additional factors were rural over-population together with educational and work opportunities in the towns. Whole Albanian *zadrugas* moved to the outskirts of towns and cities, and would occupy a number of neighbouring properties. In Kosovo's newly-urbanised areas, Albanians bought their land and built their own houses, whereas Slavs usually occupied state-owned property. Among the Albanians of Kosovo the blood-feud was still widely practised as the conservative family heads saw no other way of preserving the honour of either an individual man or of his family. In 1958 the young dissident Kosovar writer Adem Demaci published, in his novel *Serpents of Blood*, a powerful condemnation of the vendetta, the cruel social vice that haemorrhaged his own people, and of a society that did little if anything to stop it. The entire narative is imbued with love for his countrymen. Only one character - a young man who breaks the rules of patriarchal life with a decision to 'see the world' outside the cocoon in which he lives - is aware of the dangers of the suffocating air breathed by his people and makes an effort to throw off the chains of servitude. For Demaci, this character was the only hope for his countrymen's future, representing the new man, the new

28. M. Baskin, 'Crisis in Kosovo', *Problems of Communism*, March/April 1983, p. 65.

society, and a new mentality of enlightenment, tolerance and love of one's neighbour. The novel was an instant popular and literary success, and even received an award, before it came under official condemnation. Unable to publish in his own country and without work, this promising writer took to opposition politics, which in Yugoslavia inevitably led to prison.[29]

Traces of the earlier Christian faith were still to be seen in Kosovo during the 1960s. Periodically (always on a Friday) Albanian Muslims would descend from their hills to visit a Serbian monastery – the men wearing white skullcaps called *plis* and white serge trousers braided with black lace, followed by the women, who no longer wore veils – and their children. They then waited for the priest to admit them. This was done out of reverence for the Holy Mother, a saint whose icon was in the church, or some Serbian king sanctified in the monastery; they were known to help where Mohammed had failed. 'No wonder', a Serbian priest commented after one such visit; 'they were Christians once.' At this time it was also not unusual to see Albanians visiting their Christian friends on Christian holidays and joining in dancing and feasting (wine and pork were avoided), or attending weddings and baptisms.[30]

The majority of Albanians in the 1950s and 1960s lived a marginal existence of harsh poverty. Whole families would walk miles to market and try to sell perhaps one wheelbarrow-full of vegetables or lime. Every autumn Kosovar men would drift north to find work in Belgrade and other northern Serbian towns, and through the winter months they could be seen trundling along the roads carrying their light bow-saws, axes and little folding trestles in search of work as wood-cutters. Poverty and lack of education had hindered Kosovo's embryonic cultural development, but in the period 1956-60 a new generation of young Albanian authors began publishing – in Albania itself at this time, creative writing had all but vanished under the heavy hand of Stalinism. Among the leading prose writers of this first wave were Agim Gjakova (b.1935), Kapllan Resuli (b.1935), also known as Kallushi, Adem Demaci (b.1936), Anton Pashku (b.1938), Azem Shkreli (b.1938) and Ramadan Rexhepi (b.1940). However, life for the handful of Albanian intellectuals in Kosovo was not much easier than in Albania. The Serbian authorities still fiercely opposed all progress in education and

29. S. Repishti, 'Human Rights...', pp. 250-1.
30. Dragnich and Todorovich, *The Saga of Kosovo*, p. 51.

culture for the Albanian minority, and in particular targeted intellectuals who, as in Albania, presented the greatest threat to those in power. Tragically, this first generation, who might have laid the foundations for writing in Kosovo, was annihilated politically before it could give birth to a new written culture. Of the six writers mentioned above, only two, Anton Pashku and Azem Shkreli, survived unscathed. Adem Demaci was imprisoned by the Serbian authorities in 1958, Ramadan Rexhepi fled to Sweden, and Agim Gjakova and Kapllan Resuli made the bitter mistake of fleeing to Albania, where Resuli was soon in prison. Demaci, who later came to be referred to as Albania's Nelson Mandela, was arrested for criticising the expulsion of hundreds of thousands of Albanians to Turkey on the pretext that they were Turks.[31]

The 1963 constitution

Yet another new Yugoslav constitution was promulgated in 1963. It stressed the principles of constitutionalism and legality, and redefined the original right to exist of the Autonomous areas; for the first time the Republics were given the right to establish new Autonomous units and so eliminate existing ones. Thus the Autonomous units ceased to be constitutive elements of the Federation, and their very existence became a Republican perogative. Although this constitution did not basically change the foundations or the status of autonomy of Kosovo or Vojvodina, it was widely criticised for not being as clear about the guarantees of autonomy as the 1946 constitution had been. It introduced the term 'nationality' to replace the term 'national minority' previously used. Thus it was hoped to emphasise that the national rights of the nationalities were not reduced to classic national rights but that the nationalities belonged to the country and community in which they lived. The 1963 statute of Kosovo-Metohija changed the 'Regional Council' to the 'Provincial Assembly', an upgrading to the status enjoyed by Vojvodina. A section of Serbia's supreme court was also established in Pristina; hitherto, there had been one for Vojvodina

31. In 1964 Demaci was sentenced to a further fifteen years for allegedly organising a Kosovo national liberation movement. In a mock trial in 1976 he was sentenced once again to fifteen more years in prison where he remained till 1990 as one of Yugoslavia's most prominent political dissidents. R. Elsie, *History of Albanian Literature*, vol. II, New York, 1995. pp. 623-5.

but not for Kosovo, where this function had been exercised by the supreme court of Serbia. Kosovo-Metohija was also now entitled to send five representatives to the Federal Chamber of Nationalities, having previously been entitled only to four representatives compared to Vojvodina's six. Nonetheless, this increase in representation failed to bring about a greater degree of devolution for the Province.

The 1963 constitution inaugurated the trend of polycentrism, with the Republics as the essential components of the Federation. Unlike the 1946 constitution, which recognised the original right of existence of the Autonomous provinces, it transferred to the socialist republics 'the right to establish autonomous provinces in areas with distinctive national characteristics, or other distinguishing features, on the basis of the expressed will of the population of these areas' (Article 111). Thus the status of the Autonomous provinces was demoted. From constituent elements of the Federation constitutionally recognised, they became 'socio-political communities within the republic [of Serbia]' (Article 112) or 'juridicial creations' of the Republican constitution.[32] Although Kosovo was earmarked for special treatment under the 1957-61 'Social Plan for Economic Development', differences in *per capita* income, social services and job opportunities continued on account of the almost total centralisation of resource allocation. In 1953 the *per capita* social product of Slovenia was 182 per cent of the countrywide average compared to 52 per cent for Kosovo which, according to one foreign observer, had become 'a colonial dependency ruled, neglected and exploited by Serbs.'[33]

An English visitor in the mid-1960s was reminded by Kosovo's 'bustle and dust and high population' of the Central Provinces of India.[34] He decribed Kosovo as 'parched and dry in summer', particularly in the eastern part so that there was much emphasis on installing a comprehensive irrigation scheme.[35] In the countryside barefoot Albanian shepherd boys sat by the roadside playing their little wooden flutes. Pristina was still full of horses and carts. When two cars by chance appeared together in Marshal Tito Street, a teenager was heard to raise the sardonic cry 'Look!

32. Pipa, and Repishti, *Studies on Kosova*, p. 202.
33. D. Rusinow, *Kosovo: The Other Albanians*, American Universities Field Staff Reports, no. 5, 1980, p. 13.
34. B. Aldiss, *Cities and Stones: A Traveller's Yugoslavia*, London, 1966, p. 177.
35. Ibid., p. 179.

London!'[36] Prizren was now a quiet little town of 26,000 inhabitants, its narrow streets cluttered with hanging washing and strings of drying peppers. On market days the Serbs drove in carts with husband and wife side by side, while the Albanian ones contained men and boys sitting tightly packed.

> 'Even discounting market days, Prizren was still, as in the past, full of a variety of colourful costumes. For women baggy trousers were commonplace, and the costume that pads the hips, and dashing long silk pants with embroidered cuffs at the ankle; while among the men the best showing was made by lanky Albanians with their white wool trousers and jackets braided with black. Although the veil had been banned by law ten years before, in 1955, statutes had small power over custom, and one still came across even tiny girls who covered the lower part of their faces with a hand or an arm if anyone looked at them.'[37]

The colourful bustle of Prizren was in dramatic contrast to the loneliness of the monastery of Pec. Now that the Patriarchate was in Belgrade, few candles burned any longer in the nest of churches, and the grounds were tended by an ever-dwindling band of sisters.[38]

The removal of Alexander Rankovic

As the participation of Albanians in the political life of the Province increased, so too did the distrust of them by the security forces because of their continually perceived political unreliability. Many were proclaimed enemies of Yugoslavia and socialism. Many Albanians were arrested in the early 1960s. In the years 1948-60, 675 agents were smuggled into Kosovo from Albania, and 115 of them were tried in Yugoslav courts.[39] Alexander Rankovic, Vice President of Yugoslavia, had been a committed proponent of Serbo-centralism. He had direct responsibility for the security police, the UDB-a, and its operations were never exposed to supervision or review because of his political standing. He was thus able to fashion UDB-a into a strongly centralised organisation based largely in Serbia and manned mainly by Serbs. The Sixth Plenum of the Serbian Party Central Committee held in September 1966, issued a condemna-

36. Moats, 'Yugoslavia Lost', p. 152.
37. Aldiss, *Cities and Stones*, p. 187.
38. Ibid., p. 193.
39. *Borba*, 1 June 1961.

tion of 'certain sections of the State Security apparatus for discriminatory and illegal practices entirely contrary to the League of Communists of Yugoslavia's (LCY) programme and the Yugoslav Constitution', especially in relation to the Albanians.

An inter-party squaring of accounts ended with the replacement of Rankovic and his associates for clandestine and illegal activities, at the Fourth Plenum of the Party's Central Committee held on the Brioni islands in 1966. The purge of Rankovic followed revelations that he had ordered the bugging of Tito's conversations as well as those of other Yugoslav leaders. These developments marked a fresh consolidation of Tito's personal power, which had been threatened by the omnipotent State Security Service. Tito purged UDB-a of cadres loyal to Rankovic and initiated the country's further decentralisation. The Brioni Plenum, reviewing conditions in Kosovo, warned of 'Greater Serbian' tendencies within the ranks of the League of Communists; this was viewed as a potential stimulus to 'Greater Albanian' separatism. At Brioni, the political principles of decentralisation, republican/provincial parity in federal-level decision-making bodies, and ethnic affirmation within the Republic and Provinces were accompanied by the increasing dispersion of economic decision-making power to those entities.[40] Thus Brioni, which brought to light the worst excesses of the security forces, ended Rankovic's personal rule over Kosovo and humiliated and humbled the UDB-a. The Plenum also claimed to have adopted measures that would 'eliminate the consequences of the earlier deformations and create new conditions for the many-faceted affirmation of Albanian nationality'.

For the Albanians of Kosovo, therefore, the removal of Rankovic was a milestone in their campaign for the assertion of their national rights. As a result of the severe criticism of the police role in Kosovo, an emigrant from Albania was appointed chief of police in Kosovo. Other non-Serbs too celebrated Rankovic's departure: in Vojvodina there erupted a 'spontaneous and lively mass celebration' among Hungarians and among the Croats there was a 'euphoric atmosphere' as they almost universally interpreted it as a victory for Croatian interests. For the Serbs, however, the affair was viewed as an attack on the Serb nation and its position in Yugoslavia. The investigations which followed the removal of Rankovic revealed the widespread abuses and discrimination carried out against both the

40. Baskin, 'Crisis in Kosovo', p. 70.

Albanian and Hungarian minorities. Not one Albanian or Hungarian had been employed by the Republican Secretariat for Security affairs in Serbia, not one in Vojvodina, and only one Albanian in Kosovo-Metohija.[41] The London *Times* reported: 'The almost daily disclosures of brutal acts of repression, murder and torture by members of Rankovic's police against the Albanian minority there...to intimidate that minority, are astonishingly frank.'[42]

Such disclosures produced a political catharsis, bringing to the surface the emotions of the local population silenced since 1945. It eliminated the inferiority complex imposed on Albanians, and afforded them the benefit of expression. As Rankovic's power base was eroded and the nature of his policies became widely known to the Albanians, they began to agitate for reform. The limited measures of liberalisation which followed Rankovic's dismissal were used by the Albanians to begin pressing for greater autonomy. Rezak Salja, the Kosovo Provincial Prosecutor, even went so far as to call for a separate republic for the Albanians of Yugoslavia, which would have the rights of self-determination and secession.[43] Although Tito backed some measure of reform in Kosovo, he was still adamantly opposed to granting the province the status of a republic. He argued realistically that republican status alone would not solve Kosovo's problems, which could only be overcome if the Province exercised its rights more fully. However, once the majority of Kosovars became fully aware of the extent of Serbian dominance over the governmental, Party and security apparatus in Kosovo, their resentment intensified. There followed a purge of the secret police, a freeze in the process of Turkification, and especially an Albanian-sponsored drive for an ambitious educational and cultural development of the Province.

As if wishing publicly to reaffirm the decisions taken at Brioni and instill confidence in the promised political and social changes, Tito embarked in 1967 on his first-ever visit to Kosovo. An English visitor described the excitement and manic preparation for the visit:

'Suddenly there were workmen all over Pristina painting, tacking up, tearing down, kneeling here and there along Marshal Tito Street in ones and twos, filling in gaps among the cobbles, all in a bitter March wind. By then it was no longer a joke when people said,

41. S.L. Burg, *Conflict and Cohesion in Socialist Yugoslavia*, Princeton University Press, 1983, p. 66-9.
42. *The Times*, 22 September 1966.
43. *Borba*, 7 December 1968.

"Tito must be coming!" "Yes, Tito is coming", people said after hearing details of the visit on television. A member of the Kosovo League of Communists explained that this visit was an 'historic moment for Kosmet'. Tito had never been to Kosmet. Tito, who so often made tours in the six Republics. It seemed incredible that he had never been to us, only six hours away by train, much less on his special "blue train".'[44]

Flags and banners proclaiming 'LONG LIVE TITO OUR DEAR CONSCIENCE AND LEADER OF THE LEAGUE OF COMMUNISTS!' decorated the city streets. After Pristina Tito took the road south to Metohija. At Pec he ate with the Albanian tribesmen of Rugovo, sitting crosslegged on a blanket out in the mountain air, where he was offered 'bread, salt and our hearts', the traditional Balkan welcome. There had been some surreptitious talk about taking into temporary custody some Albanian youths along the route of the blue train, but commenting on the security precautions for Tito's visit, one of the journalists at Radio Pristina had said that for the first time ever Serbian extremists had been taken into custody. 'What they have to worry about from now on, after Brioni, are the Serbs and Montenegrins here in Kosovo, not the Albanians.'[45]

By removing police pressure and giving more concessions to the Albanians to secure their allegiance to Yugoslavia, the government was unwittingly encouraging the Kosovars to become more conscious not only of their national rights but also of their Albanian culture. The floodgates were now opened to a powerful revival of Albanian nationalism. At Pristina University some students wore lapel-pins commemorating the centenery of Karl Marx's birth, but most of the Albanian students wore ones of the great fifteenth-century Albanian national hero, Skanderbeg. The five-hundredth anniversary of his death fell in 1968. The pins, as well as Skanderbeg cognac, had been imported from Albania. A symposium on the hero was held in Pristina, following one in Tirana. Albanian-language paperbacks started to pour off the presses from Pristina's printing house Rilindja. Many were reprints from Tirana: instant best sellers with titles like *History of the Albanian Alphabet* or *Towards a Purification of the Albanian Language*. In April Rilindja brought out the classic *Serbia and Albania* by Dimitrije Tucovic, one of the great early Serbian socialists. Published in 1914, this book condemned

44. Moats, 'Yugoslavia Lost', p. 184.
45. Ibid., p. 188.

Serbia's imperialistic policy in Kosovo and northern Albania following the invasion in 1912. Tucovic attempted to counter the rabid Serbian propaganda of the day and make his Serbian readers see Albanians as real people, not as 'men with tails'.[46]

The development of broader cultural contacts with Albania was encouraged so that Kosovo could finally activate its role of 'bridge-building' with Albania. The departure of Rankovic had paved the way for the resumption of dialogue between Yugoslavia and Albania. Both countries felt threatened by the Soviet invasion of Czechoslovakia in 1968, which led them to reappraise their foreign policy. For the time being, Tirana saw Yugoslavia as a buffer zone against Warsaw Pact territorial ambitions. Therefore, official relations between the two countries were cordial at state level while they remained irreconcilably opposed politically and ideologically. Yugoslav-Albanian relations might have improved but in Kosovo there were signs of a steady deterioration in Serbian-Albanian relations. The Serbian Party leadership, until the November 1968 Party Congress, still largely comprised only relatively uncompromised hold-overs from Rankovic's day. At a meeting of the republican Central Committee in May 1968, two members, the historian Jovan Marjanovic and the writer Dobrica Cosic, ventured to criticise manifestations of Albanian and Magyar nationalism in Kosovo and Vojvodina. Albanian 'nationalism and irredentism' were being openly promoted in Kosovo, they said, and Serbs were suffering systematic discrimination in current employment policies in the Province. As evidence they cited the emigration from Kosovo of an increasing number of Serbs and Montenegrins, 'especially the intelligentsia'. Although both also criticised several specific manifestations of Serbian nationalism, they were condemned by their colleagues for being 'nationalistic' and opposed to 'self-management'.[47]

Meanwhile, towards the end of 1968 there were sporadic eruptions of inter-ethnic violence. Tension among the Kosovars had increased as their newly-aroused expectations remained unfulfilled. Their representatives had failed to win support in Belgrade for their demand for greater autonomy, if not republican status. They therefore took to the streets. As a prelude to the full-scale demonstrations which were soon to engulf Kosovo, large groups of students waving Albanian flags marched through the towns of Prizren, Pec and

46. Ibid., pp. 209-10.
47. Rusinow, *The Yugoslav Experiment*, p. 246.

Suhareke in October. On 27 November violent demonstrations broke out in Pristina, Gjilan, Podujevo and Urosevac. Albania's Day of the Flag, celebrating the proclamation of independence in 1912, fell on 28 November, the day before Yugoslavia's Day of the Republic. In 1968 the largest group of foreign journalists ever to visit Yugoslavia was gathering in Bosnia with Tito and all the top surviving Partisans to commemorate the first quarter-century of the New Socialist Yugoslavia, declared on 29 November 1943. It was while they were all assembled there waiting for the celebrations to begin that the Albanian students from Pristina University, on 27 November, finally made the headlines in the 1968 Year of Revolution. They gathered in front of the Faculty of Philosophy in a demonstration which turned into what the international press classified as a 'riot' with ten policemen and several students badly injured and one youth killed. Youths with banners proclaiming in Serbian 'Down with Colonialism in Kosovo' were chanting '*Duam Republik*' – 'we want a Republic'.[48] The few private cars in Pristina were overturned and had their windows smashed. Men sat in the windows of their shops, behind jagged, broken glass, on the tiny three-legged stools which were the closest Albanians traditionally got to chairs, hunched over oil-stoves and with storm lanterns at their feet, guarding their stocks. In response the authorities hurriedly deployed several army units and tanks on the streets of Kosovo's main towns.

The demonstrations spread quickly throughout Kosovo and into neighbouring Macedonia, where Albanians called for the Albanian-inhabited areas of Western Macedonia to be joined with Kosovo, to form an Albanian Republic within Yugoslavia. On 23 December 1968, following the removal of an Albanian flag by a Macedonian from an Albanian tailor's shop, a riot broke out in the predominantly Albanian-inhabited town of Tetovo in Western Macedonia. The Macedonian Communist Party had consistently failed to grant proportional representation in positions of political power to its minorities. Belated recognition by the Macedonian Party of rights for Albanians and Turks was brought about by concern in Belgrade that Macedonia was ignoring the Yugoslav nationality programme, which stressed the appointment of minority cadres in the Party apparatus. The growing discontent had eventually compelled the Macedonian leadership to improve its nationality policy, but the

48. Moats, 'Yugoslavia Lost', p. 222.

riots erupted before this programme could be even partly implemented. The League of Communists' initial response to the unrest was to detain the ringleaders, but it had a disquieting effect on the Party. Following the disturbances, the Kosovars issued a list of political and economic demands. These included republic status, equality of language, freedom to fly the Albanian flag, an independent university for Kosovo, and the dropping of the Serbian word 'Metohija' from the official name of the province.[49]

Kosovo did get the red Albanian flag with the black eagle, its talons spread wide. All over the province that October it appeared at the head of wedding processions, fixed to the leading cart or rippling over the head of the horsemen as they went to 'fetch the bride'. And throughout Kosovo incidents were reported of the flag being torn down and burned by Serbs, who saw it as an ominous prelude to Yugoslav Albanians demanding union with Albania.[50]

49. Ibid., p. 227.
50. Ibid., p. 220.

9

ALBANIAN SELF-ASSERTION GATHERS MOMENTUM

Instead of being satisfied with the considerable increase in equality and personal security which they had enjoyed since the taming of the Province's Serb-dominated UDB-a after July 1966, the politicised strata of the rapidly-growing Albanian minority, now nearly 1 million strong, were demanding more of the same and the transformation of their region into the seventh Yugoslav republic in which the Albanians, as the local majority, would be politically dominant. The demonstrations in Kosovo and their echoes in western Macedonia witnessed the return of the national question to centre-stage among Yugoslvia's problems.[1]

The victory of the Slovenian and Croatian factions in the League of Communists of Yugoslavia back in 1964 made the status of the Provinces a major stake in the struggle for power within the Yugoslav federation. Under the new constitutional amendments made in December 1968, legislative and judicial authority was passed on to the Provinces, which were given direct representation in the federal parliament. As a further concession to Albanian national sentiment, the purely Serbian geographical term 'Metohija' was abandoned in favour of the single name Kosovo. The appellation 'Socialist' was added to that of Autonomous Province for both Kosovo and Vojvodina, and the basic legal order of each was now to be established by a constitution separate from that of the Serbian Republic. Henceforth the rights and duties of the Autonomous Provinces were no longer to be determined 'within the framework of the rights and duties of the Republic of Serbia'. Kosovo was now given priority over other Yugoslav regions in the distribution of central funds. However, this resulted in piecemeal and purely cosmetic development, which did little to improve the quality of life for ordinary people. It was hoped that these measures would appease the Kosovars because their

1. Rusinow, *The Yugoslav Experiment*, p. 245.

demand for republic status was still flatly rejected by the Central Committee of the League of Communists.

In January 1969 the Serbian Parliament adopted a new constitution for Kosovo. The Province received its own supreme court together with considerable independent policy-making rights, and the Albanian, Serbo-Croat and Turkish languages were accorded equal status. An independent University of Pristina was created from what had hitherto been only a branch of the University of Belgrade. The 1969 Constitutional Amendments were another attempt to find a legal basis for enlarged Provincial autonomy. But the Albanian request to revise the borders of the Socialist Autonomous Province of Kosovo to include all Albanian-inhabited territories attached to the Socialist Republics of Serbia, Macedonia and Montenegro was once more rejected by the Politburo on 4 February 1969 as 'threatening the territorial integrity of Yugoslavia'.[2] In the light of these constitutional amendments Kosovo was now able to pass its own Constitutional Law, which it did in February 1969. Thus it officially ceased to be merely a faceless geographic entity and emerged as a fully-fledged constituent element of the federation. Relatively modest as these Albanian gains may have been, Serbs became increasingly apprehensive, dreading any transfer of land from Serb to Albanian. The growing mistrust between Slavs and Albanians resulted in a noticeable exodus of Serbs and Montenegrins from the Province after 1968: Serbs and Montenegrins started to abandon Kosovo, while Albanians from Macedonia, Montenegro, southern Serbia and Muslims from the Sandjak region began to settle there, particulary in Pristina, which had developed into Kosovo's literary and cultural centre, primarily to get schooling.

Population growth, industrial development and irredentism

During the twenty-year period 1961-81 the demography of Kosovo changed dramatically. From a comfortable two-thirds of the population in 1961, the proportion of Albanians virtually doubled, while Serbs and Montenegrins decreased from a quarter of the population to one-sixth. The 1971 census established that 73.6 per cent of Kosovo's population were now Albanian, and whereas the natural rate of population increase per 1,000 inhabitants in Yugoslavia as a

2. Repishti, 'Human Rights and the Albanian Nationality in Yugoslavia', p. 249.

whole was 9.6 that in Kosovo was 29.6.[3] In 1971 'Turks' were the sixth largest ethnic classification in Kosovo, having dropped from fourth position ten years earlier; they were found in largest numbers in the commune of Prizren – 5,794 or 5.9 per cent of the total population. What these figures failed to reveal is that much of Kosovo's population, including Albanians, were trilingual – in Albanian, Serbian and Turkish. This meant that ethnic barriers in the province were not what they might have appeared.[4]

It was not unreasonable to assume, therefore, that part of the reason for the decline of the Turkish national minority in Kosovo in the decade before 1971 was the result of their assimilation and partial absorption by the Albanian community. It seems obvious that if the authorities in Belgrade were interested in seeing a reduction in Albanian numbers, support for the Turkish minority would have gone some way to achieving this by preventing the Albanians from absorbing them. More important, support for the Turkish minority was consistent with the Yugoslav policy of promoting all national groups in order to play down the significance of the larger ethnic groups. The emergence of a Muslim national category in the population censuses since 1961, and attempts to integrate the Gypsies by appealing to their national identity were further examples of encouragement given to previously 'unrated' or 'underrated' national groups. If, through promotion of the Turks in a predominantly Albanian region, the Albanians could be persuaded to see themselves as just another *narodnost* [5] within the orbit of the 'society of socialist self-managers', then the nationality policy in Kosovo might help to differentiate the Yugoslav Albanians from the Alba-

3. According to the 1961 and 1971 census figures, the SAP of Kosovo consisted of:

	1961	% of total	1971	% of total
Albanians	646,605	67.2	916,167	73.7
Serbs	227,016	23.6	228,261	18.4
Montenegrins	37,588	3.9	31,555	2.5
Muslims	8,026	0.8	26,357	2.1
Gypsies	3,202	0.3	14,593	1.2
Turks	25,764	2.7	12,244	1.0
Croats	7,251	0.8	8,276	0.7
Macedonians	1,142	0.1	1,048	0.1

Source: Yugoslav *Statisticki Bilten*, no. 727, 1972, p. 11.
4. C.N.O. Bartlett, 'The Turkish Minority in the Socialist Autonomous Province of Kosovo', *Co-existence*, vol. 17, p. 194.
5. *Narodnost* was the 'democratic' term for 'national minority', devoid of the implication of inferiority regarding other national groups.

nians of the Albanian state. For this reason support for the Turkish minority served both Turkish and 'Yugoslav' interests and was later endorsed by the League of Communists in Kosovo.[6]

Despite the apparently diminishing number of Turks, there had been a notable growth in the first half of the 1970s of Turkish-language publishing and broadcasting in Kosovo and a new Faculty of Turkish Studies at Pristina University was opened. The Turkish community in Kosovo was thus being actively supported in the hope of somewhat diluting the Albanian nature of the province with a view to achieving the community's greater integration. There were several factors contributing to the sharp increase in the overall population in Kosovo. The public health service in Kosovo achieved important results in reducing the province's mortality rate – it had fallen from 17.0 per 1,000 in 1950 to 8.6 by 1970. A similar trend had occurred in the rate of infant mortality in Kosovo, which had fallen from 142 per 1,000 live births in 1960 to ninety in 1970. Epidemics and contagious diseases, which had earlier been rife, had been all but eradicated by 1975; by then also the full electrification of Kosovo's villages had been completed.[7] Another factor contributing to the rapid population increase was the traditional desire of Albanian women in Kosovo to have children as quickly as possible after marriage. The sooner a wife could produce a son, the sooner she could ensure her marital relationship and hence her status in her husband's house (to which she had to move after marriage). Until a son was born, a wife was on trial, and if she was unable to produce one within a few years her husband was permitted to divorce her. Also, the sooner a son was born, the quicker he would grow up and enable the wife to hand over a large part of the domestic work to her daughter-in-law. Having a large number of children, apart from other perceived advantages, was also seen as ensuring for Kosovo an Albanian as opposed to a Serbian future. Kosovo's Albanians then had the highest natural population growth-rate in Europe: 26.1 per 1,000 in 1979 compared with 8.6 for the Yugoslav national average.

This high level of fertility strained the economy and diluted further Kosovo's standard of living in comparison with the rest of Yugoslavia. Any effect of economic expansion was sharply negated by the increase in the dependent, non-working and non-productive

6. Bartlett, 'The Turkish Minority ...' p. 196.
7. Marmullaku, *Albania and the Albanians*, p. 148.

part of the population: the ever-increasing percentage of the population under the age of twenty-five continued to swell the number of unemployed. Apart from a positive migration balance and a high growth-rate, the Albanians of Kosovo also increased their share in the population by absorbing parts of other ethnic communities of Slavophone Muslims (Torbesi, Gorani, Bosnjaci-Muhadziri, Arnautasi), ethnic Turks, Roma (Madjupi) and the few remaining Circassians. At the same time, co-religionists from minority groups unwilling to pledge allegiance to the Albanian cause were given to understand that it would be wiser to try their luck elsewhere. Some Turks reportedly fled to Belgrade, just as Slavophone Muslims were heading for Sarajevo. The area was also getting too hot for Serbian – or Yugoslav – oriented Albanians lacking the 'right' nationalist attitude. A foreign visitor told of how he had often heard members of the Albanian Catholic minority expressing fear for their own safety after the Albanian Muslim majority had finally 'dealt' with the Orthodox Christians. 'Then it will be our turn,' they said. Sometimes they even spoke in favour of the policy conducted by the Montenegrin government to prevent Muslims dominating the Albanian scene in their own Republic as in Kosovo.[8]

In the late 1970s some observers suggested that one way to stifle potential irredentist tendencies among the rapidly growing Albanian population of Kosovo was to embark on a massive programme of industrialisation and job creation, which it was hoped would ease their integration into Yugoslav society. As the Albanian population increased and continued to live in predominantly agricultural settlements, they were constantly searching for more land. In the mid-1970s many large *zadrugas* still existed as independent economic units relying on the subjugation of individual interests for the general prosperity. By now they were almost all Albanian, and although several studies of the *zadruga* in Kosovo were completed by 1975, it was not possible to determine exactly how many there were. But it may be indicative that households with over nine members appeared only in 4 per cent of the cases throughout Yugoslavia as a whole, but amounted to nearly 21 per cent in the Kosovo region.[9] Following the war, Albanian 'intellectuals' were merely hastily-trained primary and secondary school teachers, and the situation remained the same until a modern Albanian élite

8. R. Gremaux, 'Politics of Ethnic Domination in the Land of the Living Past', in Duijzings, Janjic, and Maliqi (eds), *Kosovo: Kosova,* p. 20.
9. V. St. Erlich, 'The Last Big Zadrugas in the Kosovo Region', p. 244.

emerged in the mid-1970s. This replaced the traditional élite comprised of senior members of the clan or *zadruga* organisation of a few landed families whose wealth derived from past services to the Ottoman administration. This specific élite group, which played a crucial role in the articulation of Albanian nationalist perspectives, was the small established intelligentsia, composed of a few respected academics and professionals, together with a much larger number of individuals with only modest intellectual attainment or professional skill. The opening of Pristina University served to intensify inter-Albanian migration and managed, through marriages in many walks of life, to integrate the Albanian regions.

Meanwhile Kosovo's Slav population began complaining of their lack of representation in local politics, unfair hearings in courts staffed almost entirely by Albanians, and their children being forced to learn Albanian in school. As the exodus of the Slav element from Kosovo continued, there was a corresponding growth in Albanian communist regional party membership. Nevertheless, Kosovo's regional Communist Party was still controlled almost exclusively by Serbs. At the same time some small ultra-nationalist groups appeared that were affiliated to Tirana. In 1969 the Kosovo Party organisation reported that the Province continued to be plagued by both 'nihilistic' Albanian nationalists and Great State 'unitaristic' Serb nationalists. The former were always dissatisfied, belittling all achievements and blamed the socialist order and its leadership for failing to fulfill nationalist aspirations. The latter attacked concessions to Albanian nationalist ambitions as imperilling the position and rights of Serbs and Montenegrins.[10]

The policy of the increasingly Albanian-led Kosovo leadership was oriented above all towards a struggle to gain the greatest possible resources on the basis of special rights arising from the region's underdevelopment. The 1967-72 constitutional changes were intended to help resolve issues in multinational relations within the Federation and to strengthen confidence in Yugoslavia as a community of nations and nationalities enjoying equal rights. Vast sums of money were spent on such prestige projects as the huge glass and marble library in the centre of Pristina. Throughout Yugoslavia at this time the words 'Bratsvo i Jedinstvo', brotherhood and unity, were to be seen on billboards in every city. Tireless party officials hurled the slogan at mass rallies and repeated it constantly in the

10. S.L. Burg, *Conflict and Cohesion in Socialist Yugoslavia*, p. 71.

media. It was ironic that in an effort to encourage unity among the country's twenty-four national groups the government was encouraging the recognition of their diversity. Belgrade deliberately underplayed the growing Albanianisation of Kosovo by stressing the multi-ethnic character of the province with a view to achieving greater integration and actively supported other small ethnic groups such as the Gypsies and the Turks. Bosnia–Hercegovina was kept as an historic region to avoid its division between Croatia and Serbia and to create a centre for the Slav Muslims, who had been turned from a religious group into a recognised ethnicity in 1961.[11] The formal differentiation of the two terms 'nation' and 'nationality', each entitled respectively to its own Republic and Autonomous Province, was of paramount importance in the Yugoslav constitutional system. Their denial of a nation's status was perceived by the Kosovars as utterly unacceptable. Montenegrins were granted the status of a nation although they were people of mainly Serbian stock; and as late as 1961 Muslims in Bosnia-Hercegovina were similarly favoured because of their religious differentiation, although they were also of Slavic stock. So too were Macedonians, as a Serbian answer to Bulgarian claims, although up till 1945 being a Macedonian had largely meant being a Bulgarian.[12] The fact that Macedonians and Montenegrins had their own Republics was interpreted by the Albanians as discrimination against themselves.

Although by the 1970s the blood-feud had completely died out in Montenegro, it was still very much alive in Kosovo, despite having long been subject to prosecution by law as a serious crime. It was hard to estimate how many blood-feuds still survived, because everything in connection with them was handled secretively and hidden from the authorities. However, in 1975 some observers estimated that about 2,000 men were virtual prisoners in their houses since they were threatened with death as soon as they appeared in the open. They 'owed blood' mostly because of old feuds in which they personally were not involved. Twenty or more killings could

11. There was also a rise in the nationalist movement in Croatia in 1968-71. This movement consisted in part of an emotional reaction against 'unitarism' and 'centralism' in any form. It stressed the independence of the nations within the federal structure to the point of reviving the 'right to secede', which the constitution had granted first to the republics and later to the nations. - V. Meier, 'Yugoslavia's National Question', *Problems of Communism*, March-April, 1983, p. 53.

12. Pipa and Repishti, *Studies on Kosova*, pp. 222-3.

follow a quarrel among shepherds about a source of water for sheep. In the mid-1970s the attitude of individuals towards their traditional customs revealed unbroken loyalty. Young Albanians on military service in different Yugoslav garrisons were often exposed to sharp criticism because of their customs, especially the brideprice. However, they rarely in their turn criticised this custom or indeed rejected any Albanian customs. Albanian students in high schools or universities also remained surprisingly loyal to the traditional ways of their people.[13] But their resistance to the attraction of pecuniary gain and temptation was even more impressive. Many Albanian teachers and employees, in spite of working in cities far from their families, still considered themselves members of the *zadruga*, and sent home most of their salaries for which they received goods in return.[14] While the Serbs were abandoning their *zadrugas* for city life, there were still signs that the Albanian ones would continue for at least another two or three generations.

In the eyes of the province's Slav population, the normalisation of Yugoslavia's relations with Albania in 1971, and the unrestricted exchange of teachers, textbooks and other cultural exchanges that followed, further encouraged the Albanianisation of Kosovo. The Holy Synod of Bishops responded to the alleged 'destruction, arson and sacrilege of the holy shrines of Kosovo' by appealing to the official authorities of the Republic of Serbia, as well as to the Federal Executive Council, listing actual cases, but the situation was not rectified, and so on 19 May 1969 the Bishops appealed to President Tito himself. In his reply Tito expressed his regrets, agreed that the reported incidents were in violation of the constitution, and promised to do everything possible to prevent such incidents and lawless acts, and 'to secure for all citizens a safe life as well as the security of their property'.[15] A degree of vandalism was certainly directed against Orthodox Church property. The most usual incidents were the destruction of tombstones and the cutting down of trees on church property, with the wood often being sold by Albanians in the local markets. The land owned by the monasteries usually contained large areas of forest, and this was a magnet for youths looking for something to cut and sell.

At the same time, orientation towards Albania was becoming clearly visible in the sphere of language politics. The mainly Tosk-

13. Erlich, 'The Last Big Zadgrugas ...', pp. 249-50.
14. Ibid., p. 251.
15. Dragnich and Todorovic, *The Saga of Kosovo*, pp. 167-8.

based standard language of Albania was also to become the official language of the Gheg-speaking Kosovars, and this added to the estrangement between them and their old Serbophone neighbours. An elderly Montenegrin residing in Pristina told a foreign visitor: 'I used to understand them well, but now it's getting difficult. Formerly they spoke Shiptarski, but now they are trying to speak Albanski. They are turning our Shiptars into Albanians!'[16] Allowing increased cultural cooperation between Tirana and Pristina was not merely to appease the Kosovars: as mentioned above, Belgrade and Tirana were also both acutely aware of the threat posed by the Soviet intervention in Czechoslovakia in 1968, which led them to re-appraise their own vulnerability. These fears were not without foundation, since a Soviet plan for armed intervention in Yugoslavia apparently existed, as a Czech defector disclosed in early 1974. The plan included a classic pincer movement by the Warsaw Pact countries against Yugoslavia. Thus any group willing to create turmoil in Yugoslavia helped the interests of the Soviet Union, including its long-term desire for an Adriatic port. For its part, Tirana saw Yugoslavia as a buffer zone against Warsaw Pact territorial ambitions. Thus while at state level official relations between the two countries remained cordial, they were irreconcilably opposed politically and ideologically.

There was not only national disquiet among Serbs and Albanians; Croats too had explosive grievances focused especially on their perceived exploitation by Serbian hegemony.[17] The 1971 Croatian crisis was a crucial turning-point in the evolution of the nationality question in Yugoslavia: it spelled out the end of propagandistic slogans and Leninist flourishes, and of the notion that socialism made nationalism inconceivable. In 1971 there were yet further significant constitutional amendments whereby the rights and obligations of Kosovo became very similar to those of the republics. Kosovo's leaders were now encouraged to regard their Province as a constituent federal unit enjoying the same rights as the Republics, and the Kosovars themselves were also encouraged to take a more positive attitude towards the Federation. Although in 1971 Tito ordered a thorough crackdown on nationalist manifestations, national aspirations were given more consideration in the ensuing

16. Gremaux, 'Politics of Ethnic Domination ...', p. 19.
17. For an account of the Croatian Crisis see Rusinow, *The Yugoslav Experiment*, pp. 245-80.

years. The principle of statehood for the individual Republics became accepted and adopted first in the constitutional amendments of 1971 and then in the constitution of 1974.

The 1974 constitution

Yugoslavia's fourth constitution in less than thirty years was promulgated on 21 February 1974. It considerably narrowed the powers of the Federation, while extending those of the Republics and Autonomous Provinces. This meant that Kosovo was now a full constitutive element of the Federation with direct and equitable representation in all its Party and state bodies. As one of Yugoslavia's eight federal units, Kosovo was represented in the Federal Chamber of the Yugoslav Assembly and, like the Yugoslav republics, had the right to propose laws and other legal acts within the competence of the Chamber of Republics and Provinces. It was also separately represented in the Yugoslav federal court and the constitutional court. Implicit in this reform was the view that Yugoslavia could no longer be regarded as an exclusively South Slav state. Many Serbian Party leaders consequently saw the new constitution as not only deepening the division of the Serb nation but also as weakening Serbia's statehood as one of the Yugoslav Republics. The Autonomous Provinces now had a veto on all matters which affected them, and thus the Belgrade leadership had lost full control over the Serbian Republic's affairs. The 1974 constitution forbade the Republic of Serbia to intervene in Provincial affairs against the will of the assemblies in Novi Sad (the capital of Vojvodina) and Pristina.

The status of Vojvodina and Kosovo differed from that of the Republics in that the statehood of the regions was not recognised. Article 4 characterised the regions simply as 'autonomous, socialist, self-managed, democratic, socio-political communities' in which 'the nations and nationalities realise their sovereign rights.' This is the point on which the authorities of Kosovo and Vojvodina based their claims in their struggle against centralising tendencies in the Republic of Serbia. It is often asked why federalism in Yugoslavia came to be especially emphasised and anchored in the constitution in a veritably 'bourgeois' manner after the crisis in Croatia in the early 1970s. The explanation can only lie in Tito's belief at the time that he had dicovered a new political concept for Yugoslavia. He apparently thought it possible to accommodate the new realities on the state level through a federalism solidly anchored in the constitution and the legal system, while a more disciplined and centralised party would buttress both the state and the regime.[18]

The new constitution enabled Kosovo to emerge as an independent factor in the Yugoslav Federation, no longer under direct Serbian tutelage. The Province had its own national bank, supreme court and independent administration under the supervision of the provisional executive council and provisional presidency. In other areas, including economic policy, taxation, education and culture, the Republic of Serbia was empowered to pass legislation valid for the entire Republic only with the prior approval of the assembly of the Province.[19] The 1974 constitution contained the seeds of discontent for all. For Albanians the provision of autonomy did not go far enough to satisfy their demand to have a republic. Albanians were defined as a nationality of Yugoslavia, not as a nation, and for this reason they could not have a republic, but only autonomy. The sovereignty of the nation included the important right to secession. Serbs complained further that they were divided not only in Serbia but in Yugoslavia as well, and this sense of injustice was enhanced by inconsistency in granting autonomies. Vojvodina, with a majority Serb population, was given autonomy on the basis of cultural and historical identity, whereas Kosovo's autonomy, with a majority Albanian population, was based on ethnic principles. Consequently, about 21 per cent of Serbs in Serbia were not under the jurisdiction of Belgrade. Serbian grievances were further enforced by the position of Serbs in Croatia, where they comprised 14.7 per cent of the population but received no special recognition of their rights. At the same time Albanians, who accounted for 8.15 per cent of Serbia's population, were granted autonomy.[20]

The new constitution emphasised equalities and equal rights and duties. These included the right to the development and free expression of the national language, culture and history, and its recognition precipitated two trends: a spate of translations, normally from Serbo-Croat, and the demand by employers for knowledge of both Albanian and Serbo-Croat in workplaces, even where this was not actually required. The matter was aggravated when this trend received official sanction from the League of Communists of

18. V. Meier, 'Yugoslavia's National Question', p. 53.
19. Pipa and Repishti, *Studies on Kosova*, p. 235.
20. D. Kostovicova, *Parallel Worlds: Response of Kosovo Albanians to Loss of Atonomy in Serbia, 1986-1996*, Keele European Research Centre, 1997, pp. 11-12.

Kosovo and the educational and cultural authorities, including Pristina University. The new policy placed the Serb and Montenegrin nationality group as a whole at a great disadvantage, since only a few from this group spoke both Serbo-Croat and Albanian. Many members of the Serb-Montenegrin nationality group began sending their children to school outside the province because of alleged nationalistic pressure and the schools' new language equality rules.[21] The 1974 constitution caused 'positive discrimination' in favour of the Albanians in Kosovo: bilingualism became a condition for employment in public services; four-fifths of the available posts were reserved for Albanians on a parity basis; and national quotas were strictly applied when nominations were made for public functions. Thus began the virtual Albanianisation of public life in Kosovo.[22] The constitution was ambiguous and unworkable and it collapsed as soon as the slightest strain was put upon it. Several years later Edvard Kardelj, its creator who was seen as Tito's heir apparent until he died in 1979, admitted that even he believed it would cause problems for Serbia. Kardelj advised the Serbian President Ivan Stambolic and his comrades to work towards changing the constitution, but by Tito's death in 1980 no progress had been made, and afterwards the question was shelved.[23]

According to the official Yugoslav viewpoint at this time,

'Foreign observers who regarded the Albanians as one of the weak points in the Federation, based this assumption on the preoccupations of the Albanians before the socialist revolution, when 'bourgeois' Yugoslavia was a prison for them. It was natural then for their demands for secession to be stronger. Now, however, in the multinational Federal Yugoslavia in which they enjoyed equal rights and cultural, political and economic emancipation, many observers believed that they were committed to maintaining the security and integrity of their homeland.'[24]

Nothing could have been further from the truth. In 1974 more demonstrations broke out in Pristina with students calling for the union of the Albanian regions of Montenegro and Macedonia with Kosovo. The next year scores of students were jailed for organising a 'Kosovo National Liberation Movement' aimed at union with

21. RFE, Background Report/242, 16 November 1982.
22. P. Simic, *The Kosovo and Metohija Problem and Regional Security in the Balkans*, Institute of International Politics and Economics, Belgrade, 1996, p. 10.
23. L. Silber and A. Little, *The Death of Yugoslavia*, London, 1995, p. 35.
24. Marmullaku, *Albania and the Albanians*, p. 151.

Albania. From 1973 to 1975 the security forces discovered evidence of two underground separatist organisations known as the 'Revolutionary Movement of United Albanians' and the 'Marxist-Leninist Communist Party of Albanians in Yugoslavia'. Both groups undertook what the regime called 'serious propaganda actions'. The Kosovo Ministry of the Interior was fairly well informed about some of the separatist groups, but witheld its intelligence from Belgrade.

Although it was nearly a decade since the removal of Rankovic, Albanians continued to be arrested on charges of inciting nationalism and irredentism. In February 1976 the writer Adem Demaci (who had served two previous prison sentences for nationalist agitation) and eighteen other Albanians were tried in Pristina on charges of 'organising against the people and the state', 'hostile propaganda' and 'crimes endangering the territorial integrity and independence of Yugoslavia'. Demaci was accused of forming the 'National Liberation Movement of Kosovo', whose alleged goal was the unification of Kosovo with Albania. The defendants were accused also of distributing publicity material attacking the policy of the SKJ, the system of socialist self-management and the leadership of the Socialist Republic of Yugoslavia in the student quarters of Pristina University and other places in Kosovo and Macedonia. They were not accused of either using or advocating violence, so when they were sentenced to fifteen years imprisonment they were adopted as prisoners of conscience by Amnesty International.[25] Nevertheless, the majority of Kosovars were not enamoured of Enver Hoxha's condescending attitude towards them. This was reflected in a saying widely heard in Kosovo at the time: 'Enver Hoxha should remember that he is a head of state and head of a Party but not the head of a nation.' Most Kosovars saw life in Albania as far worse than it was in Kosovo, and another of their common sayings was 'The streets of Tirana are so clean because the Albanians have nothing to throw away.'

Kosovars enjoy a sense of freedom

By the late 1970s the provincial leadership, which now operated with minimal interference or restraint from either the Serbian Republic or the federal government, began to look with tolerance

25. Amnesty International, 'Yugoslavia, Prisoners of Conscience', 1985, p. 6.

on expressions of Albanian nationalism, and would not allow developments in the province to be criticised by other republics. Another form of positive discrimination in favour of Albanians resulted in Serbs and Montenegrins gaining employment in only one job vacancy out of every five. Also the tendency to publish internal information in Albanian left the local Slav population generally ignorant of important issues. Serbs saw a reversion to the days of Ottoman rule due to their perceived deprived status, and the accompanying physical and psychological pressures. Kosovo's Serbs, now with a strong victim mentality, felt that a surrogate Albanian national state had been created in Kosovo in which they had become an ethnic minority without the protection of Serbia.

On the other hand, access was granted to Albanian-language education and cultural facilities, Albanian literature and culture in Kosovo flourished as never before. It was a brief blossoming in which tremendous progress was made within a short time.[26] Adoption of the basically Tosk literary Albanian by Kosovo's Gheg-speakers in 1968 – following the decree in Tirana that it should become the standard Albanian language – had paved the way for Albanian cultural penetration in Kosovo. Albanian textbooks, together with an ever-growing number of Albanian publications, were imported from Tirana. Albanian intellectuals, who had been persecuted during the Rankovic era, were eager to discover their history and culture, and as a result played a vital part in encouraging Albanians to rediscover their national identity by studying their history, literature and traditions at the new Albanology faculty of Pristina University.[27]

Thus the Kosovars' self-perception was enhanced as they reaffirmed their cultural heritage and discovered the role their forefathers had played in the struggle for Albanian independence from the Ottomans. Albanians in Kosovo also had access to an Islamic college (the Alauddin Medrese) and to many religious publications in Albanian, and the opportunity to send numerous students to the

26. Elsie, *History of Albanian Literature*, p. 620.
27. By the late 1970s c. 95 per cent of Kosovo's children received elementary education. There were advances in the training of medical personnel and in health care for the population. Whereas in 1952 there was one doctor per 8,527 inhabitants, by 1978 the ratio was one per 2,009. Similarly life expectancy, which in the immediate post-war period was forty-five years, had risen to sixty-eight years by 1980. Pipa and Repishti, *Studies on Kosovo*, p. 133.

theology faculties in the Muslim Arab world. The close cultural ties established between Tirana and Pristina were the principal force behind the outpouring of Albanian nationalist sentiments in the 1970s, but such cultural exchanges singularly failed to build the bridge between Albania and Yugoslavia. Young Kosovars were like a parched sponge, avid to absorb anything that helped to illuminate their past history and make some sense of their present situation.[28] At the same time, Kosovo's Serbs had become dismayed and angered as their former prestige continued to wane. In 1977 a working commission of the Serbian Party gathered arguments against this enhanced provincial autonomy in what became known as the 'Blue Book'. This sought the return to Belgrade of control of the Province's judiciary, police (including state security service), territorial defence and economic policy, but because acceptance of these aims would clearly involve a new bout of repression in Kosovo, the document had a hostile reception from the Federal leadership. The *Blue Book* was never publicly discussed, but the fact of its existence allowed the issue of provincial autonomy to smoulder below the surface of Serbian politics till the 1980s, when it would acquire a new and potent charge.[29]

During the years 1971–81, Kosovo's administration operated with minimal restraint from either the Federal or the Serbian Republic government. At the May 1978 session of the State Presidency, Fadil Hoxha, then aged sixty-two, was elected Vice-President of the State Presidency, Yugoslavia's nine-member collective leadership, replacing Stevan Doronjski, a Serb from Vojvodina, whose one-year term of office in the rotating Vice-Presidential post expired on 15 May. This was the first time an Albanian had occupied such an important position as Tito's deputy in the state. He was also nominated as one of the two representatives of the League of Communists of Kosovo for membership of the Yugoslav Party Presidium, which gave many Kosovars the illusion that the Party was at last taking them seriously. In fact he was the Albanians' perennial representative at the Party summit. The second Kosovo representa-

28. Ibid., p. 190.
29. B. Magas, 'Yugoslavia: The Spectre of Balkanization', *New Left Review*, 174/1989, p. 11. The *Blue Book*, which was suppressed, partly due to objections from the Kosovo leadership, was modelled on the *Blue Book* printed for the 1899 Peace Conference in The Hague, containing diplomatic correspondence on acts of violence committed by Albanians in Kosovo, but Austria-Hungary prevented Serbian diplomats from raising the question before the international public.

tive was Mahmut Bakalli (then forty-two), President of the Kosovo Provincial Committee.[30]

However, the numerous concessions made to the Kosovars remained relatively meaningless because they were granted for political reasons without first attacking the Province's underlying national tensions and emotions, especially among the Serbs, who were strongly opposed to further devolution to the Kosovars. Little effort had been made to encourage discussion between Serbs and Albanians to adjust their demands and expectations to the reality of the current situation. Kosovo's dire economic problems should also have been addressed, since ethnic tensions intensified as the gap in prosperity between Kosovo and the other regions grew. As early as 1977 Edvard Kardelj had warned his colleagues that if the Party failed to adopt a resolute policy that would narrow the economic gap and tranquillise inter-ethnic tensions, then Kosovo would explode into violence.[31] During the 1970s Kosovo's infrastructure, as in much of Yugoslavia, improved dramatically with the construction of a network of modern roads, the arrival of electricity in all but very remote villages, and the opening of various health, educational and cultural establishments. The Academy of Sciences and Arts in Pristina greatly expanded its range of activities, and the radio and television centre there was among the most up-to-date in the whole country.

In spite of these obvious social achievements, the Province's economic development remained seriously impaired. According to one researcher, the imbalance in the economy came about mainly because the emphasis on investments was concentrated on basic industry, meaning the extractive or raw materials industries, to the relative neglect of the other branches of the economy. Furthermore, investments during this period did not benefit Kosovo as much as the major recipients of the raw materials, namely the other regions of Yugoslavia. This was also true of the electric power produced in

30. RFE, Background Report/95, 17 May 1978. After the war Fadil Hoxha divided his time between regional and federal politics. He was Prime Minister of Kosovo till 1963, when he became a member of the Yugoslav federal government in Belgrade. In 1967 he was appointed President of the Kosovo National Assembly, at the same time becoming a member of the Yugoslav Party Presidium. At the Ninth LCY Congress in Belgrade in March 1969, Hoxha was elected a member of the Executive bureau of the Yugoslav Party Presidium, and in 1974 a member of the State Presidency.

31. P. Ramet, *Nationalism and Federalism in Yugoslavia, 1963-83*, Indiana University Press, Bloomington, 1984, p. 165.

Kosovo, of which at least two-thirds flowed to other republics, leaving the Province notably behind the republics in the *per capita* use of electricity. Unable to generate capital on its own, Kosovo relied heavily on outside sources for investment funds, mainly from the Federal Development Fund,[32] but money alone was insufficient to break the vicious circle of underdevelopment. The considerable socio-economic change in the Province since the war had resulted in the emergence of new social structures. As more and more Albanian families migrated to the towns and cities of Kosovo, their social structure underwent a fundamental change.

Albanians searching for work in other parts of Yugoslavia often had difficulty getting jobs because of the language barrier, their relatively low level of technical and professional experience, and the basic prejudices they encountered throughout the country. Those who did find employment usually did menial work for low pay in the numerous tourist developments along the Dalmatian coast. In Kosovo the percentage share of educational costs to national income was more than double the average for Yugoslavia as a whole, and much of this financial burden was borne by the rest of the country. Hence many non-Albanian Yugoslavs resented having to subsidise the huge Albanian birthrate. A visitor to Kosovo in 1979 noted:

> 'Among the youth studying in Kosovo I could sense a certain vacuum, perhaps even resignation. The problem of insufficient career opportunities and impending unemployment came up repeatedly in conversations. The high level of solidarity within families seemed to mitigate the problem somewhat, without providing an alternative. The desire to get work in the Federal Republic of Germany functioned as a primary safety valve. The people with whom I spoke regarded the expansion of the economy in Kosovo primarily as a process dependent on the Yugoslav member republics. They felt excluded from assuming responsibility and showing initiative.'[33]

Throughout the post-war period, the level of investment *per capita* in Kosovo amounted to only 50 per cent of the country's average. Investments were made mainly into the mining industry which did not generate conditions for accumulation and for the creation of a large number of jobs. On the other hand, while *per*

---

32. Pipa and Repishti, *Studies on Kosovo*, p. 134.
33. Ibid., p. 114.

capita income in Kosovo was several times lower than the country's average, the natural increase of its population was several times higher. Furthermore, despite the comparatively low wages in Kosovo, the developed regions in Yugoslavia were reluctant to invest in the province. A particular reason for this was that prospective investors were wary of the indiscipline and unreliable work habits of Kosovo's workers. Kosovo was known to have a weak technological infrastructure and to be comparatively short of engineers and technicians.[34]

In the early 1980s an Albanian scholar noted that the Kosovar way of life was still governed by traditional mores and outdated customs and badly needed to be transformed. He wrote that this needed to be social no less than economic, and to address first the still patriarchal family system:

> 'The position of a woman is that of a human being deprived of
> fundamental rights. Women were still kept secluded at home when
> they did not work in the fields, they received minimal education,
> and were totally subordinate to male authority. The emancipation of
> women is the first and foremost task for the Kosovars as a people in
> order to achieve full emancipation. A community denying half of its
> members access to a full education can never be a civilised commu-
> nity.'[35]

Gradually women participated more in public life. Only ten years earlier they hardly ever left home. All the same, women still had servile domestic tasks. Hartmut Albert, a guest in an Albanian home in Pec in 1979, reported as follows:

> 'During our meal, between the tales, the patriarchal order in the
> household was evident once again. Only the men (including the 14-
> year-old son) gathered around the sofra (low table). Our host's wife
> approached only to serve our food and clear the table. Then she
> waited silently at the door with water and a hand towel until we
> wanted to wash our hands.'[36]

In the late 1970s factors that tended to hinder social progress – such as a high birth-rate, a patriarchal family structure and the influences of various religious communities, especially the clergy, were still largely present in Kosovo. Another visitor to the region in 1979 found that while the Albanians showed a natural pride in things

34. Ibid., p. 135.
35. Ibid., p. 250.
36. Ibid., p. 118.

Albanian such as the museum of the Prizren League, they also visited places of Serbian cultural interest such as the Patriarchate of Pec and the Cloister of Decan as if out of pride in a great regional historical tradition, not reserved for the Serbs only. The visitor's Albanian companions took part naturally in his conversations with Serbian monks and showed no reservation or desire to engage in polemics, but wanted to stress the contributions made by Albanian artists to the buildings and arrangements.[37]

At end of the decade, differences between the level of development in Kosovo and in the rest of the country became more obvious. While at the same time the Kosovars joked that the one thing all new buildings in Pristina had in common was a lack of what they were supposed to have – the banks had no money, the library had no books, and the huge new Grand Hotel rarely had any guests. In 1979 Kosovo still had the highest illiteracy rate in Yugoslavia for persons over ten years of age: 31.5 per cent, as against the national average of 15.1 per cent and a mere 1.2 per cent for Slovenia. In 1979 the *per capita* income in Kosovo was US$795 compared with the Yugoslav national average of $2,635, and $5,315 for Slovenia, a difference of seven times. In 1979, only 107 Kosovars per 1,000 in the active population were employed, compared with the Yugoslav national average of 253, and 427 for Slovenia – the highest in the federation, as for so much else. As late as 1978, 42.9 per cent of the population were engaged in agriculture, and 57.1 per cent were urbanised; the figures for Slovenia in the same year were 13.5 per cent rural and 86.5 per cent urban.[38] There was a massive influx of peasants from the countryside into the towns, and the élite townsmen of Prizren began complaining about the uncontrolled arrival of peasants with their dirty customs and uncivilised behaviour which had turned this once proud and clean town into a 'pig-sty'; one reason why they continued speaking Turkish was to distinguish themselves from the uneducated newcomers.

Demand grows for a Kosovar Republic

A new impetus to the Albanian quest for Republic status was provided by the festivities for the League of Prizren centennial which took place in almost every town in Kosovo in 1978, and of

37. Ibid., p. 111.
38. Ibid., pp. 131-2.

course in Albania itself. Visitors from Kosovo were allowed to travel to the festivities in Albania, but the Albanian authorities would not let Albanians visit Yugoslavia. An uneasy situation developed when national euphoria spilled over into 'illegal' distribution of leaflets, writing of slogans and open verbal confrontation with the authorities. At the University of Zagreb an Albanian student was killed by police in a skirmish following an evening of Albanian literature and songs. At Pristina University and in high schools students boycotted non-Albanian classes, ostracised 'hostile' teachers, and refused to study Serbo-Croat. During his last visit to Kosovo in 1979 Tito recognised the seriousness of the problem and asked that it be remedied 'by all means'. The result was 'massive arrests of members of the Albanian minority in Kosovo in November–December 1979', made public by Amnesty International on 30 June 1980.[39]

The central dilemma was how to integrate Kosovo into Yugoslavia while at the same time preserving the national rights of the Albanian population. The fact remained that the pragmatic solution sought for Kosovo after 1971 – *de facto* but not *de jure* Republic status – was not followed up by a broadening of the dialogue between Serbs and Albanians; this solution might then have been made more palatable to the Albanian population, and the Serbs might have been persuaded that the final step – Republic status for the provinces – could be accomplished without detriment to the rights of Serbs in Kosovo and the historic interest of Serbia in the Province.[40] The difficult task facing the political leadership in Kosovo was therefore to secure an expansion of its economy at a rate equal to population growth.[41] A large number of young people were encouraged to study in Kosovo to camouflage the high rate of youth unemployment. Although Federal funds kept pouring in, the disparity between prices for industrial and agricultural products left Kosovo in a poverty trap because agricultural and not industrial output was the major determinant of Kosovo's overall growth-rate. Had the Federal funds been invested in more labour-intensive sectors instead of low-labour, capital-intensive and higher-technol-

39. Repishti, 'Human Rights and the Albanian Nationality', p. 256.
40. Pipa and Repishti, *Studies on Kosova*, p. 237.
41. According to the 1981 census, the population of Kosovo was 1,584, 558, of whom 1,227,424 (77.5 per cent) were Albanians, 209,795 (13.2 per cent) Serbs, 50,948 (3.7 per cent) Muslims, 26,875 (1.7 per cent) Montenegrins, and 48,941 (3.1 per cent) members of other nationalities.

ogy sectors, they could have helped reduce the massive unemployment in the Province, which rose from 18.6 per cent in 1971 to 27.5 per cent ten years later. By comparison, the Slovenian unemployment rate in 1981 was a mere 2 per cent.[42]

Kosovo continued to fall even further behind the national average, and the provincial leaders claimed that the causes of this disappointing performance were 'subjective and objective' in nature, with stress on 'subjective'. This was because Pristina could not afford to antagonise the richer Republics by criticising them publicly for not providing greater investment funds to the Province despite the flow of investments from the outside. Of Kosovo's financial resources in 1977 only 7.7 per cent came from internal provincial sources and a year later this had dropped to 4.6 per cent, with over 90 per cent coming from Yugoslav and foreign banks. Another example of Pristina blaming the subjective factor occurred in the report delivered by the chairman of the Provincial League of Communists, Mahmut Bakalli, in which the current complicated situation was said to be a result of the province's low level of economic development; if these 'difficulties were not eliminated or reduced soon, there could be grave consequences'.[43] And more specifically: 'Essentially, we must reduce expenditures, trade for representational purposes, the frequent and unnecessary trips, internal and abroad, the unnecessary use of social means of transportation [a reference to the twenty-six official cars being used for private purposes], because in Kosovo this is measured not only in material but also in moral and political terms.'[44]

On the one hand, the development of generous autonomy in the 1960s and '70s failed to satisfy Kosovo's Albanian population or ensure its loyalty to the Yugoslav Federation. On the other hand, the exorbitant investments in capital-intensive plants in a region abounding in labour and natural resources but lacking capital produced frustrating results: while Slovenia and Croatia complained that much of their income was being poured into Kosovo as its economy continued to lag behind on the Yugoslav scale, Kosovo complained of the unfavourable terms-of-trade being imposed in its dealings with these developed republics to which it was selling its raw materials and energy cheaply while having to pay high prices

42. D. Rusinow, *Yugoslavia - A Fractured Federalism*, Wilson Center Press, Washington, DC, 1988, p. 71.
43. *Rilindja*, 23 May 1979.
44. RFE, Background Report/128, 7 June 1979.

for their manufactured goods.[45] During his visit to Kosovo in 1975, President Tito had told the Province's leaders: 'The question of Kosovo's development is everyone's question. In general, its accelerated development basically is also in the long-term interests of the more developed republics of Yugoslavia.' In other words, the wealthier regions of the country should in their own interest share some of their surplus with Kosovo.

The 1970s witnessed the increasing emancipation of Yugoslav society from the Party state, but at the same time economic differences between the national sub-units were increasing. In Kosovo *per capita* income declined from 48 per cent of the Yugoslav average in 1954 to 33 per cent in 1975 and to 27 per cent in 1980.[46] The largest industrial conglomerate in Kosovo during this period was the Trepca mining-metallurgical-chemical complex in the Mitrovica district, which employed 21,000 people. Unlike former times when it produced only raw materials, the Trepca industries were now increasingly engaged in processing operations and producing finished goods. The plant was seen as vital to Kosovo's economy. Agricultural productivity, however, remained very low. Among the problems causing this was the frequent fragmentation of arable land due to the splitting up of large families, and the resulting small size of plots, which precluded the use of modern agricultural equipment. As in the Sandjak and parts of Bosnia and Macedonia, wooden ploughs were still common. The result was low yields, which in turn meant meagre accumulation of capital and a shortage of produce. Faced with low grain yields and the increasing food needs of the rapidly growing population, Kosovo was obliged to turn to other regions in Yugoslavia or to foreign markets for the food grains it lacked. But the importation of food meant spending badly-needed foreign currency, a worsening balance of payments, and further economic instability. An American tourist in Kosovo reported seeing bread lines, and noted that people in villages were again eating corn bread, as they had done before and immediately after the war.[47]

The causes of Kosovo's relative backwardness were to be found not only in its underdeveloped economy but most of all in the misplaced investment policy, delayed and inefficient investments, a shortage of suitable experts, and waning productivity (one-third

45. P. Simic, *The Kosovo and Metohija Problem*, Institute of International Politics and Economics, Belgrade, 1996, p. 10.

46. Rusinow, *Yugoslavia - A Fractured Federalism*. p. 70.

47. Pipa and Repishti, *Studies on Kosovo*, p. 141.

lower than the Yugoslav average). For many years the trend had been towards developing the so-called long-term structure in investments (predominantly in power-generation and raw materials) while processing industries and handicrafts were neglected. The invested funds were not used efficiently while industrial production growth lagged. Labour productivity was constantly low and agricultural production stagnated. All this brought up the acute problem of unemployment in the region. With 67,000 unemployed in 1980, Kosovo had the highest unemployment rate, at 10.5 per cent, in the country. The pressure of unemployment was channelled into an explosive growth in the number of educational establishments and education itself. Young people graduated from secondary school or university with little chance of finding work, which was made more difficult by their ignorance of other languages besides Albanian. Certainly the lack of employment opportunities was largely due to the failure to adjust education to the requirements of the economy: both in Kosovo and other Provinces the majority of young people chose to study the humanities.

As the gap in prosperity between Kosovo and the rest of Yugoslavia widened, tensions intensified among the Kosovars. Concern was voiced almost daily in the press that the faster economic development anticipated by Belgrade had failed to materialise. The demographic explosion negated any benefits of economic expansion by increasing the dependent, non-productive population with wage-earners having to support large dependent families. Among the many negative trends in the Province was a mentality of complacency among its leaders, who concentrated on asking for as much help as possible on the basis of Kosovo's under-developed status, but failed to strive for greater self-reliance, association of labour and the pooling of resources. As more and more money poured in, no criticism or discussion was raised on the state of affairs in the Province. Indeed nothing was known of it in its broader context. The cycle of misappropriated funds went unchallenged and no discussion on ways to reduce the birthrate was forthcoming.

By the end of the 1970s it had become clear that the system of 'self-management' had totally stagnated in Kosovo. So-called 'market Socialism' had served to increase rather than help eliminate economic inequality between the Province and the rest of the country. Celebrated as a monumental achievement in the socialist world, self-management was actually a convoluted system based on 'social ownership', meaning that factories were owned by workers and their councils rather than by the state, but in fact it was difficult to define who owned what.[48] In 1979 Yugoslavia's Minister of Information, Ismail Bajra, an Albanian from Kosovo, severely criticised the state of 'cultural co-operation among various nationalities' in Yugoslavia as being 'far below the real achievements and needs of our nationalities and national minorities.'[49] He wrote:

'In particular, the cultural, artistic and scientific values of our national minorities and their national centres outside Yugoslavia have not been sufficiently presented. The self-isolation of national cultures, cultural egotism and hegemonism, state socialism, and the slow self-managing transformation of national cultures of individual nationalities and minorities in Yugoslavia, are only some of the negative factors which make greater and more permanent cultural co-operation between the republics, autonomous provinces, and nationalities impossible.'[50]

Bajra indirectly criticised the Serbs for employing 'nationalist-chauvinist' slogans, thus propagating the 'false defence of one's own nation, which leads towards national monolithism under the guise of national unity which removes all ideological differences'. Of course, this passage could also be interpreted as self-criticism: the attitude of many Albanians in Kosovo.[51]

In October 1979 President Tito paid his fifth and last official visit to Kosovo (the others were in 1950, 1967, 1971 and 1975), and in Pristina he spoke, somewhat belatedly, of 'Kosovo becoming the concern of Yugoslavia as a whole'.[52] He promised that other republics, notably Slovenia and Croatia, would invest more in its economy, thereby changing the whole economic structure of the Province. However, since his previous visit in 1975, the Kosovo leadership had become sceptical and were now telling Tito that words alone were not enough and deeds too were now expected. They warned that 'the slow pace of socio-economic development, and in the development of the self-management system, was having a negative impact on relations among the province's nationalities'.[53] Tito admitted that even then Kosovo 'was facing increasing activ-

48. Silber and Little, *The Death of Yugoslavia*, p. 34.
49. *Borba*, 27 April 1979.
50. *Borba*, 28 April 1979.
51. REF, BR/102, 8 May 1979.
52. *Kommunist*, Belgrade, 19 October 1979.
53. *Politika*, 17 October 1979.

ity on the part of various nationalists, irredentists, hostile clergy and other ideological enemies'. They all had the same goal, he said, which was 'to provoke dissatisfaction among the Albanians in Kosovo and stir up disunity among its multinational population'.[54] Tito promised economic help for Kosovo, especially after the Yugoslav Prime Minister Veselin Djuranovic, who accompanied him during the tour, admitted that since 1975 only four new factories had been put into operation there.[55]

As the end of the 1970s, the national culture of the Albanians was flourishing in Kosovo, with the right to Albanian-language teaching from primary to university level guaranteed. According to an Albanian professor at the University of Pristina, Dr Hajredin Hoxha, Kosovo's Albanians enjoyed more rights and privileges than virtually any other of the world's minority groups. He stated in an interview:

> 'I have visited more than sixty countries and I have attended the most important conferences on these problems held in different parts of the world. I have come to the irrefutable conclusion as a result of this experience that not a single national minority in the world has achieved the rights that the Albanian nationality enjoys in Socialist Yugoslavia. The Albanian nationality exercises rights equal to those of the nations. To quote but one datum, it has its own university. In the world, only the Hungarians in Romania and the Swedes in Finland have their own university; and it should be pointed out that while the University of Pristina is completely autonomous, similar universities in other countries do not enjoy full autonomy.'[56]

With unrest about to erupt in Kosovo, this statement proved over-optimistic.

54. *Kommunist*, 19 October 1979.
55. RFE, BR/236, 25 October 1979.
56. Hajredin Hoxha interview, *Vjesnik*, 9 May 1981.

10

KOSOVO'S FLIMSY BRIDGE-BUILDING ROLE COLLAPSES

Tito's death was announced on 4 May 1980 a few days before his eighty-eighth birthday, and with him went the notion of national liberation, self-management, brotherhood and unity, and the Yugoslav road to socialism. The entire country was gripped by a sense of disorientation and foreboding, but nowhere more so than Kosovo: Albanians felt they had lost their protector. With no prepared successor, Tito had devised his replacement in the form of a collective leadership comprising a rotating eight-member state presidency, with all officials elected on the basis of equal representation of the six Republics and the two Autonomous Provinces. Thus it was hoped that its multi-ethnic composition would not cause Yugoslavia to fragment. However, the world's media immediately began to contemplate whether the country would survive his departure. Tito had held the country together with skillful diplomacy against the threat of Soviet invasion, and in buying off nationalist unrest with regional autonomy. His death now posed the problem of the establishment of a new system for conflict resolution, but for this the required strength, will, political skills and, above all, the necessary social and political consensus were lacking. The old system was retained: the League of Communists was neither centralised nor federalised and an exceptionally complex system of rotation and national balance in the state and Party hierarchy took a strong hold. The system was supposed to function without a dominant leader, but it was impossible with such an incompetent *nomenklatura*, i.e. groups of leaders at the federal, republican and provincial level who retained their high positions due not to any real ability but to their unshakable loyalty to Tito.[1]

1. D. Janjic, *Conflict or Dialogue: Serbia-Albanian Relations and Integration of the Balkans*, Subotica, 1994, p. 141.

One interesting reaction to the uncertainties after Tito's death was that many people now classified themselves as Yugoslavs rather than as members of a particular nationality. When the results of the 1981 census were published, it turned out that a surprisingly large number of Yugoslav citizens – around 1.22 million or 5.42 per cent of the total population – designated their nationality as 'Yugoslav'. This was 4.3 times as many as in 1971. Undoubtedly, the fear of conflict felt so soon after Tito's death, the wish to resolve personal dilemmas such as mixed marriages, or a preference for unity and centralism influenced some respondents. In addition, some groups who were minorities in their area might have sought to protect themselves by 'national Yugoslavness'. The number of citizens declaring themselves as 'Yugoslavs' varied according to region, but in Kosovo their share of the total – 0.2 per cent – was the lowest in all of Yugoslavia.[2]

In 1981 Albanians made up roughly 77 per cent of Kosovo's population of 1,584,588, but as in previous censuses the correct number of Albanians was unclear. For example, in the 1981 census baby boys were not registered in order to avoid future conscription. The question of Slav migration from Kosovo was still as emotional an issue as the high Albanian birthrate. Statistics for the number of Serbs and Montenegrins migrating from the Province were scarce, and those available tended to vary according to the nationality of their source: the Kosovars estimated that 57-60,000 left the province between 1971 and 1981, whereas the Serbs claimed that the number for that period was over 100,000.[3] According to the census, Serbs in Kosovo decreased by 18,172 between 1971 and 1981, and Montenegrins by 4,680. This fact had economic implications of some consequence for the Province because the migrating Slavs represented a high percentage of the professionals and specialists in Kosovo's population. Their exodus meant a drain of expertise in industry, technology, science and the professions. In contrast there was a migration into Kosovo of Albanians from Macedonia, Montenegro and the south of Serbia. The opening of Pristina University had greatly intensified inter-Albanian migration. It is estimated that in the period from 1966-86, 46,000 Albanians migrated to Kosovo from other regions of Yugoslavia.

According to *Rilindja*, the daily newspaper of the Communist League of Pristina, the major causes of migration were economic:

2.   V. Meier, 'Yugoslavia's National Question', p. 55.
3.   RFE, BR/242, 16 November 1982.

widespread unemployment in the Province was cited as the main factor for the departure of the Serbs and Montenegrins. Other factors were the housing problem and unfavourable educational conditions. Many of those who moved out, the report said, did so to further their professional training or instruction elsewhere in Yugoslavia. Thus, it appeared that those who migrated from the province did so to escape the hardships of life there and to take advantage of the opportunities for a better and more prosperous life that other parts of Yugoslavia offered. It was not only Slavs who had been leaving Kosovo. From 1971 to 1981, a total of 44,808 Albanians left the province as well, chiefly for economic but also for educational reasons.[4] The local Albanian press reported that in spite of being badly needed to cater for rapid population growth, new schools were not being built. Schools with only three-hour daily programmes, in three and even four shifts, were common. Teachers were the lowest-paid of sixty-five different professions, and were quitting their jobs. According to the Provincial Vice-premier quoted in *Rilindja* (5 May 1980):

> 'We have been recruiting people unable to find jobs elsewhere. Half the teachers are unqualified to teach. Books and related educational materials are limited or not available at all in many schools. Albanians seem particularly upset by the fact that investments are made to open colleges and university branches in non-Albanian towns, while their Albanian counterparts possess hardly enough funds and space for elementary and secondary education. Libraries, cultural and artistic societies are almost starved for lack of funds.'[5]

Much Albanian thinking at this time was basically on the lines that if the Kosovars could entirely manage their own economy, they would be able to alleviate their critical state of underdevelopment. Given that in Kosovo economic equality was a precondition to social and political stability, the socio-economic disparities continued to exacerbate tensions. Only one person in ten was a wage-earner. A disproportionately high share of central government funds was channelled into the administrative sector which, like the birth-rate, grew much faster than the economy and industrial output. An obvious problem in Kosovo, as in the rest of Yugoslavia, was the pervasive bureaucracy, rightly called a 'non-productive privileged class, causing a drain on the finances of the province. As a result, a

4. Pipa and Repishti, *Studies on Kosova*, pp. 128-9.
5. Repishti, 'Human Rights and the Albanian Nationality in Yugoslavia', p. 254.

quarter of all employed Albanians was a well-paid civil servant owning a car and decently housed. These privileges were resented by many of the lower-paid and by the thousands of unemployed graduates. Kosovo could ill afford such an inflated and extravagant administration.

The Albanian riots

Despite such undercurrents of resentment, few Yugoslavs could have anticipated the vehemence of the riots that shook Kosovo in the spring of 1981, less than a year after Tito's death. They were the worst seen in Kosovo since 1968. Years of pent-up frustration and bitterness at their perceived exploited status were let loose. On the evening of 11 March 1981, a group of students began complaining about crowded dormitory conditions and the poor food at the refectory of Pristina University. At the time, the University had an enrolment of 36,000 full-time students, and 18,000 more in extension study programmes. Yet the University had been built to accommodate only one-third of its then student body. Thus, students were sometimes obliged to sleep two to a bed. The doors of the educational system had been thrown wide open, partly as a stop-gap to lighten the unemployment problem; the authorities reasoned that it was better to have the youth in the classroom than roaming the streets. Consequently, Kosovo's ratio of students was the highest in the country: 274.7 per 1,000 inhabitants, compared with the Yugoslav national average of 194.9. One out of every three inhabitants in the Province was enrolled in some kind of educational programme.[6]

Before long the instigators of the complaints were joined by hundreds of other youths, who then spilled on to the streets immediately surrounding the university. There they were met by a hastily-formed cordon of security police who were able to disperse the crowds. But this was only a temporary pause, because even more students came back onto the streets of Pristina on 26 March. This time, Serb and Montenegrin citizens were beaten, their homes and businesses burned, and their shops looted. Kosovo's Serb population were now seriously alarmed. During the night of 15 March 1981, a mysterious fire destroyed much of the old guesthouse wing of the Pec Patriarchate, including the monks' living quarters, together

6. Pipa and Repishti, *Studies on Kosova*, p. 144.

with a quantity of books and furniture. Serb public opinion was enraged by the fire and at the failure of the Kosovo police to arrest anyone for the act. According to the Albanians, however, the fire had only destroyed the convent of the Sisters at Pec, a fairly recent construction with no architectural value. But although the convent is a good distance from the Patriarchate, which was not touched by the fire, the way the incident was presented to the press suggested that the Patiarchate itself had been damaged. Albanian 'irredentists' were accused of causing the fire, but in a court investigation the Albanian Judge Hoti declared that it had been caused by an electrical fault.[7] Despite the minimal damage, the Federal government allotted surprisingly high funds to restore the convent. The case then seemed closed, until it was re-opened in 1991.

Meanwhile, the demonstrations had spread to Kosovo's other main towns. Among the many slogans and banners which now appeared were statements calling for a 'unified Albania' and 'Kosovo - Republic'.[8] Excessive force was used to stabilise the riots; tanks were deployed and a curfew was imposed throughout Kosovo. Up to 30,000 troops patrolled the Province, which the Albanian population viewed as a military occupation. Officially it was reported that eleven people had died, but Albanians say the true number was almost 1,000.[9] Before long the student demonstrators were joined by factory workers, farmers and, as was later disclosed, several members of the League of Communists of Kosovo and Albanian members of the army and police. Schools and factories were closed, and the Province came to a virtual standstill. The Federal Secretary of Internal Affairs, Stane Dolance, declared: 'Albanian irredentists are now showing their true face, they no longer talk about a republic but say 'long live Enver Hoxha'. It is quite clear that what is really involved is the integrity of the Yugoslav State. This is why we call it a counter-revolution.'[10]

However, by all accounts the disturbances were a far cry from a revolution in any sense of the word. Pristina's huge student body,

7. In 1982, when the rebuilt church was being consecrated, Serbs from all over Yugoslavia arrived in Pec to show their solidarity with their Kosovo brethren.
8. Demand for Republic status was unacceptable because it would necessitate changing Yugoslavia's internal system and thus threaten the country's territorial integrity.
9. Amnesty International learned that the Central Committee of the League of Communists of Serbia received intelligence that over 300 people had died in the course of the disturbances.
10. Tanjug, 29 September 1981.

which spent much of its time roaming the central avenues of the city, created the perfect conditions for the eruption of discontent. This very large number of students represented a political and social time-bomb. Student apathy was widespread as, compared with other Yugoslav universities, the quality of education left much to be desired. A report in the Albanian daily *Rilindja* (21 February 1981) quoted a large number of students who disclosed that they did not bother to read that newspaper and were unaware that it devoted a full page to university affairs every Wednesday. Above all, student discontent appeared strongest over the lack of material comforts at the university. The final massive demonstration was on 18 May, when thousands of students occupied the dormitories and were only dispersed the next day by police using tear gas. The authorities closed the University and ordered all students to return home. The University Council was dissolved and a 'mandatory administration' was imposed. However, the contact of homecoming students with town and village youth only inflamed the situation.[11]

In the aftermath of the riots, Yugoslav public opinion made Kosovo's education system one of its main targets for criticism because so many of the youth had taken part in the violence. Pristina University was labelled a hot-bed of Albanian nationalism, and numerous professors were named in a black-list published by the journal *Komunist*, demanding tougher measures against nationalists and opportunist teachers and mentioning all towns that had not yet taken measures against the latter.[12] The new collective Yugoslav leadership could ill afford to be seen making concessions to nationalist-inspired demands, and therefore took up an uncompromising and pragmatic position. The Belgrade paper *Borba* openly asked why Pristina University had been encouraged to grow so large when it was inconceivable that its graduates could find jobs to match their training and ambitions. As already mentioned, the majority of Albanian students were enrolled for courses in the liberal arts curricula studying Islamic art or Albanian history and folklore, and Kosovo's economy could not absorb such an abundance of graduates in these subjects. Only around 20 per cent studied science and technology. These first-generation students not only had rising aspirations themselves, but so did the members of their large extended families. Albanians now suffered from an explosion

11. Repishti, 'Human Rights and the Albanian Nationality...', p. 259.
12. RFE, Background Report/163, June 1981.

of education after having had none. The narrow cultural orientation of the new graduates inhibited the drive for development and
isolated them from the rest of Yugoslav Society. Tanjug reported
that the Provincial League of Communists of Yugoslavia had
recommended that enrolment at Pristina University be cut by 10 per
cent and that some faculties be moved to more remote parts of
Kosovo. Apart from the imbalance in the subjects studied, its hasty
establishment had resulted in little or no academic criteria being
applied to the employment of Albanian teaching staff, most of
whom were semi-competent at best. Less than half of the professors
possessed doctorates, and even those who did had generally
published little and were not considered serious scholars by their
peers in the rest of Yugoslavia. The academic environment was thus
mediocre.

At first the regime played down the riots and tried to persuade
the public that they had been caused by the 'dirty work' of traitors,
and were unanimously condemned by local Albanians.[13] However,
this facade could not be maintained for long and admission of the
scale of the violence led to criticism of the Party's entire policy on
Kosovo up to that time. The fact that the problem could only be
contained by force played into the hands of government hardliners,
who argued that the devolution favoured by the Party's liberals as a
means of appeasement had easily been turned around and exploited
as a tool of rebellion. Official Yugoslav accounts ultimately laid the
blame for the riots firmly on the political leadership of 'the League
of Communists of Kosovo and other subjective forces who did not
wage a sufficiently energetic, determined and open ideological-
political struggle against Greater Albanian nationalism and irredentism. The many years of experience should not have been reason for
such passivity.'[14] The Party leaderships of Serbia and Yugoslavia were
also blamed for not having more 'promptly realised what was
happening, and for not having taken firmer and more timely
measures in order to deal with events in Kosovo.'[15]

There was a call for more open cooperation and consultation
between the leaders of the Province of Kosovo and of the Republic of Serbia. The President of the Serbian Central Committee, Dr
Tihomir Vlaskalic, echoed common Serb sentiments: 'We have

13. Tanjug, 10 April 1981.
14. 'Relationship Between Yugoslavia and Albania', *Review of International Affairs*,
    Belgrade, 1984, p. 97.
15. Ibid., p. 99.

taken it for granted that Kosovo has its own Republic in Yugoslavia
- the Socialist Republic of Serbia.'[16] Tanjug reported that 'the
inescapable conclusion is that much of the Kosovar Party is either
implicated in the unrest in some way or is sympathetic to the growing secessionist movement. The Kosovar Party organisation and the
security apparatus are permeated with Albanian counterrevolu-
tionaries and irredentists'.[17] The unrest had caught the Belgrade
authorities by surprise, and as the search began for a scapegoat, two
main questions were being asked: why was the (Yugoslav) population at large so badly misinformed about what happened in Kosovo
and what did the Party members do during the events? Both questions directly concerned Mahmut Bakalli's responsibility in his
capacity as head of the League of Communists of Kosovo: 'How was
it possible that we learned about the whole affair only from
Comrade Dolanc's April 6th Press Conference?'[18]

The minutes of the Kosovo Party's Provincial Committee meeting held on 8 March gave no indication of the latent discontent
which led to the riots only three days later. The Belgrade daily *Politika* remarked ironically that on the very day of some of the worst
rioting the leading Kosovo daily carried a full-page advertisement for
tourist facilities in the Province; the inference was that responsibility for the breakdown of communications between Belgrade and
Pristina lay with the Regional Party.[19] As the violence escalated after
26 March, Bakalli asked the Provincial Committee to discuss police
overreaction. He pleaded that the army, which was being sent to
protect the radio and television stations, should not come, aware of
the provocation it would cause.[20] Only five days before the unrest
Bakalli made a statement that a lack of elementary consumer goods
in Kosovo could not be tolerated and that a struggle had to be waged
for the protection of the living standards of low-income workers, the
unemployed and students.[21] Bakalli's interpretation of Kosovo's social
and economic irregularities confirms the accounts of the true nature
of the unrest given by foreign reporters; that they were inspired not
by nationalism but by economic and social factors.

16. *Vjesnik*, Zagreb, 23 March 1981.
17. Tanjug, 23 June 1981.
18. RFE, BR/114, April 1981.
19. P. Artisien, 'Yugoslavia, Albania and the Kosovo Riots', *The World Today*, vol. 37, no. 11.
20. Author's interview with Mahmut Bakalli, Pristina, October 1996.
21. *Rilindja*, 8 March 1981.

Yugoslav-Albanian relations; Kosovar irredentism

Within the general context of growing ties between Yugoslavia and Albania, a major trade agreement between the two countries had been signed in early 1980 in Belgrade for the forthcoming five-year period, 1980-5. In April 1980 a contract was signed in Pristina to build a long-distance transmission line between Albania and Kosovo to make possible greater exports of electricity to Yugoslavia and beyond. Travellers along the Yugoslav-Albanian border reported intense activity in many areas of cooperation: traffic and general travel, though still modest in non–Albanian terms, were on the increase; customs areas were being expanded and roads widened and surfaced.[22] In January 1981 Albania's most renowned artist, the sculptor Odhise Paskali,[23] visited Pristina for an exhibition of his works there. According to the Albanian writer Ismail Kadare, literature from Kosovo was making ever greater inroads in Albania, and hundreds of thousands of copies of books by Kosovar authors were circulating in the country. Furthermore the magazine *Les Lettres Albanaises*, published in French for foreign readers, carried works by Kosovar authors in most issues. Thus, despite the deep social and ideological contrasts between the two sides, Kosovar-Albanian rapprochement was gathering pace. And in the early 1980s, as Yugoslavia became one of Albania's major trading partners, the ideological differences between them were played down. It was assumed that, with the death of Tito the Yugoslav state was on the verge of collapse. Albania's leaders therefore helped to instill in Kosovo a general pro-Albanian orientation. At Pristina University young Albanians cheered the name of Enver Hoxha and called for a Socialist Republic of Kosovo. The majority of Kosovars had no idea what life was like inside Albania or of how bad things were economically. They tended to see Albania through rose-tinted glasses, believing that the Tirana regime had managed to eliminate unemployment and create an egalitarian society with the order and discipline which they tended to regard as traditional attributes of Kosovar society, and so lacking in the Yugoslavia of the 1980s. They believed that if Albanians rather than Slavs could govern their society, then things would work more efficiently – as they believed was the case in Albania. Much has been said and written about the forces behind the demonstrations. Provincial and other Yugoslav

22. RFE BR/176, 17 July 1980.
23. Paskali, who studied in Italy in the 1930s, is best remembered for his statue of Skanderbeg in Tirana's main square.

leaders continued to point the finger at 'reactionary' and 'counter-revolutionary' circles both inside and outside the country (political exiles). Kosovo's state President Xhavid Nimami was more specific, naming the 'Ballists' headed by Abaz Ermeni, 'Zogists' headed by Leka Zogu (son of Albania's one-time self-proclaimed king Ahmed Zogu), and the so-called 'extremists' headed by Emin Fazliu. Although it seems entirely possible that some of these exile groups played some role in the unrest, it is the 'extremist' group that aroused particular interest, since attention was focused on so-called 'Marxist-Leninist' elements represented by the splinter communist parties in the West that accepted the Albanian brand of communism and with which Tirana was known to maintain active contacts. Many questions were being asked: why did Pristina allow any such Tirana-inspired subversive activities to be carried out in the Province? Did the Kosovo leadership perhaps miscalculate the real intentions of the Albanian Communists towards Kosovo? Or might Pristina be deliberately exaggerating the role of the 'leftists' in the riots to be able to implicate Tirana in the unrest?[24]

It was widely believed that the irredentist tendencies of Albanian nationalists in Kosovo were not of recent origin but were a continuation of various collaborationist and fascist organisations which had fought against the National Liberation Army during the war. As has been mentioned previously, the national security organs had uncovered several Albanian nationalist and irredentist organisations and groups active in Kosovo. Albanians had been responsible for a number of actual or attempted political assassinations of Yugoslav citizens since the early 1970s. Groups ideologically related to Tirana were known to be engaged in subversive activities. One of them, the Movement for the Albanian Socialist Republic in Yugoslavia, published in Switzerland its periodical: *Zeri i Kosoves* (The Voice of Kosovo). Other Tirana-orientated groups had such titles as 'Marxist Leninist Youth of Kosovo' and the 'Group of Marxist-Leninists of Kosovo'. Meanwhile, at a meeting of the provincial council to mark the forthcoming fortieth anniversary of the Kosovo Uprising and Revolution, Xhavid Nimani discussed Kosovo's provincial status. He stressed the genesis and constitutional position of the Province, repeating the official Belgrade line that giving Kosovo republican status would destroy the integrity of the country:

24. RFE, BR/125, 6 May 1981.

'The repeated slogan of the enemy, "Why aren't all the Albanians
who live in the three republics and in the Socialist Autonomous
Province of Kosovo united into one republic", is a reactionary one
and its purpose is to ruin the integrity of Yugoslavia and to destroy
the community of the federation. This slogan "united Albanians", is
destructive and reactionary in the same way as are the slogans
"United Serbs", "United Croats", and so forth.[25]

The most important of the numerous Albanian underground
organisations uncovered in the wake of the 1981 disturbances were
the Movement for the National Liberation of Kosovo, led by the
Gervalla brothers, and the Group of Marxist-Leninists of Kosovo,
led by Kadri Zeka (the Gervalla brothers as well as Kadri Zeka were
later mysteriously murdered in Germany). Several of these groups
later worked together in the Movement for an Albanian Socialist
Republic of Kosovo in Yugoslavia. Although most of these groups
were led by intellectuals, their influence was most prominent among
the peasants. All had a Communist outlook, at least nominally, and
were sympathetic to Albania and its Communist leaders Enver
Hoxha and, after his death in 1985, to his successor Ramiz Alia.
Perhaps the fact that some of these groups received help through
Albanian embassies explains their orientation towards the regime in
Tirana.[26]

On 21 July 1981 Bislim Bajrami, a machinist, Ismail Smakiqi, a
law graduate, and Jakup Rexhepi, a teacher, were tried by Mitrovica district court on charges of having formed an illegal group.
According to reports in the Yugoslav press, Bajrami was approached
in early 1980 by a member of the 'Movement for the National
Liberation of Kosovo' (MNLK) which had created a five-member
cell in Decani commune. Later he had allegedly founded a three-
member cell consisting of himself, Ismail Smakiqi and Jakup
Rexhepi. They received the statutes and clandestine émigré publications of the MNLK, paid a monthly membership subscription
and tried to recruit other members, though with little apparent
success. According to press reports, the three defendants were found
guilty of 'founding an illegal group with the aim of destroying the
constitutional order of Yugoslavia, disrupting Yugoslavia's brotherhood and unity and promoting the annexation of Kosovo to Albania'. They received sentences of from six to eight years'

25. Ibid.
26. J. Jensen, 'Human Rights and Abuses in Kosovo in the 1980s and the Response
    from the West', in Duijzings, Janjic, and Maliqi (eds), *Kosovo - Kosova*, p. 93.

imprisonment on charges of 'association for purposes of hostile activity' and 'counter-revolutionary endangering of the social order' under Articles 136 and 114 of the federal criminal code.[27]

However, there was no direct proof of Tirana's involvement in the events of 1981. On the contrary, Albania had repeatedly emphasised its interest in Yugoslavia's stability to avoid any possible Soviet intervention which would threaten its own independence as well. Albania feared that to further Soviet-Yugoslav rapprochement Moscow might approve the annexation of Albania by Yugoslavia, especially since Albania had lost the support of China during the mid-1970s. Alternately, the Yugoslavs feared that the return of Soviet influence in Albania might provide an additional magnet for the Yugoslav Albanians – on the assumption that a pro-Soviet Albania might relax its internal policies and thus heighten the aspirations of the Kosovars towards Albania (after 1978 Yugoslavia and Albania were the only Balkan countries not aligned to either of the two power blocs). Hitherto Albania's political isolation had acted as a strong deterrent to any pro-Tirana orientation on the part of Yugoslavia's Albanians. During the 1970s, the Yugoslav authorities had encouraged visits by ordinary Kosovars to Albania so that they could see the huge disparities in social conditions, and compare the locked and boarded-up mosques there with the functioning and sometimes newly-built ones in Yugoslavia.

As for Albania being involved in the disturbances – on the contrary, there was unease in Tirana over the developments in Kosovo, where Albanians were perceived as national 'purists' whose intensifying nationalism was unsettling to the authorities in Tirana because it was not subject to their control. There was also fear that the Kosovars, who had a freer life, could practise their religion and were able to travel abroad, might have caused unrest in Albania by stimulating desires for similar conditions there. Furthermore, Tirana appreciated the importance of Yugoslavia as one one of the few countries with which it then had contacts, as its most important trading partner, and as a rampart against the Soviets.[28] An American observer questioned who would end up running a Greater Albania should it come into existence:

> 'Would the Kosovars, possessing a more sophisticated social and economic infrastructure, better educated for modern life not quickly

27. *Yugoslavia - Prisoners of Conscience*, Amnesty International Publications, 1985, p. 38.
28. Meier, 'Yugoslavia's National Question', p. 59.

become the big fish in a little pond, rather than the little fish in a big pond populated by people who generally despise them. And was this not an enticing prospect for the young, nationally conscious intellectuals, embittered by low status and frustrated by lack of opportunity in Kosovo and by cultural and linguistic barriers to opportunity elsewhere in the country of their present citizenship?'[29]

During the Hoxha years, Kosovo was seen as Albania's stake in Yugoslavia - a kind of buffer zone. In the complex international situation following the Soviet invasion of Czechoslovakia in 1968, the constant fear of invasion by the Soviet Union – shared by Belgrade – led Tirana more than once to go so far as to say that if Yugoslavia were attacked, Albania would come to her aid. Consequently, the Albanian government never pleaded the Kosovar cause before such international forums as the United Nations European Commission on Human Rights or interfered directly in Kosovo's internal politics. Whenever persecuted members of illegal Kosovar groups sought shelter in Albania they were promptly handed back to the Yugoslav authorities, in what the young Kosovar activists understandably saw as intolerable violations of basic rights of asylum. The much-maligned Swiss and Federal German authorities were undoubtedly far more helpful and generous in their treatment of Kosovar asylum-seekers during these bitter and difficult years of communist betrayal of the national cause than the corrupt, complacent professional élite of Tirana. Most of the latter had never left Albania except as honoured guests of foreign partners in delegations, and had no knowledge whatever of the severe persecutions of Albanian activists in Kosovo or of the depredation of the natural resources of the region. This background of betrayal by the Tirana authorities has never been forgotten in Kosovo.

For some time, therefore, the Yugoslav leaders were reluctant to identify Tirana as the instigator of the trouble. There was no direct proof of its involvement, and because of its extreme isolationist position, Belgrade was well aware of the importance for Albania of there being a degree of stability not only in Kosovo but in Yugoslavia as a whole. So initially Yugoslav officials put the blame for the unrest squarely on foreign enemies in the West. But once Tirana had published its first major editorial in the daily *Zeri-i-Popullit* condemning Yugoslavia's handling of the crisis, the blame was at once shifted on to Tirana. Albanian-Kosovar cooperation

29. Rusinow, *Kosovo, the Other Albania*, p. 16.

now came to a near-standstill, and Albanian propaganda against Yugoslavia was intensified, especially after an Albanian report mentioned the sensitive subject of Yugoslavia's territorial integrity: 'The London and Versailles Treaties, which settled the frontiers between Yugoslavia and Albania, can no longer be imposed to the detriment of the Albanian people.'[30] In June *Zeri-i-Popullit* published an editorial headed: 'The Events in Kosovo and the Secret Soviet-Great-Serbian Collaboration', which drew attention to the deceptive silence in Moscow over the Kosovo riots. It concluded that Moscow had counted on the Serbian strong-arm soon being used in the rest of Yugoslavia, and so causing repercussions throughout the Balkans and thence to NATO via Italy and Greece. It argued that the weakening of the Yugoslav Federation would strengthen Bulgarian demands for Macedonia.[31]

This kind of reporting was in marked contrast to Tirana's previous policy of seeking to minimise the broader significance of the disturbances in the Province. Belgrade reacted promptly by severing Kosovo's cultural links with Albania; Albanian textbooks were banned, and Belgrade undertook to translate the more 'reliable' Serbian textbooks into Albanian. Events in Kosovo again directly influenced other Albanian-inhabited areas, especially Western Macedonia, where in July 1981 police and territorial defence units were put on alert after leaflets were distributed calling on Albanians to rebel. The Skopje authorities, perceiving a threat to the territorial integrity and stability of Macedonia, therefore instigated a far more intensive campaign against Albanian national culture than in Kosovo. An initiative was even launched in early 1981 to ban the use of the Albanian flag in Macedonia. The subsequent trials, purges and dismissals of Albanians resulted in a steady accumulation of frustration and anger. When the university and secondary schools closed for the summer holidays, a series of speedy trials were held, most lasting barely a couple of hours, in which nearly 300 Albanian youths were sentenced to prison terms of up to fifteen years. In June 1981 the authorities announced that 506 demonstrators had been summarily sentenced under the Code for Petty Offences, which meant fines or imprisonment for up to sixty days. According to a report in the Belgrade weekly news magazine *NIN* on 6 September, a further 245 people had been sentenced by 31 August under federal

30. *Zeri-i-Popullit*, 8 April 1981.
31. RFE, BR/199, June 1981.

law from one to fifteen years' imprisonment; another sixty people were tried and convicted in September.[32] These actions caused disapproving voices to be heard from leading officials in Croatia and Slovenia. The Croatian Education Minister warned his Serbian colleagues against conducting a policy that would only brand a great number of people as traitors – i.e. life-long opponents for themselves and unjustified 'national heroes' for other Albanians.

In the state of emergency imposed on Kosovo, over 1,000 members of the League of Communists of Yugoslavia were either formally expelled or simply struck off the membership rolls, and eleven basic party organisations were completely eliminated. The leading politicians in Kosovo were not immune to the regional political purge. One of the first steps taken was to remove Mahmut Bakalli, who had links with powerful, almost dynastic family backers in Albania through his relationship to the Hoxha family. The Provincial leadership admitted the futility of its past policy in Kosovo and failure to oppose the growth of both Albanian and Serb nationalism. Bakalli was succeeded by his predecessor, Veli Deva, who had constantly criticised Greater Serbian chauvinism in Kosovo. Deva's return to the top Party post in Kosovo indicated that Belgrade liked to have in Pristina a man who was respected among the Albanians but also had strong anti-Tirana feelings, stemming back to his anti-communist role in the Second World War. Deva's main task was to retain Kosovo for Yugoslavia. Although martial law was lifted two months after the riots, extra security forces were deployed outside the main towns, and the Province was patrolled by plainclothes men from the Federal Ministry of the Interior. At night the evening *corso* in Pristina seemed to crackle with tension as Serbs walked arm in arm one way and Albanians the other, neither group looking at the other.

By now three groups had emerged among the Albanian intellectual élite: extremists who endorsed Albanian irredentism; supporters of the League of Communists who worked to implement its policies; and 'sympathisers' – the largest group – who verbally supported the League of Communists but privately sympathised with the ideas of Albanian nationalism and irredentism. Discontent in Serbia and among Serbs elsewhere in Yugoslavia increased particularly after the Croatian, Slovenian and some Bosnian communists extended support to the Kosovo leadership. During the previous

32. *Yugoslavia - Prisoners of Conscience*, p. 12.

decade Kosovo's Slav population had found themselves within an increasingly culturally and politically Albanianised environment. The proportional employment policy had resulted in positive discrimination against the Serb and Montenegrin population. In the autumn of 1981 a dissatisfied group of Kosovo Serbs began to organise themselves, and Dobrica Cosic, the writer then seen as the contemporary spiritual father of the Serb nation, secretly advised them to write a petition and to put forward their demands. He was not their only support. They also had a silent backer: the Serbian government. A trio of local Serb activists – Miroslav Solevic, Kosta Bulatovic and Bosko Budimirovic – soon circulated their first protest petition, and it attracted just seventy-six signatures, but they were later to garner wider public support with their frequently repeated simple message: 'This is our land. If Kosovo and Metohija are not Serbian then we don't have any land of our own.'[33] In November the Central Committee of the League of Communists of Yugoslavia met to discuss Kosovo. A major report was delivered by Dobroslav Culafic, Secretary of the CC Presidium, who admitted that the main cause of the 'troubles' was erroneous policy in the past, especially concerning vital sectors of social, economic and cultural life. However, he went on to say that for the Yugoslav party there was 'no difference between the slogan: "Kosovo...a Republic" within the framework of Yugoslavia, and the slogan "Kosovo...a Republic" outside Yugoslavia'.[34]

Following the riots, however, neither side showed any moderation in its official rhetoric. While pronouncements from Belgrade lambasted Albania for interfering in Yugoslavia's internal affairs by inciting irredentism, Tirana retorted with equal force. In the words of Politburo member Ramiz Alia, the actions of Belgrade showed a 'savage chauvinistic spirit'.[35] The political campaign that followed played on the element of fear, stressing particularly the danger to peace and stability in the Balkans which could result from 'nationalist' manifestations. At the start of the new academic year in September 1981, strict censorship was imposed on the teaching of Albanian history, literature, language, culture and arts. The number of Albanian students was to be reduced each year, and in the 1980s the earlier quota which reserved two-thirds of the study places for Albanians was steadily reduced. In addition, local authorities had to

33. Silber and Little, *The Death of Yugoslavia*, London, 1995, p. 33.
34. RFE, BR/326, November 1981.
35. Albanian Telegraphic Agency, 16 September 1982.

confirm the moral and political 'reliability' of every incoming student. Despite the dramatically increased cultural contacts between Tirana and Pristina, their effect had been limited. The heavy-handed political dogmatism and Stalinist propaganda of the Albanian side was regarded by the Yugoslav authorities with a good deal of suspicion, and the broader range and eclectic, experimental nature of much theatre in Kosovo was similarly regarded by the Tirana authorities. Thus the political barrier had once again impeded the development of a unified Albanian culture.[36]

The further strengthening of the Republics and the decline of the Party's importance in the spectrum of Yugoslav institutions accelerated after Tito's death, reaching a high-point for the time at the 12th Congress of the League of Communists of Yugoslavia in 1982. Both developments were closely linked to growing economic difficulties which could not be overcome by Party resolutions alone. It also became clear that all the problems, including that of Kosovo, did not lead to strong solidarity within the Yugoslav Party but rather to an intensification of conflicts.[37] A year after Tito's death, in May 1981, Yugoslavia seemed to be pregnant with many large or small Kosovo affairs, inherited by Tito's successors from their great leader, whose 'impeccability' they had stubbornly refused to challenge. The collective presidency consisted of insignificant politicians loyal to the narrow interests of their federal units. In fact, it was precisely Tito's personality cult, his unchallenged authority, which in his life-time had successfully prevented dangerous internal confrontation both within the party and in the country, but which had led after his death to a number of serious problems, the biggest and most immediate being the chaotic economic situation. In fairness to Tito's successors, they could not be considered solely to be blamed for the untoward developments in the years after his death. In the past they had done what Tito had wanted them to do, all attempts in his lifetime to change policy having ended with one of his merci-less purges – in 1971 in Croatia, in 1972 in Serbia, Slovenia and Macedonia. As a result a loyal *nomenklatura* was created, unwilling to blame either Tito or themselves for past or present mistakes. But since in a communist dictatorship (however 'liberal") somebody had to be blamed for failure, they sought these 'somebodies' in 'foreign enemies' coming not only from Moscow and Tirana but

36. Elsie, *History of Albanian Literature*, vol. II, p. 653.
37. Meier, 'Yugoslavia's National Question', p. 53.

also from Stuttgart and New York.[38] In the wake of the Kosovo riots, these reactions could be interpreted as a measure of Belgrade's high degree of sensitivity.

Perhaps the single most important outcome of the Kosovo riots was seen in the more anti-Yugoslav line and, at the same time, more sympathetic attitude towards the Albanians of Kosovo taken by the Western press. The skillfully concealed inequality of the Serbian people in confederal Yugoslavia became an issue on which the state and ideological foundations of Tito's Yugoslavia began to crumble. Serbs argued that the policy of positive discrimination had gone too far. As well as blaming the Kosovo leadership for the province's ills, many Serbs began to talk of 'past mistakes', in effect criticising Tito without mentioning his name. They believed that Yugoslav-Albanian cooperation had been reduced too much to the narrow Kosovo-Albanian level, reflecting Tito's wish that Kosovo should be the bridge-builder in that cooperation. Many Serbs felt that Tito's successors had now to reap where Tito had sown, especially in his liberal attitude towards Tirana. In an interview Milos Minic, one of Serbia's Party leaders, said:

> 'Tito was always his own foreign Minister and Enver Hoxha used this soft line of Tito's so that an open flirtation was possible in Kosovo... We should have explained this Albanian variant of Stalinism, we should not have left our people so completely uninformed about it. If we had done so, there would be fewer misled young people in Kosovo. We now have to correct this without turning everything into a campaign against Albania and the Albanian people.'[39]

Fadil Hoxha replied: 'Greater Albanian nationalism, if it gained momentum, would also stir the spectres of Greater Serbian, Bulgarian, Greek and all the other nationalisms in the Balkans.' He went on to hint at possible Soviet interference: 'It has been realised in the world that there are sinister forces behind the events in Kosovo which do not want peace in either Yugoslavia or in the other Balkan nations.' He concluded that it was an attempt to undermine the non-aligned movement; to 'deal a blow to Yugoslavia as a pioneer and one of the most active members of the non-aligned movement'.[40] It is certainly no accident that it was precisely at this

38. RFE, BR/127, 6 May 1981.
39. *Vjesnik*, 8 May 1981
40. RFE, BR/122, 28 April 1981.

time that new polemics began between Yugoslavia and the Soviet Union over the policy and role of the non-aligned movement. During the previous few years, a fierce struggle had been waged within the non-aligned movement over its position between the two military blocs. Yugoslavia had resisted pressure from Cuba and Vietnam for an eventual rapprochement with the Soviet Union. *Borba* in Belgrade assessed the events in Kosovo saying:

'Our independence and non-alignment are the most important facets of our existence. This makes us vigilant so far as bloc tensions go and this is why we do not accept anybody's lessons concerning political evaluations of events in the world or in our own country.'[41]

There is a slim possibility that some of the rioting students were manipulated by so-called 'Cominformist' elements – pro-Soviet and mainly of Serbo–Montenegrin background. The use of 'Marx-ist-Leninist' in the names of illegal Albanian groups in Kosovo had been noticeable since the beginning of the crisis there in 1981.[42]

For the next few years a wave of 'hostile activities' swept Kosovo as well as several towns and villages in Western Macedonia and Albanian-inhabited regions of Montenegro. These activities included defacing government buildings, desecrating communist monuments and Serbian cemeteries, and secretly distributing anti-government literature. The sense of unease among the Slav population grew and helped spur on the exodus of Serbs and Montenegrins. Along with the sense of alienation from the Yugoslav community felt by the Albanians of Kosovo and other regions went the sense of persecution and oppression – albeit perceived rather than actual – experienced by the Serbs and Montenegrins of Kosovo. The events of 1966-8 that so increased mass self-confidence among Albanians also brought about increased Serbian and Montenegrin emigration from the province. If before 1981 much of this flow appeared to be of members of the intelligentsia seeking higher living standards elsewhere in Yugoslavia, subsequently emigration had taken the form of flight – reportedly encouraged by letters, threats, burnings, beatings, murders and Serbian monasteries and monuments in Kosovo being vandalised. Those Serbs who left Kosovo for good settled in places like Smed-erevo, Kragujevac, Nis, Kraljevo and Svetozarevo, as well as

41. *Borba*, 26 April 1981.
42. I. Banac, *With Stalin Against Tito*, Cornell University Press, Ithaca, NY, 1988, p. 267.

Belgrade, where they were referred to by the derogatory term '*Vrcani*' and were rumoured to suffer new social ostracism for having lived for years among the Albanians.[43]

The net emigration of Slavs from Kosovo in the decade 1971-81 was calculated at 102,000, which only served to reinforce a Serbian nationalist backlash. One important aspect of the departure of skilled Slavs from Kosovo was the decline of Serbo-Croatian culture and education in the Province, which left the remaining Slavs feeling increasingly isolated amidst a sea of Albanian culture. Serbs and Albanians began boycotting each other's shops and bakeries, cutting their sales to a fraction of their former level. A similar syndrome developed in Macedonia and Montenegro. In a dramatic appeal, the Serbian Party Central Committee called for the exodus of Slavs from Kosovo to be halted. An observer noted that if it were to continue, Serbian nationalist agitation could be stirred throughout Yugoslavia, creating new animosity in already strained relations among the nationalities. This is why the Serbian leaders warned so dramatically against a revival of nationalism.[44] The fourth plenary session of the League of Communists of Kosovo, held in October 1982, dealt with the question of migration. The main speaker, Azem Vllasi, said that no one had succeeded in realising the 'reactionary dream' of an 'ethnically clean' Kosovo, nor would the Albanian nationalists and irredentists succeed in their efforts. He added, however, that if this process continued it would have 'enormous consequences, not only for the present generation, but for future generations too'.[45]

Serb reaction and a hardening of attitudes

According to Milovan Djilas, 'Wipe away Kosovo from the Serb mind and soul and we are no more. If there had been no battle at Kosovo, the Serbs would have invented it for its suffering and heroism.' Djilas saw the plight of the Kosovo Serbs as spearheading the Serb nationalist drive:

> 'The crisis which visibly began after Tito's death, manifested itself by splitting the Communist Party into Republican and Autonomous Parties. I think the present degree of separatism is a reaction to Communism and to the nationalist discontent caused by the failure

43. M. Baskin, 'Crisis in Kosovo', *Problems of Communism*, March/April 1983, p. 72.
44. RFE, BR/142, May 1981.
45. *Rilindja*, 27 October 1982 - RFE, BR/242, 16 November 1982.

to defend the Kosovo Serbs...One reason for this sudden strengthening of national ideologies is that long after the war, Yugoslavia was a far more centralistic state than the Kingdom of Yugoslavia had ever been. In the Kingdom, the constituent nations could give free reign to their national feelings through their national parties, at least in Croatia and Slovenia. Serbia had no strictly national party as it had no real need for one.'[46]

In marked contrast to the 'Yugoslav' identity so noticable throughout the country in the 1981 census, people were now increasingly identifying with their national status, and the Albanian demonstrations were merely the most public manifestation of this trend. Fairly homogeneous national cores had been emerging inside the eight regions of Yugoslavia, and these were gradually evolving into nation-states. For the Serbs the tendency towards identifying the Republics with ethnic groups only enhanced their feelings of insecurity; they had the largest number of persons living outside their Republic, in which there was not only division, with two Autonomous Provinces, but one of them, Kosovo, was rapidly becoming a national home for Yugoslavia's Albanian minority. The Serbs therefore resisted any moves which would give yet more power to the Republics at the expense of the Federation.

The Serbian national question always presented a contradictory role in Yugoslavia. Because of the sizeable number of their people who lived outside the Serbian Republic, Serbs were particularly sensitive to any weakening of Yugoslav unity. On the other hand, any Serbian mobilisation on a nationalist basis presented a real threat to the federal structure of Yugoslavia, which still adhered to the idea that a weak Serbia ensured a strong Yugoslavia. It is ironical that the riots, while focusing on the Albanian question, also raised the Serbian national question. In marked contrast to previous events, it was the Kosovo Serbs who now had the identity crisis as they too began demonstrating against their perceived victimisation. The ideological screen suddenly collapsed, forbidden political subjects inundated the press, re-examinations of the interpretations of contemporary history began, and Serbia found itself in the paradoxical situation of having its national interests saved by the Communist Party - the main source of all its troubles.[47]

46. Unpublished interview with Milovan Djilas by G. Cirjanic, Belgrade, February 1989.
47. D. Batakovic, *The Kosovo Chronicles*, Belgrade, 1992, p. 31.

Communism had emerged as the protector of the Serbs' national interests, although under communism, according to Serbian historiography, it was Albanian as opposed to Serbian national integration that had continuity. Serbian historiography identifies 1918 as when the process of national integration and unification of the Serbian people ended with the creation of the Kingdom of Serbs, Croats and Slovenes. It was then that the Serbs conceded their national ideology to that of a Yugoslav character. Discontinuity in the development of the Serbian national movement deepened during the 1941-5 war, and turned under communist rule into a fifty-year-long vacuum which proved almost fatal for the protection of the primary national interests.[48] From 1982 onwards Belgrade engaged in a policy of political differentiation in Kosovo aimed at rooting out Albanian nationalism and purging and placing under firmer control the local League of Communists organisation. In his report to the 13th Conference of the Provincial Committee of the Kosovo League of Communists in April 1982, the Committee President, Veli Deva, gave a bleak account of the Party's accomplishments since March 1981 – one dotted with 'formalism' in democratic life, weakening of militancy, and strengthening of opportunism within the ranks. Deva reported: 'The League of Communists has not been at the centre of political life....the link with the grass roots has been continuously weakening.'[49] The Serbian leadership had thus begun exerting strong pressure on the Kosovo leadership to proceed with radical purges of those officials, academics and students held responsible for inciting nationalism and irredentism.

In the mean time, after the long summer vacation, Kosovo's high schools began ushering in the new 1982 academic year by taking drastic administrative measures to purge the Province's educational establishments of unruly elements. A specially convened League of Communists meeting of the Pristina commune and the University took such measures against a number of the teaching staff and a group of students. It was announced on 18 September that six professors who had engaged in 'organised hostile activity contrary to our legal regulations' had been expelled from the faculty and from their jobs. Nineteen students were expelled for the same reasons. The expulsions included one of Kosovo's foremost histo-

48. Ibid., p. 34.
49. M. Baskin, 'Crisis in Kosovo', p. 64.

rians, Professor Ali Hadri, who it was claimed had acted 'on the basis of the dogmatic Stalinist position adopted by the leadership of the Albanian Workers Party, following our country's conflict with Stalin and Stalinism'. Apparently Professor Hadri had failed to denounce publicly the ideological and political positions of those propagating Albanian nationalism and irredentism. In order to reduce trouble-some student numbers, the university entrance requirements were tightened. That all was not well with the Kosovar youth was high-lighted by Fadil Hoxha, still the Province's highest and most respected personality. On a visit to his home town of Djakovica, a traditional stronghold of Albanian nationalism, he said:

> 'We have not succeeded yet in turning the indoctrinated youth on to the road of the LCY, on to Tito's path. We must be especially vigilant in providing the correct education for the people, in explaining our ideas. And we cannot achieve this if we do not main-tain frequent contact with the youth, because not only do they not listen to us, but they are even calling us traitors, that we allegedly think only about our personal interests, salaries, and so forth.'[50]

The Kosovo leadership, therefore, faced the dilemma of having to combat growing Albanian nationalism without alienating the angry Albanian youth who already believed that they were acting on the orders of Belgrade. The most acute problem, it was agreed, was unemployment. Kosovo's economic development had to be accelerated, but this could only be achieved by massive loans from the West, which would be employed solely in Kosovo, or by the wealthier Yugoslav republics being prepared for sacrifices to assist development in Kosovo – an option which the stagnant atmosphere prevailing throughout Yugoslavia after Tito's death made highly unrealistic. The aim of broadening inter-ethnic ties had been a notable failure in Kosovo, where the Albanians remained glued to their television sets watching the Tirana channel or with their radios tuned to Radio Tirana, soaking up the propaganda about life across the border where Albanians 'controlled their own destiny'. In spite of knowing little of life in Albania, Albanian youth turned away from Belgrade and towards Tirana to give a direction to their own lives. The majority of young Albanians were completely indifferent to Yugoslav problems and turned away from the realities of life in the multinational Yugoslav Federation towards an almost mythical Albania that was known, yet unkown.

50. RFE, BR/200, 30 September 1982.

In defence of their actions, Albanians claimed that they felt subordinated and as a result had to act defensively. But this had not been the case since 1974, and therefore they had to assume a certain political responsibility for their actions. Albanians from Kosovo tended to blame others for their plight, seeing themselves always as exploited and as victims of circumstances beyond their control. This had certainly been true in the inter-war years but had largely ceased to be so after the fall of Rankovic. Since the 1974 Constitution the Kosovo Albanians were not repressed culturally. Kosovo was in effect an Albanian polity with the Albanian language in official use, Albanian television, radio and press, and with an ethnic Albanian government leadership. Even the courts, which were used to persecute those calling for a republic of Kosovo, were staffed by ethnic Albanian judges. The Albanian population was well served by information in its mother-tongue: the Pristina Radio and Television Centre (RTV) and seven local radio stations provided work for 1,800 editors, technicians and other staff. Television broadcast for ten hours a day in the Albanian language and the two RTV radio channels broadcast altogether for thirty-four hours a day. The publishing house Rilindja, which the Kosovo Parliament founded, had 500 employees and published more than forty newspapers and periodicals. The only daily newspaper, *Rilindja*, had been published uninterruptedly since 1945.

So, it can be said that between the 1970s and the rise of Slobodan Milosevic in the late 1980s the Albanians of Kosovo had a better situation in terms of representation and cultural autonomy than they had known at any time since the end of the Ottoman Empire and arguably in their entire history. However, the refusal to give them republican status, despite their numerical superiority over other less numerous Slav nations of Yugoslavia, which did have their own republic within the federation, showed that they had remained to some extent second-class citizens in the Yugoslav state.[51] Thus the manifest Serbian-Albanian conflict, which had begun in 1981, gradually merged into the general inter-ethnic conflict within the Federation as a whole. The riots signalled not only the end of peaceful co-existence in Kosovo but, at the same time, the beginning of the demise of Yugoslavia.

51. H. Poulton, 'The Kosovo Albanians: Ethnic confrontation with the Slav state' in H. Poulton and S. Taji-Farouki (eds), *Muslim Identity and the Balkan State*, Hurst, London, 1997.

11

'IDEMO NA KOSOVU' (LET'S GO TO KOSOVO)

The most obvious consequence of the 1981 riots was the impetus given to a resurgence of Serbian, Macedonian and Montenegrin nationalism. The post-war centralistic state had stifled national feelings, but the accelerated decentralisation after Tito's death led to a situation where the Serbs felt that no real 'Yugoslav' interest in defending their rights still existed. When Alexander Rankovic died on 20 August 1983, tens of thousands of Serbs attended his funeral in what became the first mass protest about the status of Serbs in Kosovo and in Yugoslavia generally.[1]

By now many top Pristina leaders were indicating that a tougher policy would be introduced in an effort to defuse the problem of the Serb-Montenegrin migrations from Kosovo. By far the strongest language and most revealing information on the topic of migration was delivered to a meeting of communal communist leaders by Ali Sukrija, a member of the presidium of the CC of the Yugoslav League of Communists. He vividly described the poor socio-political climate in the province, saying that 'indifference and lack of ambition' marked the attitude of Kosovo's Albanians whereas 'insecurity' was a characteristic of its Serbs and Montenegrins.[2] The Province's top officials suggested many ways of creating a secure climate in Kosovo to discourage the flight of Serbs and Montenegrins, whose catalogue of complaints included rape, robbery and the desecration of graves. Fadil Hoxha, now a member of the Yugoslav Presidency, told a large gathering in Kosovo that there was undeniable evidence in the province of both 'overt and covert' forms of pressure on Serbs and Montenegrins to leave, which had created a 'poor social climate of mutual distrust and intolerance between Serbs and Albanians'. He warned of a new tough policy, and called

1. Silber and Little, *The Death of Yugoslavia*, p. 35.
2. RFE, BR/149, 28 June 1983.

for the application of 'the most severe political, moral and administrative measures'.[3] In the aftermath of the 1981 riots, Kosovar leaders admitted that these acts did occur. Ali Sukrija appealed to a meeting of Albanians for restraint:

> 'What nation and what honourable person can be proud of the fact that the girls of Serbian nationality dare not go to school, that graves are desecrated or that church windows are broken? How would Albanian families feel if their graves were desecrated and their religious objects damaged?'[4]

But, despite the strong rhetoric, no such measures were forthcoming, and throughout 1983 Slav emigration from Kosovo continued unabated, a process that enhanced the Albanians' majority and hence their claim to the region.[5]

Regarding the high Albanian birth-rate, many Serbs became almost hysterical in their allegations that the state, with its welfare benefits and money poured into Kosovo, encouraged Albanians to breed themselves into a majority population, while Albanians were equally vociferous on the same topic, claiming that only by having large families could they secure their rights by sheer weight of numbers. Speaking against reprimanding Kosovo Albanians for their 'explosive birth rate', a prominent Croat recalled that 'even Serbs living in Kosovo' had a birth-rate three times higher than Serbs in Vojvodina. This was also true of Croats living in Bosnia-Hercegovina.[6] On the other hand, Albanians claimed that the large increase in the Albanian population of Kosovo was caused by factors other than the Kosovars' high birth-rate, namely the migration to Kosovo of Albanians from Montenegro, southern Serbia, the Sandjak and especially western Macedonia where Albanian national and cultural aspirations were becoming increasingly stifled, and any display of the Albanian flag was now forbidden. These Albanians, it was claimed, came to Kosovo because of the better schooling and

3. *Rilindja*, 11 June 1982.
4. Foreign Broadcasts Information Service (USA), 9 December 1981, p. 16. Rapes in Kosovo, however, were invariably committed by Albanians on Albanians, although the number of such crimes was among the lowest in all Yugoslavia.
5. For a discussion on the various factors relating to the emigration of Slavs from Kosovo during this period, which concludes that in up to 85 per cent of the cases the main motive for migration was discrimination rather than economic push and/or pull factors, see: M. Blagojevic, 'The Other Side of the Truth', in Duijzings, Janjic and Maliqi (eds), *Kosovo -Kosova*, pp. 70-81.
6. Repishti, *Human Rights in Yugoslavia*, p. 266.

university education to be had there. In both the 1971 and 1981 censuses Albanians and Turks pressed Roms to declare themselves respectively as Albanians or Turks, while Serbs wanted them to declare as Roms (Gypsies) in order to reduce the number of Albanians in Kosovo.[7] In an article published in 1984, the internationally respected Rom activist, Slobodan Berberski, accused (in the indigestible jargon of the time) the 'Albanian nationalistic-chauvinistic, reactionary, anti-self-managing, counter-revolutionary forces' of putting pressure on Roms to declare themselves as Albanians.[8] He mentioned the names of some Albanians from Mitrovica, and claimed that during the census Roms had been threatened that unless they declared themselves as Albanians they would be forced into exile, or Muslim imams would refuse to perform religious rituals such as funerals.[9]

By the middle of the decade, the increasing migration of Serbs and Montenegrins from Kosovo had became one of the most pressing political issues of the Yugoslav federation as a whole and of the Province of Kosovo and the Republic of Serbia in particular. The Serbs, with their psychology of insecurity and abject despondency, were deeply and emotionally involved with the issue of migration. The Albanianisation of Kosovo had led to a Serbian movement, nurtured by the Church which was determined to voice the many grievances reportedly suffered there by Serbs and Montenegrins. These Serbs thus mobilised themselves into their own Kosovo Committee and began repeatedly visiting the Federal parliament in Belgrade to protest against their continued maltreatment by Albanians. Proof exists that many Serbs and Montenegrins who decided to leave Kosovo had experienced intimidation, pressure, violence, and other severe abuses of their human rights because of their ethnicity.[10] But these incidents cannot be regarded as having been officially supported by the local Albanian government but rather as the actions of extremist groups and individuals striving for an 'ethnically clean', i.e. purely Albanian, Kosovo. There is also evidence

7. See S. Menekshe, 'Polozaj Roma u Socijalistickoj samoupravnoj pokrajini Kosovo', *Romano Allav*, no. 1, 1972.
8. S. Berberski, 'Romi i iredenta na Kosovu', *Nase Teme*, vol. 28, nos 7–8, 1984, p. 1344.
9. S. Pettan, 'The Kosovo Conflict Through the Eyes of Local Rom Musicians' in *Kosovo-Kosova*, p. 151.
10. For a discussion of pressures against non-Albanians in Kosovo, see Helsinki Watch and the International Helsinki Federation's report *Yugoslavia: Crisis in Kosovo*, March 1990, pp. 21–5.

that extreme communists destroyed property of the Serbian Orthodox Church and practised other forms of harassment against it.[11]

Kosovo Serbs bite the bullet

By now there was a growing Serbian national effort to maintain a
Slav foothold in Kosovo.[12] The underlying problem behind the
emigration issue was the long-term question of Albanian-Serb
antagonism. But, as one Yugoslav historian noted, for the significance of the Slav migration from Kosovo to be understood, it must
be viewed above all in an all-Yugoslav context. Yugoslav statistics
show the existence of a general tendency for internal migration to
be directed towards national centres: Serbs from Bosnia tended to
move to Serbia, Bosnian Croats to Croatia, Macedonian Albanians
to Kosovo and so on. This tendency was overlaid with economic
pressures arising from uneven regional development: for example,
the whole South Morava region (the poor southern area of 'Serbia
proper' adjacent to Kosovo) was becoming depopulated, as the
young and able left their villages to search for jobs in the industrial
centres further north. In all, some 4.5 million Yugoslav peasants
had left the land over the previous fifteen years since 1978, flood-
ing the cities in pursuit of employment. Kosovo, a largely agricultural area and the poorest as well, had predictably suffered most in
this way.[13]

In the mean time, the first organised protest of Serbs from
Kosovo was a petition signed by 2,000 citizens of Kosovo Polje
denouncing Albanian nationalism and separatism and published in
Knjizevne Novine on 15 January 1986. A month later, on February
26, a group of about 100 Serbs began arriving in Belgrade in what
became a series of secret visits and appeals over the coming years to
the political leadership of Serbia and Yugoslavia.[14] In the first
months of 1986 the atmosphere degenerated into one of nationalist hysteria. Yet no voice of protest reverberated as strongly as the

11. *From Autonomy to Colonisation: Human Rights in Kosovo, 1989-1993*, Interna-
    tional Helsinki Federation for Human Rights, November 1993, p. 10.
12. It is estimated that around 26,000 Serbs and Montenegrins left Kosovo
    between 1981 and 1988: J. Gow, *Legitimacy and the Military: The Yugoslav Crisis*,
    St Martin's Press, New York, 1992, p. 69.
13. Magas, *The Destruction of Yugoslavia*, p. 63-4.
14. S. Woodward, *Balkan Tragedy: Chaos and Dissolution after the Cold War*, Wash-
    ington, DC, 1995, p. 438.

draft Memorandum of the Serbian Academy of Sciences and Arts. This notorious document, known as the SANU Memorandum, officially opened the so-called 'Serbian Question': the position of Serbs in Yugoslavia. It was devised by a number of leading intellectuals, led by the writer Dobrica Cosic, as a code of Serbian political thought. The Memorandum argued that under the Federation the Serbian people had remained disunited and divided. It warned of war in Kosovo unless drastic action was taken to solve what Serbs perceived to be the province's major problems, and called for the immediate reduction of Kosovo's autonomous status, the detachment of all its links with Albania, and indeed its total de-Albanianisation. The ethnic structure of the region would need to be altered in favour of Slavs by a relocation of Serb and Montenegrins. The Memorandum acknowledged Serbian grievances in Serbia, primarily in Kosovo, but also mentioned for the first time the Serbs' unfavourable position in other Yugoslav republics. The effect of the Memorandum was far-reaching. It justified Serbs' complaints in Croatia and Bosnia-Hercegovina, but at this time the significant point was that the country's most prestigious institution aligned itself with the Kosovo Serbs.[15] Thus the Memorandum reinforced the Serbian nationalist text through an extensive critique of the Serbs' position within the Yugoslav framework, coupled with a strong denunciation of the 1974 constitution. The SANU Memorandum did not create nationalism; it merely tapped sentiments that ran deep among the Serbs, but which had been suppressed and thus exacerbated by communism. The Academy's tract echoed opinions that were being whispered throughout Serbia.[16]

Another contributory factor behind the Slav migrations, apart from economics, was insecurity. There is little doubt that, since 1966, the rapid (because belated) Albanianisation of the Kosovo administration, the new ascendancy of the Albanian language, and the accompanying cultural-national shift in the Province's schools, culture, media, etc. - all of which were made more dramatic by the fast growth of the Albanian population - had been hard for the formerly privileged Slav minority to accept. Yugoslav and Albanian policy-makers had clearly failed to anticipate the substantial problems necessarily associated with such a change. Positive

15. Kostovicova, *Parallel Worlds*, pp. 17-18.
16. Silber and Little, *The Death of Yugoslavia*, p. 31.

discrimination favouring the formerly disadvantaged Albanians had been experienced by other national groups as real injustice, so that insecurity grew among them in parallel to the growth of the new Albanian national self-confidence.[17]

As the plight of the Kosovo Serbs became more widely publicised, the third historical wave of Kosovo's Slav colonisation began, through the so-called Yugoslav Programme on Kosovo. This new policy, which received its inspiration and guidelines mainly from the SANU Memorandum, aimed to settle Serbs in the Province in order to adjust its ethnic balance. The colonists were installed throughout Kosovo but mainly in the Dukagjini plateau. Although a mere 9,-10,000 in number, the new arrivals were paid higher wages than would have been possible in Serbia proper. They were established mainly in educational and recreative institutions. The League of Communists of Yugoslavia still operated on the Marxist-Leninist premise that any resurgence of nationalism under socialism was due to economic inequalities. Therefore, large amounts of credits were pumped into Kosovo via the Special Fund for Economic Development – yet the Province still lagged further behind the other Yugoslav Federal units. The policy of trying to reduce the gap in economic inequalities had been a complete failure, and there was little point in pouring money into Kosovo if it was not going to be more wisely distributed. The annual output of 10,000 graduates from Pristina University, mainly in 'arts' subjects, was a luxury that a poor society at Kosovo's stage of development could ill afford. Between 1981 and 1989 unemployment rose from 25 per cent to 57 per cent.

Meanwhile, the increasing social mobilisation that had preceded the present political situation caused changes in the Albanian clan system. Early post-war government policy, which considered speedy industrialisation a first priority, had produced rapid urbanisation throughout Yugoslavia. Most villages in Kosovo at this time were supporting a marginal, almost self-sufficient existence on land that was grossly overpopulated. The people tended to produce food-stuffs for their own consumption, selling only a small surplus at the local market. In fact, they lived predominantly outside the system. Rural overpopulation combined with educational and work opportunities in the towns prompted whole Albanian *zadrugas* to move to the outskirts of towns and cities where they would occupy several

17. Magas, *The Destruction of Yugoslavia*, p. 64.

neighbouring properties – clear evidence of the strength of this institution among Albanians. It did not dissolve into nuclear families as in the rest of Yugoslavia, but merely split into smaller *zadrugas* on the urban periphery, which grew rapidly because of the exceptionally high birth-rate.

In the mid-1980s Kosovo's towns were heavily infiltrated with plainclothes police and military checkpoints, and most of those convicted of 'association for purposes of hostile activity' under Article 136 of the federal criminal code were Albanians. Although the 1981 demonstrations had led to clashes with the security forces and occasionally damage to property, the Yugoslav authorities appeared not to distinguish between violent and peaceful assembly, and considered any participation in Albanian nationalist activities a crime. Some Albanians on the run from the Yugoslav police fled into Albania itself, where they learned the hard way about the true nature of the regime there. Roughly half of them ended up in prison or internment camps suspected of being Yugoslav spies. One example was Mr Bukoshi, brother of the 'prime minister' of the self-proclaimed 'Republic of Kosovo'. After serving a sentence of five years in Yugoslavia for his political activities, he fled to Albania and there received a prison sentence of ten years on suspicion of political espionage.[18] The trivial nature of some of the accusations exemplifies the paranoia of the state at that time. For example, in November 1983 the twenty-eight-year-old Sherif Asllani from Urosevac was tried by Tuzla district court. According to the report of the trial in the official Yugoslav press, he was accused of possessing a book entitled *The Titoites* by Enver Hoxha and of two cigarette-holders bearing the inscription 'Kosovo - Republic', while visiting his brother in Tuzla. The court found him guilty of 'hostile propaganda' and sentenced him to four years' imprisonment.[19]

Despite such repression, terrorist activity committed by numerous Albanian organisations – the Red National Front (RNF); the Kosovar Union; the Movement for an Albanian Socialist Republic in Yugoslavia and the People's Movement for a Republic of Kosovo (MASRY) – continued throughout Western Europe. In August 1981, in Brussels, a member of the RNF, Musa Hoti, murdered Djeric Stojan and wounded Zuko Redzo, two Yugoslav consular officers. The following March two Yugoslavs were killed by Alba-

18. J. Jensen, 'Human Rights Abuses in Kosovo in the 1980s', p. 94.
19. *Yugoslavia: Prisoners of Conscience*, p. 28.

nians in a Yugoslav club, again in Brussels. On 8 November 1987 in Stuttgart several members of MASRY planned the kidnapping of the Yugoslav Consul, Imer Klokci, but were prevented by German police: they had hoped to force the Yugoslav authorities to release Adem Demaci from prison. In May 1984 six Albanians were accused of smuggling arms, ammunition and explosives into Yugoslavia. Another group was arrested in March 1984 accused of causing nine explosions in Pristina between October 1982 and March 1984. Yet other groups were accused of issuing statements threatening armed uprisings if Kosovo was not accorded the status of a Republic by peaceful means.[20] The complexity of the situation was illustrated by a Tanjug report on 10 March 1984 of seventy-two 'illegal organisations with about 1,000 members' having been uncovered between 1981 and 1983. Because of the loose central control of these organisations over individual members and local sections, and the relatively easy acquisition of firearms in the country it was difficult to establish whether or not a particular organisation had violent aims and methods. In practice certain groups operating under a particular name used violence while other groups operating under the same name firmly rejected its use or advocacy.[21]

In Kosovo itself many Albanians were being arrested on charges related to the smuggling of arms, gold and money, especially in the districts of Bujanovac and Presevo. They were also arrested for drug smuggling. Apparently, Albanians acquired at minimal prices quantities of heroin which were then sold in Western Europe. Those with Yugoslav passports took advantage of the opportunity to travel freely and serve as a link with the Albanian nationality in Turkey. Part of the Albanian nationality living and working in Western Europe and the United States sold narcotics under the control of the Albanian intelligence service or in collusion with it. Some of the money acquired in this way was delivered to activists in Pristina to buy Serb-owned land and the rest was sent to the followers of Albanian separatist movements living in Turkey and Western Europe. In 1987 an illegal laboratory was installed in Pristina for processing heroin and until it was discovered it produced at least 35 kilos of which 4 were siezed and 3 were ruined in the production process, and the rest was transferred to Madrid through smoothly organised channels. From there it went to Palermo and thence to

20. Ibid., p. 14.
21. Ibid., p. 37.

the United States. Most of the money earned in this operation was used by the separatists from Pristina – apparently in typical fashion – for purchasing property from Serbian families.[22]

By 1986 a considerable number of Yugoslav military personnel were deployed in and along the borders of Kosovo. By this time the Kosovo issue, more than any other, revealed the growing difficulty Yugoslavia faced in keeping the two spheres of political activity separate: the emergence on the one hand of ever more explicit, popular and associational protest activity, and on the other the political struggle over the constitutional relations between the Federal and Republican governments and the weakening of Federal institutions.[23] A new generation of younger and better educated Albanian leaders had now gained control of the Kosovo party organisation. Following a pattern found throughout Balkan history, Kosovo's intelligentsia increasingly came to view themselves as the bearers of the 'national cause', responsible for the progress and destiny of Yugoslavia's Albanian population. Through the establishment of newspapers and political organisations, they became increasingly active spectators and participants in Kosovo's élite structure and in the Yugoslav political system as a whole. However, Albanians and Slavs continued to be deeply suspicious of each other and to nurture a strong aversion to each other's cultural traits. Each of the two sections of Kosovo's society was used, since childhood, to stereotyping the other in images that their teachers, peers, social distance, religious differences and bigotry reinforced. This had contributed to the almost total alienation of the Albanians from the very concept of Yugoslavia.

At the end of October 1987 Federal riot police, together with army and air force troops, were deployed on the streets of Kosovo following demonstrations by thousands of Serbs in protest against a comment alleged to have been made by an Albanian leader, that incidents of Albanians raping Serbian women could be reduced if more Serbian women worked as prostitutes. We have already seen how Kosovo's unchecked birth-rate meant an ever-increasing percentage of the population being under the age of twenty-five, thus swelling the numbers of unemployed, and how Kosovo's poor economic performance, together with the almost complete Albanianisation of the Province, deepened the sense of insecurity among

22. Statement given to Interpol by Blaca Bedzeta during interrogation after which he was sentenced to ten years in prison. Cover no. 6 - Interpol Documents and Action 'Madrid' Internal Security Report 2314.8632 on 15 Dec 1987, pp. 2-5.
23. Woodward, *Balkan Tragedy*, p. 88.

the dwindling Serb and Montenegrin population. A Serbian historian wrote of the Kosovo problem at this time: 'It is now a question of the survival of the entire Serb nation. It is not the fate of the Albanian nation which is at stake but that of the Serbs. The position of the Serbs in the Balkans is much too delicate to be examined in the light of present events. The historic memory of a whole people is being wiped out, the very foundation of its national consciousness is being undermined.'[24]

Slobodan Milosevic

By now two clearly defined poles had emerged in Serbia: the one more liberal was led by Ivan Stambolic and the other more nationalistic and conservative by Slobodan Milosevic. In spite of a relatively close friendship and cooperation between them over many years, differences now emerged in their attitudes towards the growing Serb nationalism, how to work with the Kosovo Party leadership, and the character and role of the Party. Both men by now realised the potential importance of being seen to champion the Kosovo Serbs. Since April 1987 Milosevic in his speeches had attempted to equate the rights of individual Serbs with those of the nation and its unity, and to identify himself as protector of the Serb nation against external foes. Although his personal popularity was rising, Serbian public opinion was spread among competing political programmes, and Milosevic was challenged by a number of openly anticommunist nationalists, many of whom were more outspoken than he was against Albanians in Kosovo and in their support of Serbs outside of Serbia.[25] On 24 April 1987, Milosevic made a significant visit to Kosovo, which was supposed to be for talks with the local Party leadership, but which marked a turning-point for the Serbs in the Province who saw the visit as a sign that Belgrade was finally heeding their plight. Others, including the Albanian Party leadership, believed that Milosevic had been sent to calm the Serbs and bring a halt to their endless petitions and demonstrations.

Milosevic, who up till this time had been conspicuously silent over matters relating specifically to Kosovo, was given a hero's welcome. To cries of 'Slobo! Slobo!', he was mobbed by a great crowd of bedraggled-looking Serbs, who screamed for action to be

24. D. Bogdanovic, *Kniga o Kosovu*, Belgrade, 1985, p. 283.
25. Woodward, *Balkan Tragedy*, p. 99.

taken against the Albanian Party leadership for condoning attacks on Serbs and Montenegrins. Milosevic was visibly surprised at the sight of the baying mob, but he nevertheless grabbed the opportunity to tell the crowd that for the sake of their ancestors they should stay put in Kosovo. At the same time he told them that they should participate in the wider struggle then emerging in the country as a whole. The experience gave Milosevic the clear message that here in Kosovo he had the opportunity to harness the obvious discontent of the Serb population to his own plans for the country as a whole.[26] This was not Milosevic's first visit to Kosovo. Just four days earlier, on 20 April, he had been there to meet Communist Party officials, and was asked by local Serbs to make a return visit that would be entirely focused on their grievances. During those four days Milosevic's aides worked feverishly to organise the mass demonstrations which so effectively launched his Kosovo crusade. As soon as he returned to Belgrade, Milosevic, capitalising on his tremendous popular support, galvanised the CPY into debating the issue of Kosovo in order to show the other Republican leaderships the true implications of the Kosovo Serbs' situation in relation to the federation as a whole. Henceforth, the conflict between Serbs and Albanians would no longer be given ideological clothing, but treated as an ethnic issue. Thus Serbia edged closer to confrontation not only with Albanians but also with other Yugoslav Republics. Throughout that summer the Kosovo Serbs became the focus of Serbia's media. Television crews and journalists scurried down from Belgrade to report on the harrowing lives of Kosovo's beleaguered Slavs. Serbian national hats began to be worn, as did long hair and beards, and national songs were played everywhere. Rallies were held throughout Serbia.[27]

In the mean time, the intended removal of Kosovo's autonomous status had been announced in the text of the Proposal of the SFRY Presidium for Constitutional Changes of 11 February 1987. This proposal ignored the fact that the status of the autonomous Provinces could not be considered outside the total constitutional concept of federalism in Yugoslavia. The issue of constitutional changes then being discussed opened the way for the emergence of a powerful right-wing bloc which used Kosovo, as the potent symbol of Serbian nationalism, to legitimise its political rhetoric. Kosovo had become the question on which the intellectual and

26. For a concise account of the way Milosevic planned and manipulated this visit in April 1987, see Silber and Little, *The Death of Yugoslavia*, chapters 1 and 2.
27. Ibid., p. 99.

political élite of Serbia focused its constitutional debate. Often, in 1987 and 1988, entire sessions of the LCY Central Committee were devoted to the problem.

The Kosovo Party Committee was purged in late 1987. On 25 October, the Federal State Presidency suspended the authority of the provincial police and judiciary, despatching federal police units in their place.[28] A month after the 17th Plenum of the CC of the League of Communists of Yugoslavia, the Serbian leadership organised a 350,000-strong public meeting in Belgrade. A headline of the daily *Politika* proclaimed: 'No force can now stop Serbia's unification'. The Federal Party at the 17th Plenum had allowed Milosevic to trade off Kosovo against the maintenance of formal unity. Throughout the summer of 1988 street demonstrations called '*mitings*' were held all over Serbia, demanding the return of the two autonomous provinces, Vojvodina and Kosovo, to total Serbian control. Every week the '*mitings*' grew larger. Serbs and Montenegrins, waving banners that read 'DOWN WITH ALBANIAN GENOCIDE IN KOSOVO', were being called on to mount a crusade to rescue their Serbian brothers in Kosovo. Yet no speaker mentioned the central catastrophe of Yugoslav life at that time: astronomical inflation. Despite Yugoslavia having had regional self-government and open relations with the West, the Communist Party still kept its grip over the economy. Economic reforms aimed at creating a 'market economy' were instead accompanied by negative growth rates and inflation running at 250 per cent. A local friend told an English visitor to Belgrade: 'All our money goes on food now. We hunt from shop to shop like gypsies.'[29]

Following a bitter inner-Party struggle, Milosevic came to power in the League of Communists of Serbia at the end of the year. Born in 1941 in Serbia, he became a lawyer in 1964. Married to a dedicated Marxist ideologue, he worked as an executive in a state-owned company before joining the Communist Party in 1969. A few years later he became the head of a major bank. Only in 1984 did he become directly involved in politics, coming under the wing of the Communist Ivan Stambolic and learning all he could from him before taking over his position as chairman of the Central Committee of the Party when Stambolic was made President. The two men eventually fell out over the issue of Serbian nationalism following the Albanian riots in Kosovo, which Milosevic used as an opportunity to come out strongly on the side of the Serbs in the

28. Woodward, *Balkan Tragedy*, p. 88.
29. Moats, 'Yugoslavia Lost', p. 298.

Province. In a meeting with them he blamed the provincial Albanian leadership and promised the Serbs help. This meeting led to a great change in Milosevic's political personality. A Serbian journalist said: 'After that night, suddenly there was a psychological change in him. All at once, he discovered he had this power over people.'[30]

Milosevic's victory was sealed by the increasing insecurity felt throughout the Serbian Party. The call for unity behind a forceful leader appealed to many Serb Party members who wished to retain political control over Kosovo. Milosevic won his massive victory on the promise of strong leadership at a time of mounting economic difficulties and social unrest. Here was a party leader, the first since Rankovic, who addressed Serb grievances and reminded their nation of its historic task to reclaim Kosovo. An atmosphere of intense expectation now pervaded the Serb areas of Kosovo. Milosevic was easily able to align himself with the Orthodox Church which gave him a sound social base in the eyes of Serbs. Portraits of him began to appear on walls as well as in newspapers and magazines. By now the national movement in Serbia was so strong that it was impossible for the Federal leadership to have any influence over it. In October 1988 the Party leadership of Vojvodina was overthrown and replaced by Milosevic's appointees, ready to enact the desired constitutional changes that would give Serbia back the control it had once exercised over her Autonomous Provinces. The ground was thus prepared for a move to neuter the two provinces' autonomy, but before the necessary constitutional amendments could be drafted, the Provinces themselves had to give their approval, and for this it was necessary to doctor their leaderships. In October the League of Communist chiefs in Vojvodina were ousted, and on 17 November the committee of the Kosovo Party met to discuss (that is, to accept) the resignations tendered under Serbian pressure of its president Kaqusha Jashari and her predecessor Azem Vlassi, who now sat on the federal executive committee of the League of Communists.[31]

30. M. Rezun, *Europe and War in the Balkans*, Praeger, Westport, CT, 1995, pp. 126-7.
31. Azem Vlassi headed the Socialist Youth Alliance of Yugoslavia in the last years of Tito's life. After a long spell at the federal centre, he returned to Kosovo to head the local Socialist Alliance. In 1981 he was President of the Pristina Communist Party Committee. Among the first in Kosovo to call the Albanian 1981 demonstrations a 'counter-revolution', Vlassi became Kosovo party leader at the head of a younger team in 1986, following a party purge. Two years later, however, after a vociferous campaign in the Belgrade press, he was replaced in 1988 by Kaqusha Jashari. In February 1989, he was removed from the Party's Central Committee. M. Thompson, *A Paper House*, p. 135.

The miners' protest

On the morning of 17 November 1988, miners from the 'Stari Trg' mine near Mitrovica, the industrial centre of Kosovo, after completing the night shift, emerged from the 38 degrees Celsius of their pit into the freezing dawn (the first snows of winter had just fallen on Kosovo), joined forces with the day shift and began the 70-kilometre march to Pristina. Once in Pristina, they were joined by other workers and students, followed by schoolchildren and later by the older generation, coming from all parts of Kosovo (as well as Western Macedonia) in a five-day-long demonstration of national determination. The protest had two aims: to express their rejection of the proposed changes in the constitution of the Republic of Serbia; and to prevent, in that context, the enforced resignation of the two provincial leaders.[32] The marchers carried Yugoslav and Albanian flags and portraits of Tito. There were no calls to unite with Albania and Enver Hoxha was not mentioned. An Albanian from Pec told an English visitor: 'As for all that stuff about joining with Albania, I went to Albania for ten days with my aunt – she wanted to look up some relatives. My God! No Yugoslav Albanian wants to live in Albania. They have nothing!'.[33] The miners were traditional communists who continued to support the Party. They were not seccesionists but merely wished to retain the 1974 constitution. Rahman Morina emerged as Provincial Party Secretary as a response to the Serbian Party's insistance that Azem Vlassi be removed. A few Albanian 'uncle Toms' remained in the League of Communists and the Federal Assembly, but the rest were dismissed.

It did not take long then to shake the Serbs out of their dubious commitment to Yugoslavism and evoke the call of their own sense of persecution. The Serbian movement in Kosovo was skillfully used by the new communist leadership, in other words essentially by Milosevic, who introduced the populist policy to preserve the old bureaucratic structure, but to base it on rediscovered national ideas. But the accelerated disintegration of the Yugoslav federation showed that the narrow interest of the ruling communist and post-communist national élites hid underneath a heap of ethnic tensions which could hardly be overcome by democratic means.[34] Vlassi was forced to resign because he was identified with demands for increas-

32. Magas, *The Destruction of Yugoslavia*, pp. 172-3.
33. Moats, 'Yugoslavia Lost', p. 300.
34. *Kosovo Chronicles*, p. 213.

ing autonomy for Kosovo. By the beginning of 1989 Serbia had acquired four votes in the Federation, which had all but ceased to exist in anything but name. Virtually every commune in Kosovo was against the constitutional amendments. The constitution had been violated and the old post-war order overthrown along with it. The Serbian Party waited impatiently for the Kosovo Party to declare, on behalf of 'democratic centralism', its support for the constitutional changes. But it decided to go ahead with the changes with the aim of getting rid of Vlassi regardless of outside opinion. The issue revolved around the re-centralisation of Serbia. Ever since the fall of Rankovic, the Serbs had seen themselves as slowly losing their status, not only in Kosovo but, more important, in the Yugoslav Federation as a whole. They failed to understand why the Albanians were so disturbed by the new constitutional changes when 'after all Serbia was only getting what was naturally due to her.' It was now not possible for Vojvodina or Kosovo to secede. Before the changes they could influence the Serbian Constitution but Serbia had no influence on theirs.'[35]

There was certainly a legitimate argument for the constitutional changes. The 1974 constitution had placed Serbia in a Federal minority of one against eight with its two Autonomous Provinces able to vote against it. As the Federal units acquired the basic features of nation states, the Serbs felt that they were in the paradoxical position of being reduced to the status of a national minority in a part of their own Federal unit without, at the same time, enjoying genuine minority rights. Milosevic could thus exploit Kosovo as the most blatant example of the Serbs' national decline within the Yugoslav Federation. This was in spite of Serbs being still proportionately over-represented in almost every Federal institutional area. Meanwhile, the Albanians closed ranks and began their resistance to the demotion of Kosovo's autonomy.

The new year (1989) began with the resignation of the government of Prime Minister Branko Mikulic – the first occasion in post-war Yugoslavia when a government had resigned. Mikulic had been criticised for mishandling the economy and failing to find workable policies to deal with the Kosovo problem. He was also accused of using his political power to enrich his own family. He resigned in response to the Federal Assembly's failure to approve an austerity measure that would have provisionally limited public spending in

35. *Politika*, Belgrade, 25 February 1989.

1989. The Kosovo parliament then had little choice but to ratify the Serbian constitutional amendments, and in effect vote for its own dismissal. This allowed Serbia to adopt a new republican constitution.

Forcing this last step upon the Albanians in Kosovo propelled the situation out of control. In February 1989 life in Kosovo came to a standstill as, once again taking the lead. over 1,000 Albanian miners from the huge Trepca mining-industrial complex in Mitrovica went on hunger strike. They demanded the unconditional resignation of three Provincial officials, Rahman Morina (provincial party head), Husamedin Azemi (Pristina party head) and Ali Shukria (member of the Federal party central committee), who had been imposed on them that month at the insistence of the Serbian Party. Morina, also the Province's police chief, had worked his way up through the Ministry of the Interior in Belgrade and in various routine security jobs. He was one of the few Albanians in the League of Communists on whom the Serbs could rely. He was also one of the few opponents of separatist tendencies in the Albanian community and, after the 1981 disturbances in Kosovo under the Vlassi regime, found himself first appointed as Interior Minister for Kosovo Province and then as leader of the Communist Party there. Morina was a key figure in Belgrade's efforts to keep the turbulent province under control,[36] and was especially despised as a collaborator who had betrayed his people by aligning himself with Milosevic's anti-Albanian policies. Milosevic needed Morina and the handful of other 'reliable' Albanians to implement his policies in Kosovo. The strikers considered that the three leaders had shown excessive deference towards some Federal leaders and to the entire Party leadership of Serbia.

The protesters were also offended by a Serbian evaluation of the five-day demonstrations in November 1988 by some 100,000 Albanians as being in some way 'a continuation of the 1981 riots'. They claimed the contrary: that the demonstrations were spontaneous, pro-Tito and not organised by Albanian separatists. They also asked that any constitutional limitation of Kosovo's autonomy, for which Belgrade had been pressing, should be subject to democratic debate.[37] By now the Kosovo Party had all but collapsed. The Federal leadership had to accept the Serbian constitutional amendments and persuade Vlassi, Morina and Shukria to resign. After

36. J. Pettifer, *The Independent*, 19 October 1990.
37. RFE, Special Report/4, 8 March 1989.

eight days underground, the protesters emerged into an atmosphere of bitter tension between Serbs and Albanians. During that week the Province had come to a virtual standstill as Albanians abandoned workplaces, shops and schools to attend meetings in support of the miners' demands. In response, tens of thousands of Serbs demonstrated in Belgrade demanding that order be restored to Kosovo. Serbs and Montenegrins were leaving the Party *en masse* as local branches ceased to meet, while Albanians remained in it in a virtual state of paralysis. When Milosevic came to speak to the Kosovo Serbs, there were chants from a small but prominent Serbian group calling for the immediate arrest of Azem Vlassi. The next day he was duly arrested on the pretext of having given encouragement to the striking miners, and dismissed from the Party's Central Committee. Along with him all the managers of large enterprises were also arrested. These arrests and the atmosphere of fear and coercion they created signalled the end of communication between Serbs and Albanians. A curfew was then imposed on the Province.

The Albanians in their turn spontaneously walked out of their schools, closed their shops and ceased trading in the markets in an incredible show of solidarity and defiance. The authorities claimed that a 'counter revolution' was at hand and the province was placed under a state of emergency. The Trepca strike, which Albanians later interpreted as a national rebellion, united the entire Albanian population as a political entity; it was thus quite different from the mainly student demonstrations of 1968 and 1981. In spite of the resignation of the three officials, the end of the eight-day hunger strike by the Albanian miners, and the partial mobilisation of the army, the tension that remained in the Province showed up the major political differences between the Yugoslav State Presidency and Serbia's leaders on the one hand and some leaders from Slovenia and Croatia on the other.

Serbia's constitutional amendments

The abolition of Kosovo's autonomy began with the amendments to the Constitution of the Socialist Republic of Serbia on 28 March 1989. It was a centralist constitutional and juridicial settlement that undermined Kosovo's constitutional position as one of Yugoslavia's eight federal units. With the law suspending the work of the Kosovo Executive Council and the Kosovo Assembly, the Province lost its existence as a socio–political entity and was deprived of state author-ity. And the process of redefining Kosovo's constitutional and legal status was accompanied by strong police and legal repression by the Serbian state. On 3 February 1989 Serbia's National Assembly passed the amendments, which gave Serbia more direct control over the Autonomous Province's security, judiciary, finance and social planning. The Albanians immediately opposed these amendments, regarding them as a step in removing rights guaranteed to them by the 1974 constitution, which they had interpreted as the primary safeguard of their national rights. The Serbs, on the other hand, saw the amendments as a means of safeguarding the minorities in Kosovo against what they claimed were 'the genocidal tactics of the Albanian separatists'. Serbs criticised the gross ingratitude of Alba-nians who they claimed wanted to have their cake and eat it.

On 23 March Kosovo's parliament endorsed the new Serbian constitution. The Belgrade media proclaimed 'Serbia has regained her sovereignty'. Meanwhile, young Albanians stood brooding on the tense streets of Kosovo in an atmosphere of painful apprehen-sion. The new constitution defined the status of the provinces as 'a form of territorial autonomy', whereby they were given the right to create their own statutes, but with the prior agreement of the National Assembly. The southern province was again to be named Kosovo and Metohija. Serbia's constitutional order basically reverted to the principles of the 1963 federal constitution, which had stip-ulated that the rights of the provinces were to be prescribed in the constitution of the Serbian Republic. Furthermore, the controver-sial constitutional provisions of 1968, 1971 and 1974 were made null and void.[38] By stripping the provinces of their constitutional power and curtailing their legislative, administrative and judicial powers, the authorities in Serbia tried to resolve the problem of its southern province by presenting it as a matter of the legislative and executive-administrative activities of Serbia's legal bodies. The political goal of these activities was to prevent Kosovo's secession and help the phys-ical return of Serbs to the province.

The Federal leadership under Svetozar Markovic had little choice but to acquiesce to Serbia's constitutional changes because of the strength of the Serbian political machine in relation to the federation as a whole. Serious rioting followed which left twenty-

38. D. Janjic, 'Socialism, Federalism and Nationalism', *Sociology*, vol. xxxiv, no. 3, 1992, p. 319.

eight Albanians dead and many more wounded. A state of emergency was declared as sporadic rioting continued. The Slovenian and Croatian Party leaderships issued statements of support for the Albanian protesters, aware that such constitutional changes might not be restricted to Serbia alone but be extended to themselves. The Party organisations of Vojvodina, Montenegro and Macedonia supported the Serbian Party, while the Bosnian Party remained conspicuously silent. The polarisation within the federation continued with some 450,000 Slovenes signing a petition in support of their Republic's stand in criticising the Federal authority's special measures adopted to control the unrest in Kosovo. This event caused an immediate backlash elsewhere in the country. The next day more than 100,000 people took part in protest rallies in Serbia, Vojvodina, Skopje and Titograd in support of those special measures. For the fourth time since 1945, Yugoslavia's leaders had to use the army to quell disturbances in Kosovo. The pettiness continued, with the Serbian Writers' Association officially breaking off all relations with its Slovenian counterpart on 1 March 'for betraying the traditional friendship between the two nations and taking sides with the enemy of Serbia'.[39] The events in Kosovo received surprisingly extensive coverage from the media in the Soviet Union, which began to display a strongly pro-Serb slant in their reports from Yugoslavia. A report by Soviet television following the constitutional amendments introduced by Serbia commented that while the Hungarians of Vojvodina had accepted the changes, 'the Albanian nationalists had responded to them with war'. The Soviet commentator continued: 'Despite this Albanian hostility, Serbia's National Assembly adopted the amendments with the support of the higher authorities of Vojvodina, Kosovo and the majority of their populations.' Moscow's attitude suggested that it saw little hope of improving relations with Albania at that time, and perhaps Serbia was a more likely candidate for courtship.[40]

During this period some progress was made in Yugoslav-Albanian relations at the state level after they had been brought to a dramatic halt by the 1981 riots. An agreement on culture and education was signed in 1988 and in January 1989 the Deputy Foreign Ministers of the Balkan countries met in Tirana for the first international political gathering of its kind ever to take place

39. RFE, SR/4, 8 March 1989.
40. RFE, BR/62. April 1989.

there. It was a follow-up to the Balkan Foreign Ministers' Conference in Belgrade in February 1988, during which the Yugoslav press had commented that the speech of the Albanian Foreign Minister, Reis Malile had been 'delicate' and 'pragmatic' and that he had avoided stirring up any controversy; for example, he had skilfully skirted round the Kosovo issue by declaring that the national minorities should help build bridges between states. He thus echoed Tito's 'bridge-building' idea for the minorities. Malile granted an interview to the Kosovo Albanian-language daily *Rilindja* (which no Albanian official had done previously), in which he said that Albania favoured a 'high standard of integrity' in relations with Yugoslavia. He reiterated his claim that the minorities acted as bridges and, with specific reference to Kosovo, said: 'We have not demanded and do not demand anything.' This was an apparent response to Yugoslav allegations that Albania had territorial claims on Yugoslavia.[41]

For Albania the Belgrade Conference was not only a matter of prestige but also of great importance in the efforts to improve relations with its immediate neighbours. At the Conference it had been agreed not to deal with specific problems in bilateral relations but to seek to establish a general framework for cooperation. This notion was about to be put to the test by yet more unrest in Kosovo. It was the Tirana regime that had called for talks on cultural cooperation to resume, since it had far better relations with Belgrade than did the Kosovars at a time when relations among all Yugoslavia's minorities were less than promising. There was no commitment by Albania to Kosovo in any form other than the rhetorical. The general atmosphere among the largely Tosk Tirana élite, who determined Albanian foreign policy, was insular, uncertain and very conservative in its attitude to Kosovar aspirations. For a long while Yugoslavia had been Albania's major trading partner, with increasing integration of the minerals and electricity industries. The smelter at Djakovica in Kosovo was supplied with both hydro-electricity and chrome ore from Albania. In retrospect, the reaction of the Tirana leadership to the Milosevic-engineered coup in the Yugoslav party seems to have been feeble in the extreme – due perhaps to the economic collapse of Albania, which was now obvious to the leadership in Tirana. The serious human rights violations that accompanied these seminal events for the future of

41. RFE, BR/36, March 1988.

Yugoslavia were played down in the interests of peace and quiet with Belgrade.

The latest crisis in Kosovo naturally had an adverse effect on Yugoslav-Albanian relations and thereby on the spirit of Balkan co-operation so painstakingly built up over the previous year. Albania's reaction was swift and unusually extensive. A statement by Foto Cami, right-hand man to Enver Hoxha's successor Ramiz Alia, strongly criticised the Yugoslav authority's 'erroneous policies' towards their Albanian minority and warned that Belgrade's policy could not fail to have a negative impact on Balkan cooperation. Cami's statement set in motion a protest campaign throughout Albania in support of the Kosovo miners. Yugoslavia's response to Albania's barrage of propaganda was to accuse Albania of a 'dual track policy' of preaching good-neighbourliness while in practice conducting a hostile policy against Yugoslavia. But, as Ramiz Alia said at the 1987 Party Plenum, 'History has shown that Albanian relations with Yugoslavia were conditioned by the domestic situation in that state, and they improve or deteriorate in direct relation to this situation.'[42]

One reason why the hysterical propaganda was so successful in Serbia was the fact that no one in Belgrade ever went down to Kosovo. Instead they read books on Serbia's tragic-heroic past, which had emerged as best-sellers, especially those that dealt openly for the first time with Serb suffering during the Second World War at the hands of the Croatian Ustashi and the Bosnian Muslims. On 28 June (*Vidovdan* or St.Vitus's Day)[43] the Serbs had a chance to commemorate the 600th anniversary of what they perceived as the very cause of all their woes, their defeat at the Battle of Kosovo Polje, and the dark centuries of Ottoman occupation that followed. The present-day district of Kosovo Polje is nothing more than an enclave of around 20,000 Serbs surrounded by the suburbs of the predominantly Albanian-inhabited Pristina. On that warm summer day Kosovo's beleaguered Serbs were again surrounded by flags and waving banners. The event also served as a political rally where thou-

---

42. RFE, BR/41, March 1989.

43. *Vidovdan* is the celebration of St Vitus, a deity of the old Slavs to whom the Serbs remained attached even after they had embraced Christianity. St Vitus Day is by tradition, and in the Serbs' historical and mythical consciousness, the time for commemorating the legends of the Battle of Kosovo, its heroes and victims and especially the defeat. Thus the day has a special place in Serbian national and political culture.

sands of photos and posters of Milosevic were displayed – though not one of Tito. Milosevic was then generally considered the first Serbian leader since the Second World War to have defended Serbia's interests, even if it was at the expense of alienating the rest of the country. After all, ever since 1974 the constitutional set-up had satisfied all the federative units except Serbia, since it legalised all particularisms in their relations with the centre. This was the principle by which Yugoslavia claimed to have solved the national problem, and before Milosevic no leader had dared openly to challenge it. Milosevic rose to the occasion by delivering a stirring speech which, by all accounts, was relatively mild for a politician known as aggressive and uncompromising. His speech offered no hope of reconciliation for the Albanians. He openly assailed past leaders of Serbia:

> 'If we lost the Battle it was not only due to Turkish military supremacy but also to the tragic discord at the top of the Serbian leadership. This discord has followed the Serbian people throughout their history, including both World Wars and later in Socialist Yugoslavia when the Serbian leadership remained divided and prone to compromises at the expense of the people.'[44]

This suggested to his supporters that perhaps it was Serbia's current leadership under Milosevic which had re-united Serbia. He continued: 'The moment has come when, standing on the fields of Kosovo, we can say openly and clearly - no longer!' The clear implication was that the Serbs had won a significant victory in Kosovo today and that it would not be the last one. He ominously (and prophetically) concluded: 'Today, six centuries later, we are again fighting battles, they are not armed battles although such things cannot yet be excluded'. [45] Many Yugoslavs now naturally regarded Milosevic with great apprehension, believing that he had taken advantage of Serbian frustrations by appealing to their national grievances in Kosovo. When Milovan Djilas was asked what he thought of Milosevic, he replied:

> 'The other Republics see in Milosevic a Serbian Tito, inspired by Serbian not Leninist interests. He seems to them some sort of Serbian hegemonist. However, I personally agree with his policy of sorting out the relations of Serbia with her Provinces. I think he is right in that respect and the mass meetings were a positive thing. At last a Communist has realised that the absurd situation in which the

44. RFE, SR/9, 20 July 1989.
45. RFE, SR/9, 20 July 1989.

largest nation has yet to win the status which all national minorities enjoy must be put right.'[46]

Just three days before the celebrations at Kosovo Polje, the Serbs had had the opportunity to demonstrate their solidarity at what was to be the world's largest functioning Orthodox cathedral, St Sava, in Belgrade. The building of this church, begun in 1935 but halted by the war, represented the Serbs' perception of themselves as triumphant in the face of repression, and was a visible sign of the renaissance of the Orthodox Church. It stood on the site where the Ottomans had burned the remains of St Sava, founder of the Serbian Orthodox Church, and thus ever since its inception, the plan to build a church on this site has been an assertion of Serb nationalism. After the war the Church had appealed repeatedly but fruitlessly to the Yugoslav government for permission to resume work on the building, and only with the death of Tito was permission finally granted to resume work in 1984. The Orthodox Church was delighted by the Serbian Party's change of mood. Speaking later of Milosevic, a Serbian bishop told a foreign journalist: 'At last we have a leader who fills the needs of the Serbian nation. Now our culture can revive, for this younger generation of Communists in Serbia have more respect for the glory of medieval Serbia than their predecessors.'[47] According to Radio Ljubljana, the Kosovo celebrations indicated an 'obvious national rallying of Serbs who worshipped Milosevic like the legendary Prince Lazar' (who died at the Battle of Kosovo). A mood for sharper confrontation was set as the Serbian Church called for Serbs to fight against not only the ethnic but also the spiritual loss of Kosovo.

46. Unpublished interview with Milovan Djilas by G. Cirjanic, Belgrade, February 1989.
47. *The Independent*, London. 9 January 1989, p. 5.

12

THE SERBS RECLAIM THEIR REPUBLIC

By the autumn of 1989 the ever-widening gap between the Serbian and Albanian communities in Kosovo was being further exacerbated as the Republican authorities sought to establish a general administration over the Province through centralisation of government, political and propaganda pressure, and the sheer physical weight of police repression. In an ominous prelude to events soon to come, fighter jets of the Yugoslav air-force circled over Kosovo's main towns, the streets of which were now crowded with military vehicles and patrolled by heavily-armed Serbian police. On 30 October the trial of Azem Vllasi began, but it was immediately adjourned because of various objections by defence lawyers who demanded, among other things, replacement of the presiding judge and the public prosecutor. The trial resumed on 23 November but was again adjourned when the judge decided that Vlassi's defence needed more time to prepare. The trial eventually took place under very difficult circumstances with the courthouse surrounded by tanks, and access denied to foreign diplomats and human rights groups. It was clearly motivated by political considerations and a widely shared desire for revenge. In these circumstances Vlassi could not receive fair treatment, a fact which ignited fresh disturbances throughout Kosovo, including a sit-in by mineworkers.

As inter-ethnic relations steadily worsened in Kosovo, so correspondingly did relations between Yugoslavia's other republics. In Slovenia and Croatia the press called Vlassi's trial 'a judicial farce'. The Serbian press retaliated by claiming that the Croats and Slovenes did not understand what was really happening in Kosovo, especially where the grievances of Kosovo's Slav population were concerned. Serbs particularly criticised the wearing of 'I Love Kosovo' badges by young, trendy Slovenes as 'fake humanitarianism'. In a sense this description was apt: the outpouring of compassion in Ljubljana for the Kosovars was largely hypocritical since most Slovenes were no less disparaging towards Kosovar Albanians than were most Serbs, or indeed most Croats.[1] Slovenes on the whole would never think of visiting such a 'backward and primitive' place as Kosovo. Their attitude was similar towards the Albanians working in Ljubljana whom they regarded, along with others from the less developed regions of southern Yugoslavia, very much as inferior *gastarbeiters*. This hypocrisy openly manifested itself when Serbia's demands for reform of the Yugoslav Federation were at once countered by Slovenia and then by Croatia, which, covertly at first and then openly, took the side of the Kosovo Albanians, seeing them as allies in their power-struggle with Serbia. When this ended in their actual secession and the dissolution of Yugoslavia, both quickly lost interest in Kosovo.[2]

The new year, 1990, began with further civil disturbances when tens of thousands of Albanians staged initially peaceful protests in Pristina at the end of January in support of Kosovo's Communist Party leader, Rahman Morina, who had refused to receive a delegation from the newly-formed Free Students organisation demanding political reforms in Kosovo, the release of all political prisoners, and an end to political trials. Before long, however, the crowd was swelled by workers arriving from factories, and the demonstrations quickly turned violent with Albanians attacking trains, buses and cars. The protests were consequently broken up with equal violence by the security forces, which led to even more violent clashes between Albanian demonstrators and police throughout the province, leaving thirty-one dead and hundreds injured. Such was the force of the attacks on the protestors that the streets were quickly cleared and in April the federal authorities lifted the 'special measures' and removed most of the federal troops, leaving the Serbian Republican authorities to take over direct police control. Albanian police officers were immediately suspended and some 2,500 Serb policemen were brought to Kosovo from Belgrade. In

1. In the summer of 1989, the author was staying with a Croat family in Dalmatia and asked to play a tape of Albanian music bought the previous week in Prizren. When her hosts looked at the cover of the tape, they exclaimed with a look of disgust 'This is not good music, it is the same as Turkish music. They are all Albanians and gypsies in Kosovo – it is a dirty place. Why did you go there?'
2. Despite proposals from the then newly-formed Zagreb-based Society for Yugoslav Democratic Initiative that Kosovo should be governed directly by the federation, Kosovo's autonomy was in effect sacrificed by the northern republics at the recent Party Congress in order to check Slobodan Milosevic's wider aims: to secure Serbian supremacy by discrediting the federalist structure as Titoist.

a move to calm not only Albanian tempers but also condemnation from the international media,[3] Adem Demaci was released from prison on 28 April after having served nearly twenty-eight years in prison. Once the committed son striving for a better world, Demaci had now become something of a spiritual patriarch for the 3 million Albanians in Yugoslavia.[4] After his release he continually stressed the need for a peaceful solution to the present political crisis, with at most passive resistance, and publicly reiterated the dedication to the book he had published in Pristina in 1958: 'Not to those who raise their hand in crime, but to those who extend their hand in reconciliation'.[5] And indeed from the spring of 1990 the Albanians abandoned violence and embraced passive resistance, which became the hallmark of the next phase of the Albanian national movement in Kosovo.

The Serbs' programme for Kosovo

One of the key state documents from this period was the Programme for Achieving Peace, Freedom, Equality and Prosperity in Kosovo, adopted by the Serbian Parliament on 22 March 1990. In the name of its basic goal – the peaceful co-existence of all ethnic groups living in Kosovo – and specifying Albanian separatism as the main threat to that goal, the Programme announced 'specific measures for preserving law and order, peace, freedom, equality and Serbia's integrity'. It defined the problem of individual and ethnic rights as having three main aspects: guarantees of human rights for all of Kosovo's citizens; full equality for the Albanians, including the right to foster their national tradition, religion and cultural heritage; and the right to settle in Kosovo for Serbs and Montenegrins previously forced to leave the region during the Second World War. But as well as the right to settle, conditions had to exist to make it possible. However, neither the political will nor adequate financial provisions existed for effective implementation of this ambitious and contentious programme. The Albanian side no longer accepted the authority and legitimacy of its very proponent, and furthermore it came at a time

3. See *The Guardian*, 2 February 1990, for a report on the crushing of the Kosovo protesters.
4. Adem Demaci was awarded the 1991 Sakharov Prize in Strasbourg.
5. Elsie, *History of Albanian Literature*, vol. II, p. 625.

when the rift between the two ethnic communities in Kosovo had widened.[6]

There occurred at this time one of the strangest and most mysterious events to occur in Kosovo's troubles: the notorious mass poisoning of thousands of Albanian schoolchildren in the spring of 1990. According to Albanian sources, more than 7,000 cases of neuro-intoxication were observed and analysed in medical centers in March and April. Most of the victims were elementary and secondary school pupils who appeared to have suffered poisoning of the respiratory tract. The Albanians claim that neurotoxic gas was emitted via ventilation systems into schoolrooms where Albanian children were being taught. The children described how they experienced a pleasant smell but then started to feel nausea followed by other symptoms such as headache, stomach pain, dizziness, breathing problems, coughing, heart pain and hallucinations. Doctors diagnosed neuro-intoxication which they treated with infusions, vitamins and sedatives. On its fact-finding mission to investigate the poisonings, the International Helsinki Federation found that Serbian health officers accompanied by police had paid a number of visits to the hospital of the Roman Catholic convent of Binca to which numerous children with the poisoning symptoms were taken. On one occasion the police detained the nuns and forced them to send away all children with these symptoms. They then confiscated medicines on the grounds that the convent did not have official permision to keep a pharmacy, and destroyed part of the hospital's property before leaving. The Serbian authorities refused to investigate the alleged poisonings. Many hospitals and clinics were guarded by armed police to prevent Albanians from bringing their children in for treatment. According to the authorities they were suffering from 'mass hysteria'.[7]

Kosovo's autonomy removed

Meanwhile the terror being inflicted by the federal police increased dramatically after the Slovenian and Croatian contingents withdrew,

6. S. Samardzic, *Kosovo-Metohija - Political Aspects of the Problem*, Institute for European Studies, Belgrade, 1995, p. 2.

7. *Autonomy to Colonisation: Human Rights in Kosovo 1989-1993*, International Helsinki Federation for Human Rights, November 1993, pp. 23-4. A similar case of mass poisoning was reported in the predominantly Albanian-inhabited town of Tetovo in October 1996, when hundreds of Albanian pupils sought medical attention after complaining of stomach pains and shivering.

leaving exclusively Serbian units. In July 1990 the Belgrade government went one step further by depriving the provincial authorities of their power; it prevented the provincial parliament from meeting simply by expelling its members from the building. The Albanian parliamentarians then assembled on the steps outside on 2 July and proclaimed the sovereign Republic of Kosovo within the Yugoslav federation and its secession from Serbia.[8] In response Serbia dissolved Kosovo's government and Assembly three days later, and Serbia's National Assembly took administrative and executive control of the Province, now once more re-named Kosovo-Metohija. This decision was supported by the Presidency of the Socialist Federative Republic of Yugoslavia (SFRY) at its session on 11 July, thus finally removing the legal basis for Kosovo's autonomy, which had been granted under the 1974 constitution. Kosovo's parliament was also suspended with direct rule now imposed from Belgrade, which also ordered the occupation of Kosovo's radio and television stations, leaving no broadcast media in the Albanian language. There followed on 7 September a general strike by Albanians, whose deputies in the dissolved Kosovo parliament met secretly in the small town of Kacanik near the Macedonian border. Here they adopted the 'Kacanik constitution', which described the 'Republic of Kosovo' as 'a democratic state of the Albanian people and of members of other nations and national minorities who are its citizens: Serbs, Montenegrins, Croats, Turks, Romanians and others living in Kosovo'.[9]

This flurry of constitutional activity continued when Serbia's two provinces were finally defined, by the Serbian constitution adopted on 28 September 1990, as regions within the Serbian Republic. The provinces were given the usual characteristics of territorial and political autonomy with their own statutes, parliaments elected in general elections, and executive and administrative bodies (Articles 108-112). Members of ethnic minorities were guaranteed the following collective rights: official use of their mother-tongue (Article 1, Para. 2); to be educated in their mother-tongue (Article 32, Para. 3); and freedom of religion (Article 41). Kosovo's closely-knit Albanian majority did not participate, through its elected representatives, in the

8. C. von Kohl and W. Libal, 'Kosovo - The Gordian Knot of the Balkans' in R. Elsie (ed.), *Kosovo - in the Heart of the Powder Keg*, East European Monographs, New York, 1997, p. 85.
9. For the official account of these developments see *The Kacanik Resolution, Albanian Democratic Movement in Former Yugoslavia, Documents 1990-1993*, Kosova Information Centre, Pristina, 1993.

creation of the constitution and therefore those of its articles govern-
ing the Province's constitutional status and the status of the Albanian community within that framework were ignored. The concrete
deficiency of Kosovo's new constitutional status concerned the political will of the Albanians to turn the province into a state of their own
and place it out of the scope of Serbia's authority.[10] The daily newspaper *Rilindja*, with a circulation of 60-80,000 in 1990, was among
the first to feel the effects of Serbia's new 'emergency administration'.
Following the miners' strike in Stari Trg in February 1989, many of
its journalists were fired for reporting the demonstrations, and as a
result the paper appeared only irregularly. On 1 July 1990 the salaries
of the employees were frozen and *Rilindja* was closed down
completely the following month, costing 220 journalists and 170
technical staff their jobs. Chief editors and directors were removed
from their desks by force and police remained at the printing offices
for three days to ensure that nothing was printed. The Pristina radio
and TV stations and six other local radio stations which had broadcast in Albanian were also shut down. A further 1,300 Albanian staff
were dismissed and replaced by employees from Serbian radio and
televison.

Social changes under the 'emergency' administration

The imposition of 'emergency measures' on economic life in
Kosovo and the subsequent mass dismissals of Albanians from their
employment speeded up the decline of the Serbian-controlled
Kosovo Communist Party and of the trade unions under its control.
Consequently, new independent trade unions emerged and an
umbrella organisation, the Alliance of Independent Trade Unions
of Kosovo (AITUK), was founded in 1990 to coordinate their activities. The twenty-four hour general strike on 3 September 1990,
called to demand the reinstatement of dismissed Albanian workers,
was the first sign of its public activity. Following these mass
dismissals, providing financial and moral support for unemployed
Albanians and their families, whose very subsistence was at stake,
became an important function of the AITUK, which established a
solidarity fund to which all Albanian workers still employed paid 1
per cent of their salary and private Albanian firms and enterprises
paid 3 per cent. Most of the money came from Albanian guest-

10. Samardzic, *Kosovo-Metohija*, p. 3.

workers and political refugees abroad. Both the AITUK and its members were under continuous police surveillance, and their leaders and other activists were constantly harassed and imprisoned. At the same time, health care in Kosovo was placed under Serbian 'emergency management', with Albanian medical staff being dismissed and replaced by Serbs and Montenegrins.

Almost no part of Kosovo's cultural life was left untouched. The Provincial Theatre of Pristina was placed under 'emergency management' and the Albanian theatre manager was removed by police officers from his office to be replaced by a Serbian reporter from the newspaper *Jedinstvo*. This was preceded by a propaganda campaign in the Serbian media against the Albanian theatre because a photo exhibition carrying the title 'For Democracy against Violation' had taken place in the theatre lobby. The Albanian ballet was also closed down. Kosovarfilm, the local film production company, was put under new Serbian management. According to the Kosovo Ministry of Information, a great quantity of books, magazines and documents were removed from the National Library, the most precious items being transported to Belgrade and the rest to the paper factory in Lipjan for recycling. Likewise from other public libraries the majority of Albanian-language literature was removed. Most museums in Kosovo were closed, and in those that remained, exhibitions relating to Albanian culture were removed.

However, the greatest changes were in education – changes that would be severely detrimental to a whole generation of Albanian children and consequently to the future Kosovo society. In August 1990 the Serbian parliament decided to introduce a new school curricula for all regions of the Republic, including Kosovo, aimed at standardising the education system throughout Serbia. The new curricula brought major changes to the content of education: the number of hours stipulated for instruction on Serbian history and culture was significantly increased, and the teaching of Albanian language, history and literature was reduced to a minimum. In music instruction, the song-book for the first school year now contained fourteen Slavic songs and only two Albanian ones, and in physical exercises the once popular Albanian dances were omitted completely. With the introduction of the new curricula, new regulations for enrolment with a quota arrangement that gave preference to the Serbian population also took effect. Albanian pupils were not allowed to enrol in secondary school unless they passed examinations in Serbian language and literature, which only a small percentage managed to do. By December 1990 armed soldiers were patrolling the entrances to the Province's secondary schools to ensure that no Albanian children or teachers entered unless they agreed to follow the Serbian curriculum.[11]

In response to such a sudden and forceful wave of Serbianisation, Albanians began a long-overdue process of self-examination. In the midst of such a climate of violence, Albanians closed their ranks first by attempting to do away with violence among themselves. This meant challenging an integral part of their own tradition generally considered as backward and primitive: the blood-feud. A concerted effort was therefore made by enlightened students and Albanologists to stop the practice of blood vengence, which could be set off by such action as the killing of a sheepdog, an event which always started a feud. The process, which lasted a few months, resulted in reconciliation between some 2,000 families then involved in blood-feuds. About 20,000 men confined in their homes, since one feud invariably implicated all the adult males in a family, were consequently released. At great open-air ceremonies, hundreds of feuding families forgave each other and vowed not to perpetuate the cycle of revenge. The reconciliations continued despite the displeasure of the authorities, who saw them as evidence of dangerous homogenisation.[12]

Around the same time, the majority of Albanians in Kosovo seemed to think that it was necessary for them to renounce their Islamic heritage as a first step towards incorporation into Western civilisation and national unity as Albanians. Throughout 1990, as the situation in Kosovo was deteriorating daily, Muslim Albanians openly reflected on the idea of a collective conversion to Roman Catholicism. They asked themselves and their friends whether it was possible to return to the 'faith of our ancestors'. This was a time of deep collective disappointment – also a catharsis after the end of communism – and of liberation from the tutelage of the self-elected Albanian leadership in Kosovo.[13]

11. Before the academic year 1990-1, primary education in Kosovo was provided by 964 schools in three languages - Serbian, Albanian and Turkish. Classes in Albanian were attended by 304,836 pupils, in Serbian by 42,388 and in Turkish by 1,890. Secondary education was provided by 83 high schools for 69,221 Albanian, 14,678 Serbian and 389 Turkish pupils. University education was provided by six two-year post-secondary schools and thirteen University schools for 6,960 Albanian, 2,322 Serbian and 26 Turkish students. Samardzic, *Kosovo-Metohija*, p. 4.
12. Thompson, *A Paper House*, p. 141.
13. S. Maliqi, 'Albanians Between East and West', in Duijzings, Janjic and Maliqi (eds), *Kosovo-Kosova*, p. 119.

Apart from a reappraisal of social issues, the Kosovars had now to respond politically to the new constitutional changes, and the manner of their execution in Kosovo. Thus a major political turn-about in the Albanian national movement in Kosovo occurred when the old Marxist-Leninist parties and organisations disappeared from the scene and were replaced by new Albanian parties and lead-ers. By far the most significant of these was the Democratic League of Kosovo (LDK) formed on 23 December 1989 and headed by Dr Ibrahim Rugova, a quietly-spoken chain-smoker with long strag-gly hair and a perpetually weary and unkempt appearance. He was born in 1944, the son of a prosperous farmer in the village of Cerce in the district of Ostog who had been executed as an enemy of the Yugoslav state by Tito's Partisans in the chaotic final days of the war. Having studied literature in Pristina, he became a critic and in 1976 won a scholarship for a year's study in Paris, where he seems to have adopted Bohemian-cum-Gypsy attire - a red-spotted hand-kerchief wound tightly around his neck, and a lean and hungry look, aptly symbolising his people's condition at that time.

Meanwhile, the Serbian purge of the trading and industrial life of Kosovo intensified with the closing down of several enterprises, some of which may have owed their continued existence largely to the socialist policy, practised throughout Yugoslavia, of keeping unproductive enterprises alive only to provide employment. However, many of the companies shut down in Kosovo had been successful. Those which continued production were put under Serbian control and their management replaced with Serbs and Montenegrins. There also began a form of legalised looting of machinery, technical equipment and financial assets, together with the hasty merger of companies with enterprises in Serbia. This contributed to the collapse of the economy, which was spearheaded by the bankrupt Bank of Kosovo losing 66,000 individual foreign currency savings accounts worth an estimated $98 million: the money was simply confiscated by the state-owned Jugobanka in Belgrade, which refused to honour its client's obligations. The Serbian parliament then passed a law 'regulating' the proportion of workers on an ethnic basis which forced companies to recruit one Serb for every Albanian employed. All Albanian workers were required to sign 'loyalty letters' declaring allegiance to both the Republic of Serbia and the Socialist Party of Serbia; if they did not, they would lose their jobs. Many also lost their apartments, leaving them homeless and without welfare benefits. Most refused to sign and were therefore dismissed. When it is remembered that the vast majority of these workers were men with families to support, the social impact can be imagined: the resulting mass unemployment threatened the very existence of many Albanian families, who became dependent on various solidarity councils, the Union of Independent Trade Unions of Kosovo, and local charities such as the Mother Teresa organisation.[14]

Serb-Croat conflict increases tension in Kosovo

In response to their newly-defined socio-economic and political status imposed by Belgrade, the Albanians refused to recognise the legitimacy and legality of the Serbian state in Kosovo, and set about establishing a parallel, underground Albanian body politic. The Serbian authorities were not able to prevent the activities of the various Albanian political groups, the most important now being the LDK, which by the spring of 1991 had an estimated 700,000 members, and offices in several major European cities, notably in Zurich, Stuttgart and Brussels. Projecting itself as a national move-ment rather than a party, the LDK quickly became both the most numerous and the most influential organisation of Kosovo Albani-ans. Its founders were mostly members of the Yugoslav League of Communists, and as such not seen at first as a significant threat by the Belgrade authorities because of their safe and relatively reliable communist past. This complacency regarding the LDK soon faded after the outbreak of the war with Croatia. From that moment Belgrade watched to see if there were signs of the LDK being radi-cal, but its stance remained pacifist, which well suited Serbia. Groups calling for a violent response to the Serbian occupation were quickly marginalised by the LDK, which assumed the mantle of sole representative of Kosovar interests. During this period Ibrahim Rugova began to emerge on to the international stage as a human rights activist.

By now Albanians and Serbs were accusing each other of attempting to establish a 'second war front' in Yugoslavia. In the spring of 1991 reports that the Yugoslav National Army (JNA) had begun to arm Serbian and Montenegrin civilians in Kosovo began to circulate. Radio Croatia reported in its Albanian news broad-casts on May 20 and 21 that Serbs in several towns had been given

14. I. Rexhepi, 'The Province of Poverty', *War Report*, May 1996.

automatic rifles and had flaunted them in the streets. In Pec the police allegedly distributed two lorryloads of weapons and ammunition to Serbs in full public view; the Albanian opposition parties pointed out that the distribution of weapons was justified by the Serbian government's decision to step up security in Kosovo. The Serbian government appeared to be well aware of this during a session of the Committee for Domestic Politics (*Odbor za Unustrasnju Politiku*) of the Yugoslav Parliament on 30 May, when the arming of civilians throughout the former Yugoslavia, including Kosovo, was discussed. During the deliberations, the license-plate number of a car from which arms had allegedly been distributed to Serbs and Montenegrins in Kosovo was announced at the meeting by two delegates from Kosovo, Redzep Hamiti and Ramo Alihajdari. Both men claimed that 'massive' and 'public' distribution of weapons to Serbs and Montenegrins in Kosovo was occuring. At the same time, it was alleged that police in Kosovo were collecting arms – mostly hunting rifles – from Albanians even when they had permits for them.[15]

Meanwhile, the disintegration of Yugoslavia had begun in earnest, prompting the Kosovars to take action to consolidate their political response. In August, Albanian political parties in Kosovo, Macedonia and Montenegro established a joint committee under Ibrahim Rugova's chairmanship to co-ordinate their activities in order to present a unified stand to the international community. Although the Kacanik constitution had sought the solution to Kosovo's status within the framework of Yugoslavia, the secession of Slovenia and Croatia the following year had radically altered the stance of the Albanian leadership. Thus on 22 September 1991, the parliament of what Kosovars now called the 'Republic of Kosovo' approved the 'Resolution on Independence and Sovereignty of Kosovo'. This decision was put to the popular vote in a referendum organised clandestinely between 26 and 30 September. The balloting was conducted in the open in rural areas and in the privacy of homes in the towns to avoid interference by the police. Kosovo's independence was overwhelmingly supported. Out of the 87.01 per cent of all eligible voters in Kosovo, 99.87 per cent declared in favour of independence, 164 citizens voted against and 933 ballots were invalid. In accordance with the popular vote, the Kosovo

---

15. *Yugoslavia: Human Rights Abuses in Kosovo 1990-1992*, Helsinki Watch, October 1992, p. 52.

parliament amended the Kacanik constitution and declared the independence of Kosovo on 19 October 1991. Dr Bujar Bukoshi was named as Prime Minister.[16] The Serbian authorities called the referendum illegal, unconstitutional and the Province's first step towards secession and unification with neighbouring Albania. As the conflict between Belgrade and Zagreb intensified, there were numerous reports of Croatian emissaries urging the Albanians to stage an uprising. However, Croatia's President Franjo Tudjman had already alienated the Albanians by accepting Milosevic's plan to exclude their representatives from talks on the future of Yugoslavia, and by publicly declaring Kosovo to be an internal matter for Serbia. Rugova and other Kosovar leaders considered that Croatia and Slovenia had sacrificed Kosovo's autonomy in their deals with Milosevic, and were later wary of Croatian designs.[17]

Meanwhile, Kosovo's education system came under further attack when it was announced in Belgrade that no Albanian students would be allowed to register at Pristina University either for the 1991/2 academic year or subsequently; all university buildings, dormitories, laboratories and libraries were guarded against them by armed police. Some 7,000 Serb and Montenegrin students, together with a number of Greeks, who had failed to enter any Greek university, continued their studies as normal. A new Law on Universities, which took effect soon afterwards, specified in Article 10 that education should be given in Serbo-Croatian – or in a minority language if the board of the university or faculty in question so agreed.[18] But with boards nominated by the Serbian authorities and made up overwhelmingly of Serbs, such agreement would hardly be a possibility. The Albanians, in response, promptly established their own 'parallel' Albanian-language university in November 1991, at first rudimentary with classes set up in buildings lacking the basics for organised and effective teaching. Having applied to the European Community on 23 December 1991 for recognition as an independent state and been rejected, the Kosovar leadership set

16. D. Kostovicova, *Parallel Worlds*, p. 31. Back in 1989, Bukoshi had helped form the LDK and served as its Secretary General before being named Prime Minister. Since his graduation from the University of Belgrade Faculty of Medicine, he has studied, practised and taught medicine in Belgrade, Pristina and Germany. He was a faculty member at Pristina University until being dismissed in August 1990 for his political views.
17. E. Biberaj, *Kosova: The Balkan Powder Keg*, Research Institute for the Study of Conflict and Terrorism, 1993, p. 10.
18. *Official Gazette of Serbia*, 54/92, 8 August, 1992.

about consolidating its 'parallel administration' parallel to the official Serbian one.

In the wake of their declaration of independence the 'Coordinating Committee of Albanian Political Parties in Yugoslavia', with Ibrahim Rugova as chairman, passed a political declaration in October 1991 putting forth three options for the solution of 'the Albanian question in Yugoslavia'.

(1) If the external and internal borders of the Socialist Federal Republic of Yugoslavia (SFRY) were to remain unaltered, the status of a sovriegn and independent state with the right of association in a new community of sovereign Yugoslav states, was demanded. Ethnic Albanians within Serbia, Macedonia and Montenegro should enjoy the status of a nation and not be a national minority within it.

(2) Should only the internal borders of the SFRY be changed and not the external ones, the founding of an Albanian Republic was called for, incorporating, apart from Kosovo, those territories in central Serbia, Montenegro and Macedonia inhabited by Albanians.

(3) In the event of the external borders being changed, the Albanians would by referendum and a general declaration, proclaim territorial unification with Albania and the creation of 'an undivided Albanian state in the Balkans with Albanian ethnic boundries', namely, within the boundaries proclaimed by the First Prizren League in 1878.[19]

As winter approached, it appeared as if the latter option might well be on the cards. Heavy fighting was continuing in Croatia and now seriously threatened Bosnia-Hercegovina. Following the withdrawal of Yugoslav Army (JNA) units from Macedonia, most of them were redeployed in Kosovo, and by November movements of artillery and motorised units of the Serbian army were reported in all the main towns. Serbian reservist forces had been expanded with many being deployed along the Albanian border. By now there was total segregation of Slavs and Albanians in Kosovo and almost complete paralysis of all economic, political and social institutions. The current policy could not be sustained, if only because it was so disastrously unproductive. More than one-fifth of bankrupt Serbia's 1991 budget was now being absorbed in policing the one-time

19. P. Simic, *The Kosovo and Metohija Problem and Regional Security in the Balkans*, Belgrade, 1996, p. 13.

Autonomous Province and subsidising the importation of Serb and Montenegrin workers, who demanded large hardship allowances.[20]

The collapse of communism in Albania

Until the secession of Slovenia and Croatia, which marked the actual breakup of Yugoslavia, Albanians still planned their national goals within the framework of Yugoslavia. Only when it had become obvious that the country was disintegrating beyond repair did the Albanian population assert their will to secede from the rump Yugoslavia and unite with Albania. With the collapse of communism in Eastern Europe and the Soviet Union, the swift disintegration of Yugoslavia and the new process of reform under way in Albania, many Kosovars quite understandably believed that a new world order had arrived and that the Albanian national question had to be seen in a new light. The Tirana government now began issuing statements containing by far the strongest criticism so far of the policies of Kosovo's Serbian leadership. But this was more because it feared a massive influx of refugees than out of any national considerations. Albania's armed forces were placed on high alert after incidents between Yugoslav and Albanian border guards.

A deputation from the LDK – the first official delegation of Kosovars to visit Albania – came to Tirana on 22 February 1991 the day after the great statue of Enver Hoxha was toppled. There followed much coming and going by LDK representatives and other prominent Kosovars, and in late October 1991 Albania officially recognised the 'Republic of Kosovo' as a sovereign and independent state - the only country to do so. This gesture, it hoped, would spur on further international recognition of Kosovo. The LDK established a permanent office in Tirana, and Ali Aliu, once a professor at Pristina University before being sacked by the Serbs, became its first representative to Albania. The Kosovars had great but unrealistic expectations of the political assistance Tirana could provide. In an interview Aliu said optimistically:

> 'We want Tirana to treat Kosovo not just as a matter of foreign policy but as a national matter. For two years Kosovo has had no mass media. We must therefore exert maximum effort to ensure that the Albanian media based in Tirana concentrates on the Kosovo issue so as to inform the entire nation.'

20. Thompson, *A Paper House*, p. 129.

Apart from Albania giving medical and educational assistance, Aliu expressed the wish that it would also somehow accommodate the thousands of Kosovars fleeing the JNA:

> 'We want the 100,000 Albanians who are deserting the Yugoslav army to be aware that Albania can and will offer them shelter. We do not want to see our boys fleeing to Western Europe, we ask that they be given sanctuary and safety here.'[21]

This dogmatic statement demonstrated how Kosovars expected Albanians to see the Albanian national struggle in Yugoslavia as an automatic priority. This was to remain the pervading attitude among Kosovar activists despite their knowledge of the dreadful socio-economic situation of Albania. Aliu was asked why the Kosovars were waiting for the Albanian army to come to their rescue and for the Albanian people to provide them with shelter, when it was becoming well known that there was a high level of apathy - even antipathy - towards them in Albania. Aliu replied:

> 'The truth is that we did not fully comprehend what took place in Albania these last fifty years. In the 1970s I was here as a guest of the university. None of us understood the dimensions of the terror and the dictatorship. The government blinded us from reality; we saw only the facade.'[22]

Nevertheless, most Kosovars believed the poverty of Albania to be a temporary phenomenon that would be eradicated by massive injections of international economic aid shortly after the anticipated victory of the newly-formed opposition Albanian Democratic Party (DP) in Albania's forthcoming first-ever multi-party elections. At this stage the DP associated itself firmly with the Kosovar cause, claiming that once in power it would bring down the 'Balkan Wall'. In return for such stirring statements, a considerable quantity of material aid came to the DP from Kosovar diaspora groups.

The dramatic political changes then occurring in Albania were watched with avid attention by Kosovar émigré communities, which began raising funds for the DP. Campaigning equipment such as cars and fax machines were bought in Germany and Switzerland and sent to the DP before the election in March 1992. As a measure of how important the émigré factor was at that time, the notion of a 'Unified Albania' got considerably more airing in

21. *East European Reporter*, March/April 1992, p. 58.
22. Ibid., p. 58.

New York than in Albania. There are estimated to be between 350,000 and 400,000 Albanian-Americans and the leaders of their communities were active in promoting the issue of Kosovo. In 1986 Congressman Joseph DioGuardi founded the Albanian-American Civic League to bring together the various influential groups of Albanian-Americans to campaign on behalf of Albanians in Yugoslavia, and especially to raise the issue of human rights abuses in Kosovo in the US Congress.[23]

The Kosovars believed a democratic government in Albania would use its new power and energy for the benefit and progress of Kosovo. The leader of the DP, Dr Sali Berisha, told supporters that 'the DP will not stop fighting until her great dream of uniting the Albanian nation comes true'.[24] This was a provocative statement to make at this sensitive time, but Berisha was in a buoyant and expectant mood, and like many European politicians he believed that now three of the former Yugoslav republics had international recognition, Kosovo's turn must also come. Already in its initial 1990 programme, the DP had endorsed an eventual 'democratic' union with Kosovo. In common with most Albanians, Berisha believed that history was offering his nation a chance to unite. As a Gheg himself, with many close Kosovar family connections, he gave greater priority to unification with Kosovo than did many Tosk politicians.

Meanwhile, as the Yugoslav war intensified, Kosovo Albanians were still obliged to perform their twelve months' military service in the JNA with no right to conscientious objection or to alternative civilian service. Albanian conscripts in the JNA had always been treated with suspicion by their officers, but after the start of the Yugoslav war in 1991, almost all Albanian men refused to do their military service. To avoid conscription thousands fled abroad, and thousands more went into hiding in Kosovo itself, which led to routine spot-checks by police searching for them. Others crossed into Albania, making their way directly to Tirana where their arrival at first had a dramatic impact. Because of the difficult and unpredictable situation in Kosovo, Kosovars were anxious to consolidate their economic position in Albania, and together with

23. The League has since been dogged by controversy and has not perhaps fulfilled the role envisaged by its founders, although it has a strong Kosovar lobby on Capitol Hill, which developed under the leadership of Senator Robert Dole.

24. BBC/SWB, EE/1336, B/3, 23 March 1992.

returning Albanian-American émigrés, they quickly became the big fish in a little pond as their large extended families made use of widespread international connections to develop their economic interests. Even with the modest amounts of hard currency they had available, they quickly began to control several areas of economic activity, most notably, car imports, drug dealing and gun-running. Kosovar immigrants bore some responsibility for the spiralling crime rate and the growth of Mafia-type activities that became so prevalent during Albania's early transition period.

Meanwhile, the situation in former Yugoslavia deteriorated sharply after international recognition of the independence of Croatia and Slovenia in January 1992. This led directly to the escalation of the conflict into Bosnia-Hercegovina. There was a corresponding tightening of Serbian control in Kosovo, and at the end of January a large rally was held in Tirana in support of the Kosovars. The wave of euphoria and expectation which now galvanised the Kosovars in the run-up to Albania's first multi-party elections was aptly expressed by a nationalistic Kosovar academic, Rexhep Qosja, who attended a meeting at the Albanian Academy of Sciences in Tirana at the beginning of February 1992. He explained to the assembled academics and politicians the symbolism attached to his visit to Albania and what he called the 'sacred land'. His speech evoked the historical ambitions of Albania's neighbours to divide the Albanian nation:

> 'We [Kosovars] come to the land of our dreams and ideals, to the land of our symbols and apostles of Albania, where there is Kruja and Vlora, where there are the graves of Skanderbeg and Naim Frasheri. Albania's poverty has deep roots and is a result of historic injustice done to the Albanian people. The neighbouring countries try to make it impossible for us to find a solution to our national question; Serbia, Montenegro, Greece and now Macedonia have divided up our territories. So the same opponents that we had in 1878 and in 1912-13 are now against us. But neither our international position nor theirs at present is as it was 115 years ago or 80 years ago. They are not in as favourable a political position as they were then. With the correct solution of the Albanian question, the unification of the Albanians, one of the greatest injustices in Europe, will be solved.'[25]

This speech exemplified the romantic and unrealistic impression many Kosovars had about Albania and in particular the prevailing belief that they were now faced with an historic chance finally to solve the Albanian national question. Kosovars in general were convinced that a DP victory in Albania's forthcoming election would help to gain international support and understanding of their plight. When that victory eventually came in March 1992 and Sali Berisha was elected to the Albanian Presidency, it was hailed throughout the Albanian diaspora as a triumph for the whole Albanian nation. Following the collapse of the one-party state in Albania, the Albanian nation achieved, albeit briefly, a form of spiritual reunification. 'There is no Albania without Kosovo and vice versa,' declared the official Albanian press agency.[26] At DP rallies the admonition rang out: 'Let us demolish the border dividing Albanians from Albanians' - an explicit call for national reunification, which sent shock-waves through the international community whose efforts to contain the fighting in Bosnia and thus avoid any re-adjustment of borders was failing dismally. Oblivious to such international concerns, the Kosovars now hoped that the international community would quickly raise the status of Albania by means of large injections of financial aid, thereby making it a more important player on the international negotiating scene.

This hope was echoed across the Atlantic - 'Kosovo wins with Berisha' was a headline in *Illyria* (20 June 1992), the Albanian-American weekly. The belief that a politically and economically stabilised Albania could do more for Kosovo was also claimed by Ibrahim Rugova in an interview with 'Voice of America' immediately after the DP election victory: 'This victory will be significant to the Albanians in Kosovo because Albania will appear with a new authority on the international scene. It will be strengthened economically and will naturally be better able to help the general Albanian cause.'[27] However once Berisha had taken office as President and was confronted head-on by Albania's catastrophic economic situation, his priorities had to be quickly re-adjusted. Also, as Albania began to participate in the difficult negotiations concerning the Yugoslav conflict, much pressure was put on him to temper nationalistic claims – in return for which his administration was promised financial assistance. Henceforth, Tirana

25. Albanian Telegraphic Agency, 9 February, 1992.
26. Ibid., 22 March, 1992.
27. Ibid., 24 March, 1992.

stressed that the Albanian-Yugoslav border should not be forcibly changed.

The Kosovars consolidate their parallel state

In the mean time the military presence in Kosovo had been growing, with new barracks, the formation of new Serbian irregular units and the calling up of extra Serbian reservists. Serbs and Montenegrins had been supplied with weapons, and a large number of young Albanians had been forcibly drafted and sent to areas of fighting elsewhere in Yugoslavia. New border checkpoints were set up which placed Kosovo under a virtual blockade and severely restricted the movement of Albanians. In April the director of Serbian 'emergency measures' in the Province, Mr Vucovic, reportedly established a registration centre in the Grand Hotel in Pristina for volunteers for the 'Serbian National Guard' and the 'White Eagles' (*Beli Orlovi*) led by Vojslav Seselj, president of the Serbian Radical Party, who was allegedly responsible for some of the worst atrocities in Croatia. Paramilitary snipers were positioned at strategic points in Pristina, such as on the top of the Grand Hotel, the Hotel Bozur and similar buildings. Despite these activities, Seselj was then appointed professor at the Faculty of Law at Pristina University. In addition the Tigers, another paramilitary group led by Zeljko Raznjatovic, also known as 'Arkan', was becoming increasingly active in Kosovo. Raznjatovic, later named on the list of war criminals in Bosnia-Hercegovina, was alleged to be the leader of a prominent crime syndicate in Belgrade and was also wanted by Interpol for crimes committed in Western Europe. The Kosovar leadership now began strenuous efforts to obtain international recognition, visiting a variety of European capitals. In March 1992 'Prime Minister' Bukoshi visited Copenhagen, Vienna and Helsinki, and 'Deputy Prime Minister' Nike Gjeloshi visited the Vatican. Neither received anything better than feeble praise for the Kosovars' 'peaceful approach' and promises that 'Kosovo had not been forgotten.'

In a further move to consolidate their self-declared 'Kosovo Republic' and to present themselves to the International Community as a coherent and unified mini-state in the making, the Albanian political parties in Kosovo organised a parliamentary and presidential election, which was held on 24 May 1992. Election campaigning was carried out in Albanian-language newspapers and magazines, the Albanian-language programme at Radio Zagreb, and at indoor meetings throughout Kosovo. The elections themselves, which the Serbian authorities declared illegal, were carried out mostly without official interference, although in many places ballot-papers and other election materials were confiscated and some election officials were arrested.[28] Eight monitoring groups from the United States and Europe were present. A combined electoral system was used: there were 130 seats in Parliament, and 100 members were elected through direct voting, i.e. according to the majority system, and thirty seats were selected through a proportional system. The Democratic League of Kosovo, by far the largest opposition group, won the majority of seats, which were distributed as follows: 96 for the LDK, 5 for the Muslim Slav deputies,[29] and 29 for deputies from the other Albanian parties and various independent candidates.

The remaining fourteen seats which, according to the percentage of Kosovo's population and the proportional distribution of parliamentary seats, belonged to people of Serbian and Montenegrin ethnicity, were held open for the representatives of those communities who refused to take up their seats.[30] In the presidential election the only candidate, Ibrahim Rugova, represented the

28. The following political parties took part in the May 1992 elections: the Democratic Alliance of Kosova (LDK); the Parliamentary Party of Kosova (PPK); the Social Democratic Party of Kosova (PSDK); the Farmer's Party of Kosova (PFK); the Albanian Christian Democratic Party of Kosova (PSHDK); the Republican Party of Kosova (PRK); the Albanian Republican Party (PRSH); the Party of National Unity (UNIKOMB); the Liberal Party of Kosova (PLK); the Albanian People's Party (PPSH); the Albanian National Democratic Party (PNDSH); the National Front (BK); the Union of Albanian Democratic Youth (LRDSH); the Albanian Party for Democratic Union (PSHBD); the Albanian People's Movement (LPSH); the Green Movement of Kosova (LGJK); the Green Party of Kosova (PGJK); the Party of Democratic Action (PAD, a Muslim party); and the Turkish People's Party. In addition to the above parties, the People's Movement for the Republic of Kosova (KPRK) is active abroad but has many supporters also in Kosovo. *Source*: Kosovo Helsinki Committee, 15 April 1993.

29. Most of Kosovo's non-Albanian Muslims live in the districts of Pec, Istok, Prizren and Dragas. Those in Pec and Istok came originally from the Sandjak region of Serbia and Montenegro and are referred to as 'Muhadjir'. Muslims originally from Kosovo live primarily in Prizren and Dragas. In 1991 there were an estimated 40,000 *Muhadjir* and 50,000 indigenous Muslims resident in Kosovo.

LDK and was elected president of the 'Republic of Kosovo` with 99.5 per cent of the vote. Although a growing number of Albanian political leaders and intellectuals complained that the LDK had monopolised Kosovo's political life, none could mount a serious challenge to Rugova. Thus the Kosovars' parallel institutional structure was completed. During the process of their institution-building they had substantially modified their national goal. At first Albanians had fought for the preservation of the autonomy stipulated by the 1974 constitution, but Serbia's suspension of Kosovo's autonomy created a new aim – an Albanian Republic within Yugoslavia. However, the break-up of Yugoslavia caused yet another formulation of the national goal, which eventually emerged as a self-declared 'sovereign and independent Kosovo.'[31]

Despite such apparently overwhelming support, the newly-elected parliament never actually convened – partly because of severe interference by Serbian police. However, if it had convened it would have legitimised itself, and thus presented the international community with the embarrassing dilemma of not being able to recognise it officially. Instead Albanian legislators began meeting in small groups to coordinate their policy. Attention was understandably still focused on relations with the DP in neighbouring Albania, which was still reeling with euphoria over its victory. In July, in a move which suggested that the issue of gradual unification was still very much on the agenda, Albanian government officials and Kosovar leaders met to discuss socio-economic cooperation. The Albanian Prime Minister, Alexander Meksi, received Rugova in

30. The results were: Democratic League of Kosovo 574,755 votes (76.44 per cent); the Parliamentary Party of Kosovo 36,549 (4.86 per cent); Peasants Party of Kosovo 23,682 (3.15 per cent); the Albanian Christian Democratic Party 23,303 (3.10 per cent), independent (non-party) candidates 24,702 (3.29 per cent). Other electoral subjects participating in the election received less than 1.87 per cent of the vote, and so did not secure the right of participation in the proportional distribution of seats in Parliament. Albanians, Muslims, Turks, Rom, Croats and a small number of Serbs and Montenegrins participated in the elections. The parliamentary seats were allocated as follows: Democratic League of Kosovo 96; Parliamentary Party of Kosovo 13; Peasants Party of Kosovo 7; Albanian Christian Democratic Party 7; Independent (non-party) candidates 2. People of Muslim ethnicity, according to the percentage of the population and proportional distribution, had 4 deputies; whereas 1 candidate of Muslim ethnicity won in the direct voting. In the composition of the new Parliament there were two deputies of Turkish ethnicity who won as candidates of the Democratic League of Kosovo.
31. Kostovicova, *Parallel Worlds*, p. 32.

the first meeting between the LDK president and members of the new DP government. The talks concentrated on creating opportunities for cooperation between Albania and Kosovo in all fields but especially in education, and it was agreed to bring experts from Kosovo, primarily university lecturers in philosophy, law and sociology into Albanian faculties, where these subjects were totally distorted and politicised. Unable to assist Kosovo either financially or militarily, Meksi could only stress his government's unhesitating support for the cause of Kosovo's eventual independence.

By the end of the year, the impact of the mass dismissals of Albanians from all walks of public life and industry in Kosovo society had become more pronounced. Some 750,000 people were by now estimated to be without social insurance and thus denied free medical services in the state-run institutions. For those who could not afford medical care in state-run or private clinics, the only alternative was to attend the 'parallel' health centres. At the time there were said to be 166 such centres or clinics in Kosovo staffed by Albanian medical personnel dismissed from their previous posts, who did their work without payment. Most of these clinics were wholly unsuitable for medical practice, since they lacked sanitary facilities and some were even without running water. Although some equipment and medical supplies were financed and supplied by private foreign or international humanitarian organisations, this was far from adequate. Thus the medical treatment available was limited by a chronic shortage of all medicines, including the most basic, and of other supplies and equipment. In addition, the 'parallel' clinics were in constant danger of closure by the Serbian authorities, and their staff were systematically harassed and detained. Nevertheless, it must be recalled that the Albanians had in many ways mismanaged the health care programme in Kosovo when everything was under their control up till 1989. According to an American doctor who worked in Kosovo, the Albanians had put great emphasis on obtaining grandiose equipment such as heart scanners, instead of organising a far more practical sort of 'barefoot doctor' programme, such as that successfully practised in China, by going out into the villages and performing simple but effective preventive measures. Apparently the Albanians believed at the time that the Serbs were oppressing them by not providing sophisticated equipment.

By mid-1992 the Province's 170,000 Serbs and Montenegrins accounted for just 9 per cent of Kosovo's population.[32] Although

Kosovo still remained the most potent symbol of Serbian nationalism, the Slavs had long since lost the demographic war for Kosovo, and demographically the Albanians were well on their way to achieving an 'ethnically pure' Kosovo.[33] It was therefore with an air of increasing desperation that 'the Serbian Bloc for the colonisation of Kosovo' was formed in Pristina, with the aim of putting high-level pressure on the administration to accelerate the Serbian re-colonisation of the Province. In an effort to reverse the region's ethnic distribution, Belgrade offered credits, housing and, where possible, jobs to those Serbs and Montenegrins willing to settle there, but by March 1992 fewer than 3,000 Serbs had taken up the offer and many of these were from Albania's minute Slav population.

As the summer of 1992 approached, Kosovo's Slav and Albanian communities were living in an apartheid situation, virtually without communication and in a state of open hostility. By now the LDK was insisting on Kosovo's statehood as the source of the Albanians' sovereign rights, but although politicians in Belgrade now recognised the danger of Kosovo sliding into communal violence, wounded national pride failed to accept that the Serbs had lost Kosovo, not only demographically but because they could only maintain control over the province by severe police repression and military force. But few, if any, Serbs were willing to engage in negotiations over Kosovo, cut Serbia's losses, and concede to Albanian demands for self-determination. While the financial cost of keeping control over Kosovo could not be calculated with any certainty, it was estimated that since 1989 Serbia had spent more than US$6 billion maintaining 'peace' in Kosovo. However, there were no signs that the Serbs, despite their serious economic difficulties, were beginning to see the cost of maintaining their control over Kosovo

32. During 1992 virtually the entire Croat population of Kosovo fled to Croatia, mainly through fear and insecurity caused by the war in Croatia, and threats from armed local Serbian extremists. Most of these Kosovo Croats were resettled in abandoned Serbian villages in Western Slavonia.(For a description of the Croat exodus from Letnica, a small Croatian enclave in Kosovo, see Ger Duijzings, 'The Exodus of Letnica - Croatian Refugees from Kosovo in Western Slavonia', *Narodna umjetnost*, 32/2, str. 129-152, Zagreb, 1995.

33. The latest precise data on the Albanians in Yugoslavia were from 1981, because they boycotted the 1991 census. For a detailed statistical study of the demographic, and socio-economic situation in Kosovo see: S. Bogosavljevic, 'A Statistical Picture of Serbian-Albanian Relations' in *Conflict or Dialogue: Serbian-Albanian Relations and integration of the Balkans*, Subotica, 1994, pp. 17-29 and H. Islami, *Kosova dhe Shqiptaret*, pp. 30-53.

as excessive.[34]

While Albanians were busy proclaiming their ancestral right to Kosovo by broadcasting Illyrian names, such as the Hotel Dardania in Pec, as if to say: 'We were here first',[35] Serbs set about changing Albanian street-names in Kosovo's towns to ones reflecting Serbian history and culture. Meanwhile, Albanians continued their policy of passive resistance, born out of their military weakness. Ibrahim Rugova explained at the time:

> 'We have no local territorial forces like the Slovenes and Croats. All our weapons have been taken away by the Serbian police. We are not certain how strong the Serbian military presence in the province actually is, but we do know that it is overwhelming and that we have nothing to set against the tanks and other modern weaponry in Serbian hands. We would have no chance of successfully resisting the army. In fact the Serbs only wait for a pretext to attack the Albanian population and wipe it out. We believe it is better to do nothing and stay alive than to be massacred.'[36]

Consequently, the LDK continued to be a movement rather than a political party, and for that reason perhaps failed to develop a fully democratic structure.

34. Biberaj, *Kosovo: The Balkan Powder Keg*, p. 20.
35. M. Moats, 'Yugoslavia Lost', p. 295.
36. I. Rugova, *Impact International*, 10 April-7 May, 1992, p. 10.

13

NEITHER WAR NOR PEACE

By mid-1992 the atmosphere in Kosovo had become extremely tense, with a pervading sense of insecurity and a fear of impending conflict that was felt by all its citizens. However, while the war went on in the western republics, Kosovo managed to maintain its relative peace, mainly because of a balance of fear in which the leaders of both the Serb and Albanian communities recognised that any outbreak of hostilities between them would surpass even the Bosnian war in violence and consequently be fatal to the interests of both nations. Thus in spite of their mutual distrust and profoundly disrupted relations, the Serbs and Albanians of Kosovo took care not to go beyond a point where conflict would inevitably be provoked. Thus the gravest ethnic problem in Yugoslavia escaped from being drawn into the Yugoslav civil war, but relations between the two communities remained frozen in a way seen nowhere else.[1]

Ibrahim Rugova, a powerless leader

In the summer of 1992 the British government and the United Nations hosted an international conference in London in an ambitious attempt to reverse the ethnic cleansing in Bosnia and restore territory forcibly taken by the newly-reconstituted (27 April 1992) but unrecognised Yugoslav state, which now comprised only Serbia and Montenegro. Albanian representatives from Kosovo were angry that, although they had been invited to London, they were classed as observers rather than participants. The entire new Kosovar political élite turned up, only to be relegated to a side room where they had to be content with watching the proceedings on a TV monitor. This was an enormous humiliation for a people who believed their suffering to be equal to that of the Bosnian Muslims. The

---

1. P. Simic, *The Kosovo and Metohija Problem and Regional Security in the Balkans*, Belgrade, 1996, p. 3.

only marginally constructive outcome of the Conference that affected the Kosovo problem was the decision to station human rights observers in Kosovo, Vojvodina and the Sandjak, and for talks to be held on educational issues. Perhaps it was due to their isolation that the Kosovars had an inflated sense of their importance on the international scene. Whenever Berisha or Rugova travelled abroad, especially to Washington, they were convinced that the issue of Kosovo would be foremost on the agenda, but on most occasions it was only a peripheral item in talks which centred on bilateral issues. The Albanian media accorded Rugova's visits to Western countries with exaggerated importance, and as recognition of Kosovo as an independent state, even though he was always received as a delegate from a non-governmental organisation.

Although at the London conference Rugova did have conversations with the recently-elected and reform-minded Yugoslav federal Prime Minister, Milan Panic, nothing concrete was achieved. Panic may have publicly committed himself to improving conditions for Kosovo's Albanians and to reopen their schools and hospitals, but he also strongly asserted that 'Kosovo belongs to Yugoslavia'; and that while he was working to restore full human rights to Kosovars, they must first be included in the political life of Yugoslavia, ie., participate fully in the forthcoming Yugoslav elections. However, where the LDK was concerned there was little difference between Panic and Milosevic; neither was prepared to negotiate on the issue of self-determination. Talks about opening the Albanian-language schools and the university duly began in Belgrade in October 1992 between an Albanian delegation headed by Fehmi Agani and the Serbian Minister of Education, Mr Ivic, but although the Albanian demand for a dialogue on education at all levels had been accepted by Belgrade, no agreement could be reached because of the complexity of Kosovo's problems and the need for a prior political solution. It was admitted by both sides that trying to take a pragmatic approach to the problem without prejudicing the future status of Kosovo was very difficult because Kosovo's status and Albanian-language education were inextricably linked.

Meanwhile, the Kosovar leadership continued its policy of peaceful resistance amid an increasingly tense atmosphere. With the majority of the Albanian population unarmed, they were concerned to avoid at all costs the bloodshed they were witnessing in Bosnia. Serbian paramilitary units roaming throughout Kosovo appeared to be recruiting members and increasing their presence in the region as Serbia's most feared paramilitary leader, Zeljko 'Arkan' Raznjatovic paraded around the towns flanked by sharp-suited bodyguards. The key element in Arkan's strategy was to play on the fears of the Serb minority in Kosovo of an Albanian uprising in order to mobilise support for a cleansing programme, which would concentrate on ensuring that the main industrial installations of northern Kosovo, the lead mines at Trepca and the northern ferro-nickel plant at Glogovac would be firmly in Serbian hands if there were to be any ultimate division of the province between Albania and Serbia. To this end Arkan's people let it be known that they were stockpiling weapons near these installations, hidden in Serbian Orthodox monasteries or on adjacent monastic land – in particular at Djavic, a historic church and monastic buildings in remote country near Glogovac, at Samodreza near Mitrovica, and at Gracanica outside Pristina. At the time local Albanians reported widespread militia activity based on hunting clubs, together with close collaboration between local Serb leaders of the government security forces and paramilitaries in the vicinity of Pec monastery. President Slobodan Milosevic, mindful of a potential international backlash, had so far managed to keep his strongman Arkan under tight control.

The strong gains of the Serbian ultra-nationalist parties in the Yugoslav elections in December 1992 cast a pall of fear over sections of Kosovo's Albanian population. Although Milosevic's Socialist Party won forty-seven seats in the federal Parliament, thirty-three seats went to the Radical Party led by the extreme Serb nationalist leader Vojislav Seselj, who during the electoral campaign had demanded the expulsion of all Albanians from Kosovo, saying that if they did not respect the Serbian administration in Kosovo then they should go and live in their own newly-democratic national state next door. The main opposition coalition, Depos, gained a mere twenty-one seats. As expected, Kosovo's Albanians boycotted the Serbian elections despite calls from the international community to vote for Milan Panic, who promised to restore human rights and negotiate some form of autonomy for Kosovo. This angered many Serbs who did not appreciate the interference of Panic in issues concerning Kosovo, which they deemed a matter for the Serbian rather than the federal authorities.

Those Kosovars who advocated Albanian participation in the rump Yugoslav elections were dismissed as traitors by the LDK, which excused their non-participation in the December elections:

> 'The result of the elections in Serbia and Montenegro has confirmed our predictions that Milosevic and Seselj would win and that the Albanian vote would have no influence on the final result since Milosevic would manufacture the votes he needed in the same way as his regime printed as much money as it needed.'[2]

In reality, however, the million Albanian votes could undoubtedly have ousted Milosevic, but as the Kosovar leadership admitted at the time, they did not want him to go. Unless Serbia continued to be labelled as profoundly evil – and they themselves, by virtue of being anti-Serb, as the good guys – they were unlikely to achieve their goals. It would have been a disaster for them if a peacemonger like Panic had restored human rights, since this would have left them with nothing but a bare political agenda to change borders.[3] Although the fact that there were other Serbian political parties, such as Serbian National Renewal under Vuk Draskovic and the Radical Party of Vojislav Seselj, with far stronger and more lurid views on Kosovo than Milosevic's League of Communists, the Albanians wanted to have things both ways – they refused to participate in the elections but then complained that they were being represented by non-elected individuals – and war criminals.

Meanwhile, the Bosnian war showed no signs of abating. As a result, Kosovo – known as the most volatile region with the greatest degree of human rights abuse in Europe – came to look like an oasis of peace compared with the carnage going on in Bosnia. A report in the international weekly edition of *Politika* (19–25 September 1992) claimed that Turkey was supplying Kosovo with arms via Bulgaria and Skopje; they were reportedly collected in the predominantly Albanian-inhabited towns of Tetovo and Gostivar in western Macedonia and smuggled from there over the mountains into Kosovo. The Serbian public were also told that Albanians were fighting alongside Croats and Muslims against Serbs, and it was a fact that, counting on a weakening of Serbia as a result of the war in Bosnia and the possibility that this would open the way for their secession, many Albanians joined the Croatian and Muslim army. According to one observer, 'Albanians joined the Croatian army

2. *Bulletin of the Ministry of Information of the Republic of Kosovo*, no. 67, 29 December 1992.
3. *New Statesman and Society*, 5 March 1993, p. 13.

voluntarily and with their weapons. It is a well-known fact that there were many esteemed Albanian officers of high rank who joined the Croatian army and they contributed to Croatia's victories so far against the Serbian army.'[4] The LDK publicity machine responded with articles entitled 'Kosovo Serbs volunteer to fight in Croatia.'[5]

The issue of Albanian unification

Although by the end of 1992 Albanians had to put the idea of national unification into a single state 'on hold', they were resolute that the incipient process of unification was already under way, and that the Albanian nation had achieved what President Berisha termed a 'spiritual unification.' Despite his being overwhelmed with intensely serious internal problems, Berisha's outspoken support for the Kosovars had helped keep Kosovo on the international agenda and presented the world with a united Albanian front. But, as the situation in Bosnia became ever more intractable, Western pressure on Tirana to recognise the inviolability of its frontiers with Serbia and Montenegro was stepped up. The international community urged Berisha to help prevent war spreading through the Balkans through continuing restraint over the increasing maltreatment of Albanians in Kosovo. Berisha was aware that any move towards a forcible change of borders and the creation of a unified Albania would cause a bloodbath and lose Albania all of the foreign economic assistance it so desperately needed.

Yet the issue of Albanian national unification was still being hotly debated by Albanian nationalists and academics. In contrast to Rugova's moderate stand, which was evidently still supported by the overwhelming majority of the Kosovars, Kosovo's pre-eminent scholar, Rexhep Qosja, who refused to be associated with any particular political party, had emerged as the mouthpiece of a steadily growing segment of the Kosovar population who had concluded that the Albanians and the Serbs had to part ways. Qosja had publicly chastised Rugova for supposedly leading the Albanians up a dead-end with his insistence on peaceful resistance.[6] A first indication that

---

4. Behar Zogiani, 'Granic's Pro-Serbian Position on Kosovo', *Bujuku*, Tanjug, 27 February 1996.
5. *Bulletin of the Ministry of Information...*, no. 77, 5 February 1993.
6. Biberaj, *Kosova: The Balkan Powder Keg*, p. 14.

Berisha was falling out of favour with the Kosovars came at the beginning of 1993. It was symptomatic of the widely differing views on Albanian-Kosovar dialogue when in February Qosja wrote a rather hysterical open letter to Berisha accusing him of 'damaging our [the Kosovars'] historical image and rejecting our ideals.'

The trouble occurred after Berisha stated in an interview in Bujku that: 'The idea of a Greater Albania is not considered in serious Albanian political circles.' Qosja responded by accusing Berisha of

> ...confusing the term 'Greater Albania' with 'Original Albania'.
> Albania and Kosovo cannot be called a Greater Albania. There is,
> however, Mr President, an Original Albania...a natural Albania...a
> true Albania. You have belittled the sacrifices of all those Albanian
> historians, scientists and writers who have suffered in Serbian prisons
> for fighting for an Original Albania and a Republic of Kosovo. You
> also said 'Albania does not want and will not ask for any changes in
> borders'. At first this seems reasonable and understandable. Albania is
> a member of the UN and the CSCE and must comply with interna-
> tional rules and regulations. But, as President, you do not speak in
> your own name but in the name of history and the future. Albania
> has never accepted its existing borders and has always tried to remind
> international circles that these borders are unjust, dividing the
> Albanian land in two. They are borders that go through the heart of
> the Albanian people. As President, you should know the history of
> your own people and of the year 1912. None of us has the moral
> right to speak in the name of future generations.'

To this Berisha angrily replied in an open letter published in *Zeri-i-Popullit* and *Bujku*, in which he accused Qosja of being a 'radical': 'The Kosovo issue can never be solved through terrorism. The Albanian movement in Kosovo has been successful particularly because of its civilised and unterroristic methods.' Albania would not allow the changing of borders through violence, and he added: 'Other ideas that promote violence would legalise violence and aggression in the Balkans and lead to a true Balkan and Albanian tragedy.'[7] In this statement it was striking that, contrary to all the evidence, Berisha and presumably others too, believed that the Albanian movement in Kosovo had been 'successful'.

During the first years of nationalist conflict in the rest of Yugoslavia, the Albanian leadership in Kosovo had had an advantage in that the Serbian Party purges of Albanian communists in the 1980s had done the work of the anti-communist revolution for

7. *Illyria*, 3 February, 1993, p. 5.

Albanian nationalists such as Ibrahim Rugova. Serbian policies to counteract Albanian autonomism and the Kosovars' boycotts after 1988, namely by removing from formal positions the entire political, economic and cultural élite, had built extraordinary cohesion and a parallel organisation around anti-Serbianism and Rugova. But this unity could not be maintained in the changed conditions of the breakdown of Yugoslavia, the opportunity for full independence provided by international condemnation of Serbia, and increasing impatience at delays in achieving their goals. By 1993 the growing resentment at international negotiators for not according the Kosovo Albanians full status at talks held that year in Geneva, as earlier in London, had begun to shift the balance within Rugova's movement toward radical militants who preached a military solution. The lives of Albanian moderates were thus under threat.[8]

The LDK's policy of non-violence was now beginning to be challenged by newly-emerging and more radical groups, like that in Pec led by Reshat Nurboja, which demanded more active measures of resistance. Such demands came in response to both the increasing hardship suffered by most of Kosovo's Albanian population, and the realisation that they were possibly not doing enough to draw international attention to their plight. It was time for action. Thus on 24 May Adem Demaci began a hunger strike in protest against the destruction of *Rilindja* and the closing down of all the Albanian-language media. 'I shall die for the freedom of the public word,' said a defiant Demaci.[9] 'Adem Demaci must not die!' proclaimed the headlines of the LDK's information bulletin.[10] As news of the hunger strike spread, the situation became somewhat confused, if not farcical, as Kosovars in the Netherlands, Switzerland, Norway, Germany, and the United States all went on hunger strike. Needless to say, none pursued their strike to the death, and this lemming-like display of national solidarity soon collapsed.

During the first half of 1993 talks on the issue of education in Kosovo were held at intervals in Geneva (attended by both Federal and Serb representatives) but yielded no results. The talks were supposed to concentrate on education policies but moved towards more substantial political issues such as autonomy. It was agreed to proceed step by step. First, a pragmatic approach was to be adopted on immediate and urgent issues without prejudicing the position of

8. Woodward, *Balkan Tragedy*, p. 35.
9. *Bulletin of the Ministry of Information...*, no. 109, 31 May 1993.
10. Ibid., no. 110, 4 June 1993.

the parties on the broader ones. But in spite of apparent good intentions and an encouraging start, the talks broke down almost immediately on the difference between the Serbian and Albanian school curricula and the issue of minority status for the Albanians. This destroyed the format of the talks, which above all were supposed to help improve the general political climate so that dialogue could eventually begin on a permanent solution to the status of Kosovo.

Kosovar emigration

Meanwhile, the growing presence of extreme nationalist paramilitary militias prompted a continuation of Kosovar emigration abroad. Although the majority still sought refuge in Western Europe, an increasing number were crossing into Albania, where by 1993 an estimated 25,000 Kosovars had settled. Despite the obvious danger of crossing the volatile Kosovo border, where tension had increased since the start of the conflict in former Yugoslavia, small groups of young men trekked silently every night along remote, forest-clad mountain paths, dodging the nervous Serbian border guards who shot at all moving objects on sight. As the conflict in Bosnia intensified, Albanian soldiers continued to abandon the Yugoslav Army (JNA) and flee to Western Europe where they sought political asylum declaring that if they returned to Kosovo they would be recruited back into the JNA and sent to fight in Bosnia. By 1993 an estimated 400,000 Albanians had left the former Yugoslavia, most for the following countries: Germany (120,000), Switzerland (95,000), Sweden (35,000), Austria (23,000), Belgium (8,000), France (5,000), Denmark (5,000), Italy (4,000), Norway (3,500), Britain (3,000), the Netherlands (2,000), Finland (600), and Luxembourg (200); Croatia had received about 40,000, Slovenia 15,000 and the Republic of Albania 25,000. A considerable number also emigrated to the United States for the already mentioned reasons, joining the ranks of the long-established diaspora.[11] Some Albanian youths being pursued by Serbian military authorities found shelter in Former Yugoslav Macedonia where hardly any of the Albanians do not have relatives in Kosovo. The Albanians called

11. H. Islami, 'Kosova's Demographic ethnic Reality and the Targets of Serbian Hegemony', *Kosova Historical/Political Review*, no. 1, 1993, p. 33. Before the war there were an estimated 100,000 Albanians in Belgrade. By 1997 there were fewer than 20,000.

this massive exodus of young men 'silent ethnic cleansing'. At this time Macedonian leaders were gravely concerned at the likely spillover from any future conflict in Kosovo; they already had a difficult task controlling ethnic divergences at home and maintaining cohesion and stability among 'Macedonian' Slavs and Albanians. Back in the autumn of 1992, members of the Conference on Security and Co-operation in Europe (CSCE) Monitor Mission to Macedonia observed intensive activity on the border with Serbia at Tabanovce and Sopot and that with Kosovo at Blace. At all three points, temporary structures had been built to house an expected influx of refugees.[12] All of the CSCE Monitor Mission's interlocutors in Macedonia predicted a sudden, massive influx of ethnic Albanian refugees if hostilities spread into Kosovo. They also believed that unless the republic received substantial economic assistance, such an influx could not only lead to the collapse of the economy but also destabilise the government and provoke social upheaval.[13] Macedonian officials were also concerned that if Kosovo erupted the republic's north-west quadrant would become a corridor for weapons and troops.

Deteriorating socio-economic conditions

By the winter of 1993 general living conditions in Kosovo were becoming intolerable. Shops were almost empty and the population was increasingly subject to various forms of violent repression. As the Serbian military presence intensified, a situation akin to war now developed. The airport outside Pristina was now a military base, tanks surrounded the city itself, and several Albanian primary schools had been converted into hostels for Serbian army and police units, then being deployed in ever-increasing numbers throughout Kosovo. Almost daily, planes flew low over towns and villages, and machine-gun fire could be heard on most nights.

The Serbianisation programme continued steadily and had by now affected most of the public sector and local administration. A privatisation process had been implemented with enterprises selling out to Belgrade to prevent previously employed Albanian workers from becoming shareholders. The Serbian legislation provided for

---

12. CSCE Secretariat Communication no. 282, Prague, 16 September 1992, p. 7.
   CSCE-CPC Vienna, 21 September 1992.
13. Ibid., p. 15.

the setting up of private enterprises for printing and publishing, but in practice this remained extremely difficult for Albanians. Although several papers and periodicals in the Albanian language had emerged in 1992-3, their publication had ceased mainly because of lack of funds. In addition, getting a licence for a new publication involved such bureaucracy that few people were willing to complete the lengthy procedure.

The judiciary in Kosovo had come progressively under near-total Serbian control since May 1990, and by 1993, more than 300 of the 500-plus Albanian judges, district attorneys and other senior officials in the system had been dismissed and replaced by about eighty Serbian officials. The Serbian parliament had also appointed 168 judges for Kosovo of whom only twenty-five were of Albanian nationality, and of these just sixteen had been willing to take up office – the rest refused. Investigations were routinely carried out by police without authorisation from the prosecuting attorney, and trials were often used only to legalise the procedure and confirm punishments predetermined by other authorities. In many cases, sentences were passed without any trial as administrative decisions based solely on political grounds. Given that so many of the new judges were appointed on the basis of their ethnicity and loyalty to the policies of Belgrade, the Kosovo judiciary could not possibly have been regarded as independent: and the concept of fair trials appeared to have been abandoned.[14]

Since the Serbian takeover of medical care, the Albanian population largely avoided the Serbian-administered institutions, especially in the fields of gynaecology, paediatrics and surgery. Albanian women did not want their babies delivered under the supervision of Serbian doctors and thus some 85 per cent were estimated to give birth without any professional medical attention. Given the low standard of living and hygiene conditions, this led to increased maternal and infant mortality. High-risk pregnancies were recognised too late or not at all. With some 55,000 children then being born annually in Kosovo, cases of polio, tetanus and infectious diseases in general were on the increase. The majority of Kosovo's children were not being immunised against illnesses because it was widely believed that the Serbian vaccines would cause sterility as part of Belgrade's plan to reduce the high Albanian birth rate. Therefore, despite pleas by the LDK leadership for parents to have their

14. From *Autonomy to Colonisation: Human Rights in Kosovo*, p. 56.

offspring vaccinated, Kosovo's infant mortality rate of around 5.5 per cent continued to rise.

At the same time, not much education was taking place in Kosovo either. Hundreds of thousands of Albanian children were being prevented from having a normal intellectual development, as the Serbian authorities tightened their grip on the education system. In the middle of rubble-strewn Pristina, school-aged children whiled away their time playing cards or selling cigarettes. Although elementary schools still gave instruction in Albanian, all secondary and university classes had to follow the Serbian language curriculum imposed by Belgrade. The Serbs were totally dismissive of the Albanian education boycott. Miodrag Duricic, Kosovo's Belgrade-appointed minister of education, stated: 'The problem is the Albanians don't recognise Serbia or Yugoslavia; the curriculum is made in Serbian for the whole of Serbia. Albanians should accept the Serbian curriculum because Kosovo is an administrative region of Serbia.'[15] By 1994 around two-thirds of Kosovo's 450,000 Albanian pupils were being taught in private houses, church buildings, restaurants and even garages. Textbooks and teaching materials were scarce, having been confiscated by Serb police during their periodic raids on the 'illegal' classes. Although the Kosovo government-in-exile had set up a national fund to help maintain the parallel system, it could only provide around 30 per cent of the required funding. LDK finances were by now in trouble, with more and more individuals refusing or failing to pay the 3 or 5 per cent levy. As a result teachers were paid meagre and irregular salaries, and the Kosovo government's claim to be running its parallel administration successfully was beginning to look rather hollow. A growing number of young Albanians were reluctant to continue with this system of schooling, because the 'parallel' schools issued their own diplomas which were not recognised by the Serbian or any other educational authorities. As more and more Albanian children received no secondary or university education, parents began voicing their concern at the long-term effects of these crucial years without education on their children and the future of Kosovo society.

The overall living standards of the Albanian population in Kosovo, and to a lesser, but gradually increasing extent the Serbian minority, had been falling continuously since 1991. According to

15. Author's interview, 5 August 1994.

the Mother Teresa relief organisation, the number of families in need was 43,320 in 1992, 45,835 in 1993, and 57,353 in 1994. The Mother Teresa Society calculated the average family size to be 6.52 persons, which meant that by 1994 over 370,000 people, corresponding to some 20 per cent of the Albanian population of Kosovo, were wholly or partly dependent on humanitarian aid. It was also discovered that the financial support provided by relatives working abroad had been declining for two reasons. First, the guestworkers were increasingly concerned with their own economic problems, and secondly they could no longer transfer money home to their families by bank or post because of the UN sanctions, and they feared that if they took home cash, it would be taken from them by police at the border or that their passports might be confiscated.[16] Water and power restrictions, particularly in winter, contributed further to the general decline in living standards. According to a Swiss report the towns and districts populated by Albanians were worse affected than areas housing large numbers of Serbs. For example, while current in Fushe Kosove (a town housing a high proportion of Serbs) was never switched off for more than three hours at a time, power cuts in the Albanian section of the centre of Pristina lasted for up to eighteen hours. Other communes with a majority of Albanian residents, e.g. Malisheva, would sometimes remain without electricity for weeks. With outside temperatures of minus 20 degrees and a prevalence of electric heating systems the consequences are easy to imagine.[17]

Housing had also become a serious problem in Kosovo. In former Yugoslavia, most apartments were built by the state or by enterprises. The cost of building houses was covered by enterprises which then rented them to their employees or sold them on the free market. Workers could live in the apartments owned by a company for as long as they were employed by it; or, if they wished, they could buy the apartment at a relatively low price as their own private property. But, since the imposition of 'emergency measures' most Albanians had been fired and thus evicted from their apartments. At the same time, apartments were being given to Serbs who retained the right to buy them from the state. The Serbian authorities were now also blatantly inflicting financial hardship on Kosovo-Albanians as never before, and simultaneously enriching

16. *Repatriate the Expellees?*, Organisation Suisse d'Aide aux Refugiés (OSAR), Zurich, 6 February 1995, p. 12.
17. Ibid., p. 13.

the Serbian state. In the last five months of 1994, DM 229,096 and considerable sums in other hard currencies were arbitrarily seized from individuals. In November alone, the Serbian financial police confiscated 1,415 million dinars (approx. DM 1 million) belonging to private Albanian businessmen in the four communes of Pec, Istok, Decan and Kline.[18]

Although Belgrade was undeniably oppressing the Kosovars politically, it was inadvertently stimulating some of them economically. Many Albanians used the mass dismissals to organise themselves not only politically but also economically, and a sizeable proportion of those dismissed from their employment actually benefited as the result. There was the additional factor that the collapse of communism and, with it, of malfunctioning state-run industries created economic space. Those with useful contacts or initial capital started up their own small private business, particularly in trade, agencies, manufacturing and catering. Immediately several hundred cabs, vans, lorries and minibuses were registered and took over the city and intercity lines (twice as many began operating without registration). A similar process occurred with thousands of mini-markets and supporting merchandise networks, where the supply of goods was completely privatised. Tourist agencies mushroomed because a family could support itself solely from the ticket-handling fees. Coffee bars, restaurants and other enterprises were also quickly established. Many civil servants discovered latent talents for business, and did not regret losing jobs that brought them $100 a month when they found themselves able to earn three times more and make considerable profits. The same could not be said for Kosovo's Slav community. For while Albanians were finding ways to diversify their sources of income, Serbs were still employed in the administration and in decaying companies largely dependent on state subsidies. The state meanwhile was being impoverished by war and sanctions, and realising the enormous cost of supporting the Kosovar apartheid, abolished the financial privileges of Kosovo Serbs. By the spring of 1994 their average monthly salary, which had been $400 during the 'triumphal' annexation of Kosovo in 1990, was $12, according to one report.[19] On the whole, it was the Kosovar's closely-knit family structure, combined with an unprecedented

---

18. Ibid., p. 10. For a full analysis of the serious human rights abuses in Kosovo during this period, see Amnesty International reports: *Yugoslavia: Ethnic Albanians - Trial by Truncheon*, February 1994, and other reports issued in 1994.
19. S. Maliqi, *War Report*, April/May 1993, p. 14.

degree of national solidarity, which enabled them to stave off Serbia's economic pressures.

The emergence of Albanian resistance groups

During this time, a number of radical splinter groups had made themselves known. In the spring of 1993, an organisation called the Popular Front of the Republic of Kosovo distributed leaflets calling for the removal from leading positions of those Albanians who had abandoned the goal of a unified or Greater Albania. Another group, the previously mentioned National Movement for the Liberation of Kosovo, was handing out leaflets calling for a popular revolt throughout Kosovo. In May two Serb policemen were killed by Albanian gunmen in the town of Glogovac, and by October we find open acknowledgement of the existence of an Albanian resistance group when the Serbian newspaper *Jedinstvo* claimed that an enemy group, the National Movement for the Liberation of Kosovo, had been discovered in Decan and its members arrested (4 October 1993). As more reports circulated about the Albanian adoption of violence, the LDK leadership consistently denied the existence of any Kosovar military forces. It also rejected claims that the parallel government had defence and interior ministries. However, a growing number of reports were quoting Albanian underground sources, which described Kosovo's armed forces as a two-tiered organisation consisting of special forces and an army which received funds from small businesses, from smuggling and drug dealing, and from Albanians living abroad. The money was used to obtain weapons on both the black market and the open international market, and underwrite the costs of intelligence activities. Members of Kosovo's special forces were allegedly trained in two camps belonging to the Albanian armed forces, near the towns of Kukes and Tropoja. The Kosovars were illegally transported into Albania somewhere in the region of the Prokletije mountains, an area that is difficult for the Yugoslav border patrols to control. Kosovar army units were organised in four regiments deployed in the areas of Kacanik, Prizren, Pristina and Podujevo, with some 10,000 members of each regiment, making a total of 40,000 soldiers.[20]

20. A. Vasovic, 'Kosovo – Braced and Armed for Confrontation', *War Report*, January 1993, p. 19. See also article by F. Schmidt in *Transition*, 3 November, 1995, which discusses the show trials of Albanians accused of belonging to the 'Ministry of Defense and General Staff of the Army of the Republic of Kosovo'.

Although in January 1993 there were several hundred young Kosovar men living in army camps in Labinot and in the Kukes and Tropoje region of northern Albania, the report referred to above, which implied that the Kosovars were intending to abandon their hitherto passive stance, brought forth a furious response from the Albanian government, whose spokesman Gence Pollo angrily replied:

> 'We categorically deny the claim that Kosovo's special forces are being trained in Albanian armed forces camps. Indeed, we would be greatly surprised if any 'Kosovo special forces' existed. We invite international journalists to come to Albania to see that we really mean it when we say the Albanian government and the Albanian people do not want, and are not preparing for, a military solution to the Kosovo crisis.'[21]

In reality the Albanian government were loathe to admit that its army would be incapable of offering any assistance to the Kosovars. Military hardware and ammunition were in particularly short supply and morale was low after years of neglect.

In the event of conflict erupting, the Kosovars planned to withdraw their troops to the mountains along the Yugoslav-Albanian border, from where they would mount guerrilla attacks and defensive actions until the Western allies, or more specifically the Americans, came to their defence. The Kosovo army would then undertake full-scale offensive activities, providing ground support for the interventionary forces. The resistance of Serbian paramilitary troops, it was believed, would be broken by the joint action of Kosovars, regular Albanian armed forces, and the Western allies. Any Yugoslav Army resistance would be overcome by international forces. Or so it was hoped.[22] Following Milosevic's electoral victory the previous December, the United States President George Bush had warned the Serbian President not to allow the war to spread to Kosovo because 'In the event of conflict in Kosovo caused by Serbian action, the United States will be prepared to employ military force against the Serbs in Kosovo and in Serbia proper.'[23]

Meanwhile, the Kosovars once again boycotted the rump Yugoslav elections held in January 1994, which allowed not only

---

21. *War Report*, February/March 1993, p. 19. See also Albanian Telegraphic Agency report of 13 December 1992, denying claims made in *The Times* of 9 December 1992 that Albania was concentrating its military forces on the border of Kosovo.
22. Vasovic, 'Kosovo – Braced and armed for Confrontation', p. 19.
23. *New York Times*, 28 December 1992.

Milosevic to remain in power but also the election of extreme Serbian nationalists such as the notorious 'Arkan' as deputies for Kosovo. (Albanians living in Southern Serbia did, however, take part in the elections.) Of the twenty-four deputies chosen from Kosovo, twenty-one were from the ruling Serbian Socialist Party, two from the ultranationalist Vojislav Seselj's Radical party and only one was from DEPOS, the Democratic opposition. The deputies represented the Serbs' choice since the Albanians boycotted the elections. Muslims, who numbered around 60,000, had formed their own Party of Democratic Action (SDA), which also did not take part in the elections; nor did the Turkish National Party, representing the Turkish minority of roughly 12,000 people.[24] It is somewhat paradoxical that the Albanian boycott of previous multi-party elections in Serbia in 1990, 1992 and 1993 had actually strengthened the power of the leading Serbian parties. This persistent refusal by the Kosovars to participate in the electoral process caused frustration among international observers, who believed that the problem of Kosovo could not be resolved without strengthening democratic institutions in Serbia, i.e., without the political participation of the Albanian segment of the population in the political life of Serbia and the Federal Republic of Yugoslavia.

In the 1992 elections, the Socialist Party of Serbia (SPS) won thirteen mandates in the electoral district of Pristina with 42,396 votes; the Serbian Radical Party (SRS) got five mandates with 18,735 votes, and so on. The situation was repeated in the elections of December 1993 when the leading SPS in Kosovo won a total of twenty-one mandates (the SRS got two and the coalition of the opposition parties, DEPOS, got one seat). Although some prominent Albanian intellectuals from Kosovo including Shkelzen Maliqi, called on Albanians individually to take part in the Serbian elections, only two Albanian parties outside Kosovo (the Party of Democratic Activity and the Democratic Party of Albanians) came out and won two mandates in the Serbian Assembly. Had the Albanians of Kosovo exercised their electoral rights in both the Republic and Federal elections, they could have counted on taking power in twenty-four of the twenty-nine municipalities of the province, and having at least twenty-four seats in the Republic and twelve seats in the Federal parliament. As the dominant Serbian parties would then have lost an equivalent number of seats, the participation of Alba-

24. I. Berisha, 'Pristina's One Party Rule', *War Report*, February 1994, p. 12.

nians in the ballot would have considerably altered the existing political balance in the country,[25] but, as previously mentioned, the LDK had no wish whatever to assist the process of democratisation in Serbia. The experience of Serbian repression and the deterioration in relations between the two communities had only cemented the determination of the Albanians not to settle for individual human rights alone, leading many to believe that the Albanian demand for territorial rights was irreversible. Moreover, Serbia proper was not immune to the conflict. As long as Albanians could boycott every election, democracy in the republic, which many considered a precondition to any solution, would be stunted.[26]

Growing division in the Kosovar ranks

Throughout 1994 most international observers of events in Kosovo believed that unless there were some let-up in the degree of repression, Kosovo would undoubtedly explode. It was generally understood by all that Rugova's policy of peaceful resistance and parallel government enabled the Serbs effectively to control Kosovo, and to encourage Kosovar emigration by violent means, and therefore the situation was fairly stable. Rugova's policies, while relying on the international community to appreciate the justice of the Albanian cause in Kosovo, had failed to change the situation, and this led to increasing tension within both the LDK and the other smaller parties, especially the Peasants Party and the Liberals. By the autumn of 1994, the rift in the LDK between hardliners pushing for total independence for Kosovo and moderates advocating autonomy within a new Yugoslavia, was set to widen. This was the first public conflict within the LDK since its formation and was caused by Kosovars increasingly objecting to the LDK's dominance of local government. The division between the moderates and the 'independentists', not only in Kosovo but throughout the Kosovar diaspora, especially in the United States, Switzerland and Germany, began to escalate after the resignation of a number of leading LDK moderates in October 1994.

This was best witnessed in Tirana where Anton Kolaj, the LDK's vice-president, who had taken over the Kosovo embassy, sharply criticised Kosovo's Prime Minister Bujar Bukoshi for wanting to

25. P. Simic, *The Kosovo and Metohija Problem*, p. 14.
26. Woodward, *Balkan Tragedy*, p. 341.

accept autonomy. Bukoshi's representative in the Tirana office, Skender Zogaj, was ousted by Kolaj who claimed that Bukoshi had no mandate to speak for the majority of Kosovars, acting as he did from his isolated 'fiefdom' in a village outside Stuttgart. Kolaj also attacked Bukoshi's organisation in Tirana on the grounds of political misconduct and possibly misappropriating Kosovo funds. Bukoshi's people naturally denied these claims but the majority of the Kosovar diaspora leadership sided with Kolaj. The situation became tense and the resulting atmosphere of fear and suspicion led to a wall of silence within all LDK offices as officials scurried to align themselves with one of the two sides. Kosovars were becoming increasingly ready for a change in leadership with people like Shkelzen Maliqi, Veton Surroi, Mahmut Bakali (a former Communist Party leader) and Fehmi Agani gaining support. Talk about autonomy was still political suicide in Kosovo but the key issue now centred around the situation in Albania itself. There was disgust at Sali Berisha's recent change of policy in which he too, under US pressure, had accepted the notion of autonomy for Kosovo. Berisha, like Ramiz Alia before him, repeatedly called for an end to human rights violations against Albanians but stopped short of demanding any change of international borders.

Although Rugova and Bukoshi had publicly to follow Berisha's line, there followed a frenetic period of shuttle diplomacy on behalf of the Kosovar leadership and on 24 October Adem Demaci visited human rights groups in Switzerland and on 2 November Ibrahim Rugova had talks in Geneva with the two co-chairmen of the International Conference on the Former Yugoslavia, Lord David Owen and Thorvald Stoltenberg. Rugova presented the co-chairmen with the position of the Albanians on a resolution of the Kosovo problem: 'An independent and neutral Kosovo, open to both Albania and Serbia, is an optimal solution for all in the region.' To which Owen and Stoltenberg gave the now obligatory reply that the international community had not ignored the question of Kosovo and was sympathetic to the non-violent policy pursued by the Kosovars.[27] All Owen and Stoltenberg could offer Rugova was the prospect of initiating yet again a dialogue on the education issue. The following week Rugova went to the Netherlands and Belgium to meet human rights groups, while two LDK parliamentary deputies visited the Ministry of Foreign Affairs in Canada. On 22 Novem-

27. *Bulletin of the Ministry of Information...*, no. 194, 7 November 1994.

ber Rugova was in Berne meeting the Swiss Foreign Minister, and at the beginning of December he was in the United States to meet top officials. In mid-December he was back in Bonn holding talks with Klaus Kinkel, the German Foreign Minister. In all these meetings the Kosovars were promised the same thing - support for a continuation of their peaceful struggle and mediation in any dialogue process with Belgrade.

By now political life among Kosovo's Albanians was completely dominated by the LDK while the smaller political parties were marginalised. Such issues as economic development and social problems were shelved until the main issue - liberation from Serbian colonial domination - could be achieved. It could be argued that the LDK was not entirely to blame for the absence of political competition. For example, the Kosovo Democratic Union shunned cooperation with other smaller parties as not being useful. Nonetheless, the LDK did everything it could to marginalise the other political parties. As a concession to the survival of some smaller parties, the LDK agreed to participate in the formation of a Council of Political Parties of Kosovo (SPPK), which would facilitate coordination among political parties to create a movement of national liberation. However, the LDK used the Council for its own purposes, particularly to build support internationally for its own agenda, thus preventing the emergence of a national movement with a more democratic basis.[28] By now it was becoming increasingly obvious that the LDK had no clear strategy beyond boycotting official institutions and any electoral processes and hoping that eventually the international community would grant it recognition.

As the war in Bosnia-Hercegovina dragged on, external powers increasingly leaned towards the view that the republics were state entities. Therefore, Kosovo was an integral part of Serbia and under its internal jurisdiction. The international community had two reasons for insisting on Bosnia's territorial integrity. One was to safeguard European security and stability by protecting the Helsinki norm on existing borders, and the other was containment. Allowing the partition of Bosnia-Hercegovina would only have opened the door to a domino effect and increased the likelihood of war in adjoining areas. For example, if the Bosnian Serbs could create a national state and international negotiators could recognise the principle, how great was the legitimacy of Milosevic's claim that

28. Berisha, 'Pristina's One Party Rule', p. 12.

Kosovo and Vojvodina were parts of Serbia? What principle would restrain radical forces on both sides of the national conflicts in each region (Serbs for republican boundaries, Albanians and Hungarians for independence) from war?[29] Thus Rugova, like Berisha, had to beat a tactical retreat by accepting Balkan realities. Henceforth the LDK was exposed as a largely impotent human rights campaign masquerading as a political struggle. The result of this slow but steady rise in dissatisfaction with Rugova's peace policy meant that ever more younger Kosovars were considering a violent solution.

With every month that passed tension rose in Kosovo. The situation became especially acute during August 1995 when some 200,000 Croatian Serbs arrived in Serbia following Croatia's violent reintegration of the Serb-populated Krajina region. Although thousands of these refugees were sent to Kosovo, the majority of young men returned almost immediately to Serbia, and only women, young children and elderly people remained. The official argument over why the refugees were sent to Kosovo rather than to the large depopulated areas of southern Serbia proper was that the settlement of the refugees from Krajina would improve the national structure of Kosovo (only 6 per cent were now Serbs), and that a balance would help avoid eventual future national confrontations. The number of Serb refugees being resettled in Kosovo from the Krajina and Vojvodina had reached 16,000 by early October 1995. Nevertheless, despite protests from the LDK that Belgrade was trying to alter the ethnic balance of Kosovo and reverting to its inter-war policy of encouraging the settlement of Serbs and Montenegrins, the arrival of relatively so few Serbs could have had little effect on the overall demographic superiority of the Albanians. However, the capacity to absorb more refugees was virtually exhausted since the Krajina Serbs were not the first external arrivals. Many new arrivals in Kosovo were in fact Albanian. Those refugees who had arrived in the first wave that started in 1991 were mostly Albanian and Muslim returnees – Albanians and Muslims, born in Kosovo, who had gone to Slovenia and Croatia in the 1950s and '60s for economic reasons. They had returned at the beginning of the war in 1991 and been received by their families. They could not have refugee status, one of the most important conditions in deciding the status of refugees being the place of birth. Since those people were born in Kosovo, they could not be treated as refugees, and so they

29. Woodward, *Balkan Tragedy*, p. 330.

received no humanitarian aid.

According to Ruzica Simic, Secretary of the Red Cross of Kosovo, the number of 'new' refugees (those from Krajina) was 6,000-7,000. There were also around 4,000 registered Serbian refugees from Bosnia in Kosovo who had arrived previously. During the summer of 1992 several hundred Serbian refugees had already settled in Kosovo, notably 700 in the 'Pishat e Decan' holiday homes near the town of Decani. Other than the refugees, the principal beneficiaries of confiscated Albanian land and buildings at that time were Serbian soldiers. Large areas of land were confiscated in Globocice (a district in Kacanik, by the Macedonian border), notably in Xhemajl Zeka, where the army began building military installations, and in Ponoshec by the Albanian border, where reservists from the Serbian army had been settled.[30] Among the refugees many had chronic diseases causing a high death-rate, with more cases expected during the harsh winter, which was typical for Kosovo but very different from the mild climate of Krajina. The Red Cross was making a great effort to prevent a humanitarian catastrophe, and individuals were also bringing donations of food and clothing and offering the refugees accommodation.[31] Despite a real fear of an aggressive reaction to the settlement of the refugees in the Prizren area, the Serb and Albanian communities apparently showed some solidarity, owing in part perhaps to the relatively cosmopolitan makeup, and thence tolerance, of Prizren compared to other Kosovo towns. State firms, private firms and private donors brought in food and clothing, as did members of the Albanian community who offered gifts of food and money. Several Albanians also offered to accommodate the refugees in their houses, and one member of the Albanian community even wished to give 5 hectares of his land to a refugee family.[32]

Meanwhile, with its indecision and hesitation, the international community was failing dismally in its attempts to end the bloodshed in Bosnia-Hercegovina. Albanians as a nation were alarmed at the world's inability not only to stop the war but also to call Belgrade to account over abuses of human rights. Although the Kosovars had persistently tried to internationalise their problem, after the initial

30. *Dismissals and Ethnic Cleansing in Kosovo*, International Confederation of Free Trade Unions, Brussels, October 1995, p. 6.
31. Kosovo Report by the EU Humanitarian Office, ECHO, Belgrade, 9-30 August 1995, pp. 1-12.
32. Ibid., pp. 12-19.

support abroad for the Albanian national movement in Kosovo, the international community changed its attitude, taking the standpoint that any attempt at the forced secession of this province from Serbia and the rump of Yugoslavia would undoubtedly spread the conflict first to neighbouring Macedonia (a strengthening of Albanian political parties in the border area had come about in the early 1990s) and then to other neighbouring countries. Bearing this in mind, President Milosevic's visit to Kosovo on 20 July 1995 – his first in three years – was accompanied by words of reconciliation. He proclaimed his confidence that Kosovo would become 'a region of mutual understanding, cooperation, and coexistence'. This did not signal a miraculous metamorphosis from hawk to dove; rather, his latest move was inspired by the need to present himself as a serious member of the international community capable of supporting the peace process in Bosnia. During his visit, it became obvious that the Socialist Party of Serbia was not sincere in its resolve to negotiate with the Kosovar Albanians and that an understanding between Rugova and Milosevic was most unlikely. At a rally in Mitrovica, Milosevic made clear that he aimed to drive a wedge between the Kosovars and their political leadership by calling for a policy of 'national equality' in which 'every citizen will be equal'. He urged the Albanians to sideline their political leaders and embrace the Serbian administration. Visiting the Trepca metalworks, he expressed his 'deep satisfaction' over the return to work of 1,200 Albanians who had boycotted the factory since the abolition of autonomy in 1989.[33]

By October there was a generally optimistic mood internationally that the war in former Yugoslavia was coming to an end. The Kosovar leadership also hoped that the status of Kosovo would be resolved as part of a comprehensive peace settlement for former Yugoslavia, but in this they were to be gravely disappointed: any hope of a solution to the Kosovo crisis had to be abandoned by the international community in order to gain the support of Belgrade for the implementation of a peace agreement for Bosnia. When such an agreement was made at Dayton, the international commitment to the notion of settling Serb-Albanian relations in Kosovo within the framework of Serbia and the rump Yugoslavia continued.[34] At Dayton, where a peace settlement for Bosnia was finally

33. F. Schmidt, 'Strategic Reconciliation in Kosovo', *Transition*, 25 August 1995, p. 19.
34. Simic, *The Kosovo and Metohija Problem*, p. 5.

hammered out, the Bosnian Serbs were given their own republic within the Federation of Bosnia-Hercegovina, and the lifting of United Nations' sanctions against Serbia and Montenegro was not made conditional on a solution to the Kosovo problem, which was to be treated as an issue of autonomy and human rights. There was never any mention of Kosovo becoming independent.[35]

Thus the Kosovars were both surprised and bitterly disillusioned by the outcome of the Dayton Agreement, which made no specific mention of Kosovo apart from the UN Security Council's agreement to maintain an 'outer wall' of sanctions until Belgrade should begin seriously to address the Kosovo issue. It now became apparent to all that as long as there appeared to be relative peace in Kosovo, the international community would avoid suggesting any substantive changes. The Kosovars' sense of betrayal reached its height when the Albanian President Sali Berisha aligned himself with Western counterparts in supporting the solution of the Albanian question within Serbia. Berisha, who was much commended at this time by the UN and NATO for his policy of restraint over the Albanian national question, was now calling for talks between the local Kosovar leadership and Belgrade. Thus by opting for non-violent resistance the Kosovar leadership had reaped no benefits whatever. Instead they suffered humiliation and their people became more and more desperate.

A statement from the Kosovar 'Prime Minister' Bujar Bukoshi, on 31 October 1995 warned ominously: 'Let it be noted that it is in Kosovo that everything started and unless our issue is allotted due attention and deep understanding, followed by intense international pressure on Belgrade, the perspective is rather bleak.' He continued:

> 'In this regard the position of the Government of the Republic of Kosovo is as follows. First, while welcoming the good will behind the adopted decision to make Kosovo a condition of reintegration to Belgrade, the Government of the Republic nonetheless is of the opinion that, given past experience and present circumstances, autonomy for Kosovo is not an equitable and lasting solution, and therefore will not be accepted. In this context, the Government reiterates its stance that it will only be bound by the express will of the population of Kosovo for an independent republic and will work to this end only. The EU ministers have committed themselves to 'respecting the internationally recognised borders of the Federal

35. Kostovicova, *Parallel Worlds*, pp. 56-7.

Republic of Yugoslavia'. The Government of Kosovo is of the view that neither has the self-proclaimed 'Federal Republic of Yugoslavia' been recognised internationally, nor has its borders. We strongly uphold that it is the will of the peoples of the region that shall shape the borders of the remaining territory of former Yugoslavia, and only then will the world be in a position to recognise or give its blessing to a reality. Kosovo, with its defined borders, is a reality to be recognised. The sooner this reality is understood the better.'

This was the tone of an increasingly irate Kosovar leadership. At the end of 1995, moves towards rejecting Rugova's approach were gathering pace, with major speeches by Adem Demaci and a long interview in *Intervista* magazine by Rexhep Qosja. Both clearly expressed the view now held by most Kosovars that in five years Rugova's policies had achieved nothing. The LDK's leadership was accused of inflexibility and harming the Kosovar cause, and Rugova's persistent claims that the international community was taking a 'strong hand' on Kosovo were now seen to be totally false.

14

'EVERYTHING STARTED WITH KOSOVO, AND EVERYTHING WILL FINISH WITH KOSOVO'

In response to the situation after the Dayton Accords, the Kosovars, snubbed and humiliated, were forced to re-evaluate their political stance. Aware that their passive policy throughout the Yugoslav war had denied them an invitation to the peace talks, many young Albanians were no longer prepared to abide by an 'unacceptable' solution to the status of Kosovo - in other words, Kosovo remaining as an autonomous province within a new Yugoslavia. This was equally unacceptable to the Kosovo Serbs for whom it represented a return to the despised 1974 constitution.

Apartheid in Kosovo

Although by the beginning of 1996 a few Albanians and Slavs still worked together, the vast majority lived strictly apart – they used separate bars and restaurants, and while Serbs travelled on the trains, Albanians took the buses. For Albanians public contact with Serbs inside Kosovo was off-limits, and the LDK used its power to isolate those violating that unspoken rule. Only a few élite intellectuals could appear publicly on panel discussions with Serbs without fear of public censure. Other Albanians reported receiving warnings from members of the LDK to avoid anything resembling dialogue with Serbs. Not all Albanians were members of the LDK and not all LDK members supported such a rigid prohibition, but most Albanians, like most Serbs, preferred to leave contact with the other group to their political leaders.[1] For the Albanians, hardly any of whom under the age of twenty could speak or understand Serbian,

1. Julie Mertus, 'A Wall of Silence Divides Serbian and Albanian Opinion on Kosovo', *Transition*, 22 March 1996, p. 49.

Belgrade was merely the capital of a foreign state, whose police and army units were temporarily deployed as an occupying force, paid for by enormous taxes derived from semi-legal trade in a devastated economy. The two communities thus remained suspicious of each other's aspirations, and stereotypes, fears and hatreds were reinforced. While the oppression of Albanians in the first half of the decade had been overt, most police crack-downs from 1995 onwards tended to be at night and in remote rural districts. Thus the casual and especially the foreign visitor to any of Kosovo's main towns would gain an impression of calm.[2]

In the post-Dayton climate, there was a discernible trend throughout Kosovo and the large Kosovar diaspora towards rejecting the peaceful policies advocated by Ibrahim Rugova. As previously mentioned there had recently been trends in this direction, but they were gradually becoming stronger and more organised. For the majority of Kosovars the *status quo* in Kosovo could no longer be preserved. Angry and dissillusioned, they felt that their plight was ignored by the international community and that now, as in the past, their destiny was being decided without their being consulted. Despite countless statements from the LDK and human rights organisations about human rights abuses, the international community continued to ignore the issue of Kosovo's self-determination, insisting that it remained an internal issue for rump Yugoslavia. As a result the growing despair and frustration, noticeable by now among women and older people, allowed the passive policies of the Albanian resistance to be replaced by a more offensive strategy. This was accelerated by a number of simultaneous bomb attacks on five camps housing Serb refugees in several towns throughout Kosovo in mid-February 1996. By then up to 10,000 Serbs from Croatia had been resettled in Kosovo.

The underground group, the National Movement for the Liberation of Kosovo (*Levizja Kombetare per Clirimin e Kosoves*, LKCK), claimed responsibility for these attacks adding that it was only the beginning of its campaign. This was followed by a series of 'trial runs' by another underground group, the Kosovo Liberation Army (*Ushtria Clirimtare e Kosoves*, UCK), in preparation for launching a

2. One interesting by-product of the polarisation of Kosovo's Serb and Albanian populations is the changing attitude of each community towards the Rom (Gypsy) population of Kosovo: Albanians have replaced Rom musicians with inferior Albanian musicians, while Serbs have employed Roms at their weddings instead of Albanians.

guerrilla campaign with attacks on individual Serbs in several isolated incidents. Although both guerrilla groups remained shadowy, state security officials claimed that the core of the Kosovo Liberation Army and the smaller National Movement for the Liberation of Kosovo consisted of mercenaries who had fought with Muslims against the Bosnian Serbs in the war in Bosnia-Hercegovina. Many of the insurgents, who had apparently built an organised base of several thousand supporters, had received training in Albania, Iran and Pakistan.[3] Both groups appeared to be well trained and well equipped with automatic weapons, explosives and sophisticated communications. Apart from receiving money from the large and wealthy Kosovar diaspora in Western Europe, regular funding was reportedly coming direct from militant Islamic groups in the Middle East. The commanders of the UCK are former commissioned and non-commissioned officers of the regular and reserve units of the JNA and territorial defence units. Although lacking heavy weapons, the groups appeared at this stage to be well armed with mortars and automatic and semi-automatic weapons.

Where the European media were concerned, this was widely acknowledged to be the beginning of the use of violence by Albanians. Sporadic terrorist activity had begun the previous year, which saw a noticeable rise in the number of armed attacks on Serb police or soldiers, but these had gone largely unreported. The most serious of these took place in April 1995 near a frontier marker on the Albanian-Kosovo border (Pyramid D2), when a group of three Albanians attacked a Serbian border patrol using automatic weapons and grenades, killing one border guard, and badly injuring two others. This was not reported in Kosovo at all, or mentioned by the press in Albania in spite of it being common knowledge in the Kukes district. The cause or motive was revenge for the death of two young Albanian school teachers exactly one year earlier. The most serious incident inside Kosovo took place in August 1995 at Decani, when a number of armed men attacked a Serb police station, throwing a bomb inside and then firing on the police with automatic weapons, seriously wounding two. The important aspect of these incidents was the degree of organisation required. Previously, such incidents had consisted mainly of individual Serb police inspectors being shot in the back, or a grenade being dropped in to a police car, and the perpetrators were commonly believed to be individu-

3. See report in *New York Herald Tribune*, 17 February 1997.

als seeking revenge. Attacking border patrols and police stations requires a greater degree of planning and organisation.

The Kosovo Liberation Army officially announces itself

The Kosovars were further incensed by the recognition of the new Yugoslavia by several EU countries in April 1996. Bujar Bukoshi called the move premature and offensive to Albanians, claiming that it undermined the credibility of the Kosovar leadership and its efforts to avert conflict in Kosovo. Ibrahim Rugova now found himself in an increasingly difficult situation. He had won international praise, but his Gandhi-like policy had gone so conspicuously unrewarded that he was now tired and withdrawn, and fast losing credibility among his increasingly angry and disillusioned followers. We can perhaps get a sense of how deeply deceived Rugova personally must have felt after Dayton by noting his optimism back in 1991 when he explained to a British journalist the LDK's policy of non-violence in terms of patience rather than pacificism: 'Our political secret is to combine traditional and current thinking. Fighting was always the last resort for Albanians. Now, too, we have learned that non-violence is the modern European preference.'[4]

The killing of eight people at the end of April 1996 could be interpreted as a response to the EU recognition of Yugoslavia and the beginning of a careful strategy to destabilise Kosovo. Then, the day after a Serb had shot an Albanian student, six Serbs were killed and a number of others wounded when gunmen launched a series of attacks in the Decan and Pec regions of southern Kosovo. In one of the killings, at a café in Decan, the targets were civilians but elsewhere they were policemen. The sudden increase in violence caused tension throughout the region, and in a bid for calm, international observers called for immediate dialogue between representatives of the Serbian and Albanian leaderships and appealed to both sides to show restraint and avoid provocation. The initial reaction from Belgrade was to increase the police and military presence on the streets of Kosovo, a move that exacerbated Albanian resentment.

At first no group claimed responsibility for the attacks, but later, in a letter to the BBC World Service Albanian-language section, the UCK admitted killing the Serbs in Decan and Pec. The letter stated

4. M. Thompson, *A Paper House*, London, 1992, p. 139.

that 'a UCK guerrilla detatchment undertook an armed assault against Serbian aggressors' and that it was 'operating a struggle for the liberation of Kosovo that would continue until complete victory'. Although there was no doubt about the identity of this group and the credibility of the letter, which many Albanians claimed had not been written by a native Albanian-speaker, the violence continued in the final days of April with explosions in the Prizren suburb of Dusanovac, and on the road between Vucitrn and Mitrovica. The general sentiment was that whatever group had carried out the killings, they had achieved their objective of further raising tensions in Kosovo, and focusing international attention on the region.

Official LDK sources strenuously denied any knowledge of the existence of the UCK or the LKCK, and ascribed the attacks to extreme Serbian nationalists intent on forcing the Albanians out of their passive stance, and thus provide an excuse for a further military clampdown in Kosovo. The Yugoslav press, however, claimed that the terrorist activities were organised by top diplomats in the Albanian embassy in Belgrade 'under the direct control of President Sali Berisha' with the aim of destabilising the situation in Kosovo. According to Belgrade, there were two main goals behind this new campaign of Albanian violence. The first was to enhance the nationalist card in the run-up to Berisha's forthcoming election campaign. If this was the case, it was singularly ineffective: the Kosovo issue was barely mentioned anywhere in Albania during the spring of 1996 since Albanians were preoccupied with their own stuggle against unemployment, rising crime and corruption. The second goal was more plausible: to secure, in advance, a strong negotiating position in future discussions on the status of Kosovo.

Many Kosovars now seriously feared some sort of hasty post-Dayton resolution for Kosovo and were determined to prevent any compromise solution to fit in with the timing and wishes of the international community rather than those of the Albanians themselves. At Dayton it was clarified that no change of borders in Yugoslavia would be sanctioned. This stance was viewed by the Kosovars as hypocritical because the Dayton Peace Accord had allowed the Bosnian Serbs to retain their separate Republika Srpska, and even offered them prospects of confederal links with Serbia. So why then could the Albanians not have their Republika Kosova within the framework of Yugoslavia, under similar conditions? The (moral) argument used by the Albanians was that the former entity was entirely new and had been established by force, which had gained it international recognition, while the latter had already existed as a territorial entity, albeit not as a republic; the Albanians felt therefore that they should not be put at a disadvantage because they had refused so far to back up their demands with violence.[5] Thus the single most important message the Kosovars learned from Dayton was that it gave value to the armed struggle of the Bosnian Serbs by recognising, even if only partly, the Serb Republic of Bosnia. This convinced many Albanians that the international community understood only the language of armed conflict, and not that of non-violence.

Adem Demaci, leader of the LDK's main rival the Parliamentary Party of Kosovo (PPK), and chairman of the Council for the Defence of Human Rights and Freedoms in Pristina, showed his impatience when dismissing the theory that the international community would not tolerate any change of borders: 'I think that borders have changed. What is being said about borders now is absurd, since Yugoslavia no longer exists. All its borders have been destroyed, and there cannot be differing criteria – that some borders can be changed and others cannot.'[6] In a lengthy interview for the Kosovar magazine *Koha*, the then British ambassador, Ivor Roberts, explained the international position on Kosovo in the light of the Dayton Accord:

> 'With the Dayton Agreement we saw all parties eventually signing up to a solution and what we want to work towards now is a similar arrangement for Kosovo which will inevitably mean compromise on both sides, flexibility and statesmanship. We have to find a way of finding a middle path between the requirement for self-government of the people of Kosovo and respect for international borders laid down in the Helsinki Convention. ... An Albanian may say to me "but we do not accept these borders" and I understand why you say that. But I have to say that that is not a view supported by the international community. That is therefore a reality you have to live with.'[7]

Thus the international community was attempting to ensure territorial integrity for Yugoslavia, together with self-determination for the Albanians, by asking both Serbs and Albanians to find a middle way. However, this is difficult because the starting point for

5. Duizings, Janjic and Maliqi (eds), *Kosovo/Kosova*, p. xxi.
6. D. Gorani, 'The Key is Belgrade', *War Report*, May 1996.
7. *Koha*, 6 November 1996.

this middle way is the datum that Kosovo must be treated as a constituent part of Serbia. We have seen how the Great Powers determined the borders which allotted Kosovo to Serbia, and we know that there is no willingness on the part of the international community today to re-examine their past decisions; yet the consensus is that the Serbs and Albanians must find a middle path. It is natural for the Albanians to ask why the international community cannot look again at the decisions it took in 1913 and 1918, but established powers are always nervous about suggested frontier changes. The impression has been allowed to spread that the Helsinki Agreement prohibits changes of frontiers, but this is not so; what Helsinki prohibits is the use of force to change frontiers. Frontier changes by consent are theoretically possible, and many internal boundaries in Eastern and Central Europe and the former Yugoslavia have become international frontiers in the 1990s, mostly by consensual processes.[8]

The signing of the Dayton Agreement not only led to growing radicalism among young Albanians; it also urged others to advance more realistic options, similar to the kind brokered for Bosnia-Hercegovina. During 1996 some Albanians, most notably Adem Demaci, began discreetly proposing a solution within the framework of present-day Yugoslavia, i.e. an 'independent and sovereign' Kosovo within a new federal Yugoslavia as a compromise solution or temporary settlement which would keep the territorial integrity of Yugoslavia intact. Demaci's plan envisaged reviving the old concept of a Balkan rather than Yugoslav federation – *Balkanija* – with its core comprising the three republics of Serbia, Montenegro and Kosovo, while other former Yugoslav states could join later.[9]

Other proposals for a solution to the Kosovo problem came from the Serbian Renewal Movement of Vuk Draskovic, which argued in favour of a high level of autonomy; the Nationalist Party of Vojslav Kostunica backed a limited local decentralisation; and the Democratic Party of Zoran Djinjic supported a form of regionalism.[10]

8. Sir Reginald Hibbert, 'Response to Ivor Roberts on Kosovo', *Albanian Life*, no. 62, winter 1997.

9. *Kosovo-Kosova*, p. xx.

10. For a useful discussion on five possible solutions to the Kosovo problem (1. division of territory, 2. a Balkan confederation, 3. a Yugoslav mini-confederation, 4. special autonomy, 5. European Civil Peace Corps) see Alberto l'Abbate, *Kosovo: A War not Fought*, Dipartimento di Studi Sociali, Università degli Studi di Firenze, 1996.

Certainly their predominant aim was to attack Milosevic for his failure to resolve the problem. Meanwhile, the Yugoslav United Left, led by Milosevic's wife Miriana Markovic, was cultivating a more moderate line, speaking of Albanians as 'citizens' and even, in some documents, airing various autonomy proposals. For Milosevic there were two fundamental options: either to provide guarantees for the rights of the Albanians within Serbia/Yugoslavia or to divide the territory along ethnic lines. However, there would be little chance that Kosovo could be divided without serious local and regional conflict. In particular, the aspirations of the Albanians in Macedonia to unify with other Albanian lands would intensify, launching new and destabilising regional alliances. Yet the process had now been legitimised, at least in Bosnia. After Dayton the plausibility of division had increased. Certainly Milosevic's central aim was to avoid really weakening Serbia and the federation through either serious autonomy or independence, both of which would carry high political costs for him.[11]

The escalation of violence in Kosovo alarmed Albanians in neighbouring Macedonia.[12] 'If there is fighting in Kosovo we cannot just sit back and watch it unfold on television', said Menduh Thaci of the Party of Democratic Prosperity (PDPA) in an interview for Reuters (16 May 1996), 'This is the struggle of all Albanians'. Thaci agreed that shadowy Albanian groups who supported violent resistance to Serbian rule existed in both Kosovo and Macedonia, but said that his party had no contact with them and that they did not appear to form an organised force. But he and other Albanian politicians expressed concern that more young men would join such groups if Macedonia and Serbia continued to resist demands from their Albanian minorities for greater autonomy and equality of status. 'Both here and in Kosovo, Albanian leaders are holding the line against violence and calling for peaceful dialogue', said Arben Xhaferi, PDPA president, 'but our stance brings no results and people start looking for other answers'.[13] Meanwhile the violence continued. On the night of 29 May 1996 two Serbian policemen were killed and five were wounded in the town of Glogovac, in circumstances which remain

11. D. Janjic, 'Towards Dialogue or Division?', *War Report*, May 1996.
12. Official figures show that ethnic Albanians account for about 23 per cent of Macedonia's 2 million people, although some Albanians put the figure as high as 40 per cent.
13. Reuters, 16 May 1996.

unclear, and this led to the harassment of Albanians by the security forces being stepped up.

The worsening situation prompted the hurried opening in June of a US Information Office in Pristina, which was intended to reconfirm the State Department's insistence that Belgrade must show substantial progress in solving the Kosovo problem before the 'outer wall' of sanctions imposed on Yugoslavia could be removed. Speaking at the opening ceremony, John Kornblum, head US mediator for former Yugoslavia, said the the Centre's aim was to acquaint people with the society and culture of the United States and that its presence was another 'proof of permanent US interest and concern for the people of the region'. An American delegation from the US Committee in the Organisation for Security and Cooperation in Europe (OSCE) began closely monitoring the Kosovo situation, and US officials held talks with both local Serb and Albanian leaders, appealing to both sides to calm down and immediately begin serious negotiations. It appeared at first that the LDK hoped to manipulate the new Information Centre. 'Prime Minister' Bujar Bukoshi said on Albanian television on 11 June:

> 'The government of Kosovo considers the opening of the office to be of great importance and hopes that it will play not only the role of an observer and informer, but will also have a further dimension, more significant and meaningful than this. It is here that we should be insistent. With the assistance of our friends and by cooperating with the office, we should enable the US office in Pristina to play precisely this role.'

Most Serbs however saw the opening of the US Centre as yet another concession by the Serbian authorities.

Response of Kosovo Serbs to the worsening situation

For the Serbs definitely, but also probably for the Albanians who are likely to get less than they want, the most likely consequence of a resolution of the Kosovo problem will be bitter loss. Hence the anxiety pervading the Serb population, and their dilemma about whether to stay or leave. This anxiety was also due to uncertainty about what tomorrow might bring – if they were to leave, would they meet with an even worse fate than their compatriots from Croatia and Bosnia-Hercegovina? The Kosovo Serbs have not failed to notice how indifferently these refugees were received in Serbia, especially by official institutions, and how eager they were to return where they had come from.[14] Belgrade Serbs have an extremely negative attitude to the Kosovo problem, believing that it is not impossible for Serbs and Albanians to live together, whereas the Kosovo Serbs recognise positive traits in Albanians and know from their historical experience that it has been possible in the past for the two communities to live in harmony. Belgraders see the local Serb population of Kosovo as having lived for too long in the company of Muslims. In conversation with her Serbian landlord, an English teacher, then working in Pristina, asked about the problem of Serbs leaving Kosovo. The landlord replied: 'They go up to Kraljevo and Kragujevac and people call them "Half Blacks" because they come from Kosovo. They say they are dirty, call them Muslimani. A lot of them come back. They don't feel at home there. They are Kosovari.'[15]

Although most of Kosovo's beleaguered Serbian population had voted for Milosevic in the hope of securing their own future, they now felt isolated and fearful that Kosovo was in the process of being abandoned by Belgrade just as the Krajina Serbs had been the previous year. The Albanian programme, if enacted, would fatally weaken the Serb minority. However, a new group of Serbs had recently arrived in Kosovo from the Bihac region of northern Bosnia, consisting primarily of young, battle-hardened men who had made a considerable amount of money dealing with the Bihac business mogul, Fikret Abdic, at the height of the Bosnian war. Following the Dayton Peace Accord, these Serbs, some hiding from war crimes investigators, had entrenched themselves around the Serb-inhabited town of Kosovo Polje, close to Pristina. Local Serbs wisely avoided unnecessary contact with these unruly and unpredictable new arrivals. Further south in Prizren, the town's small Serbian community (9 per cent of the town's 56,000 population) waited subduded and fearful of the new prospect of Albanian revenge attacks.

Kosovo's Serbs continued to sell their land and houses to Albanian buyers, yielding to the high prices offered them. In the 1990s, Serbian sellers and Albanian buyers have found ways of circumventing the legal obstacles imposed in 1989 to prevent Serbs from selling their property to Albanians. Albanians and Serbs are even

14. M. Karan, 'Facing Reality', *War Report*, May 1996.
15. Moats, 'Yugoslavia Lost', p. 296.

prepared to enter false marriages in order to overcome these obstacles. At the August 1996 session of the municipal assembly of Istok (western Kosovo) it was decided to publish the names of those 'unpatriotic' Serbs who in the past year had sold their land to Albanians in that area where a 100-square-metre plot of Serb land fetched up to DM30,000. According to the Istok Assembly's findings, some 'senior military officials from that area, former and present ministers, high officials and businessmen have been named as being involved in the sale of land to Albanians through bogus mortgages and property deals without official transfers...'[16] Many Serbian officials in Kosovo were also doing business with Albanian tradesmen – buying petrol, cigarettes and hard currency.

The act of bringing Kosovo under Belgrade's control had brought nothing but economic grief to most of Kosovo's Serbs. Kosovo's state sector – their main employer – had suffered most from international sanctions, while its private sector, predominantly in the hands of Albanians, remained largely unscathed. Most Serbs in Kosovo have become poorer, but not only because of sanctions. Following the break-up of the former Yugoslavia, Serbia undertook to complete all projects that the federation had financed in Kosovo. They included factories, farms, schools and hospitals. By the end of 1996, 273 such projects remained unfinished A number of more recent projects initiated by Serbia, such as housing for Serb returnees, still awaited completion with the money allocated already spent. Simultaneously, existing assets had been driven to ruin, following a massive plunder of factories, mines, firms and banks. Cash, dozens of tons of copper, 300 kilos of gold, and even office equipment disappeared after Kosovo companies were taken over by Serbs.[17] The growing exodus of young Albanian men from Kosovo was highly satisfactory for Belgrade as it removed a potential opposition army from the region as well as obviating the need to train and arm Albanians in the JNA. However, the failure to attract Slavs to replace the dismissed Albanian workforce resulted in Serbs trying to woo back Albanian engineers and managers in such key industries as metallurgy and mining.

After the collapse of the federation, the Serbian Orthodox Church engaged in feverish activity, building churches and monasteries in almost every town in Kosovo. By the ruin of the Holy

16. Tanjug news agency, Belgrade, 13 August 1996.
17. Kostovicova, *Parallel Worlds*, p. 46.

Archangel church in Prizren, a new monastery is under construction and in the old Serbian quarter of the town a tiny church is being lovingly restored by local Serbs with finance from Belgrade. In Pristina a huge church has been built inside the University and another on rough ground in the city centre. But it is a forlorn gesture since the potential congregation of these new religious centres is disappearing and the nuns and priests themselves are elderly. The lifting in April 1996 of visa restrictions on Kosovars wanting to travel through the Morina border crossing to Albania was seen by many observers as a positive gesture by Belgrade to ease unnecessary restrictions on the Albanian population. At the same time, trade was boosted as up to 1,000 people a day with new, easily acquired entry visas were crossing into Kosovo from the Albanian town of Kukes to sell and buy goods in Prizren. For Prizren's Serbs, however, the relaxations at Morina were an ominous prelude to the day they dreaded, when their town would finally be united with Albania.

While Serbs in far-off Belgrade demanded an immediate crackdown on 'Albanian terrorists and separatists', those Serbs actually living in Kosovo felt increasingly threatened by the new Albanian assertiveness. In response to further attacks by the UCK in August, prominent JNA personnel were adamantly declaring that Yugoslavia would never surrender Kosovo. Lt-General Dusan Samardzic, commander of the 3rd Army, told a new intake of young officers:

> 'This is a turning point for Yugoslavia, when we need to show the world our military ability and might. Kosovo-Metohija's integrity has been threatened by Albanian secessionists, with assistance from abroad. Our ancestry and posterity would never forgive us if we surrendered the cradle of Serb culture to someone else.'[18]

Criticism of the LDK escalates

By 1996 there were more than fifteen Albanian political parties in Kosovo This suited Belgrade since the factionalisation of Albanians led to them bickering, squabbling and haranguing each other. As one Kosovar put it, 'Thank God there are Serbs here in Kosovo, otherwise we would be tearing each other apart.' It was widely agreed that a radical democratisation of Kosovar political life was

18. Tanjug news agency, Belgrade, 26 August 1996.

needed. Because the Kosovars' parliament was never constituted, and the new parliamentary election, due to be held on 24 May 1996, did not take place – both had been stipulated in the Kacanik constitution – the parallel state and the Kosovar national movement as a whole had become totally dominated by the LDK. No other Kosovar political party was able to articulate a different national programme from the LDK's or present any serious political opposition to it. The LDK leadership was increasingly criticised for its lack of creativity, its tendency to monopolise power and the tight bureaucratic grip in which it kept the Albanian movement, leaving little space for criticism and dialogue.

The most vocal attacks on the LDK came from Adem Demaci, who shattered all illusions of the parallel state by describing democracy in Kosovo as a caricature, condemning the transformation of the LDK from the Albanians' national movement into a political party, which subsequently organised party life in Kosovo. According to Demaci, this has led to an enormous waste of energy in a struggle for power in Kosovo which does not actually exist. Nor does Demaci spare the parallel state and its education system. He said that such a state was merely a shadow of the object it purported to be; education in garages, attics, cellars and private houses only meant that children were not loitering in the streets.[19]

However, the 'parallel' state was not supposed to last for more than a couple of years. An indication of how short a time the Kosovars thought they would have to go without schooling could already be seen in the spring of 1991 when Zenun Celaj, a newspaper editor and Secretary of the Council for the Defence of Human Rights and Freedoms in Pristina, said in an interview: 'Serbian school authorities are interested in halting schooling altogether for Albanians, and since we are in a state of undeclared war – occupied by an external power, which the Serbs are considered to be – Albanians are prepared to lose a year or two of school.'[20] The PKK argued that Albanians could no longer support Rugova's stance and that a more active resistance to the situation was needed. Apart from sharply criticising the LDK leadership because of its indecision, Demaci has propagated active forms of resistance, though always stopping short of an outright call for armed struggle. He has pointed out that Albanians need to exert more pressure if they want to be

19. Kostovicova, *Parallel Worlds*, p. 20.
20. *East European Reporter*, vol. 4, no. 4, spring/summer 1991, p. 20.

taken seriously, and that furthering their aims through massive popular protest might require painful sacrifices.[21]

There had been stubborn resistance by the LDK to the candidacy of Adem Demaci for chairmanship of the Kosovo parliament. When asked where that resistance had come from, Demaci said:

> 'From the leadership of the LDK! Of course only competent people should be candidates. I have no illusion that, even if the leadership were not opposed, the whole thing could be completed in 24 hours. But there has been a very deliberate delay in constituting and organising the Parliament. Those who insisted on Parliament not functioning found it more convenient to use their power for manipulative purposes, to continue improvising, and not to allow power to be exercised where it actually should be - in Parliament itself.'[22]

Although, therefore, the LDK still had much popular support, it had to some extent alienated those dissident circles which challenged its approach, and attempted to advance alternative srategies. It had also tried the patience of many international negotiators. On the intransigence of the Kosovar leadership Ivor Roberts remarked:

> 'I have felt that I wish I was making greater progress in convincing Dr Rugova of my arguments. Dr Rugova has all the persistence and conviction over his own views of someone who is of an academic bent. I come from a different background, a diplomatic background, where there are no absolutes. There are ideas and policies that you follow, but occasionally in negotiations if you can't get what you want, you have to aim a bit lower. We have a phrase in English "don't let the best be the enemy of the good".'[23]

At the end of June 1996, another series of assaults on Serb police left two policemen dead and several badly wounded in the regions of Podujevo and Kosovo Mitrovica. The attacks, with automatic weapons and hand-grenades, were once again presumed to be the work of the Kosovo Liberation Army. The killings caused a heightened sense of fear throughout Kosovo, and only small numbers of people ventured out of doors in the main towns. The Muslim festival of Kurban Bajram, which normally enticed thousands on to the streets and into the cafés, went almost uncelebrated outside the home environment. In a session of the Yugoslav lower house the

21. *War Report*, May 1996, p. 4.
22. *War Report*, May 1996, p. 4.
23. *Koha*, 6 November 1996.

Interior Minister, Vukasin Jokanovic, declared:

> 'The Albanian separatist movement in Kosovo was striving to main-
> tain a tense atmosphere and even create new tensions. Yet a stabilisa-
> tion is not in the interest of the separatist movement, particularly
> given the unequivocal stand of the international community that
> Kosovo is Serbia's internal affair.'

But patience on all sides was wearing thin. At a news conference, an
angry spokesman for the Democratic Party of Serbia accused the
authorities of pursuing an 'ostrich-like policy' in Kosovo: 'How many
more police officers have to be killed in Kosovo', he demanded, 'to
move Milosevic to get down to settling the Kosovo problem?'

At the time Milosevic was still reeling from the crisis caused by
the campaign in May to oust the governor of the National Bank of
Yugoslavia, Dragoslav Avramovic, which coincided with Montenegrin defiance of Belgrade. Milosevic, who could see his goal of a
tight federal union under threat, was particularly angry with the
Montenegrin President Momir Bulatovic for at first supporting
Avramovic. Parliamentarians of the Montenegrin Democratic Party
of Socialists (DPS) had, along with the Serbian opposition parties,
defended Avramovic, thus endangering the coalition between the
ruling SPS (Socialist Party of Serbia) and the DPS. However, just
before the final manoeuvres against Avramovic, the DPS achieved
a deal with the SPS whereby they would vote for his removal, in
return for which Montenegro would be awarded the post of federal
director of customs. Apart from a few other trade-offs, there were
rumours of outright warnings of military action against Montenegro if it did not back Milosevic. Against this background it came as
no surprise when Avramovic was eventually dismissed by a vote of
no confidence.

In the absence of any initiative from Belgrade, the situation on
the ground in Kosovo was becoming increasingly complex and
dangerous. Kosovo's Slavs, determined not to suffer the same fate of
Serbs in Bosnia and Croatia, were mobilising themselves in their
drive to keep Kosovo within the borders of Yugoslavia, and at the
same time Albanians living in southern Serbian towns were also
demanding self-determination and unification with Kosovo.[24]

---

24. On 13 August 1996 a political party representing ethnic Albanians in southern Serbia sent a 'memorandum' to leading international bodies and politicians
drawing attention to the plight of the Albanian minority under Serbian administration. The party urged unification of the region with Kosovo.

Tensions were further heightened in mid-June when a speech by the president of the Serbian Academy of Sciences, Alexander Despic, who called the Kosovo issue 'the most important strategic problem of the Serbian people's future' shocked his listeners by suggesting that, because of the overwhelming demographic superiority of the Albanians in Kosovo, the time had possibly come for a 'peaceful and civilised' secession of the region from the federation.[25] Despic elaborated on the Albanian demographic explosion by revealing that the Albanian population was younger and more fit for military service, so that around 23 per cent of Serbia's conscripts were of Albanian origin. It was soon obvious that Despic had touched a raw nerve with his frank but realistic pronouncements. The Yugoslav League of Communists immediately criticised his 'reckless' stance, calling it 'irresponsible' and dangerous for inter-ethnic relations in Kosovo. However, the LDK welcomed Despic's proposal, and its deputy chairman, Fehmi Agani, told the independent Serbian newspaper *Nasa Borba*: 'This statement is interpreted by the Albanians as proof that the original Serbian nationalist aggression has been defeated.' Far from being encompassed within one state the Serbs were still a deeply divided nation and Serbia itself had emerged from the war in the paradoxical situation of being a predominantly multi-ethnic state. Hence the hysterical reaction to the large Albanian birthrate: any discussion about the demography of Kosovo is taboo among Albanians, Catholic and Muslim alike. Having a large number of children, apart from many other perceived advantages, is seen as ensuring the Albanian, as opposed to Serbian, future of Kosovo.

The speech in the Academy of Sciences alarmed Kosovo's increasingly wary Serb and Montenegrin population who felt that Belgrade was about to sell them out. In response, several thousand Serbs gathered at Gracanica monastery for a meeting organised by the newly-formed Serbian Resistance Movement (SRM), who demanded that an internal consensus be reached, with the national interest being clearly defined, before any solution to the problem of Kosovo was proposed. Although President Milosevic declined an invitation to present his views on Kosovo in person, the meeting began with a prepared address to him read by the writer Aco Rakocevic:

25. For an Albanian response to discussions on the Albanian birthrate see H. Islami, 'Demographic Reality of Kosovo, Conflict or Dialogue' in *Serbian-Albanian Relations and Integration of the Balkans*, Subotica, 1994, pp. 30-53.

'Having seen the experience of our brothers in the Krajinas, we are anxious not to suffer the same fate. We are hearing now that Kosovo should be handed to the Albanians or divided between Serbia and Albania. This is why the Serbs and Montenegrins want to know whether at Dayton something was decided which we are unaware of. The Serbs of Kosovo refuse to be cattle peacefully led to the slaughter without knowing what awaits them.'

The meeting's participants elected a temporary committee to coordinate activities until the SRM founding Assembly could take place (it was planned for that autumn), when the new leadership would be elected. On Serbian TV, the ruling Socialist Party of Serbia swiftly condemned the SRM for trying to raise the issue of the future of Kosovo to make cheap political points in advance of the forthcoming autumn elections in federal Yugoslavia. Nevertheless, the SRM was receiving strong support from the extreme nationalist opposition in Belgrade and the Bosnian Serbs in Pale, all of whom were strongly dissatisfied with Milosevic's metamorphosis from 'warlord' to Balkan 'peacemaker'.

The education accord

Some serious dialogue on Kosovo's education problem had been in progress meanwhile between Belgrade and Pristina, mediated by representatives from the community of St Eudigio. On 2 September 1996 came one of the most promising signals yet: the signing by Milosevic and Ibrahim Rugova of an agreement to normalise the education system for Albanian children and students in Kosovo, thus enabling them to return to the state secondary schools and colleges in the coming academic year. However, the two leaders never actually met, the agreement being signed by Milosevic in Belgrade and by Rugova in Pristina. It was agreed to appoint a commission to supervise the implementation of the agreement and ensure its successful enforcement. The Education Accord was received with enormous relief not only in Kosovo and Belgrade but also abroad. The Serbian Prime Minister, Mirko Marjanovic, told Serbian radio listeners:

'The government of the Republic of Serbia welcomes this agreement and sees it as a major step of humanitarian significance because it ensures that Albanian children in Kosovo will no longer suffer from the negative consequences of political differences.'[26]

26. BBC, Summary of World Broadcasts, EE/2708 A/11, 4 September 1996.

The President of the Provincial Committee of the Socialist Party of Serbia for Kosovo, Vojislav Zivkovic, was more vitriolic in his appraisal of the agreement which, he said, 'shows how unrealistic were the plans of Albanian extremists who in the past advocated the ghettoisation of the Albanians in Kosovo-Metohija'.[27] In Pristina the Accord was hailed as a solution to one of the most important open questions facing the Kosovars. However, the texts which the two sides received did not exactly correspond as was shown in the contradictory nature of the responses. The real issues around the education problem – funding and the curricula to be followed – were not addressed. According to Tanjug, 'Under the agreement the Albanians undertook to accept the curricula in use in the schools throughout Serbia.'[28] The Kosovar education spokesman, Abdyul Rama, said: 'The Albanian side has agreed at this phase not to discuss how the education system in Kosovo should be financed,' while the LDK Vice President, Fehmi Agani, pointed out that the agreement did not mean that the Albanians were going back to Serbia's education system, but only that they would continue their education in proper school buildings: 'We shall remain in our system', he said. Bujar Bukoshi gave a guarded response to the Accord: 'This agreement should be welcomed as a gesture of the good will of the Albanians and of their hope that this is an opportunity to re-open their schools. It is a mistake, however, to feed an uncontrolled and naive euphoria, but we can speak of a very careful optimism. The experience of signed agreements by Serbia has taught us that Serbia easily signs and even more easily does not observe them be they even mediated by the UN Security Council.'[29] In the event, the Education Accord turned out to be yet another irrelevant diversion. Neither side seemingly had any intention of implementing it, and it appears with hindsight to have been a stalling tactic for both sides which wanted to be seen by the international community as able to offer at least a conciliatory gesture towards a peaceful settlement.

The year 1997 began ominously when, on 17 January a car bomb seriously injured the Serbian Rector of Pristina University, Radivoje Papovic, and his driver. This bloody reminder of the region's volatility further strained relations between the two

27. Ibid.
28. Ibid.
29. Bulletin of the Ministry of Information of the Republic of Kosova, no. 277, 9 September 1996.

communities. Both Albanians and the Serbian opposition parties claimed that the explosion was the work of Milosevic's secret police, believing that whenever Milosevic was faced with a crisis he would divert attention by creating tension in Kosovo. The bomb blast occurred as the Serbian opposition coalition *Zajedno* (Together) continued its street protests against the reversal of its election gains in the previous November's Serbian elections.[30] The number of Albanians killed because they were suspected of 'collaborating' with Serbs also increased. Following the car bomb explosion in Pristina, the municipal deputy of the Socialist Party of Serbia, an ethnic Albanian, Malic Seholi, was murdered in the town of Podujevo by an unidentified attacker. According to Seholi's family he had lately received anonymous phone calls and letters saying that he was to be killed. In May the UCK claimed responsibility for killing an Albanian in the village of Llozice near Klina because of his 'notorious and open collaboration with the Serbian occupying forces'. The UCK statement advised the international community 'not to trade off the Albanian question, as it did earlier this century'. However, many in Pristina interpreted the UCK's strongly-worded statement as a warning and a threat to the Kosovar Albanians themselves rather than to the Serbs or the international community. This pattern follows closely that of the Provisional IRA in the late 1960s when it was establishing itself in Londonderry and West Belfast – its intimidation of the local Catholic population was a warning to stay in line, and not deviate from its 'path to a United Ireland'.

Kosovo's Croat population, too, had become alarmed by the escalation of violence in the region, and were making hurried plans to move to Croatia. On 22 March 1997, sixty-five Kosovo Croat families left to settle permanently in Croatia. The families were granted permits by the Croatian Reconstruction and Development Ministry to have the use for a few years of abandoned houses in the village of Kistanje in the Zadar hinterland. By the end of May another seventy families, out of a total of 270, had settled in Kistanje. The Croat exodus continued throughout 1997: the Letnica local commune, about 12 kilometres from Kosovska Vitina, on the Macedonian border, had nearly 5,000 inhabitants before 1990 but by November 1997 it had only 650. According to a local community leader, Gega Matic, 'Living conditions are unbearable.

---

30. In December 1996 an OSCE mission found that the Serbian authorities had fraudulently reversed opposition victories in fourteen cities.

Croats have to walk 12 kilometres to Kosovska Vitina for medical treatment because Yugoslav Army troops have been accommodated in the local clinic since 1991. But the biggest problem is unemployment.' The situation in other Croat-inhabited villages in the province is similar. Between 1990 and November 1997, the population of Sasare fell from 2,800 to 280, that of Vernez from 1,500 to 150, and that of Vernaokol from 1,300 to 120. In Janjevo, the largest Croat village near Pristina, a growing number of houses have been abandoned.

Kosovars observe the discord in Albania

In March 1997 even the dangerously volatile situation in Kosovo was eclipsed by events occurring over the border. Albania itself suddenly exploded into anarchy and chaos fuelled by anger over the failure of high-risk investment schemes in which nearly every family lost hard-earned savings. As the protests grew into a chaotic anti-government insurgency, the Kosovars became profoundly confused. The sense of despair and anxiety they felt was expressed in dramatic language. 'There is no hope, the evil queen of hopelessness and chaos is reigning in the Albanian soul,' said the editorial of Pristina's Albanian-language weekly *Zeri*. Its editor Blerim Shala wrote:

> 'The troubles in Albania have psychologically weakened the negotiating position of Kosovo's Albanians. They have shown that Serbia still has better chances for reforms than Albania. What has happened in Albania makes it clear that the solution for Kosovo lies in negotiations between Serbia and Kosovo Albanians, and not in Albania or somewhere else.'[31]

The deputy chairman of the Parliamentary Party of Kosovo, Bajram Kasumi, told TV Politika in Belgrade: 'The Kosovo Albanians are experiencing the crisis in Albania as their own personal dilemma.'[32]

Kosovars watched in horror as Albanians attacked fellow Albanians. On the question of who was to blame for the bloodshed, the Kosovars were divided. Although the majority admitted, albeit reluctantly, that President Sali Berisha and the cabinet of Prime Minister Alexander Meksi were chiefly to blame for the chaos, others believed that the Albanian opposition were 'traitors to the

31. Associated Press wire service, APO (AP online), 21 March 1997.
32. Tanjug News Agency, Belgrade, 15 March 1997.

national cause', and being manipulated by the foreign media. Yet others attributed the descent into anarchy, for the second time in five years, to 'the Albanian mentality' and traditional divisions within the country. Publicly Kosovar leaders denied that events in Albania would have any impact on their struggle, but privately many voiced concern that their struggle for human rights, already difficult enough, would be made more so by an uprising in Albania. Although there was general agreement that the crisis in Albania was bad for Kosovo, a clear split appeared in attitudes to the parent country – between those who supported Berisha's way of addressing the problem and backers of the demands of the Albanian political opposition. Rugova was accused of siding with the socialist-led opposition when he asked for a new constitution and new parliamentary elections in Albania. Some observers in Kosovo believed that Rugova wanted to get even with Berisha who, having fallen out with the Americans, had recently started to advocate radicalisation of the Albanian movement in Kosovo. Towards the end of 1996, the Albanian regime's propaganda machinery had noticeably dropped its previous unconditional support for Rugova and begun to side with Demaci. Thus, the Kosovars may have lost powerful psychological support from Albania but, as LDK Vice-President, Fehmi Agani pointed out, 'the Albanian movement in Kosovo emerged and survived without help from Albania.'[33] Thus for the time being, the dream of uniting all Albanians had to be put into cold storage.

The Yugoslav war postponed the resolution of the Kosovo problem, but it also served to maintain a precarious peace in the province. Yet it remains indisputable that the maximalist objectives of both Serbs and Albanians are unobtainable without a war. The ultimate goal of the Albanians is 'an independent and sovereign Kosovo', but the United States and the European Union have clearly stated that political autonomy with guaranteed minority rights is the only internationally acceptable status for Kosovo. Yet the very word 'autonomy' sends negative signals to both Serbs and Albanians: to Albanians it is less than what they want, which is independence, and to Serbs it is coded language for the 1974 constitution.[34] A non-violent solution to the Kosovo dilemma can only succeed if it is supported by strong and sustained international pressure. The United States has consistently issued preventive threats

33. *War Report*, April 1997, p. 9.
34. Ivor Roberts, *Koha*, 6 November 1996.

warning Belgrade that it will not tolerate a Serb-instigated campaign of war and ethnic cleansing in Kosovo. Yet these warnings will only continue to be treated seriously by Belgrade if contingency plans can be enforced, coupled with the political will to back them up. One mechanism for exerting international pressure is the 'outer wall of sanctions' specified by the Dayton Accord. These sanctions continue to exclude Federal Yugoslavia from such international bodies as the United Nations and the Organisation for Security and Cooperation in Europe. However, an even more severe penalty for a country whose economy went into a steep decline after it was condemned internationally for supporting the war in Bosnia is that the sanctions also prevent Yugoslavia from getting help from the International Monetary Fund, the World Bank, and the European Bank for Reconstruction and Development. Apart from entering into dialogue on a peaceful resolution of Kosovo's status, the conditions stipulated by the international community include cooperation with the United Nations War Crimes Tribunal, as well as respect for freedom of the press.[35]

One outcome of the chaos in Albania was renewed American insistence that the Kosovars abandon their plans to hold their 'parallel' parliamentary elections scheduled for May 24. US Assistant Secretary of State John Kornblum, outgoing envoy to the Balkans, visited Kosovo on 12 April, accompanied by his successor, Robert Gelbard, and once again told the LDK, and Dr Rugova in particular, that Kosovo was a part of Serbia and should remain so. Hence, the United States would not support the Albanian's plans for parliamentary elections in Kosovo. He was more forthright on this matter than before, which was interpreted in Kosovo as a response to the chaos in Albania and the threat this posed to regional stability. The Americans were also putting strong pressure on the Kosovars over the parallel elections because they believed that for the Kosovars to take part in the Serbian elections would be more constructive, and they also did not want to see the 'parallel' state fully legitimised.

By persistently demanding an independent Kosovo, the LDK leadership had maintained among its supporters unrealistically high expectations that such a state would eventually gain international recognition. The inability of the LDK to realise its ambitions even in part had convinced a growing number of Kosovars that both the international community and Ibrahim Rugova supported the *status*

35. Aryeh Neier, 'Impasse in Kosovo', *New York Review*, 28 August 1997, p. 51.

quo in Kosovo. This was borne out at the beginning of May when Rugova acquiesced in John Kornblum's request that the 'parallel' presidential and parliamentary elections be postponed. His decision infuriated the Kosovar opposition, who were anxious, amid the growing divisions then being publicised among Albanians in Albania itself, to present as united a front as possible to the outside world. According to the Parliamentary Party of Kosovo (PPK) 'This decision was the worst possible solution for the Albanians at the present moment. The postponement of the elections paves the way for a rift in the Albanian political movement in Kosovo.'[36] Luleta Pula-Beqiri, leader of the hard-line faction in the Social Democratic Party of Kosovo, denied that Rugova's decision was based on a general agreement between Albanian parties, and asserted that by postponing the elections, he had failed to honour the Kosovar Albanians' demand for their elections to be held before the parliamentary and presidential elections in Serbia due to be held at the end of the year.[37] Albanian analysts in Pristina estimated that Rugova and the LDK would have beaten Demaci's faction in elections, and therefore the motives for his decision were not clear, since the majority of Kosovars were in favour of holding the elections in May. Belgrade interpreted the postponement as a positive step in that the Kosovars were possibly now thinking about getting involved in Serbia's political life. This was indeed what the international community wanted.

Meanwhile, the situation in Albania continued to deteriorate. The Yugoslav Army was forced to review its security along the Kosovo-Albanian border, where Albanian Army border units had fled leaving the frontier posts unmanned; it was particularly concerned about Kosovars crossing the border to seize looted weapons and other military equipment. Belgrade responded by placing additional troops along the Kosovo-Albanian border, and arresting a large number of Albanian youths suspected of belonging to the Kosovo Liberation Army. At the beginning of June, nineteen Albanians, accused of being members of the UCK, were found guilty by the district court in Pristina of 'preparation of terrorist acts, and hostile association with the intention of breaking up Yugoslavia' and sentenced to long terms of imprisonment. None of the defendants denied the charges.[38] Most said that they did not recognise the

36. V.I.P. Daily News Report, issue no. 1002, Belgrade, 2 June 1997.
37. Ibid.
38. For a detailed report on the 'Show Trials in Pristina', see *War Report*, October 1997, p. 6.

'occupying court but only a court of an independent Kosovo. They told the court: 'We are not terrorists, we are people's fighters for the liberation of Kosovo.'[39] More than 20,000 Albanians from all districts of Kosovo rallied outside the courtroom before heavily armed police dispersed them.

As the summer progressed, the UCK stepped up its attacks on Serbian police and on Albanians thought to be 'collaborators' (called 'Serb regime people' by the LDK), especially those who had joined the Serbian Socialist Party (SPS). The UCK also began calling publicly for Albanians to give the organisation financial support. During the previous few years, several Albanians had joined the Socialist Party of Serbia, following the founding of the SPS municipal council in Kosovo. Referring to this, the chairman of the SPS municipal council, Qamil Gashi, told Tanjug that interest among the Albanians in the SPS was:

'an expression of their willingnes to actively participate in the political life of Serbia, with the aim of contributing to the efforts to resolve current problems in their own environment more quickly. We should not be labelled 'traitors' to our own people because we have joined the SPS. It was us, the Socialists and the SPS leadership, who initiated actions to solve numerous economic and municipal problems more swiftly. This is in the interest of the people of the area, who are mainly Albanians employed by Feronikl and other firms or working for the health service and state bodies.'[40]

This was a direct reference to the LDK's inability to equate socio-economic issues with political ones. The fact that Albanians were even thinking of joining the SPS – an organisation which, to the majority, represented colonial exploitation and oppression – was proof that at least some Kosovars had by now accepted that the LDK did nothing more than purport to govern an imaginary and illusory state. When many Kosovars acutally confronted the stark reality of their situation, it resulted in one, albeit small sector of Kosovar society gradually drifting back into mainstream, Serb-dominated economic and civic life of Kosovo, while a younger and more militant sector chose to support a more aggresesive, if not violent position. In discussion, members of the latter group admit to an almost fatalistic belief that a violent solution to the Kosovo crisis is inevitable, and to a conviction that they will have to 'shoot

39. V.I.P. Daily News Report, issue no. 1002, Belgrade, 2 June 1997.
40. Tanjug, Belgrade, 8 February 1996. Gashi was shot by the UCK in November 1997.

their way out of Serbia' or be forever an 'enslaved' minority within it. As late as 1990 the majority of Kosovars would have sanctioned living in an autonomous province within the Yugoslav Federation, but hardly one would accept such a solution today.

A funeral

At the beginning of December 1997 the UCK made its first public appearance when three masked members of the Kosovo Liberation Army, carrying automatic rifles, arrived unexpectedly at the funeral of an Albanian teacher killed by Serbian security forces. To applause from the 20,000 mourners, one of the armed men declared: 'Serbia is massacring Albanians. The Kosovo Liberation Army is the only force fighting for the freedom of Kosovo. We shall continue to fight.'[41] The message was clear enough: we exist, do not ignore us! As one Kosovar activist declared,

> 'There is nothing unexpected, wondrous or surprising in the emergence of the UCK. At a time when the seven-year-old Kosovar movement can be pronounced a failure without any concrete results. At a time when the international community has been underestimating and seriously ignoring the Albanian factor, reducing it to a problem of minorities requiring solutions in ridiculous frameworks within Serbia, when Serbia's only way of communicating with Albanians is violence and crime, one should not be amazed if part of the people decide to end this agony and take the fate of Kosovo and its people in its own hands.'[42]

41. *Daily Telegraph*, 2 December 1997.
42. Luljeta Pula-Beqiri, *Bulletin of the Ministry of Information of the Republic of Kosovo*, no. 321, 7 December 1997.

SELECT BIBLIOGRAPHY

Aldiss, Brian, *Cities and Stones: A Traveller's Jugoslavia,* London, 1966.

Baerlein, Henry, *A Difficult Frontier,* Leonard Parsons, London, 1922.

Banac, Ivo, *The National Question in Yugoslavia: Origins, History, Politics,* Cornell University Press, 1992.

Batakovic, Dusan, *The Kosovo Chronicles,* Belgrade, 1992.

Bogdanovic, D., *Kniga o Kosovu,* Belgrade, 1985.

Brestovci, Sadulla, *Marredheniet Shqiptare - Serbo-Malazeze 1830-1878,* Pristina, 1983.

Brown, H.A., *A Winter in Albania,* Griffith, Farran, Ockenden and Welsh, London, 1888.

Buda, Alex (ed.), *Problems of the Formation of the Albanian People, their Language and Culture,* Tirana, 1984.

Cani, Bahri and Cvijetin Milivojevic, *Kosmet ili Kosova,* Belgrade, 1996.

Cirkovic, S., 'Kosovo i Metohija u srednjem veku' in: *Kosovo i Metohija u Srpskoj istoriji,* Belgrade, 1989.

Cvijic, Jovan, *Balkanski rat i Srbija,* Belgrade, 1912.

———, *La Peninsule Balkanique,* Geographie Humaine, Paris, 1918.

Dedijer, Vladimir, *Yugoslav-Albanian Relations, 1939-1948,* Belgrade, 1984.

Djakovic, S., *Sukobi na Kosovu,* Belgrade, 1984.

Djilas, J.K., *Srpske Skole na Kosovu od 1856-1912,* Pristina, 1969

Dragnic, A.N. and S. Todorovic, *The Saga of Kosovo: Focus on Serbian-Albanian Relations,* Eastern European Monographs, Boulder CO/New York, 1984.

Drini, Skender, *Bajram Curri,* Tirana, 1984.

Duijzings,G., D. Janjic, and S. Maliqi (eds), *Kosovo - Kosova: Confrontation or Coexistence,* Peace Research Centre, University of Nijmegen, 1996.

Durham, M. Edith, *Through the Lands of the Serb,* London 1904.

———, *Twenty Years of Balkan Tangle,* Geo. Allen and Unwin, London, 1920.

———, *High Albania,* Edward Arnold, London, 1909, and repr. Virago, London, 1985.

Elsie, Robert, *History of Albanian Literature,* 2 vols, Eastern European Monographs, Boulder CO/New York, 1995.

Fine, J.V.A., *The Late Medieval Balkans,* University of Michigan Press, Ann Arbor, 1994.

Forsyth, William, *The Slavonic Provinces South of the Danube,* London, 1876.

Gordon, J. and C., *Two Vagabonds in Serbia and Montenegro,* Penguin Books, 1939.

Gruenwald, O. and K. Rosenblum-Cale (eds), *Human Rights in Yugoslavia,* Irvington Publishers, New York, 1986.

Hadri, Ali, *Keshillat Nacionalclirmtare ne Kosove,* Pristina, 1974.

Hahn, J.G. von, *Albanesische Studien,* 3 vols, Jena, 1854.

———, *Putovanje kroz porecinu Drina i Vardara,* Belgrade 1876.

Hasani, S., Kosovo, *Istine i Zablude,* Zagreb, 1985.

Horvat, Branko, *Kosovsko Pitanje,* Zagreb, 1989.

Hoxha, Enver, *The Titoites*, Tirana, 1982.

Iliri i Albanci, *Srpska Akademija Nauka i Umetnosti*, Beograd, 1988.

Ippen, Theodor, *Novi pazar und Kosovo* (Das Alte Racien), Vienna, 1892.

Islami, Hivzi, *Kosova dhe Shqiptaret - ceshtje demografike*, Pristina, 1990.

Janjic, D. and S. Maliqi (eds), *Conflict or Dialogue: Serbian-Albanian Relations and Inte gration of the Balkans*, Subotica, 1994.

Jastrebov, I.S. *Stara Srbija i Albania, Spomenik Srpske Kraljevske akademije*, XLI, 36, Belgrade, 1904.

Jones, Fortier, *With Serbia into Exile*, London, 1916.

Jovanovic, J., *Southern Serbia from the End of the Eighteenth Century up to Liberation*, Belgrade, 1941.

Kindersley, Ann, *The Mountains of Serbia: Travels through Inland Yugoslavia*, David and Charles, Newton Abbot, 1977.

Kohl, C. von, and W. Libal, *Kosovo: Gordischer Knoten des Balkan*, Vienna–Zurich, Europaverlag, 1992.

Kokallari, Hamit, *Kosova*, Tirana, 1944.

Kostovicova, D., *Parallel Worlds: Response of Kosovo Albanians to Loss of Autonomy in Serbia, 1986-1996*, Keele University European Research Centre, 1997.

Krstic, B., *Kosovo between Historical and Ethnic Rights*, Kuca Vid, Belgrade, 1994.

Lendvai, Paul, *Eagles in Cobwebs*, Doubleday, Garden City, NY, 1969.

Mackenzie, G.M. and A.P. Irby, *Travels in the Slavonic Provinces of Turkey-in-Europe*, London, 1877.

Magas, Branka, *The Destruction of Yugoslavia*, Verso, London, 1993.

Maletic, Mihajlo, *Kosovo, Yesterday and Today*, Belgrade, 1973.

Maliqi, Shkelzen, *Nya e Kosoves - As Vllasi As Milosheviqi*, Ljubljana, 1990.

——, 'Kosovo: Politics of Resistance' in *Ex-Yugoslavia: From War to Peace*, Generalitat Valenciana, Valencia, 1993.

Marmullaku, Ramadan, *Albania and the Albanians*, Hurst, London, 1975.

Mihaljcic, R., *The Battle of Kosovo in History and in Popular Tradition*, Belgrade, 1989.

Mijatovic, Elodie Lawton, *Kosovo*, London, 1884.

Misovic, Milos, *Ko je trazio Republiku Kosovo 1945-1985*, Belgrade, 1987.

Mitrovic, A., *Srbija u prvom svetskom ratu*, Belgrade, 1985.

Musaj, Fatmir, *Isa Boletini*, Tirana, 1987.

Novakovic, St., *Zakonik Stefana Dusana*, Belgrade, 1898.

Obradovic, Milovan, *Agrarna reforma i kolonizacija na Kosovu, 1918-1941*, Pristina, 1981.

Petrovic, R. and Blagojevic M., *The Migration of Serbs and Montenegrins From Kosovo and Metohija*, Belgrade, 1992.

Pipa, A., and S. Repishti, *Studies on Kosova*, Columbia University Press, New York, 1984.

Popovic, Dimitri, *Borba za narodno ujdinjenje, 1908-1914*, Belgrade, 1936.

Qosja, Rexhep, *La Question Albanaise*, Fayard, Paris, 1995.

'Relationship Between Yugoslavia and Albania', *Review of International Affairs*, Belgrade, 1984.

Reuter, Jens, *Die Albaner in Jugoslawien*, Südost-Institut, Munich, 1982.

Roux, Michel, *Les Albanais en Yougoslavie: Minoritee nationale, territoire et developpe ment*, Editions de la Maison des Sciences de l'Homme, Paris, 1992.

Rushti, Limon, *Levizja Kacake Ne Kosove (1918-1928)*, Pristina, 1981.

Rusinow, Dennison A., *The Yugoslav Experiment, 1948-1974*, Hurst, London, 1977.
Rugova, I., *La Question du Kosovo* (Entretiens avec M.F. Allain et X. Galmiche), Fayard, Paris, 1994.
Shala, Blerim, *Kosovo krvi suze*, Ljubljana, 1990.
Shoup, Paul, *Communism and the Yugoslav National Question*, New York, 1968.
Skendi, Stavro, *The Albanian National Awakening, 1878-1912*, Princeton University Press, 1967.
Stojkovic, L., and M. Martic, *National Minorities in Yugoslavia*, Belgrade, 1952.
Sufflay, Milan von, *Srbi i Arbanasi*, Belgrade, 1925; repr. Mala Azurova Povjesnica, Zagreb, 1991.
Swire, Joseph, *Albania: The Rise of a Kingdom*, repr. Arno Press, New York, 1971.
Tempo, Svetozar Vukmanovic, *The Battle for the Balkans*, Zagreb, 1980.
Todorovic, D., *Jugoslavija i balkanske drzave, 1919-1923*, Belgrade, 1979.
Tomic, Jovan, *Rat na Kosovu i Staroj Srbiji 1912 godine*, Novi Sad, 1913.
Thompson, Mark, *A Paper House: The Ending of Yugoslavia*, London, 1992.
Tukovic, Dimitri, *Srbija i Arbanija*, Belgrade, 1914.
Vickers, Miranda, *The Status of Kosova in Socialist Yugoslavia*, Bradford Studies on South Eastern Europe, no. 1. University of Bradford, 1994.
——, *The Albanians: A Modern History*, I.B.Tauris, London 1995.
——, and James Pettifer, *Albania: From Anarchy to a Balkan Identity*, Hurst, London, 1997.
Vucinic, Milan, *Zasto Kosovo ne moze da bude Republika*, Beograd, 1990.
West, Rebecca, *Black Lamb and Grey Falcon: A Journey Through Yugoslavia*, 2 vols, Macmillan, London, 1942; paperback (1 vol.), 1982.
Wilkes, John, *The Illyrians*, Blackwell, Oxford, 1992.

* * *

Baskin, Mark, 'Crisis in Kosovo', *Problems of Communism*, March-April, 1983.
BBC, *Summary of World Broadcasts*.
The Central Archive of the Republic of Albania, especially the material collected in Fond no. 251.
Documents Diplomatiques, Correspondence concernant les actes de violence et de brigandage des Albanais dans la Vielle Serbie, 1898-1899, Belgrade, 1899.
Emmert, T.A., 'The Kosovo legacy', *Serbian Studies*, vol. 5, no. 2, 1989.
Further Correspondence Respecting The Affairs of South-Eastern Europe, Turkey, 3, 1903, London, 1903.
Kosova Information Centre, *Kosova Daily Report*, Pristina.
Kosova Historical/Political Review, Tirana, 1991-5.
'Kosovo Past and Present', *Review of International Affairs, Belgrade*, 1989.
Lee, Michele, 'Kosovo Between Yugoslavia and Albania', *New Left Review*, July-August 1983.
Mikic, D., 'The Albanians and Serbia during the Balkan Wars' in B.K. Kiraly and D. Djordjevic (eds), *East Central European Society and the Balkan Wars*, New York, 1987.
Prepiska o arbanaskim nasiljima u Staroj Srbiji 1898-1899, Ministry of Foreign Affairs, Belgrade, 1899.
'Relationship Between Yugoslavia and Albania', *Review of International Affairs*, Belgrade, 1984.

Rusinow, Dennison, 'Events in the SAP of Kosovo: Documentation', *Review of International Affairs*, Belgrade, 1981.

TFF, *Preventing War in Kosovo*, Transnational Foundation for Peace and Future Research, Lund, Sweden, 1994.

The Truth on Kosova, Institute of History, Academy of Sciences, Tirana, 1993.

Yugoslavia, Prisoners of Conscience, Amnesty International Publications, 1985.

V.I.P. Daily News report, Belgrade.

War Report, Institute of War and Peace Reporting, London.

APPENDIX: POPULATION DATA

ETHNIC COMPOSITION OF KOSOVO POPULATION
ACCORDING TO CENSUSES OF 1961, 1971, 1981

	1961	%	1971	%	1981	%
Albanians	647,000	67.1	916,000	73.7	1,227,000	77.5
Serbs	227,000	23.5	228,000	18.3	210,000	13.2
Montenegrins	38,000	3.9	32,000	2.5	27,000	1.7
Turks	26,000	2.7	12,000	1.0	13,000	0.8
Muslims	8,000	0.8	26,000	2.1	59,000	3.7
Other	19,000	2.0	29,000	2.4	49,000	3.1
Total	964,000	100	1,224,000	100	1,585,000	100

Source: Rilindja (Albanian-language daily), Pristina, 17 March 1982, p.7.

ETHNIC COMPOSITION OF THE LCY IN KOSOVO-METOHIJA, 1953, 1968, 1973

	1953			1968			1973		
	No.	% of Party	% of ethnic group in Province	No.	% of Party	% of ethnic group in Province	No.	% of Party	% of ethnic group in Province
Albanians	12,226	46.8	64.9	27,623	54.9	67.2	28,447	61.49	73.7
Serbs	10,052	38.5	23.5	15,799	31.4	23.6	12,258	26.51	18.4
Montenegrins	3,044	11.6	3.9	5,233	10.4	3.9	3,746	8.09	2.5
Others	809	3.1	7.7	1,661	3.3	5.3	1,805	3.91	5.4
Total	26,131	100.0	100.0	50,316	100.0	100.0	46,256	100.0	100.0

★ League of Communists of Yugoslavia

+ Includes Muslims (ethnic), Turks, Gypsies and other numerically less important nationalities.

Sources: Yugoslav Survey, vol. 14, 1973, pp. 17-19; Shoup, *Communism and the Yugoslav National Question*, Appendix B, table 3, p. 272; *Socialist Thought and Practice*,1 M. Bakali's report to the 11th Conference of L.C. Kosovo, April 1974, 4, pp. 89-98.

ETHNIC COMPOSITION OF POPULATION OF KOSOVO AND METOHIJA WITHIN CHANGED ADMINISTRATIVE BOUNDARIES, 1991

	TOTAL	SERBS AND MONTENEGRINS	ALBANIANS	MUSLIMS	TURKS	CROATS	ROM	OTHER
Vucitrn	78,877	5,687	70,000	535	66	7	1,834	748
Glogovac	53,802	26	53,771	-	-	-	-	5
Kacanik	37,055	243	36,488	4	-	5	306	9
Kosovo Polje	32,500	9,244	17,374	1,675	49	37	3,384	737
Lipljan	68,639	9,944	53,334	523	5	2,973	1,715	145
Obilic	29,523	6,190	18,944	208	3	11	3,767	400
Pristina	205,093	31,181	161,314	2,308	1,986	202	6,625	1,477
Srbica	58,399	843	57,444	11	-	-	93	8
Urosevac	95,156	8,478	81,737	1,857	7	177	2,081	819
Stimlje	23,523	986	21,743	422	-	1	266	105
Decani	49,456	799	48,267	105	-	-	184	101
Dakovica	102,947	3,194	112,888	325	15	22	2,657	1,846
Istok	57,928	7,292	46,151	2,620	-	8	1,338	519
Klina	51,723	5,890	43,1655	166	-	4	1,291	1,207
Malesevo	45,669	487	45,181	-	-	-	-	1
Orahovac	59,942	4,080	55,119	207	-	1	319	216
Pec	132,455	15,007	105,104	6,878	20	54	3,551	1,841
Prizren	175,413	11,363	132,591	19,423	7,227	41	3,963	805
Suva Reka	63,981	3,033	60,673	28	7	-	167	73
Total	1,440,081	123,967	1,221,288	37,295	9,385	3,543	33,541	11,062
%	100	8.6	84.8	2.6	0.7	0.2	2.3	0.8
KOSOVO AND DRENICA								
Count	682,567	72,822	572,149	7,543	2,116	3,413	20,071	4,453
%	47.4	10.7	83.8	1.1	0.3	0.5	2.9	0.7
METOHIJA WITH THE PRIZREN REGION AND PODRIM								
Count	757,514	51,145	649,139	29,752	7,269	130	13,470	6,609
%	52.6	6.7	85.7	3.9	1.0	0.0	1.8	0.9

Source: SZS, Statistical Bulletin 1934, 'National Structure of the Population by Municipalities', in *First Results of the 1991 Census*, Belgrade, 1992.

INDEX

Abaresh, 53

Abdic, Fikret, 298

Abdul Hamid, Sultan, 42, 44, 52, 61, 62, 69, 72

Adriatic Sea, 5, 10, 80

Agani, Fehmi, 282, 304, 306, 309

AITUK (Alliance of Independent Trade Unions of Kosovo), 246-7

Alaudin Medrese, 182

Alexander, King, 104, 114

Albania, Albanians: frontiers, 82-3, 88, 96, 97, 237, 262, 310; loses Kosovo, 86; Italian occupation, 121; growth of communism, 122ff.; relations with communist Yugoslavia, 151-4, 205, 207, 236, 238; reaction to Milosevic coup, 237; collapse of communism, 254ff.; recognises 'Republic of Kosovo', 254; multi-party elections, 255; unification with Kosovo, 269ff.; Greater Albania, 270; military aid for Kosovars, 279; descends into anarchy, 308-9; intellectuals, xiv; élite, xiv, 32; nobility, 13; and Battle of Kosovo, 13; pastoralism, 17; settle in Kosovo, 18; migration, 23, 29; religious persecution of, 24, 29; attitude toward religion, 25, 47; Islam and, 25, 26; diverge from Serbs, 26; mercenaries, 26; military, 26; Adriatic settlements, 29; resistance to Ottomans, 32-3; as Ottoman officials, 34; beys, 40; expulsion, 43; defence committees, 43; nationalism, 45, 65, 80, 146, 147, 166, 200, 216; 1878 rebellion, 46; intellectuals, 49, 57; language, xvi, xvii, 27, 51, 64, 65, 122, 157, 177, 266; strategic importance, 53; literature, 53; incursions into Serbia, 55; massacre Serbs, 59-60; conservatism of, 63; 1912 insurrection, 73, 86; identity, 75; atrocities against, 77, 93-5; resist Serb conquest, 78, 86; independence proclamation, 79; status of, 80-1; demography, 95; conservatives, 100; deportations from Yugoslavia, 118-119; Partisans, 128; diaspora, 255-6, 257; (see also Kosovo, Kosovars)

Albanian Academy of Sciences, 257

Albanian American Civil League, 256

Albanian Communist Party, 115, 124

Albanian Democratic Party (DP), 255-6, 258

Albanian League, 49; see also Prizren League

Albanian National Democratic Committee

Albanian National Liberation Conference, 132

Albanian national question/movement: xi, xiii,

Alia, Ramiz, 204, 209, 238, 282

Aliu, Ali, 254, 255

Ambassadors' Conference, London (1913), 80, 87, 88, 93

Amnesty International, 181, 188

Apis, Dimitijevic, 71

archaeology, 1-2, 3

'Arkan' (Zeljko Raznjatovic), 259, 280

Armenians, 19, 33

Arsenius IV Sakabenta, 29

Austria-Hungary, 13, 27, 29, 37, 52, 59, 60, 70, 79, 80, 92; intelligence services, 57, 87; designs on Albania, 67; annexes Bosnia-Hercegovina, 67, 75

AVNOJ, 134, 145

Avramovic, Dragoslav, 303

321